Road Traffic Law in Scotland

Road Traffic Law in Scotland

John Wheatley QC

Third edition

Butterworths/Law Society of Scotland
Edinburgh
2000

United Kingdom	Butterworths, a Division of Reed Elsevier (UK) Ltd, 4 Hill Street, EDINBURGH EH2 3JZ and Halsbury House, 35 Chancery Lane, LONDON WC2A 1EL
Australia	Butterworths, a Division of Reed International Books Australia Pty Ltd, CHATSWOOD, New South Wales
Canada	Butterworths Canada Ltd, MARKHAM, Ontario
Hong Kong	Butterworths Hong Kong, a division of Reed Elsevier (Greater China) Ltd, HONG KONG
India	Butterworths India, NEW DELHI
Ireland	Butterworth (Ireland) Ltd, DUBLIN
Malaysia	Malayan Law Journal Sdn Bhd, KUALA LUMPUR
New Zealand	Butterworths of New Zealand Ltd, WELLINGTON
Singapore	Butterworths Asia, SINGAPORE
South Africa	Butterworths Publishers (Pty) Ltd, DURBAN
USA	Lexis Law Publishing, CHARLOTTESVILLE, Virginia

© Reed Elsevier (UK) Ltd 2000

A CIP Catalogue record for this book is available from the British Library.

First published 1989
2nd Edition 1993

ISBN 0 406 98137 X

Typeset by Phoenix Photosetting, Chatham, Kent
Printed and bound in Scotland by Thomson Litho, East Kilbride

Visit us at our website: http://www.butterworthsscotland.com

Preface

Sufficient changes in road traffic law and practice, and enough new caselaw, have suggested the production of a third edition of this book. I would like to thank John Kirk of the Procurator Fiscal's office in Edinburgh for providing invaluable assistance in the preparation of this edition, as he did in the earlier editions. Any errors in the book, of whatever kind, are however all mine.

I would also like to express my deep appreciation to the Society of Solicitors and Procurators in the City and County of Perth, and also to the sheriff clerks and fiscals in Perth, all of whom made my stay in Perth between 1980 and 2000 satisfying, interesting, and when appropriate, highly enjoyable.

My gratitude is also due to the ever efficient staff at Butterworths, particularly for persuading Emeritus Professor Ken Mason and Regius Professor Tony Busuttil to provide Appendices which add qualities of excellence to the book which may be absent elsewhere.

I have deleted references to Crown Office Circulars in the authorities, partly because of the irregular frequency of their issue in recent years.

I have tried to state the law as reported up to about June 2000.

John Wheatley QC
Crook of Devon

Contents

CHAPTER 1
Definitions: identification of driver

CHAPTER 2
Dangerous and careless driving

PART 1. DANGEROUS DRIVING

CHAPTER 3
**Drink related offences (Road Traffic Act 1988 (as amended),
ss 3A, 4 and 5)**

PART 3. DRIVING OR BEING IN CHARGE OF A
MOTOR VEHICLE WITH ALCOHOL
CONCENTRATION ABOVE PRESCRIBED LIMIT:
SECTION 5

CHAPTER 4
Preliminary breath tests and provision of specimens for analysis
Sections 6, 7 and 8 of the Road Traffic Act 1988

PART 1. PRELIMINARY BREATH TEST

PART 2. PROVISION OF SPECIMENS FOR ANALYSIS

CHAPTER 5
Use of specimens and evidence in proceedings under the Road Traffic Act 1988, sections 3A, 4 and 5

CHAPTER 6
Miscellaneous; hospital patients; detention and interpretation sections 9, 10 and 11 of the Road Traffic Act 1988

CHAPTER 7
Other road traffic offences

CHAPTER 8
Licences, disqualification, endorsement and fixed penalties

CHAPTER 9
Public service vehicles and carriage of goods by road

PART 1. PUBLIC SERVICE VEHICLES

PART 2. CARRIAGE OF GOODS BY ROAD

Appendices

Index

Table of Statutes

Table of Cases

C

E

N

O

S

T

Chapter One

Definitions: identification of driver

1.1   GENERAL

The legislation provides a large number of statutory definitions and descriptions of terms used in road traffic law. Some of the most important of these have been considered and interpreted by the courts. Section 185 of the Road Traffic Act 1988 (c 52) provides a series of definitions of the term 'motor vehicle' and other expressions relating to vehicles. However, the Road Traffic Act 1991 (c 40) replaces the term 'motor vehicle' with the phrase 'mechanically propelled vehicle' in a number of the principal sections of the 1988 Act[1]. Sections 186–191 of the 1988 Act give a number of supplementary and additional descriptions relating to such vehicles. Section 192 of the 1988 Act (as amended) sets out a number of general interpretations of words and phrases used throughout the Act, and s 194 provides a definition index. Section 11 (as amended) gives a number of particular interpretations relating to ss 3A–10; ss 85 and 86 are respectively an interpretation section and a definition index relative to Part II of the Act (Construction and Use provisions); s 108 (as amended by the Road Traffic (Driver Licensing and Information Systems) Act 1989) is the interpretation section for Part III (Drivers' Licences); s 121 (as similarly amended) provides definitions for Part IV (HGV Drivers' Licences and Passenger-carrying Vehicle Drivers' Licences); and ss 161 and 162 are respectively the interpretation section and definition index for Part VI (Insurance). Further definition sections are found in ss 136–142 of the Road Traffic

---

1 See 1.2:1 below.

Regulation Act 1984 (c 27) and regulation 3 of the Road Vehicles (Construction and Use) Regulations 1986[1]. In addition, other words and phrases associated with driving offences have been the subject of judicial interpretation.

A description of some of the more commonly used statutory and other terms now follows. However, while the definition of a particular term will generally suffice for most of the occasions and purposes of its use in different contexts throughout the legislation, there are certain exceptions to this general rule which are indicated as appropriate in the text. In particular, special significance has been additionally applied to some of these terms in relation to the drink-related offences described in ss 3A–10 of the Road Traffic Act 1988, and this is discussed at 3.3:1 below.

1.2   MOTOR VEHICLES

1.2:1   General

A 'motor vehicle' was originally defined in terms of s 185(1) of the Road Traffic Act 1988 as 'a mechanically propelled vehicle intended or adapted for use on the roads'. In other words, the vehicle must be constructed for the purpose of being used on the roads, or alternatively be altered or adapted to make it suitable for that purpose[2]. Whether a vehicle has been 'adapted for use on the roads' will depend on the facts and circumstances in each case[3]. In addition, in terms of the statutory definition it is essential that the vehicle is so constructed that it can be mechanically propelled.

Section 4 of the Road Traffic Act 1991 (which came into effect on 1 July 1992) replaced, in a number of important sections, the term 'motor vehicle' with the words 'mechanically propelled vehicle'. The sections of the Road Traffic Act 1988 so affected are ss 1–4 (although not s 5), s 10, s 163, s 168, s 170 and s 181; and also s 11(1) and s 23 of the Road Traffic Offenders Act 1988. The purpose of this amendment is specifically to exclude the qualification of vehicles being 'intended or adapted for use on the road' from these sections, and thus give them a wider application. For

---

1 SI 1986/1078.
2 *French v Champkin* [1920] 1 KB 76.
3 *Taylor v Mead* [1961] 1 WLR 435, [1961] 1 All ER 626, a case where a commercial traveller adapted a private car to carry goods.

example, scrambler motor cycles, some kinds of stock cars, and certain types of building site vehicles could be described as not being intended or adapted for the purpose of being used on the roads, and would not therefore have been caught by the relevant sections as previously described. However, the term 'motor vehicle' is still extensively used in other parts of the legislation.

The words 'mechanically propelled vehicle' therefore now appear in two slightly different contexts in the legislation. Firstly, the words appear, by themselves, and without particular further definition, in the above sections of the Road Traffic Act 1988, as amended by the Road Traffic Act 1991; and secondly they continue to feature in the definition of the term 'motor vehicle' where it appears unaltered elsewhere.

In general, the words 'mechanically propelled vehicle' as used in either context should be interpreted in an ordinary as opposed to a strictly technical sense. Essentially, the phrase means precisely what it says. The definition may be applicable to a vehicle whether that vehicle is moving under its own power, whether it is capable of so moving, or whether it is temporarily out of order. However, if a vehicle is in such a condition that there are no reasonable prospects of it being mobile again, it is no longer a mechanically propelled vehicle[1]. Equally, a vehicle will not qualify for inclusion in the statutory definition if it has reached 'such a state of mechanical or structural decrepitude' that it would offend against common sense to describe it as a mechanically propelled vehicle[2].

In considering the test to be used in determining whether any particular vehicle falls within these statutory definitions, regard should principally be had to the construction of the vehicle rather than the use to which it is put. In *McEachran v Hurst*[3], a broken-down moped was being pedalled along a road; it was held that the vehicle was still a moped rather than a cycle. A vehicle, therefore, which is plainly not constructed or adapted or intended for use on the roads will not normally fall within the statutory definition of a motor vehicle. The fact that a vehicle is temporarily broken down or has had its engine removed does not necessarily take the vehicle outwith the statutory definition; even where a vehicle has had its source of motor power removed it can still properly be described as being so constructed as to be

1 *Maclean v Hall* 1962 SLT (Sh Ct) 30; *McNeill v Ritchie* 1967 SLT (Sh Ct) 68.
2 *Tudhope v Every* 1976 JC 42, 1977 SLT 2.
3 [1978] RTR 462.

mechanically propelled[1]. But if the evidence demonstrates that essential parts of the vehicle, such as the engine or gear box, have been permanently removed and are unlikely to be replaced, then such a vehicle may no longer qualify as a mechanically propelled vehicle. A mechanically propelled vehicle may be in such a dangerous condition that simply by driving it an offence is committed[2].

A further matter that may also have to be taken into account in considering whether or not a particular vehicle falls within the statutory definition of a motor vehicle in terms of s 185(1) of the Road Traffic Act 1988 is to decide if it can be said, on any reasonable view of the facts and circumstances, that one of the uses for which the vehicle was intended was a use on the public highway[3]. Accordingly, dumper vehicles used solely on building sites for construction work, and which are not in fact used or intended or designed to be used for carrying materials on public roads, will not be classed as motor vehicles[4]. This is so even though the vehicles in question could be driven on public roads or converted so that they might be appropriate for such use. The essential feature which excludes such vehicles from the statutory definition is that the vehicles are used solely off the public roads and are intended only for such use. It therefore follows that an agricultural tractor, which may well carry out many of its functions on private land and off the public roadway, but which is constructed and intended to be used for part of the time on the road, would fall within the statutory definition of a motor vehicle[5]. Such vehicles as are described in this paragraph may qualify as 'mechanically propelled vehicles'.

In defining the term 'motor vehicle' s 185(1) draws specific attention to the special provision made for invalid carriages in terms of the Chronically Sick and Disabled Persons Act 1970[6].

Section 185(1), together with s 136 of the Road Traffic Regulation Act 1984, provides further definitions of vehicle types.

---

1 *Newberry v Simmonds* [1961] 2 QB 345, [1961] 2 WLR 675, [1961] 2 All ER 318.
2 Road Traffic Act 1988, s 2A(2); *Carstairs v Hamilton* 1998 SLT 220, 1997 SCCR 311; see also Construction and Use Regulations generally.
3 *Burns v Currel* [1963] 2 QB 433; *Nichol v Heath* [1972] RTR 476; *O'Brien v Anderton* [1979] RTR 388.
4 *McDonald v Carmichael* 1941 JC 27, 1941 SLT 8; *McLean v McCabe* 1964 SLT (Sh Ct) 39.
5 *Woodward v James Young (Contractors) Ltd* 1958 JC 28, 1958 SLT 289.
6 See 1.6:8 below.

1.2:2   Towed vehicles

A motor vehicle does not cease to be classified as such when it is towed by another vehicle[1]. In terms of s 185(1) of the Road Traffic Act 1988, a trailer means a vehicle drawn by a motor vehicle. Any kind of vehicle which is towed is liable to fall within the definition of a trailer; such a vehicle may therefore be at the same time both a motor vehicle and a trailer. Accordingly, the towed vehicle will also require to be covered by insurance, and will be subject to the requirements of the Vehicles (Excise) Act 1971 and the relevant Construction and Use Regulations. This is because the vehicle, although being towed, is still 'used' on the road. Trailers are described at 1.5 below. The position of drivers of towed vehicles is referred to at 1.7:1 and 3.3:2 below.

1.2:3   General application

In terms of s 87 of the Road Traffic Act 1988 (as amended by s 17 of the Road Traffic Act 1991), an appropriate licence is required before any person can drive a motor vehicle of any class on a road; and in terms of s 143 of the 1988 Act there is a requirement that the use of a motor vehicle on a road should be covered by a policy of insurance or other security. In both those instances the definition of a motor vehicle found in s 185 of the 1988 Act should be applied. In terms of s 1(1) of the Vehicles Excise and Registration Act 1994, an excise duty is charged in respect of every 'mechanically propelled vehicle' used or kept on a public road. A 'public road' in this context has the same meaning as in the Roads (Scotland) Act 1984[2]. The phrase 'mechanically propelled vehicle' is not defined in that Act; reference should be made to 1.2:1 above.

1.2:4   Exceptions

In terms of s 189(1) of the Road Traffic Act 1988, and s 140 of the Road Traffic Regulation Act 1984, certain vehicles such as grass-cutting machines which are controlled by a pedestrian and not capable of being used or adapted for any other purpose, and

---

1 *Cobb v Whorton* [1971] RTR 392.
2 s 62: see 1.8 and 8.15:2 below.

electrically assisted pedal cycles[1] are not to be considered as motor vehicles. However, this exception might not apply to privately owned grass-mowers with a seat for the driver, which are used on a verge forming part of the road.

A cycle is taken to mean a bicycle, tricycle or a cycle having four or more wheels, and is similarly not to be regarded as a motor vehicle[2]; neither, as indicated above, is an electrically assisted pedal cycle of such a class as is prescribed by regulations. Offences connected with the riding of cycles on the roadway are found in ss 24 and 26; s 28 (as amended by the Road Traffic Act 1991, s 7) and ss 29–32 of the 1988 Act; reference should be made to 2.7 and 2.17 below. A hovercraft is a motor vehicle, whether or not it is adapted or intended for use on the road[3], but it is not to be regarded as a vehicle of any of the classes as defined in s 185 of the 1988 Act.

Within these general guidelines the question of whether any vehicle does or does not come within the statutory definition of a motor vehicle will depend on the facts and circumstances of each case. In addition to the statutory definition of a motor vehicle, there are numerous regulations governing the construction and use of all kinds of such vehicles. The principal regulations in this respect are the Road Vehicles (Construction and Use) Regulations 1986[4].

1.3 MOTOR CAR

A 'motor car' is defined in terms of s 185(1) of the Road Traffic Act 1988 as–

'a mechanically propelled vehicle, not being a motor cycle or an invalid carriage, which is constructed itself to carry a load or passengers and the weight of which unladen –

(a) if it is constructed solely for the carriage of passengers and their effects, is adapted to carry not more than seven passengers exclusive of the driver, and is fitted with tyres of such type as specified in regulations made by the Secretary of State, does not exceed 3,050 kilogrammes –

---

1 See Electrically Assisted Pedal Cycles Regulations 1983, SI 1983/1168.
2 Road Traffic Act 1988, s 192(1); 1.6:7 below.
3 RTA 1988, s 188.
4 SI 1986/1078.

   (b) if it is constructed or adapted for the conveyance of goods or burden of any description, does not exceed 3,050 kilogrammes, or 3,500 kilogrammes if the vehicle carries a container or containers for holding for the purpose of its propulsion any fuel which is wholly gaseous at 17.5 degrees Celsius under a pressure of 1.013 bar or plant and materials for producing such fuel –

   (c) does not exceed 2,450 kilogrammes in a case falling within neither of the foregoing paragraphs.'

A similar definition is provided in s 136(2) of the Road Traffic Regulation Act 1984; and regulation 3 of the Road Vehicles (Construction and Use) Regulations 1986[1] gives a simpler but essentially identical definition. The significance of the phrase 'mechanically propelled' is discussed at 1.2:1 above.

1.4   GOODS VEHICLES

1.4:1   General

A 'goods vehicle' means a motor vehicle constructed or adapted for the carriage of goods, or a trailer so constructed or adapted[2]. In the Road Vehicles (Construction and Use) Regulations 1986[3], the definition is 'a motor vehicle or trailer constructed or adapted for use for the carriage or haulage of goods or burden of any description'.

Whether a vehicle has been constructed for the carriage of goods will normally be self-evident. The question of whether a vehicle has been adapted for such use is a question of fact and degree in each case, and is likely to depend chiefly on the nature of the use to which the vehicle is put in its altered state[4].

There is special provision for the licensing of drivers of large goods vehicles[5] and the licensing of operators of goods vehicles is described at 9.11 below.

---

1 SI 1986/1078.
2 Road Traffic Act 1988, s 192(1).
3 SI 1986/1078. reg 3(2).
4 *Taylor v Mead* [1961] 1 WLR 435, 1 All ER 626; *Backer v Secretary of State for Environment* [1983] 1 WLR 1485, [1983] 2 All ER 1021.
5 See 9.12 below.

1.4:2 Goods

The term 'goods' includes goods or burden of any description; and the phrase 'carriage of goods' includes the haulage of goods[1]. It is not necessary that the goods carried on the vehicle are for sale; the term can include such diverse matters as workmen's equipment and effluent[2]. However, if a vehicle is fitted with a crane, dynamo, welding plant or other special appliance or apparatus which is a permanent or essentially permanent fixture, the appliance or apparatus shall not be deemed to constitute a load, or goods or burden of any description, but shall be deemed to form part of the vehicle[3].

1.5 TRAILERS

A 'trailer' is a vehicle drawn by a motor vehicle[4]. This definition is general and extremely wide and includes virtually anything on wheels which is towed or drawn by a motor vehicle. For example, a poultry shed being moved for sale on wheels drawn by a car will be classified as a trailer[5], as will a wheeled roadman's hut used as an office and taken onto the road[6].

In *Johnston v Cruickshank*[7], a case under the Lighting Regulations, it was held that where a mechanically propelled vehicle was drawing a trailer, the vehicle doing the towing, and not the composite vehicle, was to be regarded as the motor vehicle in terms of the requirements of the regulations.

For the purpose of drivers' hours and records, a trailer is defined as any vehicle designed to be coupled to a motor vehicle or a tractor[8].

It is important to note that for the purpose of drivers' hours and records of work (the tachograph legislation) the total weight of a commercial vehicle is to be calculated on the composite weight of

1 Road Traffic Act 1988, s 192(1).
2 *Clarke v Cherry* [1953] 1 WLR 268, [1953] 1 All ER 267; *Sweetway Sanitary Cleaners v Bradley* [1962] 2 QB 108.
3 RTA 1988, s 186(3).
4 Road Traffic Act 1988, s 185(1).
5 *Garner v Burr* [1951] 1 KB 31.
6 *Horn v Dobson* 1933 JC 1.
7 1963 JC 5, 1962 SLT 409.
8 Regulation (EEC) 543/69.

both the towing vehicle and the trailer. If this total weight exceeds the statutory minimum (currently fixed at 3.5 tonnes) then the vehicle will require to be fitted with a tachograph, and the driver will be subject to the regulations concerned with the maximum hours which it is permitted to work. Small commercial vehicles below 3.5 tonnes, currently exempt, may therefore fall under these requirements during any periods when a trailer takes the total weight including its load over the statutory minimum[1]. However, this applies only to cases where the trailer is not a 'small trailer' which is defined in the amended terms of s 60(4) of the Transport Act 1968 as one whose unladen weight does not exceed 1,020 kilograms. Such small trailers can therefore be towed without bringing the composite vehicle within the tachograph rules.

A side-car attached to a motor cycle is not normally to be regarded as a trailer.

Regulations 83–90 of the Road Vehicles (Construction and Use) Regulations 1986[2] supply detailed provisions in respect of trailers and side-cars drawn by various kinds of vehicles, and the number of trailers that can be pulled at one time.

A semi-trailer is defined as a trailer which is constructed or adapted to form part of an articulated vehicle[3].

Towed vehicles are described at 1.2:2 above.

1.6   VARIOUS VEHICLES

1.6:1   Introduction

Throughout the general legislation there are definitions provided of a variety of sorts of vehicles for different purposes. The principal relevance of these definitions is in licensing, weight limits, and construction and use regulations generally. A general description of some of the most commonly used definitions follows:

---

1 RTA 1988, s 108(1) – definition of 'permissible maximum weight'.
2 SI 1986/1078.
3 And includes a vehicle which is not itself a motor vehicle but which has some or all of its wheels driven by the drawing vehicle – Road Vehicles (Construction and Use) Regulations 1986, SI 1986/1078, reg 3.

1.6:2 Articulated vehicles

In terms of s 108(1) of the Road Traffic Act 1988, an 'articulated goods vehicle' means 'a motor vehicle which is so constructed that a trailer designed to carry goods may by partial superimposition be attached thereto in such a manner as to cause a substantial part of the weight of the trailer to be borne by the motor vehicle'. By virtue of the same section, an articulated goods vehicle combination is defined as 'an articulated goods vehicle with a trailer so attached'. The same definition applies for the purposes of Part IV of the Act[1]. The context in which these definitions are given in the Act is the licensing of drivers. For the purposes of the Road Vehicles (Construction and Use) Regulations 1986[2], the term defined is an 'articulated vehicle', which is 'a heavy motor car or motor car, not being an articulated bus, with a trailer so attached that part of the trailer is superimposed on the drawing vehicle and, when the trailer is uniformly loaded, not less than 20 per cent of its load is borne by the drawing vehicle'. An articulated goods vehicle, or an articulated vehicle is therefore regarded, when not divided, as two separate vehicles, namely the drawing vehicle (which is either a motor car or a heavy motor car (depending on the individual weight)), and the trailer. However, in terms of s 186(2), where a vehicle is so constructed that a trailer may by partial superimposition be attached to the vehicle in such a manner as to cause a substantial part of the trailer to be borne by the vehicle, that vehicle shall be deemed to be a vehicle itself constructed to carry a load. Further provision in the definition of articulated passenger vehicles is found in s 187 of the Act.

As indicated at 1.5 above, there are restrictions on the number of trailers that can be drawn by a vehicle and various conditions applicable to their use.

1.6:3 Heavy motor cars

A 'heavy motor car' for the purpose of the Road Traffic Act 1988 means 'a mechanically propelled vehicle, not being a motor car, which is constructed itself to carry a load or passengers and the

---

1 Road Traffic Act 1988, s 120.
2 SI 1986/1078, reg 3.

weight of which unladen exceeds 2,540 kg'[1]; a similar definition is
provided for the Road Traffic Regulation Act 1984[2]. For the
purposes of the Road Vehicles (Construction and Use)
Regulations 1986, a heavy motor car is defined as 'a mechanically
propelled vehicle, not being a locomotive, a motor tractor, or a
motor car, which is constructed itself to carry a load or passengers
and the weight of which unladen exceeds 2,540 kg'[3]. Heavy motor
vehicles are accordingly the heaviest class of motor vehicle and
neither the statute nor the regulations provide an upper limit on
their unladen weight. However, other regulations restrict the
laden and total weights of such vehicles. The drawing unit of
most articulated vehicles is therefore a heavy motor car, except
where it does not exceed 2,540 kilograms, when it is simply a
motor car.

1.6:4   Commercial vehicles

A 'heavy commercial vehicle' means any goods vehicle which has
an operating weight exceeding 7.5 tonnes[4].

Goods vehicles generally are described at 1.4:1 above, and the
term 'goods' is described at 1.4:2 above.

A 'large goods vehicle' is defined in s 71 of the Transport Act
1968 (as amended) for specific purposes of controlled and authorised use within the terms of that Act.

A 'medium-sized goods vehicle' means 'a motor vehicle which
is constructed or adapted to carry or to haul goods and is not
adapted to carry more than nine persons inclusive of the driver
and the permissible maximum weight of which exceeds 3.5 but
not 7.5 tonnes'[5].

A 'small goods vehicle', by virtue of the same section, is 'a
motor vehicle (other than a motor cycle or invalid carriage) which
is constructed or adapted to carry or to haul goods and is not

---

1 Road Traffic Act, 1988, s 185(1).
2 RTA 1988, s 136(3).
3 Reg 3(2).
4 Road Traffic Regulation Act 1984, s 138(1), (2), wherein also are described the
  methods of arriving at the operating weight. A similar definition is given in s 20
  of the Road Traffic Act 1988 for the purposes of s 19 of that Act (prohibition of
  parking on verges, dangerous positions etc). See also 9.12:1 below.
5 Road Traffic Act 1988, s 108, which also provides a number of definitions
  concerned with weight considerations relating to commercial vehicles.

adapted to carry more than nine persons inclusive of the driver and the permissible maximum weight of which does not exceed 3.5 tonnes'. As indicated at 1.5 above, the permissible maximum weight of 3.5 tonnes is to be calculated by including the weight of any trailer with an unladen weight exceeding 1,020 kilograms and its contents drawn by such a vehicle at the relevant time. This is of particular importance in the drivers' hours of work and tacho-graph legislation, which comes into effect when a vehicle qualifies as a small goods vehicle. Accordingly, a goods vehicle which is under 3.5 tonnes in weight, and which is not therefore subject to drivers' hours and tachograph requirements, may exceed the minimum weight limit when a trailer in excess of 1,020 kilograms is added; if this happens then the vehicle must be fitted with a tachograph, and the driver and owner of the vehicle are subject to the drivers' hours and record of work legislation. 'Motor vehicle' is defined at 1.2:1 above. The licensing of large goods vehicle drivers and the operators of goods vehicles is discussed in Part 2 of Chapter 9.

1.6:5   Passenger and public service vehicles

A 'passenger vehicle' means a vehicle constructed or adapted for use solely or principally for the carriage of passengers[1]. A passenger vehicle is also defined for the purpose of the Construction and Use Regulations as 'a vehicle constructed solely for the carriage of passengers and their effects'[2]. For the purposes of Part III of the Road Traffic Act 1988, a 'small passenger vehicle', in terms of s 108, means 'a motor vehicle (other than a motor cycle or invalid carriage), which is constructed solely to carry passengers and their effects and is adapted to carry not more than nine persons inclusive of the driver'.

A public service vehicle is defined in s 1 of the Public Passenger Vehicles Act 1981 for the purpose of that Act as 'a motor vehicle (other than a tramcar) which – (a) being a vehicle adapted to carry more than eight passengers, is used for carrying passengers for hire or reward; or (b) being a vehicle not so adapted, is used for carrying passengers for hire or reward at separate fares in the

---

1 Road Traffic Act 1988, s 187(4).
2 Road Vehicles (Construction and Use) Regulations 1986, SI 1986/1078, reg 3(2).

course of a business of carrying passengers'. There are further qualifications of this definition within s 1, and the topic is more fully discussed at 9.2:1 below.

The term 'motor vehicle' is discussed at 1.2:1 above.

1.6:6 Motor cycles

A 'motor cycle' is defined as a 'mechanically propelled vehicle, not being an invalid carriage, with less than four wheels and the weight of which unladen does not exceed 410 kg'[1]. The definition of a motor cycle for these purposes includes a variety of vehicles, including three-wheelers, motor bicycles and mopeds, each of which is governed for various purposes by further legislation.

'Learner motor cycles' are defined by section 97(5) of the Road Traffic Act 1988 (as amended) and in effect mean either electric motor cycles, those with an engine capacity no greater than 125cc or those with an engine power output which does not exceed 11 kilowatts.

For the definition of 'mechanically propelled vehicle', see 1.2:1 above. Section 23 of the Road Traffic Act 1988 imposes restrictions on the carriage of persons on motor cycles. Regulation 102 of the Road Vehicles (Construction and Use) Regulations 1986 requires that footrests are fitted for any passenger. Helmets, or protective headgear, to be used by motor-cyclists are described in ss 16-18 of the Road Traffic Act 1988.

1.6:7 Cycles

A 'cycle' is 'a bicycle, tricycle, or cycle having four or more wheels, not being in any case a motor vehicle'[2].

The Secretary of State has power to make regulations in respect of brakes, bells, etc on pedal cycles[3]. Regulations made under the corresponding power in prior legislation are the Pedal Cycles (Construction and Use) Regulations 1983[4].

---

1 Road Traffic Act 1988, s 185(1); Road Vehicles (Construction and Use) Regulations 1986, SI 1986/1078, reg 3(2).
2 Road Traffic Act 1988, s 192.
3 RTA 1988, s 81.
4 SI 1983/1176.

Reference should also be made to the Electrically Assisted Pedal Cycles Regulations 1983[1]. Offences concerned with the riding of cycles are found in ss 24 and 26; s 28 (as amended by s 7 of the Road Traffic Act 1991); and ss 29–32 of the Road Traffic Act 1988; reference should be made to 2.7 and 2.17 below.

A police officer has the power to stop any person riding a cycle on a road[2].

1.6:8 Invalid carriages

An invalid carriage is 'a mechanically propelled vehicle the weight of which unladen does not exceed 254 kg and which is specially designed and constructed, and not merely adapted, for the use of a person suffering from some physical defect or disability and is solely used by such a person'[3]. Special provision for the use of such invalid carriages on the roads is provided by s 20 of the Chronically Sick and Disabled Persons Act 1970[4]; and s 21 of the same Act (as amended by s 35 of the Road Traffic Act 1991) makes provision for the issuing by local authorities of badges for display on motor vehicles used by disabled persons. Wrongful use of a disabled person's badge is an offence[5]. Aiding and abetting such an offence is specifically prohibited by s 119. Special parking provisions for the disabled are discussed at 7.9:1 below.

For the phrase 'mechanically propelled vehicle', see 1.2:1 above.

1.6:9 Breakdown and recovery vehicles

These are two distinct categories of vehicle. A recovery vehicle is described in the Vehicles and Excise Registration Act 1994, Sch 1, para 5, and a breakdown vehicle in regulation 3 of the Goods Vehicles (Plating and Testing) Regulations 1988[6].

---

1 SI 1983/1168.
2 RTA 1988, s 163(2).
3 Road Traffic Act 1988, s 185(1); Road Vehicles (Construction and Use) Regulations 1986, SI 1986/1078, reg 3(2).
4 As amended by the Road Traffic Act 1991, Sch 4, para 3.
5 Road Traffic Regulation Act 1984, s 117.
6 SI 1988 1478.

1.6:10   General

It should be noted in considering the foregoing paragraphs that certain vehicle term definitions are provided for particular purposes such as construction and use regulations, licensing and so on. Care should therefore be taken in considering the context of any definition provided in the legislation. As indicated above[1], there are a large number of further statutory definitions of various kinds of vehicles and features relating thereto in the definition sections of the principal Acts and Regulations.

1.7   DRIVERS: DRIVING

1.7:1   General

The courts in Scotland have generally held that the driver of a motor vehicle is someone who is either in the driving seat or in control of the steering wheel, and in addition has something to do with (although not necessarily complete control over) the propulsion of the vehicle. In *Ames v McLeod*[2], a motorist steered his car (which had run out of petrol) down an incline by walking beside it with his hand on the steering wheel, and in these circumstances he was held on appeal to be driving the vehicle at the material time. The Lord Justice-General (Clyde) indicated[3] that it was not essential for the purposes of determining whether a person was driving that it is established that the engine was running or that the accused should be sitting in the driving seat. The true test was whether the accused is 'in a substantial sense controlling the movement and direction of the car'; or, in other words, whether the extent of the accused's intervention with the movement and direction of the vehicle was sufficient to establish that he was driving. It should be noted, however, that in almost identical circumstances an opposite conclusion was reached in England[4]. *Ames v McLeod*[5] was followed in *Lockhart v Smith*[6]; in that case a

---

1 At 1.1.
2 1969 JC 1 (followed in *McArthur v Valentine* 1990 JC 146, 1990 SLT 732, 1989 SCCR 704).
3 At 3.
4 *R v MacDonagh* (sub nom *MacDonald*) [1974] QB 448, [1974] RTR 372, [1974] 2 All ER 257.
5 1969 JC1.
6 1979 SLT (Sh Ct) 52.

boy who on instruction from the milkman released the handbrake of a milk float so that it rolled downhill, but who did not touch the steering wheel, was held not to be driving.

The person behind the steering wheel of a towed vehicle will in normal circumstances be regarded as driving the vehicle. In *Wallace v Major*[1] it was observed that such a person might not fall within the definition of a driver because he had no control over the propulsion of the vehicle[2]. However, although this case has not been overturned, in *McQuaid v Anderton*[3] a disqualified driver was held to be driving when steering a towed vehicle. There appears to be no reason why anyone behind the steering wheel of a towed vehicle should not be regarded as driving for most of the purposes of the road traffic legislation.

Whether or not a person is in fact driving at the material time, or is to be regarded as 'the driver' of a vehicle for the purposes of a particular prosecution, will depend on the facts and circumstances of each case, in the context of the particular offence in question. However, it has been decided that it is possible that, at any one time, more than one person can fall within the definition of being the driver of the vehicle at that time[4]. For example, a learner driver and an instructor may well be regarded as both driving at the same time if in practice both have some measure of control over both the steering and the propulsion of the vehicle[5]. Further, where a person acts as a steersman of a motor vehicle, the Road Traffic Act 1988, s 192(1) provides that he is to be included in the term 'driver' as well as any other person engaged in the driving of the vehicle. This provision is specifically excluded from applying to prosecutions under s 1 of the Act. However where a driver has been effectively prevented or dissuaded from driving his vehicle, he can no longer be regarded as driving[6]. In *Farrell v Stirling*[7], a case involving careless driving under summary procedure, a diabetic experienced for the first time an attack of hypoglycaemia shortly before an accident, and the court there concluded that he could not be described as driving his vehicle at the material time. In *McLeod v Mathieson*[8], however, this defence

---

1 [1946] KB 473.
2 At 477 per LCJ Goddard.
3 [1980] RTR 371 (followed in *Caise v Wright* [1981] RTR 49).
4 *Tyler v Whatmore* [1976] RTR 83.
5 *Langman v Valentine* [1952] 2 All ER 803.
6 *Edkins v Knowles* [1973] QB 748 at 757, [1973] RTR 257.
7 1975 SLT (Sh Ct) 71.
8 1993 SCCR 488.

was not available to a driver who knew he suffered from such a condition.

The question of whether a motorist was driving or not at any material time may be a relevant issue in many different situations other than those described above, such as where someone is called upon to produce documentation, or to comply with a direction given by a police officer.

Not infrequently the prosecution has to establish that an accused has been driving a vehicle in the absence of direct evidence by reference to the surrounding facts and circumstances[1].

Further definition of the nature of driving in the context of the drink/driving legislation is found at 3.3:2 below.

1.7:2   Attempting to drive

The question of whether a motorist is attempting to drive his vehicle is a question of fact. The phrase has its principal significance in offences under ss 4(1) and 5(1) of the Road Traffic Act 1988, and is more fully described at 3.3:3 below.

1.8   ROAD

1.8:1   General

In the Road Traffic Act 1988 as originally framed, and in earlier legislation, the majority of road traffic offences occurred if the driving or other conduct complained of took place 'on a road'. The principal exceptions to this rule were the drink driving offence sections[2] where the offence occurred if it took place 'on a road or other public place'. Accordingly, two lines of authority developed, namely what was meant by 'a road', and what was to be understood by the phrase 'other public place'. The cases involving the latter normally involved drinking and driving charges; and there were, and are, features common to both definitions.

---

1 See e g, *Henderson v Hamilton* 1995 SCCR 413.
2 Road Traffic Act 1988, ss 4, 5 and 6.

By virtue of the terms of ss 1, 2 and 3 of the Road Traffic Act 1991, the qualification of the offence taking place 'on a road or other public place' is extended to cover ss 1, 2, 3 and 3A of the 1988 Act. Accordingly, offences under ss 1–6 inclusive of the Road Traffic Act 1988 as amended occur if the driving or other conduct complained of takes place 'on a road or other public place'. In the majority of the other sections of the legislation offences are established if the actions of the motorist take place simply 'on a road'.

The legislation therefore seeks to extend the ambit of the most serious driving offences beyond the public roadway, to other places to which the public resort. One example of such places is forestry roads; provision for special events and certain exemptions from prosecution are found in the Road Traffic Act 1988, s 13, and s 13A[1]. The Roads (Scotland) Act 1984 makes a number of provisions in respect of the use of roads and highways, a detailed discussion of which is outwith the scope of this book. However, in general terms the Act gives extensive powers to the roads authority (normally the local council or, in the case of special or trunk roads, the appropriate minister) to control works and excavations, and traffic[2] and to prevent obstruction and interference[3]. Reference should also be made to the New Road and Street Works Act 1991 (c 22). The Road Traffic Act 1988, s 33 prohibits the use of footpaths and bridleways for motor vehicle trials; and s 34 prohibits the driving of motor vehicles elsewhere than on roads.

1.8:2   Road

The statutory definitions of a road are found in the Roads (Scotland) Act 1984, s 151(1)[4], as that definition is amended by the Road Traffic Act 1991, Sch 4, para 78. The definition as contained in the 1984 Act is:

'any way (other than a waterway) over which there is a right of passage (by whatever means) and includes the road's verge, and any bridge (whether permanent or temporary) over which, or tunnel through which, the road passes; and any reference to a road includes a part thereof.'

---

1 As introduced by the Road Traffic Act 1991, s 5.
2 Roads (Scotland) Act 1984, Pt V.
3 R(S)A 1984, Pt VIII.
4 Which is incorporated into the Road Traffic Act 1988 by s 192(2) of that Act.

To this must be added the further description of the term found in the Road Traffic Act 1991, Sch 4, para 78, which provides:

'and (b) in relation to Scotland, means any road within the meaning of the Roads (Scotland) Act 1984 and any other way to which the public has access, and includes bridges over which a road passes.'

These additional provisions are not intended to affect the exceptions contained in s 151(3) of the Roads (Scotland) Act 1984, which relate to certain public paths, footpaths and recreational ground.

For convenience the entire collated statutory definition of 'a road' is as follows:

'a "road" means ... (a) any way (other than a waterway) over which there is a public right of passage (by whatever means) and includes the road's verge, and any bridge (whether permanent or temporary) over which, or tunnel through which, the road passes; and any reference to a road includes a part thereof; ... (and) ... (b) ... means any other way to which the public has access, and includes bridges over which a road passes.'

The definition of a 'road' has therefore gone through three historical stages. Prior to the Roads (Scotland) Act 1984, a number of cases described a road as essentially a highway or other road to which the public had access, or had obtained access thereto without having to overcome a physical obstruction or in defiance of an express or implied prohibition[1]. This reflected the terms of s 121(1) of the Road Traffic Act 1930, which was common to both Scotland and England, and which provided a definition in effect as 'any highway and any other road to which the public has access'. The principal feature of the definition introduced by the Roads (Scotland) Act 1984 was that there should exist a public right of passage over the way in question. The effect of this was to diminish the significance of public access other than by right in any particular case. In *Young v Carmichael*[2] a driver was found on the lawn attached to a private apartment block, onto which he had driven from one of two car parks adjacent to the building. Access to the building was gained from a public road which passed through a gap in the fence surround-

1 E g *Harrison v Hill* 1932 JC 13; *Purves v Muir* 1948 JC 122, 1948 SLT 529; *Hogg v Nicholson* 1968 SLT 265.
2 1993 SLT 167, 1991 SCCR 332.

ing the apartment block and its amenity grounds. The car parks were used by residents, their guests, tradesmen and police. There were signs at the entrance indicating that the car parks were private and for the use of residents only. In the Appeal Court it was held (a) that as the public had no right of access to the car park it was not a road, and (b) that as there was no evidence that members of the public had access to the car parks in the sense that they normally resorted to it and so might be expected to be there, the car park was not 'a public place'. The report also considers the history of the definition of the terms 'road' and 'other public place' to that date. *Young v Carmichael*[1] therefore concluded that cases decided under earlier legislation which in general terms defined a road as a 'highway or any other road to which the public has access' were of limited value.

However, the additional definition provided by the Road Traffic Act 1991, Sch 4, para 78, passed after the decision in *Young v Carmichael*, seeks to re-introduce the idea of public access into the definition of the term 'road'. Accordingly the case of *Young v Carmichael* is not the final word on this subject and cases decided before the 1984 Act may again be of interest.

A footway associated with a carriageway, or a footpath not so associated, are included in the definition of a road[2]. A lay-by or verge is also part of the road[3], as is a parking area next to a place of public resort such as an inn, on the basis that it is a way over which there is a public right of passage[4]. The car deck of a ferry was held to be a road when connected to a ramp on the dock in *Dick v Walkingshaw*[5]. The court is entitled to understand that the M90 is a motorway and therefore a road[6].

In *Adair v Davidson*[7] the drive to a private house was held to be a road, but this was doubted by Lord Guthrie in *Hogg v Nicholson*[8] at 268; see also *Carmichael v Wilson*[9].

---

1 1993 SLT 167, 1991 SCCR 332.
2 Roads (Scotland) Act 1984, s 151(2).
3 Roads (Scotland) Act 1984, s 151(1); *MacNeill v Dunbar* 1965 SLT (Notes) 79.
4 *Beattie v Scott* 1991 SLT 873, 1990 SCCR 435.
5 1995 SLT 1254, 1995 SCCR 307.
6 *Donaldson v Valentine* 1996 SLT 643, 1996 SCCR 374.
7 1934 JC 37, 1934 SLT 316.
8 1968 SLT 265.
9 1993 SLT 1066.

1.8:3   Other public place

The phrase 'other public place' means a place to which the public may resort by express or implied permission. The principles which apply are in some respects similar to the question of whether a road is public or not. For example, an isolated farmyard where there were few visitors or passers-by and where in general there would be little if any expectation that the public might be present is not a public place[1], whereas a private road commonly walked by fishermen and hill walkers is a public place[2]. A field used as a car park at the Highland Show was held to be a public place[3], as was a spare piece of ground used as an overflow parking area at a cattle mart[4]. The prosecution may have to prove the right to resort to a particular area[5]. In certain circumstances a dock road may be a public place[6]. A driveway from a public road to a hotel, even where the proprietors of the hotel reserved the right to exclude certain members of the public, may still be a public place[7]; similarly, a private camping and caravan site occupied by persons who had gained access through the permission of the site owners was held to be a public place even although other members of the public were effectively excluded from the site[8]. A car park attached to a public house may also be a public place as well as a road[9]. On the other hand, a private car park attached to an apartment block signposted as private was held not to be a public place[10].

A garage forecourt is a public place; in *Brown v Braid*[11] it was observed that the test was 'whether the forecourt was a place on which members of the public might be expected to be found and over which they might be expected to be passing, or over which they are in use to have access.' Reference should also be made on the question of whether the public has access to a particular place[12].

---

1   *Alston v O'Brien* 1992 SLT 856, 1992 SCCR 238.
2   *Thomson v MacPhail* 1992 SCCR 466.
3   *Paterson v Ogilvy* 1957 JC 42, 1957 SLT 354.
4   *McDonald v McEwen* 1953 SLT (Sh Ct) 26.
5   *Elkins v Cartlidge* [1974] 1 All ER 829; *Pugh v Knipe* [1972] RTR 286.
6   *Renwick v Scott* 1996 SLT 1164.
7   *Dunn v Keane* 1972 JC 39.
8   *DPP v Vivier* [1991] RTR 205.
9   *Vannet v Burns* 1999 SLT 340, 1998 SCCR 414.
10   *Young v Carmichael* 1993 SLT 167, 1991 SCCR 332; see 1.8:2 above.
11   1985 SLT 37, 1984 SCCR 286, 1984 CO Circulars A/22.
12   *Rodger v Normand* 1995 SLT 411, 1994 SCCR 861; *Aird v Vannet* 1999 JC 205, 2000 SLT 435, 1999 SCCR 327; *Vannet v Burns* 1999 SLT 340, 1998 SCCR 414.

1.8:4 Motorways

Driving on motorways is governed by the Motorways Traffic (Scotland) Regulations 1995[1]. The court is entitled to assume from its own knowledge that the M90 is a motorway[2].

1.9 ACCIDENT

Whether or not an accident has occurred will depend on the facts and circumstances of each case. A satisfactory definition of the word is not easy to provide, having regard to the variety of circumstances under which what might be described as an 'accident' can occur. No definition of the term appears anywhere in the legislation, and the courts have not been anxious to provide a general or all-purpose definition of the word, preferring normally to draw conclusions from the circumstances of each case. It has been suggested that an appropriate test might be to consider whether an ordinary man who witnessed what happened would say that in all the circumstances there had been an accident. It is, however, clear that an accident can arise out of a deliberate act, and need not involve another vehicle. It is also clear that an impact does not have to take place before it can be said there has been an accident[3].

The matter was considered by the Appeal Court in *Pryde v Brown*[4], where two pedestrians walking on a main road were obliged to take evasive action when a vehicle came round a bend at speed on the wrong side of the road. In holding that this had been an 'accident', the Appeal Court said:

'We do not think that any precise definition of the word "accident" . . . can be formulated. We do not think that any of the tests adumbrated in the cases referred to are wholly satisfactory in every circumstance. We do not think that only unintended occurrences can be included in the word "accident", as the word may obviously include occurrences which may have been intended. We do not think it can be limited to untoward occurrences having an adverse physical result, because it is possible to visualise an "accident" having no adverse physical result at all. It seems to us

---

1 SI 1995/2507.
2 *Donaldson v Valentine* 1996 SLT 643, 1996 SCCR 374.
3 *Bremner v Westwater* 1994 SLT 707, 1993 SCCR 1023.
4 1982 SLT 314, 1982 SCCR 26.

to be more appropriate to proceed on the basis that it will depend on the circumstances of each case whether a happening can properly be described as an "accident". The test is one of common sense rather than conformity with a definition difficult to formulate and providing an exhaustive cover.'

The circumstances in which an accident can be said to have occurred are therefore wide and general. Incidents where a vehicle has been required to take avoiding action as a result of the conduct of another vehicle, where an obstruction or object, as opposed to another vehicle or person, has been struck, or where something has happened as a result of the way a vehicle is being driven completely outwith the awareness of the driver, may all be termed as accidents. Section 170 of the Road Traffic Act 1988[1] envisages that an accident has occurred if injury is caused to any other party or damage is caused to any other vehicle, to specified animals or to any property constructed on, fixed to, growing in or otherwise forming part of the land on which the road is situated or land adjacent thereto. The *de minimis* rule would seem to have very little relevance, if any, in the interpretation of the word.

The question of whether or not an accident has taken place may be of particular importance inter alia in prosecutions under the breathalyser legislation[2]; in charges of failing to stop after an accident[3]; and in respect of prosecution restrictions in terms of s 2(1) of the Road Traffic Offenders Act 1988. The duty on a driver to stop after an accident is discussed at 7:6.3 below.

1.10   USING, CAUSING AND PERMITTING

1.10:1   General

Throughout the legislation there are a number of offences which are committed when an accused person uses a vehicle, or causes or permits a vehicle to be used, in a particular way. The terms 'use' or 'using', 'causing' and 'permitting' have always to be considered in the context in which they are employed; however, certain general observations may be made on these terms.

---

1 As amended by the Road Traffic Act 1991, Sch 4, para 72.
2 Road Traffic Act 1988, s 6(2).
3 RTA 1988, s 170.

1.10:2   Using

The most common offences involving use are those which contravene s 143 of the Road Traffic Act 1988 (compulsory insurance), s 87 of the same Act (licensing of drivers) or the use of vehicles in a manner contrary to many of the Road Vehicle (Construction and Use) Regulations 1986[1]. An offence involving 'use' as opposed to 'causing' or 'permitting' normally involves strict liability and the question of *mens rea* is irrelevant. The word has been interpreted in a wide sense and, for example, convictions for using a car without insurance are commonplace where the only use made of the vehicle is to park it on the street. Even if a vehicle is broken down and unable to move by its own power, it will be regarded as being used on the road for the purpose of s 143. 'Driving' involves the use of a vehicle.

A vehicle being towed will also be regarded as being used for all relevant purposes of the legislation[2]. A corporate entity may be guilty of an offence involving use of a vehicle, and because most of such offences carry absolute liability, the employer of a driver who drives or uses a vehicle which contravenes the construction and use regulations may well be guilty of an offence even although the employer had no direct or personal knowledge of the defect which caused the offence[3]. The word 'use' can also mean 'have the use of' and two people may therefore be using a vehicle at the same time[4].

However, the nature of 'use' has been qualified in certain circumstances. In *Hamilton v Blair and Meechan*[5] it was held that an owner of a vehicle who had hired it out for an excursion to a third party (who was to supply the driver) was not 'using' the vehicle at the material time, nor was the hirer 'using' the vehicle at a time when she was not within the vehicle. In the latter instance, Lord Carmont[6] indicated that the hirer, although not using the vehicle, may have been causing or permitting its use. In *Valentine v MacBrayne Haulage Ltd*[7] (a sheriff court case) it was held that where a statute penalised both using and causing as well as permitting use of a vehicle, the category of 'user' should be

1 SI 1986/1078.
2 *Cobb v Whorton* [1971] RTR 392.
3 *Swan v MacNab* 1977 JC 57, 1978 SLT 192, 1978 CO Circulars A/13.
4 *Dickson v Valentine* 1989 SLT 19, 1988 SCCR 325.
5 1962 JC 31, 1962 SLT 69.
6 At 76.
7 1986 SCCR 692.

confined to the driver of the vehicle and his employer at the material time, and should not be extended further. The report usefully considers the principal authorities on the term 'using'. If the vehicle in question is the subject of a hire agreement, then the person who is 'using' the vehicle at the material time is the hirer and not the hire firm[1].

Whether a vehicle is being 'used' or not may depend upon the particular offence in question. Thus in *Tudhope v Every*[2] it was held that a vehicle which was immobile and parked on a road was being used in terms of s 143 of the Road Traffic Act 1972 (which required vehicles used on a road to be covered by insurance), but was not being used on a road in terms of s 44(1) of the same Act (which requires vehicles used on a road to be covered by an MOT certificate).

The reason for this differing treatment of the same word is that the meaning of the term 'use' contemplated in the two sections of the Act, and the nature of the prohibition involved in each case, is different. A parked car, even when immobile, may cause or be involved in an accident; therefore it must be insured. However, the MOT certificate is designed to cover other areas of use which an immobile vehicle could not perform, and accordingly such a vehicle is not being used for that purpose.

Nothing in the Road Traffic Acts authorises a person to use on a road a vehicle so constructed or used as to cause a nuisance, or affects the liability, under statute or common law of the driver or owner[3].

1.10:3   Causing or permitting

'Causing' and 'permitting' are two separate ideas. In practice their meanings may overlap. Corporate entities may be guilty of causing or permitting. The principal application of the terms is again in the Road Traffic Act 1988, s 87 (licensing of drivers) and s 143 (compulsory insurance) and in the Construction and Use Regulations.

The two words are used, normally together, in slightly different ways and contexts throughout the legislation, and consideration

---

1 *Mackay Brothers & Co v Gibb* 1969 JC 26, 1969 SLT 216; *Farrell v Moggach* 1976 SLT (Sh Ct) 8.
2 1976 JC 42, 1977 SLT 2.
3 Road Traffic (Consequential Provisions) Act 1988, s 7.

has to be given to the particular nature of the offence in each case. For general purposes, the term 'causing' involves some measure of direction or control by the accused towards or over a third party in a matter where the accused has the proper capacity to make such a direction or exercise such control. In other words, actual or constructive knowledge of the offence must be established, as well as some measure of participation in allowing the offence to take place, or failing to take reasonable steps to stop it happening. The most common example of 'causing' in practice is where an employer instructs an employee to drive the employer's vehicle.

For an accused to be convicted of 'causing' a third party to commit an offence, the prosecution will normally have to establish both that the accused directed or controlled the substantive acts complained of, and that he was aware or should have been aware that those acts constituted an offence. In other words, actual or constructive knowledge of the offence must be established, as well as some measure of participation in allowing the offence to take place; a failing to take reasonable steps to stop it happening. This is notwithstanding that most of the offences in which the terms are used involved strict liability.

In *Smith of Maddiston Ltd v Macnab*[1], a limited company was charged with using, or causing or permitting to be used, a vehicle with an insecure load. The company had hired out to a third party a vehicle and a driver to transport a load. The driver, who was experienced in such matters, elected to secure the load in an ineffective manner although he had been supplied with suitable securing material. The Appeal Court (overruling *Hunter v Clark*[2]) held that the company could not be guilty of the offence as it neither knew nor should have known of the contravention of the relevant regulations, and could not therefore be said to have caused or permitted the use complained of.

In *Macdonald v Wilmae Concrete Co Ltd*[3], it was held that a company was not guilty of causing or permitting a vehicle to be used with a defective brake in circumstances where it was not proved that any responsible official of the company knew of the defect. In particular, it was held to be insufficient for a conviction simply to show that the company took no action or even that this system of

1 1975 JC 48, 1975 SLT 86, 1975.
2 1956 JC 59.
3 1954 SLT (Sh Ct) 33.

inspection was not perfect. However, in *Brown v Burns Tractors Ltd*[1], it was held (following *Smith of Maddiston Ltd v Macnab*[2]) that knowledge, in relation to a statutory provision, includes 'the state of mind of a man who shuts his eyes to the obvious and allows another to do something in circumstances where a contravention is likely, not caring whether a contravention takes place or not'. In other words, wilful blindness, or culpable ignorance, in respect of the relevant statutory provisions on the part of an accused in a charge of causing or permitting is not a defence. In this context, reference may also be made to *Clydebank Co-operative Society v Binnie*[3]; *Mackay Bros v Gibb*[4]; and *Farrell v Moggach*[5].

'Permitting' means simply giving permission, or allowing a third party to do something. The permission must, however, be proved to be something which the accused can properly give. In addition, for conviction it must be shown, as in the case of 'causing', that the accused was aware that what was permitted constituted an offence; actual or constructive knowledge of the offence has to be demonstrated, as well as direct or indirect evidence of permission. The same general considerations that apply to 'causing' described above apply also to 'permitting'.

In *MacDonald v Howdle*[6] a driver who offered his car to another on condition that he got it insured was held not to have permitted its use, when the other driver drove without getting insurance. A discussion of what may be meant by the term 'permitting' is found in *Elsby v McFadyen*[7].

It is competent and common practice for accused persons or corporate entities to be charged with 'using' and 'causing or permitting' as alternatives.

1.11   IDENTIFICATION OF DRIVER

1.11:1   General

Except in some limited cases where there is specific statutory exemption, corroborative evidence of the identity of the driver of

1 1986 SCCR 146.
2 1975 JC 48, 1975 SLT 86.
3 1937 JC 17, 1937 SLT 114.
4 1969 JC 26, 1969 SLT 216.
5 1976 SLT (Sh Ct) 8.
6 1995 SLT 779, 1995 SCCR 216.
7 2000 SCCR 97.

a vehicle is required for the purposes of prosecution of road traffic offences[1].

Accordingly, if the only evidence of identification is that of two police officers who speak to an admission by the driver that he was driving at the material time, this is insufficient for conviction[2]. Reference in this respect should be made to para 7.5:8 below.

A car driver will not be considered in normal circumstances to be a person in a special capacity in terms of s 255 of the Criminal Procedure (Scotland) Act 1995[3]; however, an accused charged with driving while disqualified will be regarded as being in such a special capacity and so in those circumstances the need for corroborative evidence does not arise[4]. Production of an extract conviction does not amount to waiver by the Crown of the right to rely on this section[5].

An admission by a driver, made to a police officer or any other person, that he was driving at the time of the alleged offence can be sufficient evidence of identification if the surrounding facts and circumstances confirm that identification[6].

A statement made in reply to a caution, or a caution and charge, if properly administered by a police officer, is competent evidence

---

1 *Mitchell v MacDonald* 1959 SLT (Notes) 74; *Sinclair v MacLeod* 1964 SLT (Notes) 60.

2 *Sinclair v McLeod* 1964 SLT (Notes) 60.

3 *Cruickshanks v MacPhail* 1988 SCCR 165.

4 *Smith v Allan* 1985 SLT 565, 1985 SCCR 190.

5 *Paton v Lees* 1992 SCCR 212; see also *Campbell v HM Advocate* 1999 JC 147, 1999 SLT 399.

6 *Copeland v Shields* 1959 SLT (Sh Ct) 50; *Sinclair v Clark* 1962 JC 57 (per LJ-C Thomson at 62), 1962 SLT 307; *Lockhart v Crockett* 1987 SLT 551, 1986 SCCR 685; see also *White v MacDonald* 1964 SCCR Supp 5; *Douglas v Pirie* 1975 at 61, 1975 SLT 206; *Miln v Fitzgerald* 1978 SCCR Supp 205, 1978 CO Circulars A/9; *McDonald v Smith* 1978 SCCR Supp 219; *MacNab v Culligan* 1978 SCCR Supp 222, 1978 CO Circulars A/26; *Lodhi v Skeen* 1978 SCCR Supp 197; *Wright v Tudhope* 1983 SCCR 403; *Cummings v Tudhope* 1985 SCCR 125; *Tudhope v Dalgleish* 1986 SCCR 559; *McClure v McLeod* 1987 SCCR 274; *Lockhart v Crockett* 1987 SLT 551; *MacLennan v Macdonald* 1988 SCCR 133; *Cruickshanks v MacPhail* 1988 SCCR 165; *Rowley v Hamilton* 1989 SCCR 211; *Frew v Jessop* 1990 JC 15, 1990 SLT 396, 1989 SCCR 530; *Hingston v Pollock* 1990 JC 138, 1990 SLT 770, 1989 SCCR 697; *Fisher v Guild* 1991 SLT 253, 1991 SCCR 308; *McClory v McInnes* 1992 SLT 501, 1992 SCCR 319; *Souter v Lees* 1995 SCCR 33; *Winter v Heywood* 1995 JC 60, 1995 SLT 586, 1995 SCCR 276 (which is authority for the proposition that one source of identification together with the fact that the accused is the registered driver is not enough); *Henderson v Hamilton* 1995 SCCR 413; *Templeton v Crowe* 1999 JC 47, 1999 SCCR 7). These cases are all subject in practice to the appeal in the case of *Brown v Stott* 2000 SLT 379, currently before the Privy Council.

as to both the identity of the driver and any other relevant matters included in the statement.

1.11:2   Statement made in response to a question

At common law, an admission by an accused that he was the driver at the time of an alleged offence in response to a question from a police officer may be admissible in evidence[1]. The test as to whether such an answer is admissible or not is to be determined having regard, in all the circumstances, to the principle of fairness to the accused. In considering that test, regard must be given to the accused's circumstances and position, and also to the public interest in ascertaining the true facts of each case, and the detection of offences. If, having regard to all these matters, it is decided that the request for information imposes unfairness on the accused, the evidence will generally be inadmissible; equally, if no unfairness is caused to the accused, the evidence will be allowed[2].

1.11:3   Duty to give information to police

In terms of s 172(2) of the Road Traffic Act 1988, as amended by s 21 of the Road Traffic Act 1991, where a driver of a vehicle is alleged to be guilty of any road traffic offence (apart from certain exceptions listed within the section), the keeper of the vehicle or any other person may be required by a police officer to give information as to the identity of the driver at the material time. The phrase 'any other person' includes the alleged driver himself[3]. An admission by the driver under this sub-section is presently admissible in evidence[4] and, as in the case of other forms of admission, can satisfy the test of corroborative evidence if there is supporting evidence from another credible source[5]. The requirement to give this information is not a breach of the European Convention on Human Rights[6]. However, in a case currently under appeal to the

1 *Miln v Cullen* 1967 JC 21, 1967 SLT 35.
2 *McClory v McInnes* 1992 SLT 501, 1992 SCCR 319.
3 *Foster v Farrell* 1963 JC 46, 1963 SLT 182, overruling *Stewart v McLugash* (1962) 78 Sh Ct Rep 189.
4 *Foster v Farrell* 1963 JC 46, 1963 SLT 182.
5 *Galt v Goodsir* 1982 JC 4, 1982 SLT 94, 1981 SCCR 225.
6 *Jardine v Crowe* 1999 SCCR 52.

Privy Council[1], it has been held in Scotland that it may be in breach of the convention to use that admission as evidence in court. Section 172 is discussed in more detail at 7.5:6, 7.5:7 and 7.5:8 below. This and other duties to provide information are described at 2.6 and ch 7 below.

1.11:4 Exceptions

The evidence of a single witness will suffice to establish certain statutory offences[2]. Details of the fixed penalty procedure for traffic light and speeding offences which in the first instance does away with the common law evidential requirements of identification are found at 7.8:3 below.

---

1 *Brown v Stott* 2000 SLT 379.
2 Road Traffic Offenders Act 1988, s 21, as amended by the Road Traffic Act 1991, Sch 4, para 89; ch 7 below, *passim*.

Chapter Two

Dangerous and careless driving

PART 1
DANGEROUS DRIVING

2.1   DANGEROUS DRIVING

Section 1 of the Road Traffic Act 1988[1], as amended by s 1 of the
Road Traffic Act 1991[2], provides that it is an offence to cause the
death of another person by driving a mechanically propelled
vehicle dangerously on a road or other public place. Section 2 of
the Act (as similarly amended) makes it an offence to drive
dangerously. Section 1 therefore creates a specific and separate
offence if death results from such driving. The term 'dangerously'
has exactly the same meaning in both ss 1 and 2. Charges under
s 1, however, must be taken on indictment; s 2 cases may be taken
on summary complaint. Servants of the Crown are not exempted
from prosecution under either section, or in respect of other
driving offences[3].

The statutory offence of causing death by dangerous or reckless
driving was introduced by the Road Traffic Act 1960[4]. Prior to
1960, the only method open for the prosecution of proceedings
against a motorist where death resulted from the driving of a

---

1 c 52.
2 c 40.
3 Road Traffic Act 1988, s 183.
4 c 16.

vehicle was to charge him with culpable homicide. However, in many such cases, juries were disinclined to return such a verdict, and a statutory alternative was therefore introduced. The offence of causing death by dangerous or reckless driving again appeared in the Road Traffic Act 1972[1], s 1; the word 'dangerous' was deleted from the statutory definitions of ss 1 and 2 of the 1972 Act by the Criminal Law Act 1977, s 50(1). Cases prior to this amendment which relied on evidence of 'dangerous driving' are now of limited value in considering current charges. However, by virtue of the Road Traffic Act 1991, s 1, Parliament reverted to describing the offending course of driving as 'dangerous', and abandoned the term 'reckless.' The significance of, and reasons for, this change are given at 2.3:2 below.

2.2   CULPABLE HOMICIDE AND SECTION 1

2.2:1   Procedure and penalties

It is, however, still open to the Crown to bring charges of culpable homicide against a motorist rather than to undertake a prosecution under the Road Traffic Act 1988, s 1. This procedure is normally adopted only in the most serious cases. It is submitted that the standard of driving to be considered on a charge of culpable homicide should nonetheless be for all practical purposes identical to the standard to be applied in the statutory charge. However, in such a charge there will normally be other features in the circumstances of the case, and in the quality of the driving, which distinguish it from the ordinary case under s 1. A charge of culpable homicide is taken on indictment. The penalties available to the court where culpable homicide is committed by the driver include an unlimited prison sentence, obligatory disqualification for a minimum period of two years[2], and obligatory endorsement of the driver's licence. In the unlikely event of disqualification not being imposed, 3-11 penalty points must be endorsed on the licence[3]. In terms of s 36 of the Road Traffic Offenders Act 1988, a driver convicted of culpable homicide and

---

1   c 20.
2   Road Traffic Offenders Act 1988, s 34(4), as amended by the Road Traffic Act 1991, s 29(4)(a).
3   RTOA 1988, Sch 2, Pt II, as amended by RTA 1991, Sch 2.

thereafter disqualified must re-sit and pass the extended driving test after the period of disqualification has expired before he can apply to have his licence back. The level of custodial sentences are normally those applicable in other forms of culpable homicide[1].

Similarly, obligatory disqualification and endorsement follow a conviction under s 1 of the Act[2]. The minimum period of disqualification is two years[3]. A sentence of up to ten years' imprisonment is available[4]. The driver must re-sit and pass the extended test before he can regain his licence[5]. Particularly serious penalties are imposed in s 1 cases if it is shown that the driving may have been affected by the consumption of alcohol.

Statutory offences under s 1 or s 2 of the Act may be separately and alternatively libelled on culpable homicide indictments[6]. A jury is specifically entitled to bring in certain alternative verdicts even where the alternative is not charged[7]. It should be noted, however, that these provisions do not allow a jury to bring an alternative verdict of guilty in terms of s 1 in a case of culpable homicide, where that alternative is not separately libelled. Directions to the jury on the alternative verdict under s 2 do not necessarily have to be given in every case[8].

2.2:2   Warning or notice of intended prosecution: dangerous driving; contents of charge

In respect of an alternative charge in terms of s 2 of the Road Traffic Act 1988 to a charge of culpable homicide, it should be noted that the provisions of s 1 of the Road Traffic Offenders Act 1988, as amended by the Road Traffic Act 1991, Sch 4, para 80, do not apply[9]. The provisions of s 1, which require either that a police officer warns the accused at the time that the offence was committed that a prosecution may follow, or, alternatively, that

1 *Brodie v HM Advocate* 1992 SCCR 487.
2 RTOA 1988, Sch 2, Pt I, as amended by the RTA 1991, Sch 2, para 5.
3 RTOA 1988, s 34(4), as amended by RTA 1991, s 29(4)(a).
4 Criminal Justice Act 1993, s 67.
5 RTOA 1998, s 36.
6 See, eg, *Dunn v HM Advocate* 1960 JC 55.
7 RTOA 1988, s 23(1), as amended by RTA 1991, Sch 4, para 90; and RTOA 1988, s 24, as amended by the RTA 1991, s 24.
8 *McDonald v HM Advocate* 1999 SLT 243.
9 See RTOA 1988, s 2(5), as amended by RTA 1991, Sch 4, para 81.

within 14 days of the incident a notice of intended prosecution should be served on the accused, are pre-requisites of any prosecution under s 2 (though not of s 1) of the Road Traffic Act 1988, and of the other offences specified in Schedule 1 to the Road Traffic Offenders Act 1988[1]. The requirement in such cases for either a prosecution warning or the service of a complaint must be strictly observed; a verbal warning must be given at the time[2]and the warning must be clear and specific[3]. In *Lindsay v Smith*[4] it was held that for police officers to caution and charge the accused was sufficient to comply with the terms of s 1; and that it was desirable that advance notice be given when the accused wishes to rely on a failure to observe this requirement. Moreover, s 1(3) of the Road Traffic Offenders Act 1988 assumes that the requirements of s 1(1) have been observed in every case until the contrary is proved, and s 2(1) provides exemption from the general requirements in the cases of offences involving accidents. Further, s 2(3) provides that failure to observe the conditions set out in s 1(1) will not bar conviction where the accused cannot be traced despite the exercise of reasonable diligence or where the accused himself contributes to the failure.

Any fatal accident inquiry into the circumstances of an incident which subsequently gives rise to a prosecution under s 1 or 2 of the Road Traffic Act 1988 normally takes place after any criminal proceedings have been concluded.

Dangerous driving under s 2 of the Road Traffic Act 1988, if charged alone, is normally taken on summary complaint. The time and place of the alleged offence must be given, but not necessarily the exact nature of the driving[5].

Differences between the copy of the complaint served on the accused and the court copy will be ignored if there is no prejudice[6]. However, where particular incidents of driving were spoken to in evidence as having taken place on streets not mentioned in the libel, such evidence was held to be inadmissible[7].

---

1 See, eg, *McGlynn v Stewart* 1973 JC 33.
2 *Cuthbert v Hollis* 1958 SLT (Sh Ct) 51.
3 *Watt v Smith* 1942 JC 109, 1943 SLT 101.
4 1991 SLT 896, 1990 SCCR 581.
5 *Todrick v Dennelour* (1904) 7 F 8, (1904) SLT 573; *Watkin v HM Advocate* 1989 SLT 24, 1988 SCCR 443; see also 2.2:1 above.
6 *Suttenfield v O'Brien* 1996 SLT 198; *Walker v Higson* 1998 SLT 131.
7 *Symmers v Lees* 2000 JC 149, 2000 SLT 507, 2000 SCCR 66.

2.3   SECTION 1 OF THE 1988 ACT

2.3:1   Ingredients of the offence

Section 1 of the Road Traffic Act 1988 as amended by the Road Traffic Act 1991, s 1, provides:

'A person who causes the death of another person by driving a mechanically propelled vehicle dangerously on a road or other public place shall be guilty of an offence.'

For a conviction against a motorist under s 1 of the 1988 Act as amended, the Crown must prove (i) that the driving complained of was dangerous; (ii) that it was a cause of the death of some other person (who may be a passenger in the car driven by the accused or indeed any other category of person); and (iii) that the driving took place in a 'mechanically propelled vehicle' and on a 'road or other public place'.

In terms of s 24 of the Road Traffic Offenders Act 1988, where a motorist is charged under s 1, alternative verdicts under ss 2 and 3 are also available[1].

2.3:2   Definitions

Driving:– see 1.7:1 above. The definition section of the Road Traffic Act 1988[2] specifically excludes from s 1 prosecutions the extended provision of which includes a steersman in the category of driver, and which otherwise applies for the purpose of the statute.

Dangerous driving: It is submitted that, in Scotland at least, dangerous driving is intended by Parliament, in terms of the amendment provided by s 1 of the Road Traffic Act 1991, to be the same as reckless driving in the repealed ss 1 and 2 of the Road Traffic Act 1988. What constituted 'reckless driving' was fully and definitively described in the case of *Allan v Patterson*[3]. The full definition given by the Lord Justice-General (Emslie) in the Appeal Court was as follows:

1 See 2.2:1 above.
2 s 192.
3 1980 JC 57, 1980 SLT 77, 1979 CO Circulars A/20.

'Section 2 [of the 1972 Act] as its language plainly, we think, suggests, requires a judgment to be made quite objectively of a particular course of driving in proved circumstances, and what the court or a jury has to decide using its common sense, is whether the course of driving in these circumstances had the grave quality of recklessness. Judges and juries will readily understand, and juries might well be reminded, that before they can apply the adverb "recklessly" to the driving in question they must find that it fell far below the standard of driving expected of the competent and careful driver and that it occurred either in the face of obvious and material dangers which were or should have been observed, appreciated and guarded against, or in circumstances which showed a complete disregard for any potential dangers which might result from the way in which the vehicle was being driven. It will be understood that in reaching a decision upon the critical issue a judge or jury will be entitled to have regard to any explanation offered by the accused driver designed to show that his driving in the particular circumstances did not possess the quality of recklessness at the material time.'

The court also approved the description of reckless driving submitted by the Crown. In the Crown's submission, reckless driving meant

'a piece of driving which, judged objectively, is eloquent of a high degree of negligence – much more than a mere want of due care and attention – and supports the inference that material risks were deliberately courted or that these risks which ought to have been obvious to any observant and careful drivers were not noticed by reason of gross inattention. Driving "recklessly", accordingly, is driving which demonstrates a gross degree of carelessness in the face of evident dangers'.

It is plain from the decision of the Appeal Court that reckless driving was not confined to driving which had been embarked upon wilfully or deliberately in the face of known risks of a material kind. Driving which occurred in circumstances where there were potential dangers, which were only liable to arise, can nonetheless be described as 'reckless'. Further, an examination of the state of knowledge of a driver charged with reckless driving, or of his intentions at the material time, was not relevant. Similarly, the particular skill, capacity or ability of the driver in question was not to be considered. In other words, the tests applied to the driving under consideration had to be regarded objectively in the context of the proved circumstances of the driving; and had to relate purely to the quality of the driving in fact.

Section 1 of the Road Traffic Act 1991, which provides replacement sections for ss 1 and 2 of the Road Traffic Act 1988, also contains a section which defines the meaning of 'dangerous driving'. Section 2A of the Road Traffic Act 1988 provides:

'(1) For the purposes of sections 1 and 2 above a person is to be regarded as driving dangerously if (and, subject to subsection (2) below, only if) –
(a) the way he drives falls far below what would be expected of a competent and careful driver, and
(b) it would be obvious to a competent and careful driver that driving in that way would be dangerous.'

The Appeal Court has emphasised on a number of occasions that the court or jury must be satisfied that the driving complained of has failed both parts of the test described in section 2A(1)(a) and (b) before a conviction is possible[1].

Further on in the same section, additional definition is given:

'(3) In subsections (1) and (2) above "dangerous" refers to danger either of injury to any person or of serious damage to property; and in determining for the purposes of those subsections what would be expected of, or obvious to, a competent and careful driver in a particular case, regard should be had not only to the circumstances of which he could be expected to be aware but also to any circumstances shown to have been within the knowledge of the accused.'

It is submitted that the foregoing statutory definition of what is meant by dangerous driving substantially reflects the essential features of the nature of reckless driving described by the Lord Justice-General in *Allan v Patterson*[2]. Accordingly (and unless and until the Appeal Court decides differently), the standard of dangerous driving, and its necessary ingredients, are for all practical purposes the same as for reckless driving.

The Appeal Court has made it clear that the specific directions contained in *Allan v Patterson* were to be given to juries in all cases of reckless driving[3]. Equally, these directions have to be considered by sheriffs in considering summary complaints of dangerous driving. It is submitted that the precise terms of the definitions contained in *Allan v Patterson* should be employed, substituting the word 'dangerous' for the word 'reckless' where it occurs.

---

1 See, eg *Aitken v Lees* 1993 JC 228, 1994 SLT 182, 1993 SCCR 845.
2 1980 JC 57, 1980 SLT 77.
3 *Crowe v HM Advocate* 1990 JC 112, 1990 SLT 670, 1989 SCCR 681.

Dangerous driving may occur where, although there is no actual danger, the potential for such danger exists[1].

It may be dangerous driving to drive a vehicle which the driver knows has a dangerous defect[2].

Reference should also be made to 2.3:4, 2.3:5 and 2.3:6 below. Throughout the rest of the treatment of dangerous driving in this book, references to reckless driving in the cases before the 1988 Act should be regarded for practical purposes as applying equally to dangerous driving.

Causes the death: For a conviction for reckless driving under s 1, it must also be demonstrated that the death resulted from the driving complained of. The course of driving need not necessarily be the only or indeed the principal cause of the resulting death. Unless the cause or connection between the driving and death is *'de minimis'*, a motorist can be convicted under this section if the driving is shown to be one of several causes which result in the death of the victim[3]. In *McCluskey v HM Advocate*[4], a driver who caused injuries to an unborn child, which died as a result shortly after birth, was convicted under this section.

In *R v Shelton*[5], a driver took a lorry which was in a dangerous condition onto the road, where it broke down and blocked the nearside lane of a motoway. Some time later another lorry drove into the back of it and the driver of the second lorry was killed. It was held that there was a sufficient link between the driving and the death to allow the case to go to a jury.

Mechanically propelled vehicle: – see 1.2:1 above.

Road or other public place: – see 1.8:1, 1.8:2 and 1.8:3 above.

2.3:3   Evidence

It is competent to introduce evidence in the prosecution of a charge of culpable homicide that the motorist had consumed alcohol or drugs such as would be adversely liable to affect his ability to drive. In *McKie v HM Advocate*[6] an accused driver was charged, after an accident, with driving while unfit through

---

1 *Mitchell v Lockhart* 1993 SCCR 1070.
2 See 2.3:8 below.
3 *R v Hennigan* [1971] RTR 305, [1971] 3 All ER 133; *Watson v HM Advocate* 1978 SCCR Supp 192.
4 1989 SLT 175, 1988 SCCR 629.
5 [1995] Crim LR 635, [1995] RTR 635.
6 1958 JC 24, 1958 SLT 152.

drink. Subsequently it was discovered that another person had died as a result of the accident. The driver was charged with culpable homicide and, at his trial, evidence of a medical examination in relation to the drunk driving charge was held admissible. In *Burrell v Hunter*[1] it was held to be competent for a motorist to be charged with dangerous driving whilst suffering 'from a nervous disorder aggravated by the consumption of alcohol'. If such evidence of previous alcohol consumption is adduced, then it must be for the purpose of demonstrating that the consumption of alcohol affected or was liable to affect the driving complained of, or that it was in the circumstances a reasonable inference that the consumption of alcohol had adversely affected the driving. It is of course competent to charge a motorist with further offences in an indictment containing a charge under s 1 or s 2. Additional charges, such as driving a motor vehicle when under the influence of alcohol or with an alcohol concentration above the prescribed limit in terms of s 4 or 5 of the Act, can, and regularly are, added to such indictments where appropriate. It is submitted that, notwithstanding the rule of evidence in the cases of *McKie v HM Advocate*[2] and *Burrell v Hunter*[3], it is proper practice for the prosecution to libel such additional offences if reliance is to be placed on the consumption of alcohol in securing convictions under s 1 or s 2 prosecutions.

Amendment of the *locus* of a charge or other matters by the Crown may be allowed at the discretion of the court, especially if there is no prejudice[4]. Reference might also usefully be made to Schedule 3 to the 1995 Act.

The manner of earlier driving, and the consequences of a course of driving, are relevant in assessing whether the driving was dangerous, and such consequences may, if appropriate, be libelled in the charge[5].

If it is not shown that the driving was the cause of death, the driver can still be found guilty of s 2 and s 3[6] or even a breach of

---

1 1956 SLT (Sh Ct) 75.
2 1958 JC 24, 1958 SLT 152.
3 1956 SLT (Sh Ct) 75.
4 Criminal Procedure (Scotland) Act 1995, s 195; *Craig v Keane* 1982 SLT 198, 1981 SCCR 166; *Brown v McLeod* 1986 SCCR 615; *Fenwick v Valentine* 1993 SCCR 892; *Gullett v Hamilton* 1997 SLT 1207.
5 *McCallum v Hamilton* 1986 JC 1, 1986 SLT 156, 1985 SCCR 368; *Mundie v Cardle* 1991 SCCR 118; *MacDonald v HM Advocate* 1999 SLT 243.
6 Road Traffic Act 1991, s 24, introducing a new s 23 into the Road Traffic Act 1988.

the peace[1]. The alternative of a breach of the peace conviction depends upon the provisions of the Criminal Procedure (Scotland) Act 1995 Sch 3, para 14.

Lengthy sentences of imprisonment have been imposed where alcohol is involved in dangerous driving cases[2].

2.3:4 Section 2: Dangerous driving

Section 2 of the Road Traffic Act 1988, as amended by s 1 of the Road Traffic Act 1991, provides:

'A person who drives a mechanically propelled vehicle dangerously on a road or other public place is guilty of an offence.'

Dangerous driving is therefore an offence by itself where no fatality occurs. Precisely the same standard and considerations apply in determining whether or not a particular course of driving should be described as dangerous as apply in the cases brought under s 1. A charge under s 2 of the Act may be brought under either solemn or summary procedure, at the option of the Crown. The particular nature of the driving complained of as being dangerous need not be specified in the charge although it is of course necessary to give sufficient details of the time and place of the alleged offence[3]. Careless driving may be and often is charged as an alternative to dangerous driving on the same indictment or complaint. The alternative verdict is always available to a jury (Road Traffic Act 1988, s 24 as amended by the Road Traffic Act 1991, s 24). On conviction under s 2 of the Act, the maximum prison sentence in solemn prosecutions is two years, and six months in summary cases[4] with obligatory endorsement, and disqualification for a minimum period of 12 months[5]. After

---

1 *Horsburgh v Russell* 1994 SLT 942, 1994 SCCR 237; *Vannet v Davidson* 1996 JC 17, 1996 SLT 626.
2 Eg *Hamilton v HM Advocate* 1992 SLT 555, 1991 SCCR 282; *Murray v HM Advocate* 1994 SCCR 781; *Russel v HM Advocate* 1992 SLT 25, 1991 SCCR 790; *Murray v HM Advocate* 1994 SCCR 674.
3 *Todrick v Dennelar* 1904 7 F (J) 8, (1904) SLT 573; see also *Watkin v HM Advocate* 1989 SLT 24, 1988 SCCR 443.
4 Road Traffic Offenders Act 1988, Sch 2, as amended by the Road Traffic Act 1991 Sch 2, para 6.
5 Road Traffic Offenders Act 1988, s 34.

the expiry of any period of disqualification the driver must re-sit and pass the extended driving test before getting his licence back[1]. If for any reason disqualification is not imposed, 3-11 penalty points must be endorsed on the licence[2]. For cases where s 2 is charged as an alternative to culpable homicide, reference should be made to 2.2:1 above.

Whether or not driving in a particular case is to be regarded as dangerous will of course depend upon the facts and circumstances that are proved to have prevailed in each case. However, it is not essential for a successful prosecution under this section that there should have been a collision involving another vehicle, or indeed an accident of any sort. Each case will depend on its own facts and all the aspects of the driving complained of require to be considered. Dangerous driving may be inferred from a given set of facts and circumstances where, for example, a vehicle behaves in an abnormal fashion without any explanation for that behaviour being proved.

As in cases under s 1, the matter has to be considered objectively, and the ability or state of mind of the motorist is not a relevant consideration. Driving which can properly be described as dangerous as defined in the case of *Allan v Patterson*[3] is not likely to arise from a momentary lack of attention or a simple error of judgment. Similarly, the intentions of the driver are irrelevant. A test sometimes applied in these circumstances is for the judge or jury to satisfy themselves on the evidence as to what in fact took place, and then put themselves in the position of a bystander and from that viewpoint consider whether the driving proved to have taken place can properly be characterised as dangerous in terms of the definitions found in *Allan v Patterson*[4]. Evidence of driving earlier in the course of a particular journey, prior to the conduct complained of in the indictment or complaint, may be admissible. However, it is considered good practice for the prosecutor to give full notice by way of the description of the *locus* where all of the driving complained of took place.

More than one driver may be guilty of dangerous driving out of the same single incident[5].

---

1 RTOA 1988, s 36.
2 RTOA 1988, Sch 2, as amended.
3 1980 JC 57, 1980 SLT 77, 1979 CO Circulars A/20.
4 See 2.3:2 above.
5 See *Watson v HM Advocate* 1979 SCCR Supp 192.

2.3:5   Highway Code

The most readily recognisable tests of dangerous driving may be found within the provisions of the Highway Code. Section 38(7) of the Road Traffic Act 1988 provides in effect that failure to observe the Highway Code may tend to establish liability for reckless driving; however, in terms of the subsection, a violation of any of the provisions of the Highway Code does not necessarily mean that the driver should be prosecuted. Clearly, therefore, a judge or jury, in considering dangerous driving, may competently have regard to the provisions of the Highway Code in determining whether or not a particular course of driving was dangerous[1], but equally the fact that a driver has failed to observe a particular rule in the Highway Code does not necessarily mean that he should be convicted. The Highway Code is published by The Stationery Office and is available from its outlets and other bookshops.

2.3:6   Nature of danger

As indicated above, in s 2A(3) of the Road Traffic Act 1988 (introduced by s 1 of the Road Traffic Act 1991), 'dangerous' refers to danger either of injury to any person or of serious damage to property. The prospect of injury to any person includes injury to the driver himself[2]. The subsection does not define what is meant by 'serious damage to property', but any question as to whether serious damage can be distinguished from trivial is almost certainly academic.

2.3:7   Speed in dangerous driving

Excessive speed may be the single most important constituent of a charge of dangerous driving but, if so, it must occur in circumstances which allow the driving to be described as dangerous. In *Frame v Lockhart*[3], a driver was travelling at 50 mph on an esplanade where the speed limit was 15 mph. Although there was no other traffic, either vehicular or pedestrian, on the esplanade at

---

1 See, eg, *McCrone v Normand* 1989 SLT 332, 1988 SCCR 551.
2 *Fraser v Lockhart* 1992 SCCR 275.
3 1985 SLT 367, 1984 SCCR 377.

the material time, the circumstances were such that a large number of pedestrians were in the immediate area and were liable to pass over the esplanade. It was held that, having regard to all the material facts, the speed at which the vehicle was being driven could properly be described as reckless. However, this was a majority decision of the Appeal Court and Lord Robertson's dissenting judgment is worthy of consideration for the contrary view.

Frame v Lockhart was followed in *O'Toole v McDougal*[1]. In that case, a motorist drove for more than 11 miles on the A74 just before midnight at speeds between 100 and 120 mph, the speed limit for that part of the road being 70 mph. The road in question is a dual carriageway with many junctions and gaps in the central reservation and is used by pedestrians and vehicular traffic. While there was no evidence of any actual danger or inconvenience to any other road user, it was held that, in the circumstances, the driver showed a complete disregard for any potential dangers which might have arisen, and that accordingly the speed was so excessive that a conviction for reckless driving was justified. In delivering the opinion of the Appeal Court, the Lord Justice-General (Emslie)[2] said:

'If consideration is given to the time at which this chase took place in the hours of darkness, if consideration is given to the character of the roadway and the dangers presented by its particular features of construction which the sheriff has described, if attention is given to the fact that the road was carrying lorry traffic and motor traffic, it appears to us that the sheriff was entitled and indeed well entitled to conclude that anyone who drives on that stretch of road in the face of the potential dangers which it obviously carried at a speed of between 100 and 120 mph is driving recklessly, however skilful he may be in controlling the vehicle at whose wheel he sits. In our judgment the sheriff was perfectly right to be satisfied – not only entitled to be satisfied but we think right to be satisfied – beyond reasonable doubt that in all the circumstances in the findings in fact which are eloquent of potential danger, the appellant's speed was so excessive that it would be regarded as a piece of reckless driving as a whole.'

This case is therefore authority for emphasising that the material risks referred to in the case of *Allan v Patterson*[3] which have to

1 1986 SCCR 56.
2 At p 59.
3 1980 JC 57, 1980 SLT 77.

be observed, appreciated and guarded against are not confined to dangers which actually arise during the course of the journey complained of, but include also potential dangers which are likely to or liable to arise.

In *Deans v Skinner*[1], a driver who had neither a licence nor insurance was driving at an excessive speed. He was pursued by a police car and panicked, going through a red light without being aware of doing so, and passed vehicles halted at traffic lights on the inside. This was considered to be a narrow case, but the driving was judged to be reckless.

It now seems clear that very little is required, in addition to grossly excessive speed, to justify a conviction for dangerous driving[2]. However, excessive speed is not always necessarily sufficient by itself[3].

2.3:8 Dangerous defects

Section 2A(2) of the Road Traffic Act 1988[4] specifically provides that a driver may be guilty of driving dangerously if it would be obvious to a careful and competent driver that driving the vehicle in its current state would be dangerous. For example, if a driver takes to the road in the knowledge that his vehicle has defective brakes and an accident occurs as a result of that defect, the driver may be convicted of dangerous driving. This confirms the position which existed previously without particular statutory sanction. In *R v Robert Miller (Contractors) Ltd*[5], a lorry driver took to the road knowing that one of his tyres was defective. The defect caused an accident which resulted in a death, and the driver was convicted under s 1. Similarly, where a driver embarked upon a journey with an insecure load, knowing that it might fall off, and the load in fact fell off and killed a pedestrian, a conviction for reckless driving followed[6].

---

1 1981 SCCR 49.
2 *Fraser v Lockhart* 1992 SCCR 275; *Abbas v Houston* 1993 SCCR 1019; *Trippick v Orr* 1995 SLT 272, 1994 SCCR 736; *McQueen v Buchanan* 1997 JC 16, 1997 SLT 765, 1996 SCCR 826; *Howdle v O'Connor* 1998 SLT 94.
3 *Brown v Orr* 1994 SCCR 668; *McQueen v Buchanan* 1997 JC 16, 1997 SLT 765, 1996 SCCR 826.
4 As amended by the Road Traffic Act 1991, s 1.
5 [1970] 2 QB 54, [1970] 2 WLR 541, [1970] 1 All ER 577.
6 *R v Crossman* [1986] RTR 49.

In *Carstairs v Hamilton*[1], a driver was convicted of dangerous driving when he drove on a public road a go-kart which had no windscreen, roof, suspension and so on, which in effect provided no protection for the driver, and in addition could not easily be seen by other road users. Reference should also be made to *R v Shelton*[2], where a driver took a defective lorry onto the road and was charged with dangerous driving after it broke down, and another lorry drove into it. For any specific mechanical defect to be relevant, it must be one which would make it obvious to any competent and careful driver that it was likely to affect the driving of the vehicle[3].

2.3:9   Jurisdiction

In *R v Robert Millar (Contractors) Ltd*[4], a lorry was driven in England with a defective tyre, and the driver and the company who employed him and who owned the vehicle were both aware of the defect. An accident was caused by the defective tyre, and the court in England concluded that not only was the driver therefore guilty of dangerous driving, but that the directors of the company, which was situated in Scotland, were equally liable.

2.3:10   General

For other cases under ss 1 and 2 of the Road Traffic Act 1988 see *Watson v HM Advocate*[5]; *Earnshaw v HM Advocate*[6]; *Campbell v Johnston*[7]; *Connorton v Annan*[8]; *Cooper v HM Advocate*[9]; and *Fraser v Lockhart*[10].

---

1 1998 SLT 220, 1997 SCCR 311.
2 [1995] Crim LR 635, [1995] RTR 635.
3 *HM Advocate v Campbell* 1994 SLT 502.
4 [1970] 2 QB 54, [1970] 2 WLR 541, [1970] 1 All ER 577.
5 1978 SCCR Supp 192.
6 1982 JC 11, 1982 SLT 179, 1981 SCCR 279.
7 1981 SCCR 179.
8 1981 SCCR 307.
9 1982 SCCR 87.
10 1992 SCCR 275.

2.4 COMMON LAW

At common law any reckless conduct which causes injury is criminal[1]. A charge of this kind is sometimes brought by the Crown where it cannot be proved that the driving took place on 'a road or other public place'; if the driving complained of does not have the necessary ingredients of dangerous driving, the Crown may have recourse to s 34 of the Road Traffic Act 1988.

2.5 DEFENCES

In the case of *Allan v Patterson*[2] it was emphasised that in reaching any decision on whether a particular course of driving should or should not be described as reckless, the judge or jury is entitled to have regard 'to any explanation offered by the accused driver designed to show that his driving in the particular circumstances did not possess the quality of recklessness at the material time'.

A special defence of automatism or the inability of the accused to form the necessary criminal intent is a competent defence to any criminal charge, including driving offences[3]. Three conditions must be satisfied if such a defence is to be successfully established. Firstly, the inability of the accused to form the necessary *mens rea* must be due to some external factor, which was not self-induced. Secondly, the external factor must not be something that the accused was bound to foresee. Thirdly, the external factor must result in a total alienation of reason amounting to a complete absence of self-control on the part of the accused. The standard of proof required to sustain such a defence is high[4]. For example, the defence did not succeed in *Cardle v Mulrainey*[5], where the accused was aware that he was committing the offences charged but maintained that he was unable to stop himself because of drugs introduced into his

1 *HM Advocate v Harris* 1993 JC 150, 1993 SLT 963, 1993 SCCR 559, overruling *Quinn v Cunningham* 1956 JC 22, 1956 SLT 55, which had held that any reckless conduct, such as the furious driving of a vehicle, could only be an offence if it was to the danger of the lieges (see also 2.14 below).
2 1980 JC 57, 1980 SLT 77, CO Circulars A/20.
3 *Ross v HM Advocate* 1991 SLT 546, 1991 SCCR 823, partly overruling *HM Advocate v Cunningham* 1963 SLT 345; and affirming *HM Advocate v Ritchie* 1926 SLT 308, where a claim that the accused was suffering from a 'temporary mental disassociation due to toxic factors' was successfully pled.
4 *Sorley v HM Advocate* 1992 SLT 867, 1992 SCCR 396; *McLeod v Napier* 1993 SCCR 303.
5 1992 SLT 1152, 1992 SCCR 658.

drink; nor did it succeed in *Ebsworth v HM Advocate*[1],where the accused took an excessive amount of prescribed drugs to relieve pain. Reference should also be made to 8.5:4C below.

In summary procedure, the defence of automatism was considered but held not to be established in *Stevenson v Beatson*[2]. In *Farrell v Stirling*[3], a diabetic who went into a state of hypoglycaemia (never having experienced such a condition in the past) just before an accident was held by the court not to be 'driving' and thus not guilty of careless driving. Such a defence could not have succeeded if the accused had had previous experience of the condition and appreciated that it was liable to affect him while he was driving[4].

It may be possible to put forward a defence of mechanical defect, provided that it is shown that the way in which the vehicle was driven at the material time was due to a complete and unexpected loss of control as a result of some mechanical failure which was not caused in any way by the fault of the motorist. It is therefore considered that such a defence would be unlikely to succeed if the motorist knew, or perhaps should have known by the exercise of reasonable diligence, that the fault existed[5].

A defence of necessity is competent, and if successful will lead to an acquittal[6]. However, the standard which this defence must reach is high; the defence can only succeed where the driver is found to have acted under an immediate danger of death or great bodily harm to himself, or another, and any reasonable alternative to the offending behaviour must be taken[7]. While the circumstances should not be scrutinised with absolute strictness, it may be difficult to justify driving beyond the point where it is no longer necessary. Examples of cases where this defence was considered are *McLeod v McDougall*[8]; *Hamilton v Neizer*[9]; *Lees v McDonald*[10] and *Dolan v McLeod*[11].

---

1 1992 SLT 1161, 1992 SCCR 671.

2 1965 SLT (Sh Ct) 11.

3 1975 SLT (Sh Ct) 71.

4 *McLeod v Mathieson* 1993 SCCR 488; see also 2.3:8 above.

5 *R v Spurge* [1961] 2 QB 205, [1961] 3 WLR 23, [1961] 2 All ER 688; *R v Robert Millar Contractors* [1970] 2 QB 54, [1970] 2 WLR 541, [1970] 1 All ER 577.

6 *Tudhope v Grubb* 1983 SCCR 350, *Moss v Howdle* 1997 JC 123, 1997 SLT 782, 1997 SCCR 215.

7 *Dawson v Dickson* 1999 JC 315, 1999 SCCR 698 (sub nom *Dawson v McKay* 1999 SLT 1328); *Dolan v McLeod* 1999 JC 32 1998 SCCR 623.

8 1989 SLT 151, 1988 SCCR 519.

9 1993 SLT 992, 1993 SCCR 63.

10 1997 SCCR 189.

11 1999 JC 32, 1998 SCCR 623.

It would appear to be reasonable to assume that there is also scope for a defence of compulsion or duress along the same lines as the defence of necessity, so that the capacity or intent of the driver is also excluded.

Section 34(3) of the Road Traffic Act 1988 allows a driver to drive off the road, if he does so in order to save a life, put out a fire or deal with a similar emergency.

Emergency services are not excluded from the ambit of ordinary duties applicable to other drivers[1] apart from the regulations concerning speed limits[2], but drivers of emergency vehicles may be able to plead extenuating or mitigating factors.

Circumstances which do not amount to a special defence of duress may form the basis of mitigating circumstances[3].

2.6 DUTY TO GIVE NAME

Any driver of a mechanically propelled vehicle who is alleged to have committed an offence in terms of s 2 or s 3 of the Road Traffic Act 1988 is obliged to give his name and address to any person having reasonable grounds for requiring this information[4]. A failure to provide such information by the driver is an offence, and such a failure will make him liable to arrest without warrant by a police officer who considers that he has committed an offence of reckless or careless driving[5]. Such a request by the police for information, if made in good faith, does not have to be accompanied by an allegation that an offence has taken place[6]. Reference should also be made to 1.11:1 and 1.11:3 above (duty of driver or keeper of vehicle to give information) and to ch 7.

---

1 *Husband v Russell* 1997 SCCR 592; see also 2.12 above.
2 Road Traffic Regulation Act 1984, s 87.
3 *McLeod v MacDougall* 1989 SLT 151, 1988 SCCR 519; *Connorton v Annan* 1981 SCCR 307.
4 Road Traffic Act 1988, s 168 as amended by the Road Traffic Act 1991, Sch 4, para 71.
5 RTA 1988, s 167.
6 *McMahon v Cardle* 1988 SCCR 556; see also *Galt v Goodsir* 1982 JC 4, 1982 SLT 94, 1981 SCCR 225 (followed in *Hingston v Pollock* 1990 JC 138, 1990 SLT 770, 1989 SCCR 697).

2.7   DANGEROUS CYCLING

It is an offence to ride a cycle dangerously on a road[1]. The term 'dangerously' has the same meaning as in s 2 of the Road Traffic Act 1988[2]. The word 'cycle' is defined at 1.6:7 above, and the word 'road' is defined at 1.8:2 above. Sections 167 and 168 of the 1988 Act apply in respect of such charges.

2.8   ART AND PART: AIDING AND ABETTING

That the accused in any case may be guilty either as principal actor or art and part is implied in all charges brought in Scotland whether on indictment or by means of summary complaint, as is aiding and abetting, counselling or procuring or inciting a contravention of any enactment[3]. Any accused found guilty art and part is liable to the same penalties as the principal actor. However, it has been suggested that all members of a gang in a getaway car may not be guilty art and part of all of the offences committed by the driver in attempting to make good his escape[4].

The offence of aiding and abetting provided by s 176 of the Road Traffic Act 1972 is not repeated in the current legislation, presumably because it is considered to be unnecessary. What constituted the idea of aiding and abetting was discussed in *Valentine v Mackie*[5] and *Manion v Smith*[6].

Section 176 of the Road Traffic Act 1972 made it an offence to counsel another to commit an offence against the Act. A solicitor advised a client not to report an accident to the police. It was held that in the absence of an averment that by the time the advice was given it would still have been reasonably practicable for the accused to have reported the accident, the complaint was irrelevant[7]. Although s 176 of the Road Traffic Act 1972 has not

1 Road Traffic Act 1988, s 28 as amended by the Road Traffic Act 1991, s 7.
2 See 2.3:2 above.
3 Criminal Procedure (Scotland) Act 1995, s 239(1).
4 *Webster v Wishart* 1955 SLT 243.
5 1980 SLT (Sh Ct) 122.
6 1989 SLT 69.
7 *Martin v Hamilton* 1989 SCCR 292.

survived into the Road Traffic Act of either 1988 or 1991, the case of *Martin v Hamilton*[1] may be relevant in common law charges of counselling or incitement, or in cases involving the accused acting art and part.

Section 119 of the Road Traffic Regulation Act 1984 makes it an offence to aid, counsel, procure or incite another to commit an offence against that Act or its relative regulations.

Section 34(5) of the Road Traffic Offenders Act 1988 (which deals with disqualification, for certain offences) applies the preceding provisions of that section to any conviction of an offence committed by aiding, abetting, counselling or procuring, or inciting to the commission of an offence involving obligatory disqualification, as if the offence were an offence involving discretionary disqualification.

2.9 CORPORATE LIABILITY

In *R v Robert Millar Contractors*[2], a lorry was driven in England with a defective tyre. The driver and the company who employed him and who owned the vehicle were aware of the defect. An accident was caused by the defective tyre, and a court in England concluded that not only was the driver therefore guilty of dangerous driving but that the directors of the company, which was situated in Scotland, were equally liable.

2.9:1 Overloaded vehicles

In certain circumstances, rather than prosecute under the foregoing provisions, s 40A of the Road Traffic Act 1988 (as amended) is used when the number of passengers, or the manner in which they are carried, is said to be dangerous. In such cases the risk must arise out of the way the vehicle is actually being used[3].

---

1 1989 SCCR 292.
2 [1970] 2 QB 54, [1970] 2 WLR 541, [1970] 1 All ER 577.
3 *Akelis v Normand* 1997 SLT 136.

PART 2
CARELESS DRIVING

2.10   CARELESS AND INCONSIDERATE DRIVING: SECTION 3

2.10:1   General

Section 3 of the Road Traffic Act 1988 (as amended by the Road Traffic Act 1991, s 2) provides:

'If a person drives a mechanically propelled vehicle on a road or other public place without due care and attention or without reasonable consideration for other persons using the road or place, he is guilty of an offence.'

Section 3 prosecutions are undertaken summarily; penalties on conviction are again found in Schedule 2, Part I of the Road Traffic Offenders Act 1988. Disqualification is optional, and normally the disposal involves the imposition of penalty points, endorsement of the licence and a fine.

   Section 3 provides for two quite separate descriptions of driving either of which, if proved against the motorist, constitute the offence. In the first place it is an offence for a motorist to drive a car on the road without due care and attention; secondly, it is also an offence for a motorist to drive a vehicle on a road without reasonable consideration for other persons using the road. A particular course of driving could conceivably contravene both aspects of the section. The scope of both aspects of this section is extremely wide.

2.10:2   Definitions

Driving. See 1.7:1 above.

Mechanically propelled vehicle. See 1.2:1 above.

Road. See 1.8:2 above.

Other public place. See 1.8:3 above.

Due care and attention: A formal definition of these words is not appropriate and has not been attempted by the courts. The question of whether a driver in any particular case has driven without due care and attention is invariably a matter of fact. In general terms the test is concerned with an assessment of whether the driver was exercising the degree of care and attention expected of a reasonable and prudent driver. The circumstances which can produce careless driving are virtually unlimited in nature. The words are therefore to be construed in their ordinary and everyday sense, having regard to the test described at 2.10:3 below.

Reasonable consideration: Similarly, no formal definition can be given for this phrase; the words must be considered in their normal sense having regard to the test described at 2.10:3 below.

Other persons using the road: This includes passengers in the accused's vehicle: *Pawley v Wharldall*[1].

2.10:3   Character of offence: test to be applied

A description of the kind of situations in which careless or inconsiderate driving may arise is virtually unlimited. For example, driving without due care and attention may arise out of simple acts of carelessness or failure to pay sufficient attention in the circumstances, a lack of judgment, momentary inattention or lack of concentration, or a simple mistake, up to and including all cases of extremely bad or objectionable driving which do not attain the high standard required for a charge of dangerous driving.

Typical cases of driving without reasonable consideration for other persons using the road may include (among a wide variety of examples which might be given) the driving of a vehicle too close to the driver in front thus causing the preceding driver to be distracted, lose concentration and be liable to make driving errors; driving with full beam headlights at night, dazzling and inconveniencing oncoming drivers; driving needlessly in the outside lane of a motorway or dual carriageway, or overtaking in the inside lane, thus inconveniencing other road users; or even driving deliberately at high speed through pools of water causing pedestrians to be splashed with water. It does not appear to have been established in Scotland whether the prosecution is required to prove that actual inconvenience was caused to other road users, or whether such inconvenience was merely liable to occur.

1 [1966] 1 QB 373.

In England, it has been held that actual inconvenience must result[1]. It is submitted that this authority might not be followed in Scotland[2].

The test to be applied in all cases is whether the particular course of driving proved in the circumstances, demonstrates that the driver was or was not exercising the degree of care, skill and attention which the reasonable, competent and prudent driver could be reasonably expected to show in the circumstances[3]; driving without reasonable consideration for others involves carelessness.

The same general approach is applied whether the driver is alleged to have driven without due care and attention or without reasonable consideration for other persons using the road. The test as to whether a particular course of driving contravenes this section of the Act therefore involves the application of an objective and fixed standard, which means that the same requirements are imposed on all drivers irrespective of their status, capacity and experience. For example, no distinction is drawn, for the purpose of this section, between a learner driver and a qualified driver[4]. However, the tests are applied to the facts and circumstances of each case and it therefore follows that it may be appropriate in certain situations to take into account variable factors such as weather and traffic conditions. Driving carelessly, or without reasonable consideration for others, may arise whether the driving complained of was deliberate or unintentional. It is not necessary for there to have been a collision between two vehicles, or contact between a vehicle and some other person or thing, for careless driving to be established; charges may be brought where, for example, the conduct of the accused on the road requires another motorist or road user to take evasive or emergency action. Equally, the fact that two vehicles have been in collision does not necessarily mean that either or both have been guilty of careless driving. Driving deliberately embarked upon to harass or intimidate other motorists or road users may found a contravention of the section.

---

1 *Dilkes v Bowman Shaw* [1981] RTR 4.
2 See *O'Toole v McDougall* 1986 SCCR 56.
3 *Wilson v MacPhail* 1991 SCCR 170.
4 *McCrone v Riding* [1938] 1 All ER 157.

2.10:4   Car telephone cases

In *MacPhail v Haddow*[1] a driver drove off from traffic lights and round a corner while using a car telephone. It was held that no offence had taken place, as no danger or inconvenience was caused to any other road user, and there appeared to be no opportunity for such danger or inconvenience to arise during the course of the journey observed. However, in *Rae v Friel*[2] it was held that where a driver overtook five vehicles at speed while operating his car telephone, he would have been unable to react appropriately to any danger or emergency that arose. Reference may also be made to *Stock v Carmichael*[3].

2.11   CHARGES

In a charge of dangerous driving under the earlier legislation, it was held to be competent for the prosecution to allege that the motorist had committed the offence while suffering from a nervous disorder aggravated by the consumption of alcohol[4]. However, in a case of careless driving, it is not competent to include in the complaint a reference to the effect that the victim has been killed as a result of the driving complained of[5]. In *Sharp v HM Advocate* 1987[6], the appeal court said it was wrong for a sheriff to take into account the fatal consequences of a piece of careless driving in considering sentence. However, it is relevant to consider (and libel) other consequences of driving, such as a collision or the vehicle leaving the roadway in order to determine whether the driving was dangerous or careless[7].

There is no limit to the number of charges which may be included in a complaint, as long as these charges represent distinct and different offences and each can individually be

---

1 1990 SCCR 339.
2 1992 SCCR 688 (distinguishing *MacPhail v Haddow*).
3 1993 SCCR 136.
4 *Burrell v Hunter* 1956 SLT (Sh Ct) 75.
5 *McCallum v Hamilton* 1986 JC 1, 1986 SLT 156, 1985 SCCR 368.
6 1987 SCCR 179.
7 *McCallum v Hamilton* 1986 JC 1, 1986 SLT 156, 1985 SCCR 368; *Mundie v Cardle* 1991 SCCR 118.

proved on the evidence[1]. It is competent to libel the two alternative offences described in s 3[2].

No complaint should contain any charge which reveals that the accused has been disqualified by a court order or has any previous convictions[3]. A necessary and solitary exception to this rule is made only in charges of driving or obtaining a licence while disqualified in terms of s 103 of the Road Traffic Act 1988[4]. Reference should also be made to 2.3:3 above.

2.12   EVIDENCE: GENERAL RULES

Each case of driving carelessly or without consideration for other road users depends ultimately on its own facts and circumstances. However, there are a number of reported decisions which afford some general assistance by illustrating general rules. Some of these decisions are civil cases.

A driver who makes a signal for a manoeuvre which may lead to another person on the road observing and acting upon that signal may be under a duty to see that his signal has been appreciated and understood by that other person[5]. A motorist who signals to turn and then drives straight on and collides with another vehicle which had relied on that signal may be guilty of careless driving in respect that the other driver was entitled to rely on his false signal[6]. A driver who follows another driver on the road is bound, in so far as is reasonably practicable, to adopt a position on the road and to drive in such a fashion that will allow him to deal successfully with all traffic exigencies reasonably to be anticipated, particularly in relation to the vehicle in front[7]. If a driver turns right into the path of an overtaking car, the test to be applied is whether he ought to have seen the overtaking vehicle[8]. Where a vehicle has skidded, this is not necessarily by itself evidence of carelessness on the part of the driver; however, the skid

---

1 *Archibald v Keiller* 1931 JC 34, 1931 SLT 560; *Harris v Adair* 1947 JC 116, 1947 SLT 356.
2 *Archibald v Keiller* 1931 JC 1, 1986 SLT 156, 1985 SCCR 368.
3 Criminal Procedure (Scotland) Act 1995, ss 101 and 166.
4 See, for example, *Moffat v Smith* 1983 SCCR 392.
5 *Sorrie v Robertson* 1944 JC 95, 1944 SLT 332.
6 *Another v Probert* [1968] Crim LR 564.
7 *Brown & Lynn v Western SMT Ltd* 1945 SC 31.
8 *Millar v Dean* 1976 SCCR Supp 134.

may well be a factor which has to be considered in all the circumstances of the case[1]. In circumstances where a vehicle went off a stretch of road, then travelled for 120 feet along the roadside verge and thereafter collided with a rock face, it was held, on appeal, that there was on the face of such objective facts, evidence of faulty driving[2]. There is no general rule of law to the effect that a driver requires to drive at night at a speed that will enable him to stop within the limit of vision supplied by his headlights[3].

If the evidence establishes that traffic lights are showing green in one direction then the court may be entitled, in the absence of any evidence to the contrary, and if it is shown that the light system is working properly, to assume that the traffic lights showing the other way are at red[4]. However there must be evidence to support this conclusion[5]. There may be circumstances where the driver on a major road may have to take into account the conduct of the driver on a minor road, if the conduct of the latter indicates that he is about to drive his vehicle in such a manner as will affect the driving of the vehicle on the main road, and the driver on the main road has reasonable opportunity to accommodate such interference[6]. This case is of particular interest in this area because in the course of his opinion Lord Robertson considered in detail a number of earlier authorities on the respective duties of drivers on major and minor roads.

Where a driver drove off on his lorry despite the fact that children were playing thereon, he was found guilty of careless driving although not of reckless driving[7]. Again, where the driver of a large articulated vehicle reversed slowly along a road without assistance, using only his mirrors, in an area where he was aware children were playing, and ran over one of the children, he was found guilty of careless driving because he had reversed without having clear vision to the rear, or assistance to allow him to reverse safely. This decision was reached notwithstanding that the lorry was showing a variety of lights, including

---

1 *McGregor v Dundee Corpn* 1962 SC 15; *Thomson v Brankin* 1968 SLT (Sh Ct) 2; *Crawford v O'Donnell* 1999 SCCR 39.
2 *Pagan v Fergusson* 1976 SLT (Notes) 44; see also *Ryrie v Campbell* 1964 JC 33.
3 *Morris v Luton Corpn* 1946 KB 114.
4 *Pacitti v Copeland* 1963 SLT (Notes) 52.
5 *Inwar v Normand* 1997 SCCR 6.
6 *Ramage v Hardie* 1968 SLT (Notes) 54.
7 *McDonald v Thomson* (1954) 70 Sh Ct Rep 288.

hazard lights[1]. The ordinary tests which apply to all cases of careless driving apply to a police officer answering an emergency call[2]. The same considerations apply to the driver of an ambulance or others engaged in emergency work[3].

It is not necessary in any charge under s 3 that a collision should have occurred as result of the way in which the offending vehicle has been driven. Moreover, the fact that there has been a collision between the two vehicles does not thereby imply that one of them is necessarily guilty of an offence of careless driving. However, it must be remembered that the facts and circumstances surrounding any particular course of driving may justify the inference that an offence under s 3 has been committed. Further, even where there are no eye-witnesses, the facts surrounding an incident may entitle the court to conclude that careless driving has taken place[4].

For other cases of careless driving for general purposes see *King v Cardle*[5]; *Sigourney v Douglas*[6]; *Holmes v Stewart*[7]; *Dunlop v Allan*[8]; *Melville v Lockhart*[9]; *McCrone v Normand*[10]; *Brunton v Lees*[11] and *Husband v Russell*[12].

2.13   HIGHWAY CODE

As in the case of dangerous driving, one of the most easily recognised tests of whether the driving in any particular case has been careless can be ascertained by reference to the provisions of the Highway Code. Section 38 of the Road Traffic Act 1988 provides that failure to observe the Highway Code may tend to establish

---

1 *Farquhar v McKinnon* 1986 SCCR 524, followed in *McCrone v Normand* 1989 SLT 332, 1988 SCCR 551.
2 *Wood v Richards* [1977] RTR 201; *Marshall v Osmond* [1983] 2 QB 1034, [1983] 2 All ER 225.
3 *R v Lundt-Smith* [1964] 2 QB 167, [1964] 2 WLR 1063, [1964] 3 All ER 255; *Husband v Russell* 1998 SLT 377, 1997 SCCR 592. In the latter case the driver was given an absolute discharge.
4 *Ryrie v Campbell* 1964 JC 33; *Pagan v Fergusson* 1976 SLT (Notes) 44.
5 1981 SCCR 22.
6 1981 SCCR 302.
7 1983 SCCR 446.
8 1984 SCCR 329.
9 1985 SCCR 242.
10 1989 SLT 332, 1988 SCCR 551.
11 1993 SCCR 98.
12 1997 SCCR 592.

liability for careless driving[1]. Equally, as in the case of dangerous driving, the fact that the motorist has violated any of the provisions of the Highway Code does not necessarily mean that he should be prosecuted, and if he is prosecuted does not necessarily mean that he should be convicted.

The Highway Code is published by The Stationery Office, and copies of the Code and other driving publications can be purchased at its outlets and some bookshops.

2.14 COMMON LAW

At common law, any reckless conduct which causes injury is criminal[2]. Accordingly the reckless driving of a vehicle may be an offence and such a charge may be used, for example, where it cannot be proved that the driving took place on a road or other public place.

Offences affecting or relating to traffic on the public roads are not confined to statutory offences. In *MacPhail v Clark*[3], a farmer was charged at common law with culpable negligence and causing danger to the lieges by recklessly endangering the safety and lives of the occupants of two vehicles travelling on a road next to his farm. The accused had set fire to a quantity of straw, causing thick smoke to drift across the road so that the drivers of the two vehicles, whose vision was obscured, collided. It was held that this was a relevant charge and the accused was convicted and fined.

Driving a vehicle in a disorderly manner likely to create alarm or annoyance may constitute a breach of the peace; also a driver may be charged with assault if he uses his vehicle in a way that constitutes an attack on another person.

2.15 DEFENCES

As in the case of offences under ss 1 and 2 of the Road Traffic Act 1988, the court must always take into account, in assessing

---

1 See, eg, *McCrone v Normand* 1989 SLT 332, 1988 SCCR 551.
2 *HM Advocate v Harris* 1993 JC 150, 1993 SLT 963, 1993 SCCR 559, overruling *Quinn v Cunningham* 1956 JC 22, 1956 SLT 55, which had held that any such reckless conduct had to be to the danger of the lieges.
3 *MacPhail v Clark* 1983 SLT (Sh Ct) 37.

whether or not the driving complained of was careless, any explanation tendered by the driver or any other person.

Defences are sometimes raised on the ground that the accused driver was confronted by an untoward incident or unforeseen emergency. Examples of such incidents are that the accused was dazzled by the headlights of an oncoming vehicle, was confronted suddenly by some vehicle, person or object which unexpectedly came into his path, or was stung by a wasp. As in the case of convictions, all such defences depend for their success on a consideration of all the material facts and circumstances. It is submitted that such defences can only succeed when it is shown that the unforeseen circumstances deprived the driver of control or vision and led directly to the accident or other consequences of the driving. Even if it is shown that some sudden or unexpected emergency occurred, the driver still has a duty thereafter, in so far as is reasonably practicable, to drive his vehicle with reasonable care; such emergencies will not necessarily excuse all further driving actions on the part of the driver. Further, it is submitted that an unforeseen emergency brought about by the driver's own negligence, such as carelessly dropping a lighted cigarette into his lap, or stepping on the accelerator rather than the brake, will render a defence of unforeseen emergency extremely difficult to establish. Any contribution to the unforeseen emergency by the accused will therefore proportionately reduce the effectiveness of any such defence. Where a motorist has been placed in a position of emergency or difficulty through circumstances outwith his control, he may be able to argue in his defence that in effect the standard of driving reasonably expected of him in the circumstances is lower than would normally be the case[1]. Reference should also be made to the paragraph on defences to charges of dangerous driving (2.5 above) which are also relevant to charges of careless or inconsiderate driving; and also to 3.10 below.

The driver of an emergency vehicle is not in a special position[2] however in such a case there may be particular scope for mitigation[3].

2.16   DUTY TO GIVE NAME

See 2.6 above.

---

1 *Johnston v National Coal Board* 1960 SLT (Notes) 84.
2 Except in the case of adhering to the speed limits: see the Road Traffic Regulation Act 1994, s 87.
3 *Husband v Russell* 1997 SCCR 592; 2.12 above.

2.17 CARELESS CYCLING

It is an offence to drive a cycle on a road carelessly or without reasonable consideration for other persons using the road[1]. The terms 'without due care and attention' and 'without reasonable consideration for other persons using the road' have the same meaning as in motor vehicle offences[2]. The word 'cycle' is defined at 1.6:7 above, and the word 'road' is defined at 1.8:2 above. Sections 167 and 168 of the Road Traffic Act 1988 apply in respect of such charges[3].

1 Road Traffic Act 1988, s 29.
2 See 2.10:2 and 2.10:3 above.
3 See 2.6 above.

Chapter Three

Drink related offences

PART 1
INTRODUCTION AND SPECIAL DEFINITIONS

3.1 INTRODUCTION

Sections 4–11 of the Road Traffic Act 1988 (as amended by the Road Traffic Act 1991) deal with drinking and driving offences. These sections have generated a considerable number of reported cases and this area of law in particular is constantly being considered and revised. A practitioner must keep abreast of all such developments by constant reference to the reports which contain road traffic material. There is sometimes a marked difference in the development of case law in Scotland as distinct from England. For example, there has been a number of English cases following upon *DPP v Warren*[1], which was concerned with what a police officer should tell a driver about whether there are any medical reasons for not giving blood samples for analysis after arrest. These cases have wrestled with a number of problems which have simply not troubled the Scottish courts to anything like the same extent[2]. Drinking and driving offences are among the most numerous of contested cases dealt with in the sheriff court, and are usually regarded as the most important and contentious of road traffic matters.

Cases are normally taken on summary complaint. The penalties available are found in Schedule 2 to the Road Traffic Offenders Act 1988. Reference should be made to 2.3:3 above for conclusions of evidence.

3.2 GENERAL

3.2:1 General scheme

It is helpful to have a general overall view of these eight important sections of the Road Traffic Act 1988. Section 3A (which was introduced by section 3 of the Road Traffic Act 1991) makes it an offence to cause the death of another person by careless driving when the driver (1) is at the material time unfit to drive through

---

1 [1993] AC 319, [1992] 4 All ER 865, [1992] WLR 884, [1993] RTR 58.
2 See *McLeod v McFarlane* 1993 SLT 782.

drink or drugs, (2) is above the permitted level in respect of a sample of breath, blood or urine or (3) fails to provide a specimen for analysis in terms of s 7 within 18 hours. Section 4 makes it an offence to drive or attempt to drive, or to be in charge, of a motor vehicle on a road or in a public place while unfit to drive through drink or drugs. In s 4 prosecutions there does not have to be any specimen taken for analysis from the motorist, although such specimens may properly be required during the police investigation of such a case. An offence under this section occurs simply if, in the judgment of others formed at the relevant time, the driver's ability to drive properly is for the time being impaired. It is not therefore necessary, for conviction, to establish the precise level of alcohol or drugs in the accused driver. This section is the only one available to the prosecution in respect of a charge of driving while affected by drugs. While the technology exists which can determine that various drugs are present in the system of a motorist, no system has yet been devised to quantify the amount of such drugs; in general terms, most of the devices presently available can only identify that any one of a range of particular drugs has been ingested by testing saliva, sweat, urine or blood. There is accordingly no approved device for testing for drugs. Section 5 makes it an offence for a person to drive or attempt to drive, or to be in charge of, a motor vehicle on a road or other public place after consuming so much alcohol that the proportion in his breath, blood or urine exceeds the prescribed limit. This offence is therefore established following the taking of such specimens from the driver. Section 6 of the Act makes general provision for breath samples to be required of drivers by a police officer as a preliminary step to further procedure. This is the process commonly known as the breathalyser or roadside test. This test must be carefully distinguished from the breath specimen supplied by the motorist to determine the level of alcohol in his body for the purposes of s 5 and in terms of s 7. Section 7 of the Act provides in detail for the provision of specimens of breath, blood or urine for analysis in the course of an investigation as to whether a person has committed an offence under s 4 or s 5. Section 8 provides that the lower of the two specimens given is to be used, and if that lower specimen contains not more than 50 microgrammes of alcohol in 100 millilitres of blood then the motorist may require that it be replaced by a specimen taken in terms of s 7(4). Section 9 contains special provisions for hospital patients in respect of the tests that may be required under ss 6 and 7. Section 10 allows the police to detain any person required to give a specimen of breath or blood or urine, at a police station, until it appears that such a person would no longer be contravening s 4 or s 5. Section 11 is an interpretation section relating to ss 3A–10[1]. In addition, s 15 of the Road Traffic Offenders Act 1988[2] and s 16 of the same Act contain significant evidential provisions relating to ss 3A, 4 and 5 of the Road Traffic Act 1988.

3.2:2 General procedure

It is still envisaged that the first step in normal circumstances will be the requirement by a constable for a motorist to take the preliminary breath test. This is sometimes known as the roadside test, and is carried out by the motorist blowing into an Alcotest, Alcolmeter or similar device. The current Breath Test Device Approval Order lists all the approved devices currently available, and is described in Appendix B. Thereafter the Act envisages that the principal method of procedure (other than in cases under ss 3A(1)(a) and 4) will be the provision of a breath specimen for analysis by an accused driver. A blood or urine specimen can only be required if, for whatever reason, a reliable breath analysis device is not available, or if the lower of the two breath specimens given is below 50 microgrammes of alcohol in 100 millilitres. The current legislation places little emphasis on procedural, technical or formal requirements which were the subject of many reported decisions under previous law. In particular, it must be emphasised that the provision of a positive breath test in terms of s 6 and the arrest of the accused driver is not now a prerequisite before a specimen of blood, breath or urine may be required for the purpose of establishing whether an offence has been committed in terms of ss 3A(b), 4 or 5.

3.3 SPECIAL DEFINITIONS

3.3:1 Introduction

Sections 3A(1)(a), 4(1) and 5(1)(a) of the Road Traffic Act 1988 contemplate an offence where a person drives or attempts to drive a mechanically propelled vehicle or a motor vehicle on a

1 See the Road Traffic Act 1991, Sch 4, para 44.
2 As amended by RTA 1991, Sch 4, para 87.

road or other public place. Sections 4(2) and 5(1)(b) of the Act provide that an offence may occur if a person is in charge of a mechanically propelled vehicle or a motor vehicle which is on a road or other public place. The definition chapter (Ch 1) provides general descriptions of the various terms used in ss 4 and 5, but in addition, for the purpose of these drink driving offences, special consideration has to be given to the words and phrases 'drives', 'attempts to drive', 'in charge of a motor vehicle' and 'road or other public place'.

3.3:2   'Drives'

The reported cases in recent years dealing with the question of whether a person is or is not driving in the context of prosecutions under ss 4 and 5, or their historical equivalents, have been concerned principally with three particular issues: firstly, whether, in the proven circumstances of the case, a motorist was driving or not; secondly, whether the motorist was driving, as opposed to being in charge of, the vehicle; and thirdly, whether a driver in the circumstances was to be regarded as still driving his vehicle or whether his driving had come to an end.

On the first question, as to whether a person is to be held as driving a vehicle as opposed to not driving it, the position for all practical purposes is as outlined in the definition chapter under the heading 'Drivers and driving' (See 1.7:1 above). This means that a person will generally be held to be the driver of a vehicle if he is in the driving seat or in control of the steering wheel, and in addition has some measure of control over the propulsion of the vehicle[1]. More than one person may be driving the vehicle at a particular time[2]. The driver of a towed vehicle was convicted of driving while disqualified in *McQuaid v Anderton*[3]. Despite what was said in *Wallace v Major*[4], there appears to be no reason why the driver of a towed vehicle should not be convicted of any offence arising out of ss 3A, 4 or 5 of the Road Traffic Act 1988.

---

1 *Ames v McLeod* 1969 JC 1; *McArthur v Valentine* 1990 JC 146, 1990 SLT 732, 1989 SCCR 704.
2 *Tyler v Whatmore* [1976] RTR 83; *Langman v Valentine* [1952] 2 All ER 803; Road Traffic Act 1988, s 192(1).
3 [1980] RTR 371 (followed in *Caise v Wright* [1981] RTR 49).
4 1946 KB 473 (at 477 per LJC Goddard).

A passenger was convicted in *Valentine v Mackie*[1] of aiding and abetting a driver with excess alcohol in his blood. In *Farrell v Stirling*[2] (a summary case) a driver was held not to be driving at the time he experienced a totally unexpected attack of hypoglycaemia.

It has also been held in England that to pedal a moped is driving, even although the engine was not operating or operational[3]; the moped did not cease to be a motor vehicle merely because there was, or might have been, a temporary loss of engine power.

The second category of cases involving drinking and driving, in which the nature of the driving has been in issue, is concerned with whether the motorist was at the material time driving, as opposed to being in charge. This distinction is not quite so significant as it was formerly. Under earlier legislation, a police constable had no power to require a roadside breathalyser test of a driver who was in charge of his vehicle rather than driving it. However, the current terms of s 6 of the Road Traffic Act 1988[4] allows a police constable to require a driver to provide a roadside breathalyser test if he is in charge of a vehicle and the constable has reasonable cause to suspect that he has alcohol in his body or has committed a moving traffic offence. Accordingly, the significance chiefly attaching to the distinction between driving and being in charge of a vehicle prior to 6 May 1983 no longer applies. However, a complaint may libel an offence in terms of s 4 or s 5 in the alternative; that is to say, the driver may be charged with driving or alternatively being in charge of a vehicle in contravention of either of these sections. Having regard to the difference in penalties that may be imposed in respect of these alternatives, the distinction between driving and being in charge of a vehicle will remain of importance. Accordingly, reference should be made to 1.7:1 above and this paragraph for consideration of the nature of driving, and reference should be made to 3.3:4 below for consideration of what is involved in being in charge. There appears as yet to be no Scottish authority dealing specifically with the distinction

---

1 1980 SLT (Sh Ct) 122.
2 1975 SLT (Sh Ct) 71.
3 *Floyd v Bush* [1953] 1 WLR 242, [1953] 1 All ER 265; *R v Tahsin* [1970] RTR 88.
4 Which repeats the terms of the Road Traffic Act 1972, s 7, as amended by the Transport Act 1981, s 25(3) and Sch 8 and introduced by virtue of the Transport Act 1981 Commencement Order 1983, SI 1983/576 on 6 May 1983.

between driving and being in charge; the matter is generally one of fact which will be determined by the circumstances in each particular case.

The third question involving the nature of driving which the courts have considered in the past was whether a driver in the proven circumstances of the case was to be considered as still in the course of his journey, and therefore driving his vehicle, or whether his driving was to be regarded as having come to an end. Under previous legislation, the roadside breathalyser test could only be required of a motorist by a police constable if the constable had reasonable cause to suspect that the motorist had alcohol in his body while the vehicle was in motion and before the motorist had completed his journey. This issue was at the centre of a large number of cases decided between 1972 and 1983[1]. Apart from the question of whether there is reasonable cause for suspicion, these cases now have only marginal relevance, if any, because of the current terms of s 6(1)(b) and (c) of the 1988 Act. As indicated above, this section replaces the terms of the previous s 7 which came into force on 6 May 1983. In terms of s 6(1)(b), a breath test may be required of a person who 'has been driving or attempting to drive or been in charge of a motor vehicle on a road or other public place', and in terms of s 6(1)(c) where 'a person has been driving or attempting to drive or been in charge of a motor vehicle on the road or other public place and has committed a traffic offence whilst the vehicle was in motion'. It is therefore clear from the terms of the subsections that the question of whether a police officer makes the requirement for a breath test while the motorist is still engaged on his journey, or whether he has completed his journey and is no longer driving, is now entirely academic[2]. The section was specifically framed to exclude the defence, available to a driver before 1983, that he had completed his journey, and therefore could not thereafter be suspected of having alcohol in his body and thus be required to take a breath test. To underline this, the current legislation imposes no time limit of any kind on the right of a police constable in appropriate circumstances to require a roadside breathalyser specimen, except in the case of prosecutions under s 3A(1)(c) of the Road Traffic Act 1988.

---

1 Eg *Edkins v Knowles* [1973] 1 QB 748, [1973] RTR 257; *Ritchie v Pirie* 1972 JC 7, 1972 SLT 2.
2 And see *Allan v Douglas* 1978 JC 7.

Whether a driver can be said to have driven to a place where he is found will depend upon an examination of the facts and circumstances[1].

3.3:3 Attempting to drive

In terms of both ss 4(1) and 5(1)(a) of the Road Traffic Act 1988, it is a separate offence to attempt to drive a motor vehicle while affected by drink or drugs. The idea of attempting to drive is also relevant to prosecutions under s 6. It would appear to be the intention of the Act that this offence should cover the position when the vehicle is not in motion. The question of whether a motorist is attempting to drive at the material time is one of fact. In this context, the meaning of the word 'drive' has exactly the same meaning as in 'driving' as described in the preceding paragraph. In assessing the proven facts in any case, regard will be had principally to the actions of the driver and, where appropriate, to his intentions, expressed or implied. Thus, even where a car is *de facto* incapable of being driven through mechanical defect, anyone attempting to drive such a vehicle may be convicted under these subsections[2]. Again, someone attempting to start a car with the wrong key is attempting to drive that vehicle[3]; the fact that the attempt failed because of ineptitude, inefficiency or insufficient means does not mean that the attempt to drive was not made.

In terms of s 24(2) and (3) of the Road Traffic Offenders Act 1988 a charge under s 3A of the Road Traffic Act 1988 will not authorise a conviction of attempting to commit the offence, but charges under ss 4(1) and 5(1)(a) will.

Each case will depend on its own circumstances: in *Guthrie v Friel*[4] it was observed that making preparations for driving may not be the same thing as attempting to drive. Someone trying to repair a broken-down vehicle may not be attempting to drive[5].

Anyone who has been effectively stopped or dissuaded from driving cannot be considered as still being within the category of persons driving a vehicle[6], or, it is submitted, of persons attempting to drive a vehicle.

1 Eg *Henderson v Hamilton* 1995 SLT 968; 1995 SCCR 413.
2 *R v Farrance* [1978] RTR 225.
3 *Kelly v Hogan* [1982] RTR 352.
4 1993 SLT 899, 1992 SCCR 932.
5 *Ritchie v Pirie* 1972 JC 7, 1972 SLT 2.
6 *Edkins v Knowles* [1973] QB 748 at 757, [1973] 2 WLR 977.

Persons found not to be attempting to drive a car as in the foregoing illustrations may still be in charge of their vehicle.

3.3:4   'In charge'

Sections 4(2) and 5(1)(b) of the Road Traffic Act 1988 provide that offences occur when a motorist, having consumed alcohol, is 'in charge' of, as opposed to driving, or attempting to drive, his vehicle. Being in charge of a vehicle therefore only arises before driving has started or after it has ceased. In *Crichton v Burrell*[1], a motorist who was standing beside his vehicle with the keys in his possession, waiting for an employee to come and drive the vehicle, was held to be not in charge. The appeal court in that case held that to be 'in charge' meant that the motorist must be in some measure in *de facto* control of the vehicle. The circumstances of that case would therefore appear to indicate that by standing outwith the vehicle and making arrangements for another to drive, the accused had effectively surrendered control of the vehicle. In such a case, the statutory defence provided by s 4(3) would also now be available to the motorist.

The English courts have taken a fundamentally different approach to the idea of being 'in charge' of a vehicle; there, the view is taken that some person must be in charge of a vehicle unless that vehicle has been completely abandoned. It follows from this that a person remains in charge of a vehicle until he surrenders control thereof to some other person. Accordingly, the motorist in *Crichton v Burrell*[2] would have been convicted in England. It is not thought that such an approach will be followed in Scotland; the large number of English cases on the subject are likely to be of little value.

The following are some examples of Scottish decisions. The supervisor of a learner driver has been held to be in charge of a vehicle[3]. A driver sitting in his vehicle (a taxi) which had broken down and was waiting for another vehicle to tow him away was held to be in charge[4]. A mechanic repairing a broken-down vehicle by the roadside was held not to be in charge of the

---

1 1951 JC 107, 1951 SLT 365.
2 1951 JC 107, 1951 SLT 365.
3 *Clark v Clark* 1950 SLT (Sh Ct) 68.
4 *MacDonald v Crawford* 1952 SLT (Sh Ct) 92.

vehicle[1]. A person who was unconscious in the back of the vehicle which had been made mechanically incapable of being driven was held not to be in charge of the vehicle[2]. The owner of a vehicle who was sitting in the passenger seat at a time when the vehicle's engine was running and the person in the driver's seat was unlicensed, was held not to be in charge of the vehicle[3]. A driver who left his vehicle and gave a friend the keys to drive the car home was deemed not to be in charge of his vehicle[4]. Reference may also be made to *MacDonald v Bain*[5]; *McDonald v Kubirdas*[6]; *MacDonald v MacDonald*[7]; and *Thaw v Segar*[8].

It is not a coincidence, however, that all of these authorities predate the amended terms of the Road Traffic Act 1972. Although these cases are still relevant, the extended powers now available to the police to require breath tests in terms of s 6 means that the occasions when being in charge of a vehicle is of significance will become less frequent. However, cases of being in charge of a vehicle are by no means rare. In *Lees v Lawrie*[9], a supervisor of a learner driver was held to be in charge of a vehicle, but obtained an acquittal by proving that there was no likelihood of him driving. *Cartmill v Heywood*[10] contains many of the features of a typical case.

3.3:5 'Road or other public place'

In the Road Traffic Act 1988 as originally framed, and in earlier legislation, the vast majority of offences occurred if the conduct complained of took place on 'a road'. The only exceptions were the principal sections of the drink-driving legislation (then ss 4, 5 and 6). The terms of ss 1, 2 and 3 of the Road Traffic Act 1991 extend the application of a 'road or other public place' to ss 1, 2, 3 and 3A of the 1988 Act. The general position, and definitions of

1 *Adair v McKenna* 1951 SLT (Sh Ct) 40.
2 *Dean v Wishart* 1952 JC 9, 1952 SLT 86.
3 *Winter v Morrison* 1954 JC 7.
4 *Farrell v Campbell* 1959 SLT (Sh Ct) 43, (1959) 75 Sh Ct Rep 24.
5 1954 SLT (Sh Ct) 30.
6 1955 SLT (Sh Ct) 50.
7 1955 71 Sh Ct Rep 17.
8 1962 SLT (Sh Ct) 63.
9 1993 SCCR 1.
10 2000 SLT 799.

the terms 'road' and 'other public place', are discussed at 1.8:1, 1.8:2 and 1.8:3 above.

PART 2
CARELESS DRIVING, DRIVING OR BEING IN CHARGE OF A VEHICLE WHEN UNDER THE INFLUENCE OF DRINK OR DRUGS

3.4   SECTION 3A

3.4:1   Introduction

Section 3A of the Road Traffic Act 1988[1] provides:

'(1) If a person causes the death of another person by driving a mechanically propelled vehicle on a road or other public place without due care and attention, or without reasonable consideration for other persons using the road or place, and –
  (a) he is, at the time when he is driving, unfit to drive through drink or drugs, or
  (b) he has consumed so much alcohol that the proportion of it in his breath, blood or urine at that time exceeds the prescribed limit, or
  (c) he is, within 18 hours after that time, required to provide a specimen in pursuance of section 7 of this Act, but without reasonable excuse fails to provide it,

he is guilty of an offence.

(2) For the purposes of this section a person shall be taken to be unfit to drive at any time when his ability to drive properly is impaired.
(3) Subsection (1)(b) and (c) above shall not apply in relation to a person driving a mechanically propelled vehicle other than a motor vehicle.'

This section was introduced in the Road Traffic Act 1991 to meet a perceived need to cover those cases where death results from a course of driving which could not be described as reckless, as opposed to careless, and where the driver has been drinking. Broadly, section 3A contains an amalgam of existing ideas. Care has been taken to incorporate into the new offence the original

---

1 Introduced by the Road Traffic Act 1991, s 3.

notions of careless driving, drinking while unfit to drive through drink or drugs, and consumption of so much alcohol that the proportion of it in the breath, blood or urine exceeds the prescribed limit. The only original concept included in this offence is that there is a time limit of 18 hours from the time of the accident after which the requirement to provide a specimen in pursuance of section 7 of the Act cannot be made. In general, identical considerations are to be applied to the various component parts of this section as are relevant to their source in other parts of the legislation.

The possible penalties for this offence, which must be taken on indictment, include imprisonment for up to ten years, and obligatory disqualification[1].

By virtue of the Road Traffic Offenders Act 1988, s 24, as amended, provision is made for alternative verdicts in terms of ss 4(1), 5(1) and 7(6) to a charge under s 3A. However, unlike charges libelling offences under ss 4(1) and 5(1)(a), a charge under s 3A cannot authorise a finding that the motorist is found guilty of an alternative verdict of attempting to commit the offence.

3.4:2   Definitions – general

'Causes the death': see 2.3:2 above.

'Driving': see 1.7:1 and 3.3:2 above.

'Mechanically propelled vehicle': see 1.2:1ff above.

'Road or other public place': see 1.8:1, 1.8:2 and 1.8:3 above.

'Driving without due care and attention, or without reasonable consideration': see Chapter 2, Part 2 above.

'Breath, blood or urine exceeding prescribed limit': see Chapter 3, Part 4 below.

'Driving while unfit to drive through drink or drugs': see Chapter 3, Part 3 below.

'Reasonable excuse': see 4.14:3 and 4.14:7 below.

'Without due care and attention': see 2.10ff above.

---

1 Road Traffic Offenders Act 1988, Sch 2, as amended by the Road Traffic Act 1991, Sch 2, para 7 and the Criminal Justice Act 1993, s 67.

'*Without reasonable consideration*': see 2.10ff above.

'*Unfit to drive*': see s 3A(2) of the Road Traffic Act 1988 and 3.6:1 below.

It will be noted that s 3A(3) maintains the difference that exists between mechanically propelled vehicles in s 4 and motor vehicles in s 5; reference should be made to 1.2:1 above.

3.4:3   Defences

Apart from the usual common law defences, (See 3.10 below) the statutory defence contained in s 15(3) of the Road Traffic Offenders Act 1988, as amended by the Road Traffic Act 1991, Sch 4, para 87, is available in prosecutions under s 3A(1) of the Road Traffic Act 1988. This topic is discussed at 3.9:1 and 3.17:1 below; see also Appendix E.

3.5   SECTION 4(1)

3.5:1   Introduction

Section 4(1) of the Road Traffic Act 1988[1] provides:

'A person who, when driving or attempting to drive a mechanically propelled vehicle on a road or other public place, is unfit to drive through drink or drugs shall be guilty of an offence.'

This section is generally used in cases where for a variety of reasons it is not possible to determine the proportion of alcohol present in the motorist by reference to the analysis of specimens of breath, blood or urine. It may be that the accused is so drunk that he is incapable of being subjected to the various statutory procedures, or that such procedures, for whatever reason, cannot appropriately be carried out in the circumstances. There is a tendency also for prosecutors to use this section in respect of an accused who appears in custody and who wishes to plead guilty; such a charge can be prepared without first having an analyst's report on specimens which may have been provided. However

---

1 As amended by the Road Traffic Act 1991, s 4.

information from the analysis can competently be placed before the court in s 4 prosecutions if available.

Prosecutions under s 4 are normally taken under summary procedure. The penalties following conviction are found in Schedule 2 to the Road Traffic Offenders Act 1988[1], and include obligatory disqualification for a minimum period of one year[2], endorsement of the licence (with 3-11 penalty points if disqualification is not imposed), a maximum prison sentence of six months and a fine at level 5, or both. As noted at 3.2:1 above, this section is the only provision for charging a motorist with driving under the influence of drugs.

3.5:2 Definitions – general

'Driving or attempting to drive': see 1.7:1, 3.3:2 and 3.3:3 above.

'Unfit to drive': see 3.6:1 below.

'Mechanically propelled vehicle': see 1.2:1ff above.

'Road or other public place': see 1.8:1, 1.8:2 and 1.8:3 above.

3.5:3 Special definitions: drink and drugs

In a prosecution under s 4 of the Road Traffic Act 1988, the issue is whether the motorist is unfit to drive through drink or drugs, as distinct from s 5 cases where the issue is whether the motorist exceeds the prescribed limits of alcohol in his breath, blood or urine. Although there is no definition of the word anywhere in the legislation, it has never been disputed that the word 'drink' means an alcoholic drink[3]. The question of what constitutes a drug is also not comprehensively defined in the legislation and prior to 1983 was not defined at all. In *Armstrong v Clark*[4] it was held that insulin was included in the term 'drug', and that a motorist who had taken the correct and prescribed dose of insulin, but still thereafter became unfit to drive as a result, could properly be convicted in terms of s 5(1). However, in the broadly

---

1 As amended by RTA 1991, Sch 2, para 8.
2 Road Traffic Offenders Act 1988, s 34(1).
3 See *Armstrong v Clark* [1957] 2 QB 391 at 394 per LJC Goddard.
4 [1957] 2 QB 391.

similar case of *Watmore v Jenkins*[1], the appeal court declined to interfere with an acquittal in such circumstances imposed by a lower court; and in *Farrell v Stirling*[2], a driver in similar circumstances to the accused in *Armstrong v Clark* was held not to be driving. In *Armstrong v Clark*[3], the court decided that a 'drug' meant medicine given for the purposes of treating a medical condition. It appears that the court did not intend that this definition should be exhaustive and it is clear that the meaning of the word is not confined to medicines designed to treat some medical conditions. In *Duffy v Tudhope*[4], the accused drove while under the influence of toluene, which he had inhaled in the course of sniffing glue. The appeal court, following *Bradford v Wilson*[5], held that as the substance had a drugging effect, it was clearly a drug and the accused could properly be convicted.

Following all of these cases, the Transport Act 1982, s 25(3) and Sch 8[6] introduced the current interpretation provisions now found in s 11 of the Road Traffic Act 1988. Inter alia, these provide that 'a drug includes any intoxicant other than alcohol'[7]. It has never been doubted that the main types of drug contemplated by this section are those substances which are the subject of the Misuse of Drugs Act 1971.

3.5:4   Driving under the influence of drugs: general

All prosecutions where the motorist is said to be under the influence of drugs must be taken under s 4 of the Road Traffic Act 1988; s 5 makes no provision for driving while affected by drugs. The section therefore caters for the effect on the human metabolism of different kinds of drug, whether they are those mentioned in the schedules to the Misuse of Drugs Act 1971 or whether they are other kinds of drugging agents. The precise quantification of any particular drug present in any case is not a process currently available, and there are no established degrees of intoxication

---

1 [1962] 2 QB 572.
2 1975 SLT (Sh Ct) 71.
3 [1957] 2 QB 391.
4 1984 SLT 107, 1983 SCCR 440.
5 [1983] Crim LR 482.
6 Which came into force on 6 May 1983 by virtue of SI 1983/576.
7 Road Traffic Act 1988, s 11(2), as amended by the Road Traffic Act 1991, Sch 4, para 44.

related to drug quantities as there are with alcohol. This position is likely to continue for some time. There are devices which can detect the presence of drugs in a driver's system. However, it is not enough for the prosecution to show that the driver has ingested drugs; s 4 requires that the accused is shown to be unfit to drive because of the drugs. Whether or not the accused's ability to drive is impaired is always a question of fact, but in the absence of authority it seems to be accepted that the mere presence, particularly of a controlled substance, goes some way to provide the necessary grounds for conviction. Current practice, however, appears to be based on what is called field impairment tests, not dissimilar in character to the old tests for drinking and driving, such as walking along a straight line, to allow investigating officers to reach a conclusion on the question of impairment. Considerable research is currently being undertaken in an effort to produce effective devices in this field. In the meantime reference might be made to 3.6:1 below.

3.5:5 Driving under the influence of drugs: special provision

If a constable arrests a motorist because he suspects that he has been driving or attempting to drive or been in charge of a vehicle while under the influence of drink or drugs, in terms of s 4 of the Road Traffic Act 1988, and the constable is advised by a medical practitioner that the condition of the motorist may be due to some drug, the constable may require the provision of a blood or urine sample as opposed to the normal primary requirement of two specimens of breath for analysis[1]. This requirement is competent even where the motorist has already provided, or has been required to provide, two specimens of breath for analysis. This provision is designed to deal with the absence of a reliable device to detect the presence of drugs in the sample given by the motorist; such drugs are more readily detected from the analysis of a blood or urine specimen. However, it will be noted that to take advantage of this power of requirement, the police constable must receive medical advice that the motorist's condition might be due to drugs, and cannot opt to require a blood or urine specimen on his own initiative.

1 Road Traffic Act 1988, s 7(3)(c).

3.6   SECTION 4(1): THE TEST

3.6:1   General

The test of unfitness to drive in terms of this subsection is whether the driver's ability to drive properly is for the time being impaired through drink or drugs[1]. The question is one of fact. The kind of evidence which is used to support such a charge, whether of driving or attempting to drive when under the influence of drink or drugs, is usually that of medical examination and tests[2]. General observations of the motorist's conduct may also be relevant to the charge.

The results of the analysis of specimens of breath, blood or urine taken in terms of other parts of the procedure may also be used. If the accused provides such a specimen of breath, blood or urine, the results of that analysis must in all cases be taken into account and it shall be assumed that the proportion of alcohol in the accused's breath, blood or urine at the time of the alleged offence was not less than in the specimen[3]. However, in terms of s 4(5) the test is whether the ability to drive is impaired, and, accordingly, it is theoretically possible (although perhaps highly unlikely in practice) that a motorist could be acquitted of the charge even where there is evidence that the results of analysis of a blood or other specimen proved to be in excess of what is permitted in terms of s 5 of the Act. In *McNeill v Fletcher*[4] an accused was found to have nearly four times the permitted maximum of alcohol in his blood, he was unsteady on his feet, his eyes were glazed and his breath smelt of alcohol; nonetheless, the police surgeon refused to certify the driver as unfit to drive. On appeal it was held that he was entitled to do so. However, in *Murray v Muir*[5], the evidence demonstrated that a motorist had driven along a main road without any cause for criticism shortly before being taken for an examination by a police surgeon, and this was held not to create any presumption of sobriety which could not be overcome by medical or other evidence.

---

1 Road Traffic Act 1988, s 4(5).
2 *Murray v Muir* 1950 SLT 41.
3 Road Traffic Offenders Act 1988, s 15(2).
4 1966 JC 18.
5 1950 SLT 41.

In *Reid v Nixon; Dumigan v Brown*[1], a Full Bench laid down general guidelines which are to be followed in cases where the evidence turns on a medical examination by a police surgeon. As cases might arise out of a great variety of circumstances it was recognised that rigid rules for universal application could not be imposed; however, any departure from these guidelines normally requires to be justified. The procedure to be adopted in terms of the guidelines is as follows:

Firstly, the suspect should be cautioned in the usual way by the police and invited formally to give his consent to a medical examination. If he is not first cautioned without good reason, the medical evidence is inadmissible.[2] The accused should be advised of his right to refuse to consent to such medical examination, and it is proper practice that this intimation should be established by full corroborative evidence, although the evidence of one witness only on this matter has been held to be sufficient[3]. However, the requirement to advise the accused of his right to refuse to consent to medical examination may be rendered unnecessary when the accused specifically states that he has no objection to undergoing such an examination[4]. It should also be made clear to the accused that the results of such examinations and tests may be used in evidence.

Secondly, the accused should be told that he has the right to summon a doctor of his own choice, and given facilities for doing so[5]. However, the police examination is not to be delayed until this other doctor is present.

Thirdly, the medical examination should normally proceed outwith the presence of the police officers.

Fourthly, any questioning of the accused by the doctor in respect of recent events must be directed solely to testing the accused's memory and coherence and not to eliciting information bearing on his guilt and any such information incidentally obtained must not be communicated by the doctor to the police officers.

Fifthly, if the accused refuses to consent to the examination, his refusal can be spoken to in evidence, and if the police doctor has been summoned, he should confine himself to observing the accused and should not carry out any examination or tests.

1 1948 JC 68, 1948 SLT 295.
2 *Gallacher v HM Advocate* 1963 SLT 217.
3 *Farrell v Concannon* 1957 JC 12, 1957 SLT 60.
4 *Taylor v Irvine* 1958 SLT (Notes) 15.
5 Overruling *Harris v Adair* 1947 JC 116.

Should a medical examination be carried out in the case of a motorist suspected of having ingested drugs, there appears to be no reason why the same general principles should not be applied.

3.6:2   Evidence

In practice, evidence in support of a prosecution under s 4 is usually given by police and medical evidence. However, there is nothing to prevent such cases proceeding on the basis of lay evidence, provided that such testimony is sufficient in quality and quantity to allow the court to conclude beyond reasonable doubt that the accused's ability to drive at the material time had been impaired through drink or drugs. For cases on the sufficiency of evidence in a charge of this kind, see *Wallace v McLeod*[1] and *Kenny v Tudhope*[2]. Evidence of the levels of alcohol in a specimen of blood, breath or urine which subsequently becomes available may be referred to.

3.7   SECTION 4(2): IN CHARGE OF A VEHICLE

3.7:1   General

Section 4(2) of the Road Traffic Act 1988[3] provides:

'Without prejudice to subsection (1) above, a person who, when in charge of a mechanically propelled vehicle which is on a road or other public place, is unfit to drive through drink or drugs, is guilty of an offence.'

The subsection is designed to cover the situation when the vehicle in question is not in motion, and when the driver is not in the process of concluding a driving operation, and does not fall into the category of a person attempting to drive the vehicle. Whether a motorist is in charge of his vehicle, as opposed to not being in charge, or as opposed to driving or attempting to drive, is a matter of fact and evidence.

1 1986 SCCR 678.
2 1984 SCCR 290.
3 As amended by the Road Traffic Act 1991, s 4.

3.7:2 Definitions

'In charge' – see 3.3:4 above.

'Mechanically propelled vehicle' – see 1.2:1ff above.

'Road or other public place' – see 1.8:1, 1.8:2 and 1.8:3 above.

'Unfit to drive' – see 3.6:1 and 3.6:2 above.

'Drink or drugs' – see 3.5:3 above.

3.7:3 Procedure and penalties

Prosecutions under s 4(2) of the Road Traffic Act 1988 are normally taken summarily, and may be charged as an alternative to s 4(1). Penalties are given in Schedule 2, Part I of the Road Traffic Offenders Act 1988. Disqualification is discretionary, and ten penalty points must be endorsed on the licence if disqualification is not imposed. A maximum prison sentence of three months or a fine at level 4 (or both) is available.

3.8 SECTION 4(3): STATUTORY DEFENCE (1): NO LIKELIHOOD OF DRIVING

3.8:1 General

Section 4(3) of the Road Traffic Act 1988[1] provides:

'For the purposes of subsection (2) above, a person shall be deemed not to have been in charge of a mechanically propelled vehicle if he proves that at the material time the circumstances were such that there was no likelihood of his driving it so long as he remained unfit to drive through drink or drugs.'

Section 4(3) therefore provides a statutory defence in prosecutions under s 4(2). A driver will be regarded as not being in charge of a vehicle if he proves that at the material time there was no likelihood of him driving during the period that he remained unfit to drive through drink or drugs. Whether such a defence can be

---

1 As amended by the Road Traffic Act 1991, s 4.

successfully established will be a question of fact and evidence. Once a prima facie case is made out by the prosecution the burden of proof in this defence rests on the accused, and the standard of proof is on the balance of probabilities[1]. If this standard is not reached, but the defence case in any way casts a reasonable doubt on the guilt of the accused in the circumstances of the case, the accused will be entitled to an acquittal. Where appropriate, this defence may be established by uncorroborated evidence, including testimony from the accused driver himself.

For a successful defence of this kind, the accused requires to demonstrate that there is no likelihood of him driving so long as he is affected by drink or drugs to the extent that his ability to drive is impaired. Put another way, the accused has to establish when his ability to drive would no longer be impaired in addition to showing that there was no likelihood of him driving up to that point. In considering such a defence, the court will have regard to the accused's intentions, express or implied, in the light of all the other facts and circumstances of the case[2]. Reference should be made to 3.9:1 below (defence of post-incident consumption of alcohol in terms of the Road Traffic Offenders Act 1988, s 15(3)) for evidential considerations relating to the time when a driver may be said to be no longer unfit to drive.

The circumstances in which a defence under s 4(3) may be presented can conceivably overlap with some of the earlier cases where it was found that an accused was not in charge of the vehicle (see 3.3:2 and 3.3:4 above), and these authorities may be of assistance in determining whether a motorist can demonstrate that he is not likely to drive while affected by drink or drugs.

In *Lees v Lawrie*[3], the supervisor of a learner driver was held to be in charge of the vehicle, but established that there was no likelihood of him driving it and was acquitted.

The statutory defence under s 4(3) is only relevant in prosecutions in cases where the accused is in charge of the vehicle under s 4(2), and does not apply to s 4(1) (cases of driving or attempting to drive). In addition, in considering this defence, regard has to be had to s 4(4) (see 3.8:2 below). The s 4(3) defence is similar to that provided by s 5(2)[4].

---

1 *Neish v Stevenson* 1969 SLT 229.
2 *Morton v Confer* [1963] 1 WLR 763, 2 All ER 765.
3 1993 SCCR 1.
4 See 3.16:1 below, similar considerations will in general apply to both; see also Appendix E.

3.8:2 Section 4(4): Injury and damage to be disregarded

Section 4(4) of the Road Traffic Act 1988 provides:

'The court may, in determining whether there was such a likelihood as is mentioned in subsection (3) above, disregard any injury to him and any damage to the vehicle.'

In determining whether there is any likelihood that the accused will drive his vehicle while his ability to do so is impaired, the court may disregard any injury to the driver or damage to the vehicle. Thus it is not necessarily fatal to a prosecution if the evidence shows that either the driver or the vehicle in question is not in a condition to proceed further; the accused may in such circumstances still be deemed to be in charge of the vehicle.

3.9 SECTION 15(3) OF THE ROAD TRAFFIC OFFENDERS ACT 1988 – STATUTORY DEFENCE (2): POST-INCIDENT DRINKING

3.9:1 Statutory provisions

Section 15 of the Road Traffic Offenders Act 1988[1] provides:

'(1) This section and section 16 of this Act apply in respect of proceedings for an offence under section 3A, 4 or 5 of the Road Traffic Act 1988 (driving offences connected with drink or drugs); and expressions used in this section and section 16 of this Act have the same meaning as in sections 3A to 10.

(2) Evidence of the proportion of alcohol or any drug in a specimen of breath, blood or urine provided by the accused shall, in all cases (including cases where the specimen was not provided in connection with the alleged offence), be taken into account and, subject to subsection (3) below, it shall be assumed that the proportion of alcohol in the accused's breath, blood or urine at the time of the alleged offence was not less than in the specimen.

(3) That assumption shall not be made if the accused proves –
 (a) that he consumed alcohol before he provided the specimen and –
  (i) in relation to an offence under section 3A, after the time of the alleged offence, and
  (ii) otherwise, after he had ceased to drive, attempt to drive or be in charge of a vehicle on a road or other public place, and

1 As amended by the Road Traffic Act 1991, Sch 4, para 87.

(b) that had he not done so the proportion of alcohol in his breath, blood or urine would not have exceeded the prescribed limit, and, if it is alleged that he was unfit to drive through drink, would not have been such as to impair his ability to drive properly.'

It is not clear what the phrase 'including cases where the specimen was not provided in connection with the alleged offence' in s 15(2)[1] is intended to mean. One purpose of this provision may be to avoid any difficulty that may arise when a driver is asked to give a specimen in terms of s 7 of the Road Traffic Act 1988 in an investigation under s 5 and it is eventually decided to prosecute under s 4; alternatively it may be designed to avoid questions of competency in respect of the requirement of a specimen on the ground that such a general requirement, in line with certain English authorities, might leave the motorist in doubt as to the particular purpose for which the specimen is required and thus render the specimen invalid through uncertainty. As the subsection now reads, however, it would seem to allow a prosecution to be based, for example, on a blood specimen taken at a hospital for the purpose of treating a motorist injured in an accident; but such an interpretation would require to accommodate the provisions for protection of hospital patients provided by s 9. A further reason for, and consequence of, this amendment may be to cure procedural defects which occur before, as opposed to after, the specimen has been taken. It is also always open to the court to discount such evidence if, for example, it is established that the specimen has been obtained illegally, by deception or under duress, or not in accordance with the provision of the Act.[2]

The terms of this amendment make it plain that Parliament wishes to diminish even further the technical prerequisites for obtaining specimens for analysis.

Further discussion on the evidential implications of s 15(2) is found at 5.3–5.3:5 below, to which reference should also be made.

Section 15(3) therefore furnishes the guidelines for what is often referred to as the defence of post-incident or post-driving drinking. In English authorities, this has sometimes been described as the 'hip-flask defence', although this can be an inappropriate title. Unlike s 4(3) of the Road Traffic Act 1988, which provides a defence only to s 4(2) prosecutions, a s 15(3) defence

---

1 Introduced by RTA 1991, Sch 4, para 87.
2 *R v Fox* (sub nomine *Fox v Chief Constable of Gwent*) [1985] RTR 337 (at 343 per Lord Fraser), [1985] WLR 1126, [1986] AC 281.

can be applied in charges under both subsections (1) and (2) of s 4, as well as to charges under s 5(1)(a) and (b). Accordingly, this defence is available in all cases where the prosecution relies in any way on the results of an analysis of breath, blood or urine specimens. Although such specimens are normally used as the basis of prosecutions in terms of s 5, they can be, and sometimes (for the purposes of particular cases) are, used in s 4 cases. The subsection in addition specifically contemplates the possibility of such a defence in s 4 cases generally. The defence is also available in charges taken under s 3A.

3.9:2   Onus and standard of proof in defence of post-incident drinking

The onus of proof in establishing any offence remains on the Crown. However, in order to overcome the assumption referred to in s 15(3) of the Road Traffic Offenders Act 1988 there has to be evidence that a certain amount of alcohol had been consumed after driving and that this was such as to cast reasonable doubt as to the validity of the assumption[1]. However, because of the powerful evidential value given to the assumption made in the section, the quality of the evidence required to establish this defence successfully is high. At the same time, in appropriate circumstances, the accused may not have to prove the exact amount of alcohol subsequently consumed[2].

It is submitted that in the normal case in prosecutions under s 4(1) or (2) where the accused seeks to establish this defence, the following considerations will apply. Firstly, the accused will have to show in evidence, with a substantial degree of accuracy, the amount and nature of the alcohol, if any, that has been consumed prior to the time when, in terms of the section, he ceased to drive, attempt to drive, or be in charge of the vehicle. In particular, it will normally be of considerable importance for the accused to provide detailed information as to exactly when or over what period any such alcohol was consumed. Alternatively, if it is claimed that no alcohol was consumed prior to the cessation of any driving operation, this too will have to be proved. The accused will then have to demonstrate that he ceased to drive,

---

1 *Ritchie v Pirie* 1972 JC 7, 1972 SLT 2; *Campbell v Mackenzie* 1982 JC 20, 1982 SLT 250, 1981 SCCR 341.
2 *Hassan v Scott* 1989 SLT 380, 1989 SCCR 49.

attempt to drive or be in charge of his vehicle and when this cessation took place. Next, the accused will require to prove the amount and nature of the alcohol which he thereafter consumed before the specimen was given or the observations on the impairment of his ability to drive occurred, and the period of time over which this consumption took place. Finally, the accused will have to demonstrate, on the balance of probabilities, that but for the intake of the alcohol subsequently consumed, his ability to drive, attempt to drive or be in charge of the vehicle would not have been impaired at the material time. In most cases in practice, it will be essential that expert evidence be given on the effect and consequences of the subsequent drinking proved to have taken place. It is possible to envisage circumstances where the accused can establish that he had consumed no alcohol at all prior to the material time, and that his subsequent condition was wholly accounted for by post-incident drinking, but in practice such cases appear to be relatively unusual. However reference should be made to *Hassan v Scott*[1].

In such cases, expert evidence is usually adduced in respect of a number of aspects. The effect of the consumption of alcohol varies significantly depending on the amount and nature of the alcohol consumed, the height and weight of the motorist, and other factors. Expert witnesses have recourse to tables indicating the given effect of given quantities and types of alcohol on persons of differing physiques. Further, once consumed, alcohol begins thereafter to metabolise within the body and the level of alcohol therefore reduces, after the consumption of alcohol has ceased. Again, expert witnesses have recourse to tables which indicate in general terms the rate at which the body absorbs alcohol and levels reduce accordingly. These tables have not apparently been challenged by the Crown when produced by the defence, on the basis that such evidence is given by properly qualified experts who are entitled to consult such tables as being referable to their particular expertise. The tables, which are produced by the British Medical Association, have been judicially endorsed in England[2], and are partly reproduced in Appendix A.

A successful defence of post-incident drinking therefore depends on the consideration of a number of matters which, taken together, will establish that at the material time an offence in terms of the Act has not been committed. Careful preparation

---

1 1989 SLT 380, 1989 SCCR 49.
2 *R v Somers* [1963] 3 All ER 808.

and proper presentation of this evidence is essential, and each case will depend upon its own facts and circumstances. It should also be remembered that even in cases where a motorist success-fully establishes that he has consumed alcohol after he has ceased to drive or attempt to drive a motor vehicle on a road or other public place, he may well, if he is still in the vicinity of his vehicle, be regarded as 'in charge' of that vehicle.

The presumption raised by s 15(2) (as amended) can be over-come by, for example, leading evidence that the accused has in fact consumed no alcohol[1].

Evidence of post-driving drinking, where it does not go suffi-ciently to provide a defence, is competent as evidence in mitiga-tion[2].

Reference should also be made to Appendix E.

This defence can be established on the evidence of a single witness only[3].

3.9:3   Level of alcohol higher than reading: back calculation

The way in which s 15(2) of the Road Traffic Offenders Act 1988 is phrased suggests that, while it may be open to an accused to estab-lish that subsequent consumption of alcohol demonstrates that the level of alcohol in his body did not exceed the permitted level, it is also possible for the prosecution to establish, on the same princi-ples, that a specimen analysis which was taken some time after driving had ceased, and was at that time lower than the permitted levels, could nonetheless demonstrate that the level of alcohol in the accused's body at the material time exceeded the permitted level. This would be proved by a process sometimes known as 'back calculation'. In other words, the Crown would base its cal-culations on the level of alcohol observed in the specimen analy-sis; and thereafter, by computing the time between the provision of the specimen and the metabolic rate of reduction, demonstrate that the true level of alcohol in the body exceeded the permitted level at the time the accused was driving the vehicle. It will be recalled that s 15(2) assumes that the level of alcohol in the accused's breath, blood or urine at the time of the alleged offence is 'not less' than in the subsequently taken specimen; it is obvious

---

1 *Cracknell v Willis* 1988 RTR 1.
2 *Lees v Gilmour* 1990 SCCR 419.
3 *King v Lees* 1993 SLT 1184, 1993 SCCR 28.

therefore that the level of alcohol at the time of the alleged offence could be significantly more. The courts have been very reluctant to endorse this process and appear to be prepared to countenance 'back calculation' only in exceptional circumstances[1]. However, prosecutors may argue that the terms of s 3A of the Road Traffic Act 1988[2] suggest that Parliament has now specifically endorsed the principle of back calculation by contemplating, in s 3A(1)(c), the provision of specimens for analysis up to 18 hours after the driving which is concerned in the charge.

In *Hain v Ruxton*[3], the Crown proposed to lead evidence that the level of alcohol in the accused's breath was 39mg. The sample, taken over four hours after he had stopped driving, demonstrated by back calculation that his breath alcohol level at the time he was driving might have been 67mg. In 1983 the Crown Agent had intimated that he would not take proceedings on the basis of a reading of less than 40mg (see 3.15 below). It was held that the prosecution was bound by this undertaking and the prosecution failed. The Crown Agent's letter of 1983 was thereafter qualified in August 1999, when it was intimated that in future no proceedings would be taken under s 3A or s 5 of the Act on the basis of a reading of 39mg or less except in cases where (1) in terms of s 7(3)–(6) the machine is considered to be unreliable, (2) cases under s 7(3)(bb), and (3) where the Crown seeks to rely on back calculation.

3.10   DEFENCE AT COMMON LAW

Apart from the normal non-statutory defences (which usually are concerned with an error or failure in the procedure, or with an error or failure in the identification of the driver), coercion, or necessity, where a driver is genuinely compelled to drive where otherwise he would not have done so, may provide a successful defence to a charge of driving while unfit through drink or drugs[4]. In the latter case it was held that a defence of duress or necessity was available where a driver acted under immediate danger of death, or serious bodily harm to himself or another. The standard

---

1 *Gumbley v Cunningham* [1989] RTR 49; *Millard v DPP* [1990] RTR 201.
2 Introduced by the Road Traffic Act 1991, s 3.
3 1999 JC 166, 1999 SLT 789, 1999 SCCR 243.
4 *Moss v Howdle* 1997 JC 123, 1997 SLT 782, 1997 SCCR 215.

of such a defence is therefore particularly high. Any reasonable alternative to the offending behaviour must be taken accordingly. This sort of defence is not available indefinitely[1]. However, even where a defence of duress or necessity is not fully made out, the circumstances may produce useful mitigation. Equally, driving in a medical or other emergency may provide a defence, but again normally the court will have to be satisfied that no other reasonable alternative method of dealing with the emergency has been ignored; alternatively, such a crisis may allow the court not to disqualify the driver[2]. Reference may also be made to 2.5 and 2.15 above; see also Appendix E.

3.11 SECTION 4(5): DEFINITION OF UNFITNESS TO DRIVE

Section 4(5) of the Road Traffic Act 1988 provides:

'For the purposes of this section, a person shall be taken to be unfit to drive if his ability to drive properly is impaired.'

The test of whether the ability to drive is impaired is therefore a question of fact to be determined by the court on the evidence. Reference should be made to 3.6:1 above for the circumstances under which a medical examination should be conducted. In arriving at its conclusions the court may properly have regard to the subjective opinion of witnesses, whether police, medical or anyone else. The phrase 'for the time being' means the time at which the driving took place; however, evidence of the driver's conduct before and after the driving occurred is both competent and relevant.

3.12 SECTION 4(6): POWER OF ARREST

Section 4(6) of the Road Traffic Act 1988 provides:

'A constable may arrest a person without warrant if he has reasonable cause to suspect that that person is or has been committing an offence under this section.'

1 *MacLeod v MacDougall* 1989 SLT 151, 1988 SCCR 519.
2 *Watson v Hamilton* 1988 SLT 316, 1988 SCCR 13.

This subsection therefore gives a constable wide powers of arrest, and such an arrest is usually effected in proceedings under s 4. What is reasonable cause will depend on the facts and circumstances of the case. The test as to whether a person is properly arrested in terms of this subsection is whether the constable has reasonable grounds for his suspicions that the motorist is or has been committing an offence in terms of the section, and not whether the suspicion turns out to be justified or unjustified. If a constable arrests a motorist without reasonable cause, that arrest will be invalid even if subsequent investigations establish that the motorist has committed an offence under the section; equally, the fact that a motorist is shown not to have committed an offence will not invalidate an arrest made by a constable who properly has reasonable cause to suspect that an offence has been committed. Reference should also be made to 4.2:2 below.

Further, the subsection makes it clear that the suspicion does not have to arise in the constable's mind while the alleged offence is in the course of being committed; the suspicion may equally be that the accused has been committing an offence under the section but is no longer doing so. Accordingly, the case of *Breen v Pirie*[1], which decided under previous legislation that an arrest could not properly be made if the suspicion had arisen in the constable's mind after the driver's journey had been completed, is no longer applicable. The power of arrest may, under the current provisions, be exercised after the driver has left the vehicle, or at any time after the suspicion has been correctly formed in the constable's mind. The subsection does not prescribe any time limit within which the power of arrest may be exercised.

The question of corroboration is not relevant to the power of arrest; the suspicion and the subsequent entitlement to arrest can be carried out by one officer acting alone. Cases in which the matter of what constitutes reasonable grounds for suspicion was noted are *McLeod v Shaw*[2] and *Smith v Ross*[3].

1 1976 JC 60, 1976 SLT 136.
2 1981 SLT (Notes) 93, 1981 SCCR 54.
3 1983 SLT 491, 1983 SCCR 109.

A valid arrest is not a prerequisite of further procedure under the legislation; if the arrest is judged to be improper the motorist may still be convicted under s 4 or s 5 of the Act if the other evidence in the case shows that he has committed an offence. See also 5.3:3 below.

3.13   SECTION 4(7) AND (8): NON-APPLICATION TO SCOTLAND

These subsections provide firstly that in order to exercise the right to arrest without warrant contained in s 4(6) of the Road Traffic Act 1988 the constable may enter (if need be by force) any place where that person is, or where the constable has reasonable cause to suspect him to be. Section 4(8) provides that s 4(7) does not extend to Scotland and that nothing in that section shall affect any rule of law in Scotland concerning the right of the constable to enter any premises for that purpose. It would appear that the express statutory power to enter premises conferred by s 4(7) on the constable was excluded from application in Scotland because it was considered by Parliament that the police in Scotland already have such powers at common law. This view was given substantial support in the case of *Cairns v Keane*[1], where the police entered the accused's home without invitation and in pursuit of the accused, whom they suspected of having driven while under the influence of alcohol. The court held that the urgency of the situation justified the invasion or trespass of the accused's house. This decision was upheld on appeal, although the appeal court declined to deliver any opinion on the matter.

Reference may also be made to *Binnie v Donnelly*[2] where Scottish police officers followed a suspect vehicle over the border into England, and were held to be then entitled to require him to give a breath specimen, and to *Mackenzie v Hingston*[3] where, similarly, police officers followed a suspect onto a boat moored in a harbour.

---

1 1983 SCCR 277.
2 1981 JC 92, 1981 SLT 294, 1981 SCCR 126.
3 1995 SLT 966, 1995 SCCR 386.

PART 3
DRIVING OR BEING IN CHARGE OF A MOTOR VEHICLE
WITH ALCOHOL CONCENTRATION ABOVE PRESCRIBED
LIMIT: SECTION 5

3.14 SECTION 5

3.14:1 General

The broad purpose of this part of the present legislation is to provide a method of ascertaining the proportion of alcohol present in a specimen of breath, blood or urine. Underlying all of the current provisions is the intention that the principal method of determining the proportion of alcohol should be by way of a specimen of breath at a police station in terms of s 7(1)(a) of the Road Traffic Act 1988[1]. The wording of s 7, read as a whole, makes it clear that a police officer must always, in the first instance, require a breath specimen, unless a reliable device is not available at the police station. The only qualification to this rule is found in s 8(2). This topic is discussed more fully in ch 4. Parliament, in considering the present terms of ss 7 and 8 of the Act, was intent on diminishing the previous significance of procedural and technical requirements which were features of earlier legislation and which had proved to be a fruitful source of contention in drink-driving prosecutions. The current terms of ss 7 (as amended) and 8 were grafted onto the Road Traffic Act 1972 by s 25(3) and Schedule 8 of the Transport Act 1981, which came into force on 6 May 1983[2]. Case law in respect of formal requirements concerning s 5 prosecutions arising before 6 May 1983 is therefore of limited relevance.

3.14:2 Preliminary test

The provision of a preliminary breath test in terms of s 6 of the Road Traffic Act 1988 (sometimes known as the roadside or preliminary breath test and conducted by means of a breathalyser) is still seen as being normally the first step in the statutory procedure. However, it should be emphasised that, in terms of the

1 As amended by the Road Traffic Act 1991, Sch 4, para 42.
2 By virtue of SI 1983/576.

current provisions, such a roadside test is by no means an essential prerequisite for a prosecution in terms of s 5. A description of what is involved in roadside tests is described at 4.2:1ff below.

3.14:3 Section 5(1)

Section 5(1) of the Road Traffic Act 1988 provides:

'If a person –

(a) drives or attempts to drive a motor vehicle on a road or other public place, or
(b) is in charge of a motor vehicle on a road or other public place,
after consuming so much alcohol that the proportion of it in his breath, blood or urine exceeds the prescribed limit he is guilty of an offence.'

3.14:4 Special definitions

'Drives'. See 1.7:1 and 3.3:2 above.

'Attempting to drive'. See 3.3:3 above.

'Motor vehicle'. See 1.2:1 above.

'Road or other public place'. See 1.8:1, 1.8:2 and 1.8:3 above.

'In charge'. See 3.3:4 above.

3.14:5 The prescribed limits

The prescribed limits as provided in the Road Traffic Act 1988, s 11(2)[1] are 35 microgrammes of alcohol in 100 millilitres of breath, 80 milligrammes of alcohol in 100 millilitres of blood, and 107 milligrammes of alcohol in 100 millilitres of urine. Unlike the original provisions of s 6 of the Road Traffic Act 1972, which required that the readings be 'ascertained from a laboratory test' for the purpose of which the specimen was given, the present provisions impose no restriction or qualification, technical or procedural, on the method of determining levels of alcohol.

---

1 As amended by the Road Traffic Act 1991, Sch 4, para 44.

The rules governing the provision of specimens of breath, blood or urine for analysis are found in s 7 of the Road Traffic Act 1988, and are discussed more fully in ch 4. These rules should be read in the context of the evidential provisions of ss 15 and 16 of the Road Traffic Offenders Act 1988, which are discussed in ch 5.

3.14:6   Procedure and penalties

These offences are normally prosecuted summarily. Penalties for s 5(1)(a) offences, include obligatory disqualification for a minimum of 12 months, a prison sentence of up to six months and a fine at level 5 (or both). Three to 11 penalty points must be endorsed if for any reason disqualification is not imposed. For s 5(1)(b) offences disqualification is discretionary, and a prison sentence of up to three months or a fine on level 4 of the standard scale, or both, may be imposed. Ten penalty points are obligatory where there is no disqualification. Reference may be made to the Road Traffic Offenders Act 1988, s 34 and Sch 2, as amended by Schedule 2 to the Road Traffic Act 1991.

3.15   PUBLIC POLICY

In *Lockhart v Deighan*[1], the Crown Office had indicated publicly that prosecutions would not be taken in cases where the level of alcohol determined by a breath test in terms of s 6 of the Road Traffic Act 1988 did not exceed a certain level. The prosecution in the case based its charge on a specimen taken shortly before this public announcement which did not exceed that level. On appeal it was held that nonetheless the charge was based on a specimen properly and competently taken, and the motorist was convicted. However, in *Benton v Cardle*[2], and *McConnachie v Scott*[3] a motorist provided two specimens of breath of less than 50 microgrammes of alcohol which were also lower than the level below which the Crown Office had indicated proceedings would not be taken. In these circumstances it was held to be incompetent for a police

---

1 1985 SLT 549; 1985 SCCR 204.
2 1988 SLT 310, 1987 SCCR 738.
3 1988 SLT 480, 1988 SCCR 176.

officer to require the motorist to provide a specimen of blood or urine in terms of s 8(6) of the Road Traffic Act 1972[1].

In *Hain v Ruxton*[2] it was held that the Crown could not back-calculate a breath alcohol reading below 40mg in an attempt to secure a conviction. Thereafter in August 1999 the Crown Agent issued a further letter indicating that no prosecution for a contravention of s 3A or s 5 will libel a breath alcohol level of 39mg or less. However, the letter goes on to indicate that proceedings may in future be taken, even where two samples of a suspect's breath have been analysed and a lower reading of 39mg or less obtained, if (1) in terms of s 7(3)(b) of the Road Traffic Act 1988, as amended, the investigating officer requests a blood or urine sample because the machine is considered to be unreliable, (2) in terms of s 7(3)(bb) of the Act the officer requires the accused to provide a specimen of blood or urine because he has reason to believe that the device has not produced a reliable indication of the proportion of alcohol in the breath, or (3) where the readings are obtained in circumstances where a back calculation indicates that the suspect had a breath alcohol level in excess of the prescribed limit at the time the driving is alleged to have occurred.

3.16   SECTION 5(2): STATUTORY DEFENCE (1): NO LIKELIHOOD OF DRIVING

3.16:1   General

Section 5(2) of the Road Traffic Act 1988 provides:

'It is a defence for a person charged with an offence under subsection 1(b) above to prove that at the time he is alleged to have committed the offence, the circumstances were such that there was no likelihood of his driving the vehicle whilst the proportion of alcohol in breath, blood or urine remained likely to exceed the prescribed limit.'

Section 5(2) therefore provides a statutory defence to a charge under s 5(1)(b). It will be noted that the defence is not available in charges under s 5(1)(a). If a driver who is proved to have been, or accepts that he has been, in charge of a vehicle after consuming so much alcohol that the proportion of it in his blood, breath or urine

---

1 Now the Road Traffic Act 1988, s 8(2).
2 1999 JC 166, 1999 SLT 789, 1999 243.

exceeds the prescribed limit, he is entitled to escape conviction if he proves that at the time the offence alleged against him was committed, there was no likelihood of his driving the vehicle whilst the proportion of alcohol in his breath, blood or urine remained likely to exceed the prescribed limit. Whether such a defence can be successfully established will in each case be a question of fact and evidence. It is submitted that such a defence, where appropriate, may be established by uncorroborated evidence, including testimony from the accused driver himself. It should be noted, however, that for a successful defence of this kind to be established, the accused requires to demonstrate that there is no likelihood of him driving, so long as the proportion of alcohol in his body exceeds or remains likely to exceed the prescribed limit. The accused therefore has to demonstrate when the proportion of alcohol in his body would have diminished to below the prescribed limit, as well as proving that there was no likelihood of him driving up to that point. In virtually all cases of this kind, proof of when the level of alcohol in the accused's body decreased to a point below the prescribed limit will depend on expert evidence, the general nature of which is discussed at 3.9 above and 3.17 below. In this type of defence equal care may have to be taken in establishing, so far as possible, the point in time when the accused would next have driven.

In *Lees v Lawrie*[1] a supervisor of a learner driver was held to be in charge of a vehicle but not in any way likely to drive the vehicle; whereas in *Williamson v Crowe*[2] a driver in similar circumstances failed to establish a s 5(2) defence when it was accepted that he might have taken the wheel as a last resort.

It is submitted that the standard of proof on the accused in these circumstances is on the balance of probabilities[3]. In considering this defence, the court will have regard to the accused's intentions, express or implied, in the light of all the other circumstances of the case[4]. In deciding the issue, the court may disregard any injury to the driver or damage to the vehicle[5]. Thus it is not necessarily fatal to a prosecution if the evidence shows that either the driver of the car, or the car itself, was not in a condition to proceed further; the accused even in those circumstances may still be deemed to be in charge of the vehicle.

---

1 1993 SCCR î.
2 1995 SLT 959.
3 *Neish v Stevenson* 1969 SLT 229.
4 *Morton v Confer* [1963] 1 WLR 763, [1963] 2 All ER 765.
5 Road Traffic Act 1988, s 5(3).

The circumstances in which a defence under s 5(2) may be presented can conceivably overlap with some of the earlier cases where it was found that the accused was not in charge of the vehicle (see 3.3:2 and 3.3:4 above). The s 5(2) defence is similar to that provided by s 4(3) (See 3.8 above) and similar considerations will in general apply to both. Reference should also be made to Appendix E.

3.17 SECTION 15(3): STATUTORY DEFENCE (2): POST-INCIDENT DRINKING

3.17.1 Statutory provision

Section 15 of the Road Traffic Offenders Act 1988[1] provides:

'(1) This section and section 16 of this Act apply in respect of proceedings under section 3A, 4 or 5 of the Road Traffic Act 1988 (driving offences connected with drink or drugs); and expressions used in this section and section 16 of this Act have the same meaning as in sections 3A to 10.

(2) Evidence of the proportion of alcohol or any drug in a specimen of breath, blood or urine provided by the accused shall in all cases (including cases where the specimen was not provided in connection with the alleged offence), be taken into account and subject to subsection (3) below, it shall be assumed that the proportion of alcohol in the accused's breath, blood or urine at the time of the alleged offence was not less than in the specimen.

(3) That assumption shall not be made if the accused proves –
   (a) that he consumed alcohol before he provided the specimen and –
      (i) in relation to an offence under section 3A, after the time of the alleged offence, and
      (ii) otherwise, after he had ceased to drive, attempt to drive, or be in charge of a vehicle on a road or other public place, and
   (b) that had he not done so the proportion of alcohol in his breath, blood or urine would not have exceeded the prescribed limit and, if it is alleged that he was unfit to drive through drink, would not have been such as to impair his ability to drive properly.'

Section 15(2) of the Road Traffic Offenders Act 1988[2] therefore now requires that such readings, irrespective of how they are obtained, must be considered; the section now reads –

1 As amended by the Road Traffic Act 1991, Sch 4, para 87.
2 As amended by RTA 1991, Sch 4, para 87(3).

'Evidence of the proportion of alcohol or any drug in a specimen of
breath, blood or urine at the time of the alleged offence shall, in all cases
(including cases where the specimen was not provided in connection
with the alleged offence), be taken into account, and ... it shall be
assumed that the proportion of alcohol in the accused's breath, blood or
urine at the time of the alleged offence was not less than in the
specimen.'

Accordingly, it is in general open for the court in a prosecution
under s 5 to ignore any defects, omissions or failures in any procedural aspect of the Act involving the taking of the specimens. It is
not clear what the phrase 'including cases where the specimen
was not provided in connection with the alleged offence'[1] is
intended to mean. This topic is more fully discussed at 3.9:1
above.

3.17:2   Onus and standard of proof in defence of post-incident drinking

This topic has already been dealt with at 3.9:1 and 3.9:2 above but
is repeated here for convenience.

Section 15(3) of the Road Traffic Offenders Act 1988 furnishes
the guidelines for what is often known as the defence of post-incident drinking. In English authorities this has sometimes been
referred to as the 'hip-flask defence', although this may be an
inappropriate and misleading title. Unlike s 5(2) of the Road
Traffic Act 1988, which provides a statutory defence only to
s 5(1)(b) prosecutions, a defence under s 15(2) of the Road Traffic
Offenders Act 1988 can be applied to charges under both subsections (1)(a) and (1)(b), as well as to a prosecution under s 4 of
the Road Traffic Act 1988 where that prosecution relies in any
way on the results of specimen analysis.

The onus of proof in establishing any offence remains on the
Crown. However in order to overcome the assumption referred to
in s 15(3) there has to be evidence that a certain amount of alcohol
had been consumed after driving and that this was such as to cast
reasonable doubt as to the validity of the assumption[2]. However,
because of the powerful evidential value given to the assumption

---

1 Introduced by RTA 1991, Sch 4, para 87.
2 *Ritchie v Pirie* 1972 JC 7, 1972 SLT 2; *Campbell v Mackenzie* 1982 JC 20, 1982 SLT
   250, 1981 SCCR 341.

made in the section, the quality of the evidence required to establish this defence successfully is high. At the same time, in appropriate circumstances, the accused may not have to prove the exact amount of alcohol subsequently consumed[1]. Corroboration of this evidence by the defence is not necessary[2].

It is submitted that in the normal case in prosecutions under s 4(1) or (2) where the accused seeks to establish this defence, the following considerations will apply. Firstly, the accused will have to show in evidence, with a substantial degree of accuracy, the amount and nature of the alcohol, if any, that has been consumed prior to the time when, in terms of the section, he ceased to drive, attempt to drive or be in charge of the vehicle. In particular, it will normally be of considerable importance for the accused to provide detailed information as to exactly when or over what period any such alcohol was consumed. Alternatively, if it is claimed that no alcohol was consumed prior to the cessation of any driving operation, this too will have to be proved. The accused will then have to demonstrate that he ceased to drive, attempt to drive or be in charge of his vehicle and when this cessation took place. Next, the accused will require to prove the amount and nature of the alcohol which he thereafter consumed before the specimen was given or the observations on the impairment of his ability to drive occurred, and the period of time over which this consumption took place. Finally, the accused will have to demonstrate on the balance of probabilities, that but for the intake of the alcohol subsequently consumed, his ability to drive, attempt to drive or be in charge of the vehicle would not have been impaired at the material time. In most cases in practice, it will be essential that expert evidence be given on the effect and consequences of the subsequent drinking proved to have taken place. It is possible to envisage circumstances where the accused can establish that he had consumed no alcohol at all prior to the material time, and that his subsequent condition was wholly accounted for by post-incident drinking, but in practice such cases appear to be relatively unusual. However reference should be made to *Hassan v Scott*[3].

In such cases, expert evidence is usually adduced in respect of a number of aspects. The effect of the consumption of alcohol varies significantly depending on the amount and nature of the

1 *Hassan v Scott* 1989 SLT 380, 1989 SCCR 49.
2 *King v Lees* 1983 SLT 1184.
3 1989 SLT 380, 1989 SCCR 49.

alcohol consumed, the height and weight of the motorist, and other factors. Expert witnesses have recourse to tables indicating the given effect of given quantities and types of alcohol on persons of differing physiques. Further, once consumed, alcohol begins thereafter to metabolise within the body and the level of alcohol therefore reduces, after the consumption of alcohol has ceased. Again, expert witnesses have recourse to tables which indicate in general terms the rate at which the body absorbs alcohol and levels reduce accordingly. These tables have not apparently been challenged by the Crown when produced by the defence, on the basis that such evidence is given by properly qualified experts who are entitled to consult such tables as being referable to their particular expertise. The tables, which are produced by the British Medical Association, have been judicially endorsed in England[1].

A successful defence of post-incident drinking therefore depends on the consideration of a number of matters which, taken together, will establish that at the material time an offence in terms of the Act has not been committed. Careful preparation and proper presentation of this evidence is essential, and each case will depend upon its own facts and circumstances. It should also be remembered that even in cases where a motorist successfully establishes that he has consumed alcohol after he has ceased to drive or attempt to drive a motor vehicle on a road or other public place, he may well, if he is still in the vicinity of his vehicle, be regarded as 'in charge' of that vehicle.

It is also important to note that while it may be open to an accused to establish a defence on the basis as above described, there would appear to be nothing to prevent the Crown from proving, on the same principles that a specimen analysis which was taken some time after a driving operation has ceased and which was lower than the permitted limit, could nonetheless demonstrate that at the time the motorist was driving, attempting to drive or was in charge of his vehicle he had more than the permitted level of alcohol, and is thus liable to conviction (See 3.9:2 above). Evidence of post-driving drinking, where it does not go sufficiently far to provide a defence, is competent in mitigation[2]. Reference should also be made to Appendix E.

---

1 *R v Somers* [1963] 3 All ER 808; see Appendix A.
2 *Lees v Gilmour* 1990 SCCR 419.

This defence can be established on the evidence of a single witness[1].

3.18 DEFENCE AT COMMON LAW

See 3.10 above, and Appendix E.

1 *King v Lees* 1993 SLT 1184, 1993 SCCR 28.

Chapter Four

Preliminary breath tests and provision of specimens for analysis

Sections 6, 7 and 8 of the Road Traffic Act 1988

PART 1. PRELIMINARY BREATH TEST

PART 1
PRELIMINARY BREATH TEST

4.1   SECTION 6: GENERAL

Section 6(1) and (2) of the Road Traffic Act 1988 allows a police constable to require a motorist to provide a specimen of breath for a breathalyser test in a wide variety of situations. This procedure is variously referred to as the preliminary breath test, the breathalyser test or the roadside breath test, and is completely distinct from (and is given into an entirely different device from) the specimens of breath for analysis described in s 7, and which form the basis for conviction in charges under s 5 of the Act. The provision of a preliminary breath test in terms of s 6 is seen as normally the first step in the statutory procedure. The test is undertaken by the motorist giving a breath specimen into an approved device. If the device registers that the specimen is positive, the motorist is in normal circumstances formally arrested. The motorist is then taken to a police station where he is required to provide a specimen of breath, blood or urine in terms of s 7 of the Act. There is special provision for the taking of specimens of blood or urine should the motorist have to be taken to hospital[1]. Notwithstanding the current terms of the legislation, the provision of a positive preliminary breath test is not an essential step before the procedure under s 7 is embarked upon; a constable may require any motorist to provide a specimen in terms of s 7 even though no preliminary test under s 6 has been taken, or presumably even where such a test has been taken and proved negative.

1 Road Traffic Act 1988, ss 6(5) and 9.

Considerations of public policy are noted at 3.15 above. The current Breath Test Device Order, which lists the devices presently approved and a description of the more commonly used devices, is found in Appendix B.

4.2   PRELIMINARY BREATH TEST

4.2:1   Section 6(1)

Section 6(1) provides:

'Where a constable in uniform has reasonable cause to suspect –
(a) that a person driving or attempting to drive or in charge of a motor vehicle on a road or other public place has alcohol in his body or has committed a traffic offence while the vehicle was in motion; or
(b) that a person has been driving or attempting to drive or been in charge of a motor vehicle on a road or other public place with alcohol in his body and that that person still has alcohol in his body; or
(c) that a person has been driving or attempting to drive or been in charge of a motor vehicle on a road or other public place and has committed a traffic offence whilst the vehicle was in motion;
he may, subject to s 9 of this Act, require him to provide a specimen of breath for a breath test.'

4.2:2   Definitions

A constable. A constable means any member of the police force irrespective of rank, and includes a special constable.

A constable in uniform. This phrase has not been judicially considered in terms in Scotland. However, it is submitted that the matter is essentially one of fact. In English cases, a constable otherwise in uniform but without his helmet[1]; and an officer with a raincoat over his uniform[2] were both held to be entitled to make the requirement. If the question of whether the constable was in uniform is not raised specifically in the evidence, there must be facts and circumstances from which the court can infer that the constable was in uniform[3]. In a case under s 2 of the Road Safety Act 1967 it was held

---

1 *Wallwork v Giles* [1970] RTR 117.
2 *Taylor v Baldwin* [1976] RTR 265.
3 *Richards v West* [1980] RTR 215; *Cooper v Rowlands* [1971] RTR 291.

that a uniformed constable could make the requirement on the basis of information supplied by a plain clothes officer[1].

In *Orr v Urquhart*[2] there was no evidence that the constable who required the specimen was in uniform. This was held not to invalidate further procedure under s 7, although in such circumstances no conviction could follow under s 6. The fact that the constable was in uniform does not have to be corroborated[3].

Reasonable cause to suspect. It has to be established that, before requiring the specimen for a breath test, the constable has to have reasonable cause for his suspicion. Whether or not such cause is reasonable is a matter of fact in each case and depends upon the proven facts and circumstances. In the case of *Copeland v McPherson*[4], the suspicion was held to be reasonable when it arose out of information given to the constable by another officer. In *Dryburgh v Galt*[5], the information came from an anonymous phone call. The suspicion may arise from the way in which the vehicle is being driven, but it is clear that obviously erratic conduct of the vehicle is not the only method by which such suspicions may arise[6]. In particular, the suspicion in the constable's mind may arise after the vehicle has been stopped for whatever proper and legal purpose. The suspicion must relate to at least one of the three situations covered by the section.

A police constable has wide powers to stop motor vehicles in terms of s 163 of the Road Traffic Act 1988 and the only qualification on these powers would seem to be that they are not exercised capriciously or oppressively. It would therefore seem to be in order that a constable may stop a motorist purely with the intention of seeing whether or not he had been drinking[7] so long as there is no question of mispractice, malice or caprice. However, once the vehicle has been stopped, the constable must then have reasonable cause to suspect that the motorist has alcohol in his body. The usual reasons given are that alcohol is smelt on the motorist's breath, or that his speech is slurred, his eyes glazed or his movements are unco-ordinated. However, in *Thomson v Ritchie*[8], it was observed that the reasonable cause for suspicion

1 *Copeland v McPherson* 1970 SLT 87; *Allan v Douglas* 1978 JC 7.
2 1993 SLT 404, 1992 SCCR 295.
3 *MacLeod v Nicol* 1970 JC 58, 1970 SLT 304.
4 1970 SLT 87.
5 1981 SLT 151, 1981 SCCR 26.
6 *Sinclair v Heywood* 1981 SCCR 63.
7 *Chief Constable of Gwent v Dash* [1986] RTR 41, [1985] Crim LR 674; *Normand v McKellar* 1995 SLT 798; *Stewart v Crowe* 1999 SLT 899, 1999 SCCR 327.
8 2000 SLT 734, 2000 SCCR 38.

may arise before the vehicle has been stopped. A constable need not indicate to the motorist the reason for his suspicions; and if in all the circumstances the requirement is legally and properly made, it does not matter if a constable claims to have relied at the time upon grounds for his suspicion that subsequently proved to be improper[1]. It therefore follows that the constable's suspicion, whatever it may be, does not have to be subsequently confirmed as accurate or justified; all that has to be established is that the constable's suspicions were at the material time reasonable in the circumstances. It would accordingly not be a defence to a charge of failing to provide a specimen in terms of this section that the driver has not been drinking or even that he was not the driver at the material time, provided that the constable's suspicions are reasonable[2]. If the constable purports to make the requirement on an unjustified basis but proper grounds exist, then the requirement will be held to have been properly made.[3]

The question of reasonable cause for suspicion also arises in the power of arrest available under s 4(6) (See 3.11 above).

Driving or attempting to drive. See 1.7:1, 3.3:2 and 3.3:3 above.

In charge. See 3.3:4 above.

Motor vehicle. See 1.2:1ff above.

Road or other public place. See 1.8:1, 1.8:2 and 1.8:3 above.

A traffic offence. This is defined in s 6(8) and means 'an offence under –
(a) any provision of Part II of the Public Passenger Vehicles Act 1981,
(b) any provision of the Road Traffic Regulation Act 1984,
(c) any provision of the Road Traffic Offenders Act 1988 except Part III or
(d) any provision of this Act except Part V.'

Require. To require means to ask[4]. The requirement must be corroborated[5]; however, the other points of the procedure need not[6].

---

1 *McNaughton v Degnan* 1981 SLT (Notes) 105, 1981 SCCR 97.
2 See *McNaughton v Degnan* 1981 SLT (Notes) 105, 1981 SCCR 97; and *McNicol v Peters* 1969 SLT 261.
3 *McNaughton v Degnan* 1981 SLT (Notes) 105, 1981 SCCR 97.
4 *Milne v McDonald* 1971 JC 40 (per Lord Justice-Clerk Clyde at p 42), 1971 SLT 291.
5 *Carmichael v Gillooly* 1982 SCCR 119.
6 *MacLeod v Nicol* 1970 JC 58, 1970 SLT 304.

A specimen of breath for a breath test. By virtue of s 11(2) of the Road Traffic Act, a breath test means 'a preliminary test for the purpose of obtaining, by means of a device approved by the Secretary of State, an indication of whether the proportion of alcohol in a person's breath or blood is likely to exceed the prescribed limit'.

The evidence should indicate that the device is approved; however in the absence of challenge this may be presumed[1].

4.2:3 General application

Section 6(1)(a), (b) and (c) of the Road Traffic Act 1988 therefore allow a police constable to require a motorist to provide a specimen of breath for a breath test in a wide variety of circumstances. The only qualifications on this power are that the constable must have reasonable grounds for his suspicions, and that the test must be administered at or near the place where the requirement is made, or in the case of an accident where the requirement is made in terms of s 6(2) and the constable making the requirement thinks fit, at a police station[2]. Apart from these considerations, s 6(1) allows a constable to make the requirement of any person who is, or who has been, driving, attempting to drive, or in charge of a vehicle when the constable has reasonable cause to suspect that the person has alcohol in his body, or (after completing his journey) that he still has alcohol in his body, or that he has committed a moving traffic offence. Accordingly, the requirement may be made where the constable has reasonable cause to suspect that the motorist has been driving, in the absence of direct evidence on that matter, as well as having reasonable cause to suspect that the motorist has alcohol in his body. Further, unlike s 3A(1)(c), there is specifically no time limit imposed in respect of the making of the requirement; so long as the constable has reasonable cause to suspect that the motorist has been driving, and that he has, or has had, alcohol in his body or has committed a traffic offence, the requirement can be made at any time thereafter.

The test must be carried out in accordance with the device manufacturers' instructions (See Appendix B and 4.11:4 and 4.14:4 below). However, the provision of a specimen of breath for a breath test is not a prerequisite of further procedure under s 4 or

---

1 *McIlhargery v Herron* 1972 JC 38, 1972 SLT 185; reference may also be made to 4.5:3 and 4.9:2 below.
2 Road Traffic Act 1988, s 6(3).

s 5, and any failure in the procedure, either by the constable or the motorist, has relevance only in a charge of failing to provide a specimen in terms of s 6(4)[1].

4.2:4 Procedural nature of test

The administration of the preliminary breath test is essentially a procedural matter, and can therefore be spoken to in evidence by one witness only[2]. However, a charge of failing to provide a specimen will have to be supported by the corroborated evidence.

4.2:5 Safeguards for hospital patients

All the provisions of s 6(1) and (2) of the Road Traffic Act 1988 are subject to the safeguards for hospital patients described in s 9 (See 6.1:1ff below.)

4.3 REQUIREMENT FOR BREATH TEST FOLLOWING ACCIDENT (S 6(2))

4.3:1 Section 6(2)

Section 6(2) of the Road Traffic Act 1988 provides:

'If an accident occurs owing to the presence of a motor vehicle on a road or other public place, a constable may, subject to section 9 of this Act, require any person who he has reasonable cause to believe was driving or attempting to drive or in charge of the vehicle at the time of the accident to provide a specimen of breath for a breath test.'

4.3:2 Definitions

Accident. See 1.9:1 above.

Reasonable cause to believe. It should be noted that in terms of this subsection the requirement imposed on the constable is signifi-

---

1 *Carmichael v Wilson* 1993 SLT 1066, 1993 SCCR 290.
2 *McLeod v Nicol* 1970 JC 58, 1970 SLT 304; *Wither v McLennan* 1978 CO Circulars A/30.

cantly higher than in s 6(1) of the Road Traffic Act 1988. In particular, in terms of s 6(1) the constable may require a specimen of breath for a breath test in a variety of circumstances if he has reasonable cause to suspect that the accused has been driving and has alcohol in his body. In terms of s 6(2), however, the constable must have reasonable cause to believe that the accused was driving or attempting to drive or be in charge of a vehicle at the time of an accident. It is submitted that clearly the word 'believed' is intended to convey a higher standard of conviction on the part of the police constable than the word 'suspect'. In *Merry v Docherty*[1], the appeal court discussed in some detail both the need for the prosecution to establish that an accident has taken place as a result of the presence of the vehicle on the road, and further what has to be established in order that it can be shown that a constable has reasonable cause to believe that the accused was driving at the time. In particular, in view of the way in which the section is now phrased, it would seem to be essential for any requirement under this particular subsection that the constable knows of the accident in question at the time when he makes the requirement for a breath specimen. In other words, there has to have been an accident, and a police constable's suspicion or belief that there has been one may not be enough. However, the nature and extent of the constable's knowledge of the accident need not be prescribed in any way, and in a case where police officers had received an anonymous call describing the circumstances of the accident, and the accused's vehicle was found to be in a condition consistent with that description, it was held that the police could have reasonable cause to believe that the accused had been driving his motor vehicle at the time of the accident[2]. English cases that may be of assistance in comprehending this phrase are inter alia *Baker v Oxford*[3]; *Moss v Jenkins*[4]; and *Johnson v Whitehouse*[5].

In terms of s 6(2), the constable does not have to be in uniform, nor does he have to have any suspicion that the accused has had alcohol in his body. Again, as in s 6(1) requirements, there are no time limits imposed by the subsection on when the requirement must be made.

---

1 1977 JC 34, 1977 SLT 117.
2 *Glass v Milne* 1977 CO Circulars A/7; *Topping v Scott* 1979 SLT (Notes) 21; but see also *Breen v Pirie* 1976 JC 60, 1976 SLT 136.
3 [1980] RTR 315.
4 [1975] RTR 25.
5 [1984] RTR 38.

In *Binnie v Donnelly*[1], a motorist was involved in an accident on the Scottish side of the Scotland/England border, then drove his car across the border to where he was involved in a further accident. In these circumstances it was decided that there was nothing to stop Scottish police officers pursuing the accused over the border and requiring a breath specimen when he was apprehended. In *MacKenzie v Hingston*[2] police officers similarly pursued a suspect onto a fishing boat.

4.4 THE LIMITS: PLACE WHERE TEST TO BE GIVEN (s 6(3))

As indicated above, once the reasonable grounds for suspicion have been properly established in the constable's mind, there is no time limit within which either the requirement be made, or the test administered. However, in terms of s 6(3) the specimen of breath must be given at or near the place where the requirement is made. This phrase does not appear to have been judicially considered in Scotland; it is thought that the subsection will be construed with reasonable strictness, and if the specimen is provided at a place which is in any way significantly distant from the place where the requirement is made, then the specimen will be regarded as invalid.

Section 6(3) provides no restriction on when the requirement to provide a specimen in terms of that subsection should be made; normally the requirement will be made when the suspicion in the constable's mind is formed. If the requirement is made at a police station, the test need not be administered at the same station[3].

4.5 FAILURE TO PROVIDE A SPECIMEN OF BREATH (s 6(4))

4.5:1 Section 6(4)

Section 6(4) of the Road Traffic Act 1988 provides:

1 1981 SLT 294, 1981 SCCR 126.
2 1995 SLT 966, 1995 SCCR 386.
3 *Milne v McDonald* 1971 JC 40, 1971 SLT 291.

'A person who, without reasonable excuse, fails to provide a specimen of breath when required to do so in pursuance of this section shall be guilty of an offence.'

4.5:2 Definitions

Fail. In terms of s 11(2) of the Road Traffic Act 1988, the word 'fail' includes refuse.

Further, in terms of s 11(3) of the Act, 'a person does not provide a specimen of breath for a breath test or for analysis unless the specimen (a) is sufficient to enable the test or the analysis to be carried out, and (b) is provided in such a way as to enable the objective of the test or analysis to be satisfactorily achieved'.

There is no requirement on the constable administering the test to advise the motorist that failure to comply with the procedure may result in prosecution; however the appeal court has recommended that such a warning be given[1]. Such a warning must be given under s 7 procedure.

Breath test. See 4.2:2 above. A driver may refuse a test even though the equipment is not yet readily available[2].

4.5:3 Approved devices

The principal devices approved by the Secretary of State for use in Scotland are the Alcotest 80/A, the Alcolyser and the Lion Alcolmeter S-L2A (currently being replaced by the Lion Alcolmeter SL-400A (see the Breath Test Device (Approval) Order 1997 and Appendix B). Approval is about to be given in Scotland to a further device, the Alco-Sensor IV. In respect of the Alcotest, the device must be correctly assembled in accordance with the manufacturer's instructions printed thereon, and it must not be out of time in respect of the expiry date which is also printed on the device. In respect of the Alcotest 80/A, the Alcolyser and the Lion Alcolmeter, the constable must explain clearly to the motorist the method by which the test is to be administered, in accordance with the manufacturer's instructions. Any failure in respect of the

---

1 *O'Sharkey v Smith* 1982 SLT 91, 1981 SCCR 189.
2 *R v Wagner* [1970] RTR 422, [1970] Crim LR 535.

foregoing matters will invalidate the test[1]. However, if the instructions have been complied with, the motorist must properly and correctly carry through the test, unless he has a reasonable excuse for not doing so (See 4.5:4 below). An offence under s 6(4) of the Road Traffic Act 1988 will accordingly be committed if the motorist fails to co-operate with the request to provide a specimen in any material way or if he fails to comply with the manufacturer's instructions in respect of the particular device used at the material time. A description of these devices and their operating instructions is given in Appendix B.

The evidence should indicate that the device is approved; however in the absence of challenge this may be presumed[2]. The approval order in respect of such a device does not have to be produced[3]; and the working of such devices is normally within judicial knowledge[4].

4.5:4 Reasonable excuse

The majority of cases about reasonable excuse for failing to provide a specimen relate to the provision of a specimen for analysis in terms of s 7(1) of the Road Traffic Act 1988 rather than to the roadside test. What follows is a general statement based in part on those cases that would also seem relevant to the provision of s 6(4).

It can in general terms be a reasonable excuse to fail to provide such a specimen only if the person concerned is physically or mentally unable to provide it, or if to do so would involve a substantial risk to his health[5]. Once the prosecution has established that the accused has failed to provide a specimen, and there were no, or insufficient, reasons for the refusal, it is for the accused to demonstrate that his failure was justified. However once the issue of reasonable excuse has been sufficiently raised by the defence, it is for the prosecution to rebut it, and in that event the court will have to determine, on the basis of all the evidence

---

1 *Jeffrey v MacNeill* 1976 JC 54; see also cases at 4.11:4 below.
2 *McIlhargey v Herron* 1972 JC 38, 1972 SLT 185.
3 *Lee v Smith* 1982 SLT 200, 1981 SCCR 267.
4 *Valentine v MacPhail* 1986 JC 131, 1986 SLT 598, 1986 SCCR 321; however see also 7:8:2 below.
5 *R v Lennard* [1973] 1 WLR 483, [1973] RTR 252; *Williams v Critchley* [1979] RTR 46; *McGregor v Jessop* 1988 SLT 719, 1988 SCCR 339.

led, whether or not it has been established beyond reasonable doubt that the motorist failed to provide the specimen without reasonable excuse[1]. In the normal case, the accused may well have to lead medical or other evidence in support of his claim that he had a reasonable excuse to refuse to take the test. However the uncorroborated evidence of the accused, if accepted, can be sufficient to establish a defence. In exceptional cases it may be possible to proceed on the basis of a statement of facts agreed between the prosecution and defence, preferably by way of a joint statement of admissions.

It must be emphasised that the reasonable excuse claimed by the accused must relate to the taking of the test, and not to any other matter. It is therefore not a reasonable excuse for the driver to maintain that he has not in fact consumed alcohol as a reason for refusing to take the test[2], or that he was not in fact the driver at the material time[3]. Nor is it a reasonable excuse that an earlier requirement to give a specimen was made but properly withdrawn[4]. Further, the fact that the reasonable cause of suspicion or belief entertained by the constable turns out in the event to be unjustified, unfounded or inaccurate will not invalidate the request to justify the refusal on the grounds of reasonable excuse. Reference may also be made to the cases described at 4.14:3 and 4.14:7 below which deal with the onus of proof and reasonable excuse in charges of failing to provide a specimen for analysis in terms of s 7(6). The circumstances of the latter offence usually involves different consideration to an offence under s 6(4), but there may be general similarities in cases under these two sections.

In *Duncan v Normand*[5] a driver initially agreed to provide a specimen and then refused to co-operate; it was held that he could not then argue that the prosecution had not established that his failure to provide a specimen was without reasonable excuse. In *Lorimer v Russell*[6], a driver deliberately failed to give a sample into the Camic machine, but then gave a blood sample. The following day she gave a satisfactory breath sample to get her car back. In

1 *Earnshaw v HM Advocate* 1982 JC 11, 1982 SLT 179, 1981 SCCR 279; *McGregor v Jessop* 1988 SLT 719, 1988 SCCR 339; *Pringle v Annan* 1988 SLT 899, 1988 SCCR 423.
2 *McNicol v Peters* 1969 SLT 261.
3 *McGrath v Vipas* [1984] RTR 58.
4 *Nelson v McGuillivray* 1981 SCCR 70.
5 1995 SLT 629, 1994 SCCR 508..
6 1996 SLT 501.

these circumstances it was held that she could be charged with failing to give a breath sample even although she had given a blood sample; and that the court could consider the successful subsequent breath test in considering the failure to give the first one.

4.6   ARREST: SECTION 6(5)

Section 6(5) of the Road Traffic Act 1988 provides:

'A constable may arrest a person without warrant if –
(a) as a result of a breath test he has reasonable cause to suspect that the proportion of alcohol in that person's breath or blood exceeds the prescribed limit; or
(b) that person has failed to provide a specimen of breath for a breath test when required to do so in pursuance of this section and the constable has reasonable cause to suspect that he has alcohol in his body, but a person shall not be arrested by virtue of this subsection when he is at a hospital as a patient.'

The phrase *'reasonable cause to suspect'* is defined at 4.2:2 above.

This section gives a police officer the power to arrest an accused if he has given a positive breath test or failed to give a breath test. It should be noted, however, that neither the provision of a positive breath test, nor the failure to provide a specimen of breath, nor the arrest itself is now a necessary prerequisite of further procedure in prosecutions under s 5 or s 6 of the Act. The officer who effects the arrest is usually, but need not necessarily be, the same officer who required the specimen of breath; but if a different officer arrests the accused, then that officer must have been in a position to have observed the requirement taking place[1].

In the latter case one constable administered a breath test to a motorist and the procedure was observed by another constable who then arrested the motorist. It was held that in fact the test had been carried out by both constables within the meaning of the Act as they were both clearly acting together, and it was observed that the underlying purpose of the section was to give power of arrest only to a constable who observed the test and its positive result.

1 *Stewart v Fekkes* 1977 JC 85.

In the absence of evidence that the constable was in uniform (which will invalidate procedures under s 6(4)), further procedure under s 7 will not be affected[1].

4.7 GENERAL

4.7:1 Powers of entry: (s 6(6) and 6(7))

Section 6(6) of the Road Traffic Act 1988 gives a police constable in England the power to enter (if need be by force) any property or place where he has reasonable cause to suspect a person to be in order to effect an arrest under s 6(5). Section 6(7) specifically excludes this provision from applying to Scotland, presumably on the grounds (as in the similar provisions contained in s 4(7) and (8)), that in Scotland a police constable already has common law powers to effect such entry in these circumstances[2].

4.7:2 Traffic offences (s 6(8))

Traffic offences are defined in this subsection for the purpose of s 6(1)(a) and (c) of the Road Traffic Act 1988. The subsection provides:

'In this section "traffic offence" means an offence under –
(a) any provision of Part II of the Public Passenger Vehicles Act 1981,
(b) any provision of the Road Traffic Regulation Act 1984,
(c) any provision of the Road Traffic Offenders Act 1988 except Part III, or
(d) any provision of this Act except Part V.'

4.7:3 Procedure and penalties

A charge of failure to provide a specimen of breath in terms of s 6(4) of the Road Traffic Act 1988 is normally taken on summary complaint and the penalties are found in Schedule 2 to the Road

---

1 *Orr v Urquhart* 1993 SLT 406, 1992 SCCR 240.
2 *Cairns v Keane* 1983 SCCR 277; *MacKenzie v Hingston* 1995 SLT 966, 1995 SCCR 386.

Traffic Offenders Act 1988. Unlike s 7(7) of the Act, there is no provision in s 6 which requires the constable administering the test to warn the motorist that failure to comply with the procedure may lead to prosecution. Penalties include a fine and discretionary disqualification.

PART 2
PROVISION OF SPECIMENS FOR ANALYSIS

4.8   INTRODUCTION

4.8:1   Section 7

Section 7 of the Road Traffic Act 1988[1] and the Criminal Procedure and Investigations Act 1996, s 63(1) provides as follows:

'(1) In the course of an investigation into whether a person has committed an offence under section 3A, 4 or 5 of this Act a constable may, subject to the following provisions of this section and section 9 of this Act, require him –
    (a)   to provide two specimens of breath for analysis by means of a device of a type approved by the Secretary of State, or
    (b)   to provide a specimen of blood or urine for a laboratory test.
(2) A requirement under this section to provide specimens of breath can only be made at a police station.
(3) A requirement under this section to provide a specimen of blood or urine can only be made at a police station or at a hospital, and it cannot be made at a police station unless –
    (a)   the constable making the requirement has reasonable cause to believe that for medical reasons a specimen of breath cannot be provided or should not be required, or
    (b)   at the time the requirement is made a device or a reliable device of the type mentioned in subsection (1)(a) above is not available at the police station or it is then for any other reason not practicable to use such a device there, or
    (bb) a device of the type mentioned in subsection (1) (a) above has been used at the police station but the constable who required the specimens of breath has reasonable cause to believe that the device has not produced a reliable indication of the proportion of alcohol in the breath of the person concerned, or

---

1 As amended by the Road Traffic Act 1991, Sch 4, para 42.

(c) the suspected offence is one under section 3A or 4 of this Act and the constable making the requirement has been advised by a medical practitioner that the condition of the person required to provide the specimen might be due to some drug;

but may then be made notwithstanding that the person required to provide the specimen has already provided or been required to provide two specimens of breath.

(4) If the provision of a specimen other than a specimen of breath may be required in pursuance of this section the question whether it is to be a specimen of blood or a specimen of urine shall be decided by the constable making the requirement, but if a medical practitioner is of the opinion that for medical reasons a specimen of blood cannot or should not be taken the specimen shall be a specimen of urine.

(5) A specimen of urine shall be provided within one hour of the requirement for its provision being made and after the provision of a previous specimen of urine.

(6) A person who, without reasonable excuse, fails to provide a specimen when required to do so in pursuance of this section is guilty of an offence.

(7) A constable must, on requiring any person to provide a specimen in pursuance of this section, warn him that a failure to provide it may render him liable to prosecution.'

4.8:2 General application

This section (subject to the provisions of the Road Traffic Act 1988, ss 8 and 9) governs the provision of specimens for analysis in the course of an investigation as to whether a person has committed an offence under s 3A, 4 or 5 of the Act. It is clearly intended that the principal procedure under this section is to be the provision by the motorist of two breath specimens into an approved device situated in a police station. The higher of these two readings is to be disregarded[1]. Only where any one of the three sets of circumstances described in s 7(3) applies does the situation arise where the requirement of the breath specimens cannot be made, and the constable in charge of the procedure must turn instead to the alternative requirement of a specimen of blood or urine. It is, however, open to a motorist who has provided two specimens of breath, where the lower of such specimens does not exceed 50 microgrammes of alcohol in 100 millilitres of breath, to claim that the breath specimen should be replaced by a specimen of blood or

---

1 Road Traffic Act 1988, s 8(1).

urine[1]. Unlike the provision of a preliminary breath test under s 6 of the Act, the constable making the requirement must warn the accused that failure to provide a specimen in terms of this section may render him liable to prosecution[2]. The Crown cannot amend at the end of the case to alter a charge of failing to supply a specimen of breath to one of failing to supply a specimen of blood[3]. However amendment will be allowed if there is no significant change to the essence of the charge[4].

4.9   PROVISION OF SPECIMENS FOR ANALYSIS (S 7(1))

4.9:1   Section 7(1)

Section 7(1) of the Road Traffic Act 1988 (as amended) provides:

'In the course of an investigation into whether a person has committed an offence under section 3A, 4 or 5 of this Act a constable may, subject to the following provisions of this section and section 9 below, require him –
(a) to provide two specimens of breath for analysis by means of a device of a type approved by the Secretary of State, or
(b) to provide a specimen of blood or urine for a laboratory test.'

4.9:2   Definitions

'In the course of an investigation'. This phrase has not come to the notice of the courts; it is submitted that the question is one of fact and that the meaning of the words is plain.

'A constable'. See 4.2:2 above. For the purpose of administering the provision of breath specimens into an approved device, only certain police officers have been trained in the use of such devices and are authorised by the Chief Constable for the area to use them. There is nothing in s 7 or s 8 which says that the officer administering the test and requiring the two specimens of breath has to be appropriately trained or authorised; however, if the evidence indicates that the operator of the device is unskilled or

---

1 RTA 1988, s 8(2).
2 RTA 1988, s 7(7).
3 *McArthur v MacNeill* 1987 SLT 299, 1986 SCCR 552.
4 *Fenwick v Valentine* 1994 SLT 485, 1993 SCCR 892; see also 2.3:3 above.

unauthorised, the Crown may have difficulty in proving, for example, that the device was unreliable. There is no requirement that the constable supervising the procedure be in uniform.

To 'require'. To require means to ask[1]. The requirement of a specimen is something different from the provision of a specimen. The requirement must be corroborated[2].

'Specimen of breath'. Section 11(3) of the Road Traffic Act 1988 provides that a person does not provide a specimen of breath for a breath test or for analysis unless the specimen (a) is sufficient to enable the test or analysis to be carried out, and (b) is provided in such a way as to enable the object of the test to be satisfactorily achieved.

Section 7(2) makes it clear that a specimen of breath can only be provided at a police station; in other words, an approved device cannot be located anywhere else.

'An approved device'. The breath specimen analysis devices currently approved for use in Scotland are the Camic Datamaster, the Lion Intoxilyzer 6000 UK and the Intoximeter EC/IR, which are approved in terms of the Breath Analysis Devices (Scotland) Approval Order 1998 as from 31 July 1998. For many years the original Camic device was commonly used throughout Scotland, however it now seems that the Intoximeter EC/IR enjoys widespread currency. Previous authority based on the Camic device will no doubt be relevant in considering the operation of other devices. The Approval Order and a brief description of the Camic and Intoximeter devices are given in Appendix C. The prosecution is entitled to a presumption that the device is approved within the meaning of the section, but there must at least be oral evidence that the device was used[3]; and it is unnecessary to produce the relevant Approval Order[4]. Further, where the device has done what it should have done if it was in proper working order, there is a presumption that the machine is in proper working order and has been correctly maintained[5].

---

1 *Milne v McDonald* 1971 JC 40 at 42 (per LJC Clyde), 1971 SLT 291.
2 *Carmichael v Gillooly* 1982 SCCR 119.
3 *Knox v Lockhart* 1985 JC 32, 1985 SLT 248, 1984 SCCR 463; *Davidson v Aitchison* 1986 SLT 402, 1985 SCCR 415; *Valentine v Macphail* 1986 SLT 598, 1986 SCCR 321; but see also *Pickland v Carmichael* 1995 SLT 675; 1995 SCCR 76.
4 *Lee v Smith* 1982 SLT 200, 1981 SCCR 267.
5 *Tudhope v McAllister* 1984 SLT 395, 1984 SCCR 182.

'*Specimen of blood*'. Section 11(4) of the Road Traffic Act 1988 provides: 'A person provides a specimen of blood if and only if he consents to its being taken by a medical practitioner.' This definition is applied for the interpretation of ss 4–10 of the Act[1].

Section 15(4) of the Road Traffic Offenders Act 1988 provides: 'A specimen of blood shall be disregarded unless it was taken from the accused with his consent by a medical practitioner.' This definition is provided for the purposes of proceedings under s 3A, 4 or 5 of the Road Traffic Act 1988[2].

Section 16(2) of the Road Traffic Offenders Act 1988 provides: 'Subject to subsections (3) and (4) below, evidence that a specimen of blood was taken from the accused with his consent by a medical practitioner may be given by the production of a document purporting to certify that fact and to be signed by a medical practitioner.' Subsections (3) and (4) are concerned with the requirements of service.

Section 11(3) of the Road Traffic Act 1988 provides that a specimen for analysis must be sufficient and provided in a way to enable the objective of the analysis to be satisfactorily achieved. A blood specimen will be inadmissible if the court is satisfied that full and proper consent has not been given to the taking of the specimen[3].

'*Specimen of urine*'. The procedure for the provision of a specimen of urine is described in s 7(5) of the Road Traffic Act 1988.

'*Laboratory test*'. Although this phrase is not defined in the legislation, s 16(1)(b) of the Road Traffic Offenders Act 1988 describes the evidential procedure in respect of findings of the proportion of alcohol or any drug found by an authorised analyst in a specimen of blood or urine; and section 16(7) gives a definition of an authorised analyst.

4.9:3   General application (s 7(1))

As indicated above, it is the intention of the Road Traffic Act 1988 that the principal method of procedure should be by the way of two specimens of breath for analysis by means of an approved device. It is only where any of the circumstances described in

1 Road Traffic Act 1988, s 11(1).
2 Road Traffic Offenders Act 1988, s 15(1).
3 *Friel v Dickson* 1992 SLT 1080, 1992 SCCR 513.

s 7(3) apply that the alternative procedure of providing a specimen of blood or urine can be invoked. Any of such specimens of breath, blood or urine may be used to found a charge under s 4 as well as ss 3A and 5. The provisions of s 7(1) must of course be read in the context of the other subsections of s 7, and are also qualified by the provisions for hospital patients contained in s 9.

4.9:4 Previous procedure unnecessary

It is not necessary that the procedural requirements of the preliminary breath test under s 6 of the Road Traffic Act 1988 (including the power of arrest) need be observed before this section can apply, although in practice such a test normally will and should be taken. If not, the court will no doubt look closely into the circumstances of why these preliminary steps were not followed in the light of any defence offered by the accused. However, it is submitted that even an illegal arrest will not make the provision of the specimens obtained under this section inadmissible in evidence; the arrest of the motorist in terms of s 4(6) or 6(5) is not required before the procedure under s 7 is embarked upon[1]. In *Orr v Urquhart*[2] there was no evidence that the police constable who required the preliminary breath specimen was in uniform; it was held that this did not invalidate the procedure under s 7.

4.9:5 Where only one breath specimen given

Although the requirement in terms of s 7(1)(a) of the Road Traffic Act 1988 is to provide two breath specimens, a conviction has been upheld on the strength of one only, where the accused, in a considered attempt to frustrate the procedure, failed to provide a second specimen[3]. It is submitted that the English decisions which suggest that in such circumstances the driver could be charged under s 5(1), and with failing to provide a specimen under s 7(6) (but could not be found guilty of both), is correct, but the point has not yet been settled; see *Cracknell v Wilks*[4];

---

1 *Carmichael v Wilson* 1993 SLT 290.
2 1993 SLT 406, 1992 SCCR 295.
3 *Reid v Tudhope* 1986 SLT 136, 1985 SCCR 268.
4 [1988] RTR 1.

Burridge v East[1]. Clearly, offences under these two subsections are mutually exclusive. On the other hand, where a driver gave a successful first specimen at the first attempt, but was refused a second chance after failing in his first attempt to give a second specimen in circumstances where both failures were genuine, it was held that in declining to give the accused a second chance to provide the second specimen the police had not given him a fair opportunity for the provision of the specimen[2]. In this respect the relevant test as to whether a proper opportunity has been given to the accused to provide a specimen is considered to be that of fairness to the accused in the light of his own actings.

4.9:6   Right to contact solicitor

An accused has the right to contact a solicitor on being arrested in terms of s 17 of the Criminal Procedure (Scotland) Act 1995, but it is not a reasonable excuse in terms of s 7(6) of the Road Traffic Act 1988 to refuse to give a specimen until that solicitor arrives[3].

4.10   REQUIREMENT FOR A BREATH SPECIMEN TO BE MADE AT A POLICE STATION (S 7(2))

Section 7(2) of the Road Traffic Act 1988 provides:

'A requirement under this section to provide specimens of breath can only be made at a police station.'

This does not necessarily mean that both the requirement and the subsequent provision of the specimens need be made at the same police station; where the requirement was made at one station and it was then discovered that the approved device was not working there, it was held to be in order to take the specimens at another station[4].

---

1 [1986] RTR 328.
2 *Douglas v Stevenson* 1986 JC 178, 1986 SCCR 519.
3 *Manuel v Stewart* 1986 SLT 593, 1986 SCCR 121.
4 *Milne v McDonald* 1971 JC 40, 1971 SLT 291; *Tudhope v Fulton* 1987 SLT 419, 1986 SCCR 567.

4.11   CIRCUMSTANCES WHERE A BREATH TEST IS NOT APPROPRIATE (s 7(3))

4.11:1   General

This important subsection in effect prescribes the only circumstances under which breath specimens are not to be provided; in other words, unless one of the circumstances described in the subsection applies, the provision of breath specimens must be required. The first situation described in the subsection is where the constable making the requirement has reasonable cause to believe that for medical reasons a specimen of breath cannot or should not be provided. The second situation is where an approved device is not present in the particular police station or alternatively where there is such a device but it is not reliable or it is not for any other reason practicable to use the device. A third situation exclusively relates to s 4 prosecutions and arises where the constable making the requirement had been advised by a medical practitioner that the accused's condition might be due to some drug. All these situations, however, are subject to the important proviso that if they arise after the provision of two breath specimens or after just the requirement to provide them has been made, the police constable making the requirement is not precluded from then requiring a specimen of blood or urine.

4.11:2   Section 7(3)

Section 7(3) of the Road Traffic Act 1988 (as amended by the Road Traffic Act 1991, Sch 4, para 42 and the Criminal Procedure and Investigations Act 1996, s 63(1)) provides:

'A requirement under this section to provide a specimen of blood or urine can only be made at a police station or at a hospital; and it cannot be made at a police station unless –
(a)   the constable making the requirement has reasonable cause to believe that for medical reasons a specimen of breath cannot be provided or should not be required; or
(b)   at the time the requirement is made a device or a reliable device of the type mentioned in subsection (1)(a) is not available at the police station or it is then for any other reason not practicable to use such a device there; or
(bb)   a device of the type mentioned in subsection (1) (a) above has been used at the police station but the constable who has required the

specimens of breath has reasonable cause to believe that the device has not produced a reliable indication of the proportion of alcohol in the breath of the person concerned, or

(c)   the suspected offence is one under ss 3A or 4 of this Act and the constable making the requirement has been advised by a medical practitioner that the condition of the person required to provide the specimen might be due to some drug;

but may then be made notwithstanding that the person required to provide the specimen has already provided or been required to provide two specimens of breath.'

4.11:3   Medical reasons (s 7(3)(a))

A breath specimen will not be required if the constable making the requirement has reasonable cause to believe that the specimen cannot or should not be provided for medical reasons. This section has not been considered in the courts in Scotland but it is submitted that the following considerations are relevant.

Firstly, the test is that the constable must have reasonable cause to believe that the medical reasons do exist, not simply that he may have reasonable cause to suspect that such medical reasons may exist. The decision of the constable is intended to be an entirely subjective one and the Road Traffic Act 1988 does not require him to consult medical advice (*Dempsey v Catton*)[1]. However, there do have to be grounds for the constable's decision. The term 'medical reasons' is therefore thought to be subject to a reasonably broad interpretation, and can include physical causes such as asthma, and psychological causes such as repugnance[2]. The responsibility of the motorist to reveal any medical condition which may preclude the provision of a specimen is described at 4.14:3 below.

4.11:4   No device or reliable device available (s 7(3)(b) and s 7(3)(bb))

Secondly, the requirement to provide two specimens of breath is set aside when there is not an approved device at a particular station, or where at the material time the device is not 'reliable', or where it is for any other reason not practicable to use the device,

---

1 [1986] RTR 194.
2 *Johnson v West Yorkshire Metropolitan Police* [1986] RTR 167.

or where the constable in charge of the test has reasonable cause to believe that the device has not produced a reliable indication of the proportion of alcohol in the breath of the person concerned.

Not all police stations are currently equipped with a breath analyser device. Further, as indicated above, only certain officers in any police force are trained in and authorised to work the device, and it appears that if no such officer is on duty at the material time then that will constitute 'any other reason' that it is not practicable to use the device and the alternative procedure should be adopted[1].

Alternatively, it may be that the device in the particular station is not 'reliable' usually because at the material time it is not properly operational or functioning. Whether the device is or is not reliable will be a question of fact decided by the court. In terms of the proviso to this section, it may be that the fact that the machine is not functioning correctly will become evident while the two specimens of breath are being provided and, if this is so, it will not preclude a further requirement to provide a specimen of blood or urine. However, the prosecution has to prove that the machine is not reliable in the course of evidence if it is to rely on the alternative procedure. The principal issue in such circumstances, as demonstrated by the reported cases, is whether the information shown within the statement or print-out automatically produced by the device is of such a character that, by virtue of that information alone, the device can be considered not reliable. The question of the reliability of the device is to be assessed at the time the requirement to give a specimen is made[2].

Whether the machine is reliable or not may have to be considered in the light of the manufacturer's instructions[3].

If the Crown claims that the device is unreliable, it also has to show that it is the only device available in the police station[4]. The fact that the device is the only one available may be inferred from the circumstances of the procedure[5]. If there is no device, or no

---

1 *Chief Constable of Avon & Somerset v Kelliher* [1987] RTR 305, [1986] Crim LR 635.
2 *Ramage v Walkingshaw* 1992 SCCR 82; see also *Wilson v Webster* 1999 SCCR 747.
3 *Jeffrey v MacNeill* 1976 JC 54; *Sloan v Smith* 1978 SLT (Notes) 27; *Hogg v Smith* 1978 CO Circular A/37 (all cases involving the roadside breathalyser device); and *Allan v Miller* 1986 SLT 3, 1985 SCCR 227; *Fraser v Mcleod* 1987 SCCR 294 (cases where observation of the manufacturer's instructions was not required).
4 *Houston v McLeod* 1986 JC 96, 1986 SCCR 219; *Walker v Walkingshaw* 1991 SCCR 695.
5 *Welsh v McGlennan* 1992 SCCR 379.

reliable device, available at one police station, the accused may be taken to another station and required to give a specimen there[1].

In a case where the accused failed to give a specimen, the Crown did not have to prove that the Camic device was working properly[2].

The question of informalities in the print-out and whether the machine is in the circumstances reliable or unreliable, and the relevant cases thereon, are dealt with at 5.8:5ff below.

Section 7(3)(bb) of the Road Traffic Act 1988 has been introduced to anticipate projected developments in breath analyser devices which can detect the substances which interfere with the true analysis of the proportion of alcohol in the motorist's breath, a situation not covered by s 7(3)(b). However, having regard to the broad terms of this subsection, it may be used more freely by prosecutors.

4.11:5   Section 7(3)(c)

This section has not so far come to the attention of the court, and its application is essentially a matter of fact. It should be noted that this part of the subsection is restricted to prosecutions under ss 3A and 4 of the Road Traffic Act 1988. This situation can arise only once a medical practitioner has suggested that the accused's condition may be due to some drug. The Act appears to impose no obligation on the constable to seek such medical advice; however, once the constable has received such advice from a medical practitioner, he must act on that advice whatever the circumstances, and has no discretion to do otherwise.

4.11:6   Definition: medical practitioner

The legislation does not provide a definition of what is meant by a 'medical practitioner'. However, it is submitted that a medical practitioner is an appropriately qualified doctor who is authorised to be in medical practice in this country. There appears to be no reported case where the status of the medical practitioner has been challenged.

---

1 *Tudhope v Fulton* 1987 SLT 419, 1986 SCCR 567.
2 *Simpson v Lowe* 1992 SLT 425, 1991 SCCR 728.

4.12 PROVISION OF SPECIMEN OF BLOOD OR URINE (S 7(4))

4.12:1 Section 7(4)

Section 7(4) of the Act provides:

'If the provision of a specimen other than a specimen of breath may be required in pursuance of this section the question whether it is to be a specimen of blood or a specimen of urine shall be decided by the constable making the requirement, but if a medical practitioner is of the opinion that for medical reasons a specimen of blood cannot or should not be taken a specimen shall be a specimen of urine.'

4.12:2 Definitions

See 4.9:2 above.

4.12:3 General application

It is clear from the terms of s 7(4) of the Road Traffic Act 1988 that the option of which specimen (either blood or urine) the accused is to provide in circumstances where a breath specimen is not to be taken rests entirely within the discretion of the constable making the requirement[1]. Section 7(4) states unequivocally that this is so; there is no provision for the motorist's preference or view to be taken into account by the constable. In this respect s 7(4) is somewhat different from the position under s 8(2) (See 4.16:3 below). *McLeod v MacFarlane*[2] contradicts earlier authorities which suggested that for the provision of the specimen under this section to be properly made the constable making the requirement must tell the motorist of the choice that he has to make and then come to an informed decision about which specimen to require[3]. These cases are now specifically overruled[4].

---

1 *McLeod v MacFarlane* 1993 SCCR 178, overruling *Carmichael v MacKay* 1991 SCCR 953.
2 1993 SCCR 178.
3 See, eg, *Hobbs v Clark* [1988] RTR 36; *DPP v Byrne* [1991] RTR 119; *Carmichael v MacKay* 1991 SCCR 953.
4 *McLeod v MacFarlane* 1993 SCCR 178; *DPP v Warren* [1992] 3 WLR 884.

The officer who makes the requirement does not have to be the same constable who required any previous breath specimen under s 7(3). The only qualification to the constable's power is where a medical practitioner expresses the opinion that for medical reasons a blood sample should not be required. There is, however, again no apparent obligation on the constable to seek out such a medical opinion in this matter. Neither does the Act require a constable to justify his choice of the specimen required. Unless a doctor is of the opinion that, for medical reasons, a breath specimen cannot or should not be taken, the constable has complete discretion as to whether the motorist should in these circumstances be required to provide a sample of blood or urine.

If a motorist cannot provide a blood or urine sample when required the police can competently go on to require the alternative specimen[1].

Reference should also be made to 4.14:3 below.

4.12:4   Other provisions

Section 7(4) of the Road Traffic Act 1988 has to be read in the context of the other provisions of s 7, and is subject to the provisions of s 11(3) and (4) of the Road Traffic Act 1988 and ss 15(4) and 16(2) of the Road Traffic Offenders Act 1988.

4.13   PROVISION OF URINE SPECIMEN (s 7(5))

4.13:1   Section 7(5)

Section 7(5) of the Act provides:

'A specimen of urine shall be provided within one hour of the requirement for its provision being made and after the provision of a previous specimen of urine.'

4.13:2   General application

In terms of this subsection, two specimens of urine have to be given within one hour of the requirement. While the two samples

---

1 *McGregor v Jessop* 1988 SLT 719, 1988 SCCR 339.

have to be given within an hour of the requirement, there is no stipulation as to when, during the hour, the samples must be given. For practical reasons, the first sample is usually given at the beginning of the period, and the second one towards the end. Unlike the previous legislation, there is no express provision that the first specimen shall be discarded. Reference again requires to be had to s 11(3) of the Road Traffic Act 1988.

The terms of this subsection are simpler than under the previous legislation which also required the provision of two samples of urine and described the circumstances under which a failure would arise.

In a prosecution under the former legislation, where the second urine specimen was provided just over an hour after the requirement, but exactly an hour after the first specimen was provided, it was held to be competent to convict the accused on the basis of the second specimen[1]. However, the accused was convicted on the basis of the specimen which he had provided, not on his failure to provide a specimen within the terms of s 9(5) of the former [1972 Act] legislation. As the present subsection requires that both specimens shall be given within an hour, it may be that the particular circumstances of *Tudhope v Stevenson*[2] would lead under the present law to an acquittal.

In *MacDougall v MacPhail*[3], the accused was asked to give a urine specimen, but police officers gave evidence that insufficient was produced to divide the specimen into two parts. It was held that the duty on the accused was to provide a specimen of sufficient quantity to be divided into two parts[4]; and that while the sufficiency of a specimen for analysis can be spoken to only by an analyst, the best evidence as to whether the specimen could be divided into two was that of the supervising police officers. In particular, although s 15(5) of the Road Traffic Offenders Act 1988 provides that the specimen is divided into two parts only when the accused requests a specimen at the time, any specimen given must obviously be capable of division; accordingly[5] the question of sufficiency of the specimen does not depend on a request by the accused for a part of the specimen.

---

1 *Tudhope v Stevenson* 1980 SLT (Notes) 94 (following *Roney v Matthews* [1975] RTR 273).
2 1980 SLT (Notes) 94.
3 1991 SLT 801, 1991 SCCR 358.
4 Road Traffic Act 1988, s 11(3).
5 Overruling *Aitchison v Johnstone* 1987 SCCR 225.

4.14   FAILURE TO PROVIDE A SPECIMEN (s 7(6))

4.14:1   Section 7(6)

Section 7(6) of the Road Traffic Act 1988 provides as follows:

'A person who, without reasonable excuse, fails to provide a specimen when required to do so in pursuance of this section is guilty of an offence.'

4.14:2   General application

Failure includes refusal[1]. The specimens provided must be sufficient to enable the analysis to be carried out. Section 11(3) of the Road Traffic Act 1988 makes it clear that if the specimen given either for a preliminary breath test or for analysis is not sufficient to enable the test or analysis to be carried out, or further is not provided in such a way as to enable the objective of the test or analysis to be achieved satisfactorily, then the person will be deemed not to have provided a specimen and thus be liable to conviction under this section.

If the Crown alleges that the specimen provided is not sufficient to allow proper analysis to be carried out in terms of s 11(3) of the Act, expert evidence to this effect will normally be required[2]. However, in the case of a specimen which is incapable of being divided into two parts, the best evidence may come from the police officers who took the specimen[3].

If a reliable device is not available at the police station to which the accused is first taken, the test can competently be carried out at another police station[4].

The prosecution does not have to prove that the Camic device is working properly where it is alleged that the accused has refused to give a specimen[5].

Where an accused was unable to provide a second specimen of urine, the police are entitled to require a blood specimen, and should do so[6].

1 Road Traffic Act 1988, s 11(2).
2 *Carmichael v Gillooly* 1982 SCCR 119.
3 *MacDougall v MacPhail* 1991 SLT 801, 1991 SCCR 358.
4 *Tudhope v Fulton* 1987 SLT 419, 1986 SCCR 567.
5 *Simpson v Lowe* 1992 SLT 425, 1991 SCCR 728.
6 *McGregor v Jessop* 1988 SLT 719, 1988 SCCR 339.

4.14:3 Reasonable excuse: onus of proof

The Crown must prove that the motorist had no reasonable
cause for refusing to provide the specimen of whatever kind[1].
This is normally done by police officers testifying that no
apparent cause existed for the refusal. Alternatively the officers
may describe the reasons, if any, given by the accused for
declining to give the sample and thereafter the Crown requires
to justify the proposition that such reasons did not amount to a
reasonable excuse in the circumstances[2]. At the same time,
while it is for the prosecution to demonstrate that no reasonable excuse exists for the refusal, if the accused wishes the
court to consider the question of whether he has a reasonable
excuse, or whether his excuse is reasonable, then he may have
to raise the issue and put it properly into evidence at the
appropriate time.

The position is different in England and Scotland. In England
it has been held that the duty to give a specimen includes a duty
to advise the police of any reason why the specimen cannot be
given[3]. This view was specifically rejected in *Pringle v Annan*[4]. In
that case the motorist suffered from injuries in a car accident
that precluded him from giving a breath specimen, and these
injuries were not obvious to the police officer making the
requirement. The appeal court held that if the motorist had been
asked if there was any reason for his inability to provide a
breath specimen he would have been obliged to answer, but
that there was no general duty on a motorist to inform the
police of any reason for his inability to provide a specimen. In
McClory v Owen-Thomas[5] it was observed that there was nothing
in the section which required the motorist to disclose anything
to the police, or which relieves the Crown of the burden of
proving the absence of reasonable excuse if the motorist fails or
refuses to provide a specimen without explanation, even where
the condition which justifies the failure is well known and of
long standing.

---

1 *Stewart v Aitcheson* 1984 SCCR 357.
2 *Earnshaw v HM Advocate* 1982 JC 11, 1982 SLT (Notes) 179, 1981 SCCR 279;
   McLeod v Murray 1986 SCCR 369; *McGregor v Jessop* 1988 SLT 719, 1988 SCCR
   339; *Milne v Westwater* 1990 JC 205, 1990 SCCR 46.
3 *Teape v Godfrey* [1986] RTR 213 at 221.
4 1988 SLT 899, 1988 SCCR 423.
5 1990 SLT 323, 1989 SCCR 402.

4.14:4   Instructions to provide specimen

The Act does not indicate what instructions are to be given by the police officers to the motorist to enable him to provide the specimens properly. However, it seems clear that sufficient and proper instructions should be given, and whether or not that is done in any case is a matter of fact for the court to decide on the evidence[1]; it therefore appears to follow that, if inadequate instructions are given, and this can be related to the failure to provide a specimen, the accused may be able to claim that he had a reasonable excuse for not providing the specimen required. Cases which feature instructions in respect of particular devices are *Jeffrey v MacNeill*[2]; *Sloan v Smith*[3]; *Hogg v Smith*[4]; *Allan v Miller*[5]; and *Fraser v McLeod*[6].

Two of the principal devices are described in Appendix C.

4.14:5   Agreement to provide sample

An accused must unequivocally agree to provide a specimen or sample, otherwise he will be deemed to have failed to comply with the provisions of the Act. It is therefore insufficient for the accused, in response to a request for a sample, merely to say 'please yourself' and such an answer will constitute the offence of failure to provide a specimen[7]. Which part of the body a sample of blood is taken from is at the discretion of the doctor[8].

A conditional acceptance is also not sufficient and will be deemed to be a refusal[9]; eg *Rushton v Higgins*, a case where the driver agreed to give a sample but insisted that it be taken from his big toe[10]. Immediately a failure or refusal occurs, the offence is committed and complete, and the situation cannot be redeemed

---

1 *Kelly v McKinnon* 1985 SLT 487, 1985 SCCR 97; *Fleming v Tudhope* 1987 CO Circulars A/16.
2 1976 SLT 134.
3 1978 SLT (Notes) 27.
4 1978 CO Circulars A/37.
5 1986 SLT 3, 1985 SCCR 227.
6 1987 SCCR 294.
7 *MacPhail v Forbes* 1975 SLT (Sh Ct) 48; *Milne v Elliot* 1974 SLT (Notes) 71; *MacDonald v MacKenzie* 1975 SLT 190; *Beveridge v Allan* 1986 SCCR 542, *Lorimer v Russell* 1996 SLT 501.
8 *Cader v Galt* 1976 SCCR Supp 116.
9 *Solesbury v Pugh* [1969] 1 WLR 1114; [1969] 2 All ER 1171.
10 *Rushton v Higgins* [1972] RTR 456 and *Pettigrew v Northumbria Police Authority* [1976] RTR 177.

by the accused changing his mind and offering subsequently to comply with the request to provide a specimen[1]. Moreover the accused can not complain if he is given further opportunity to provide a specimen after he has initially failed to do so[2].

The prosecution must prove that the accused has given his full consent to the test[3].

Where an accused failed to give a breath specimen, and then agreed to provide a blood sample, it was held that it is still possible for a charge of failing to provide a specimen to be made, and evidence of a successful breath specimen given the following day for the purpose of retrieving the car from the police could competently be referred to in evidence[4]. In *Brannigan v McGlennan*[5] it was held to be appropriate for the police to require a specimen of blood after an accused had been charged with failure to supply a specimen of breath.

4.14:6 Reasonable opportunity to provide specimen

The accused motorist must be given a fair and reasonable opportunity of providing the specimens required. What is a fair and reasonable opportunity is a matter for the court. In *Douglas v Stevenson*[6] a driver failed at his first attempt to provide a breath specimen into a Camic device, but succeeded at his second attempt. He then failed at his first attempt at providing a second specimen, and was not given a second chance to provide the second specimen. It was held that the police had not acted fairly in refusing the accused a second opportunity to provide the second specimen, and he was acquitted. Equally, the police may give the motorist several opportunities to provide a specimen[7]. A conviction has been upheld on the evidence of one specimen where the accused deliberately attempted to frustrate the procedure by deliberately failing to give a second specimen[8].

1 *Harris v Tudhope* 1985 SCCR 305; *Beveridge v Allan* 1986 SCCR 542; *Thomson v Allan* 1989 SLT 868, 1989 SCCR 327; *Duncan v Normand* 1995 SLT 629, 1994 SCCR 508.
2 *Thomson v Allan* 1989 SLT 868.
3 *Friel v Dickson* 1992 SLT 1080, 1992 SCCR 513, [1992] RTR 366.
4 *Lorimer v Russell* 1996 SLT 501.
5 2000 SCCR 12.
6 1986 SCCR 519.
7 *Thomson v Allan* 1989 SLT 868, 1989 SCCR 327.
8 *Reid v Tudhope* 1986 SLT 136, 1985 SCCR 268.

4.14:7 Reasonable excuse

Section 7(4) of the Road Traffic Act 1988 makes it an offence to fail to provide a specimen for analysis without reasonable excuse. The courts have traditionally taken a narrow view of what is to be regarded as a reasonable excuse. The failure to give proper instructions might justify a refusal[1], or might be regarded as a failure properly to require a specimen in the first place. In *McLeod v Murray*[2] the accused had been assaulted by the police and refused to give a specimen for analysis because he could not trust the police not to tamper with it; this was held to be a reasonable excuse. However, not every apprehension about the conduct of the police will justify a refusal[3].

The majority of cases involving reasonable excuse have been concerned with the question of whether the accused is physically or mentally able to give a specimen: or whether the provision of a specimen will involve a serious risk to the accused's health. The courts have normally regarded the standard of evidence and proof that the accused has to produce in order to demonstrate that he was not capable of giving a sample to be a high one. In *Hogg v Lockhart*[4] it was established that the accused had a very powerful repugnance to blood and hypodermic needles and in those circumstances the court held that his refusal to give a blood specimen was reasonable. In *McGregor v Jessop*[5] it was held that a motorist who made several genuine attempts to provide a second urine sample but was unable to do so could be said to have a reasonable excuse for failing to provide a specimen. In *Lockhart v Stanbridge*[6] it was held that a mental condition of a very extreme character which rendered the accused unable to provide a specimen was a reasonable excuse; in that case medical evidence from a specialist in clinical psychology was led. In *Pringle v Annan*[7] an accused was physically unable to give a specimen of breath because of chest injuries he had just received in a car crash. Reference should also be made to 4.5:4 above and 8.5:3F below.

---

1 *Kelly v MacKinnon* 1985 SLT 487, 1985 SCCR 97, (although it did not do so in that case).
2 1986 SCCR 369.
3 *Gallacher v Scott* 1989 SLT 397, 1989 SCCR 61.
4 1973 SLT (Sh Ct) 40.
5 1988 SLT 719, 1988 SCCR 337.
6 1989 SCCR 220.
7 1988 SLT 899, 1988 SCCR 423.

On the other hand, a mere fear of needles is not a sufficient excuse[1], even where the fear amounts to a phobia which does not amount to an invincible repugnance[2]. Nor is embarrassment a reasonable excuse[3]. Where an accused had a medical condition but deliberately declined to give a specimen he was held not to have a reasonable excuse[4]. In *Milne v Westwater*[5] the accused's claim that he was terrified of needles was disbelieved.

It is not a reasonable excuse that the accused was not in fact driving or in charge of the vehicle[6]. However, in such a case disqualification is not obligatory (See 4.14:3 above). Nor is a refusal justified because the accused wishes to wait until his solicitor arrives[7]. It would appear from the terms of this section that a failure to arrest the accused under s 6(6) would not constitute a reasonable excuse for the accused to provide a specimen. However, if the requirement to provide a sample of blood or urine is refused following what the police consider was a failure by the accused to provide a proper second breath specimen, the Crown will be required to prove that the breath analyser device is unreliable before it can proceed to hold that the accused refused to provide a specimen of blood or urine[8]. In that case, police officers considered that the accused had failed to provide a proper specimen, and charged him under s 7(6). Thereafter, they discovered that the breath analysis device had produced proper readings, but the print-out was inaccurate in other respects. It was held that before the Crown could secure a conviction in these circumstances, it was necessary to prove that the machine was unreliable before it could properly require a blood or urine sample. As the Crown had not proved this, the accused was acquitted. On the other hand, where an accused only pretended to blow into the Camic device, and the machine produced a 'breath invalid' print-out, the prosecution does not require to show that the device was reliable[9].

The Crown does not have to prove that the other breath analyser device is working properly if the court is satisfied that

---

1 *Glickman v McKinnon* 1981 JC 81; see also *R v Lennard* [1975] RTR 252.
2 *McIntosh v Lowe* 1991 SCCR 154.
3 *Palmer v Killion* [1983] RTR 46.
4 *Singh v McLeod* 1986 SCCR 656.
5 1990 JC 205, 1990 SCCR 46.
6 *McLellan v Tudhope* 1984 SCCR 397.
7 *Manuel v Stewart* 1986 SLT 593, 1986 SCCR 121.
8 *Tudhope v Quinn* 1984 SCCR 255.
9 *Simpson v Lowe* 1992 SLT 425, 1991 SCCR 728.

the driver has deliberately failed to provide a specimen[1]. A driver cannot claim that he has a reasonable excuse if he first agreed to give a sample and then refused to co-operate[2]. Reference should also be made to 4.5:4 above.

It should be noted that if in terms of s 6(4) and 7(6) a motorist has a reasonable excuse for failing to supply one or other of a specimen of blood or urine, then it is still open for the police to further require a specimen of the remaining alternative[3]. What may be a reasonable excuse for failing to provide one kind of specimen will not necessarily (or indeed normally) be a reasonable excuse for failing to provide a different kind of specimen.

What duties are incumbent upon a motorist to reveal the nature of any disability to provide a specimen are described at 4.14:3 above.

4.14:8   Procedure and penalties

Proceedings for refusal to provide a specimen are taken summarily, and the penalties are given in Schedule 2 to the Road Traffic Offenders Act 1988. It appears from the Schedule that obligatory disqualification only applies in cases where the accused was driving or attempting to drive. If it is established that the accused was not in fact driving or attempting to drive, disqualification is discretionary[4].

Where the charge libelled is a failure to provide a specimen of breath, the Crown cannot amend the complaint at the end of its case to a charge of failure to supply a specimen of blood[5]. However, where an accused was taken to a police station where it was discovered that the Camic device was not working, and was then taken to another police station, the Crown was allowed to amend the *locus* in the complaint to include the second police station[6]. Similarly, amendment to the complaint will be allowed if the alteration is not material[7].

---

1 *Simpson v Lowe* 1992 SLT 425, 1991 SCCR 728; see also *Brannigan v McGlennan* 2000 SCCR 12.
2 *Duncan v Normand* 1995 SLT 629, 1994 SCCR 508.
3 *Hall v Allan* 1984 SLT 199, 1983 SCCR 520.
4 See also *Aird v Valentine* 1986 SCCR 353.
5 *McArthur v MacNeill* 1986 JC 182, 1987 SLT 299, 1986 SCCR 552.
6 *Tudhope v Fulton* 1987 SLT 419, 1986 SCCR 567; see also *Belcher v MacKinnon* 1986 CO Circulars A/55.
7 *Fenwick v Valentine* 1994 SLT 485, 1993 SCCR 892; see also 2.3:3 above.

4.15 WARNINGS (s 7(7))

4.15:1 Section 7(7)

Section 7(7) of the Road Traffic Act 1988 provides as follows:

'A constable must, on requiring any person to provide a specimen in pursuance of this section, warn him that a failure to provide it may render him liable to prosecution.'

4.15:2 General application

It seems clear that the Road Traffic Act 1988 intends that the accused will be warned at the same time as the requirement is made that failure to provide the specimen in terms of the requirement may result in prosecution. The Act, however, provides no sanction in the event of such a failure. It must be assumed that if the constable making the requirement fails to give a clear and unequivocal warning that such failure to provide a specimen may lead to prosecution, then this will invalidate the entire procedure and lead to the specimen being considered inadmissible in evidence. This is despite the terms of s 15(2) of the Road Traffic Offenders Act 1988 which provides that evidence of the proportion of alcohol or any drug in a specimen of breath, blood or urine provided by the accused shall be taken into account 'in all cases'. The provisions of s 15(2) must presumably be construed as meaning that such specimens will be taken into account in all cases so long as the specimens are taken in accordance with the provisions of the Act[1].

4.16 CHOICE OF SPECIMENS OF BREATH (S 8)

4.16:1 Section 8

Section 8 of the Road Traffic Act 1988 provides:

'(1) Subject to subsection (2) below, of any two specimens of breath provided by any person in pursuance of section 7 of this Act that

1 *R v Fox* [1985] RTR 337 at 343, per Lord Fraser; [1985] 1 WLR 1126.

with the lower proportion of alcohol in the breath shall be used and
the other shall be disregarded.
(2) If the specimen with the lower proportion of alcohol contains no
more than 50 microgrammes of alcohol in 100 millilitres of breath, the
person who provided it may claim that it should be replaced by such
specimen as may be required under section 7(4) of this Act and, if he
then provides such a specimen, neither specimen of breath shall be
used.
(3) The Secretary of State may by regulations substitute another proportion of alcohol in the breath for that specified in subsection (2) above.'

4.16:2 General application

This section contains two significant provisions. Firstly, the
Crown case can only proceed on the basis of the lower of the two
readings produced by the breath analyser device, the higher one
being ignored for the purposes of prosecution. Secondly, if that
lower reading is not higher than 50 microgrammes of alcohol in
100 millilitres of breath, the accused may exercise the option of
having the breath specimen replaced by one of blood or urine in
terms of s 7(4) of the Road Traffic Act 1988, and if such an
alternative specimen is given, then that is used and both breath
specimens are ignored. However, if for any reason the alternative
specimens are not given, the Crown may still secure a conviction
on the basis of the original breath specimens[1].

4.16:3 Choice of blood or urine specimen

If the lower of the two breath specimens is below the 50 microgrammes level, then it is for the police constable to indicate to the
accused that the option of giving a blood or urine sample is open
to him, and this alternative choice must be given fairly and fully.
In *Hamilton v Jones*[2] an accused gave a breath sample lower than
50 mg and was then told simply to give a sample of blood only.
He refused and was acquitted because the constable had a
statutory duty to inform the motorist in these circumstances that
he had the option to have the breath specimen replaced with a
specimen of blood or urine in terms of s 8(2) of the Road Traffic

---

1 *Bain v Tudhope* 1985 SCCR 412; *Wilson v Webster* 1999 SCCR 747.
2 1989 SCCR 1.

Act 1988. In *Pelosi v Jessop*[1] the police again advised the motorist that he could choose to give an alternative specimen of blood only; it was conceded by the Crown that the procedure had not been followed, in that the motorist should have been advised that the alternative was a specimen of blood or urine.

Once the motorist has been made aware that in terms of s 8(2) an alternative of a blood or urine specimen is available, and elects to supply such an alternative specimen, the choice of whether the specimen is to be one of blood or urine is entirely at the discretion of the officer making the requirement (see 4.12:3 above). Whether this line of authority is applicable to the requirement of a specimen of blood or urine at a hospital was raised but not decided in *Anderson v McClory*[2].

The constable need not advise the driver that he can decline to take the test on medical grounds; it is enough that he is told that it is an offence to refuse to give a specimen without reasonable cause[3]. There is a long line of partly unresolved case law in England on this subject, following on the case of *DPP v Warren*[4], but this does not concern Scottish practice.

In *Bain v Tudhope*[5], an accused who gave a breath specimen reading of 42 microgrammes elected to exercise his right under s 8(2) to provide an alternative specimen under s 7(4). He was required to provide a urine sample and failed to do so. He was accordingly convicted on the original breath specimen reading. The accused appealed on the ground that he should have been required to give a blood specimen; but this was rejected on the ground that the decision of which of the two specimens should be given under s 7(4) should in all circumstances be left wholly to the discretion of the constable. Reference should also be made to *McLeod v MacFarlane*[6] and *Simpson v McClory*[7]; the constable does not have to consider the motorist's views on which choice of specimens should be given. Where the motorist is considering his right to exercise his option under s 8(2) to provide an alternative specimen under s 7(4), it is incorrect for the police officer to give the accused advice about which option he should choose, but such advice will not necessarily invalidate the conviction if the

---

1 1990 JC 273, 1991 SLT 155, 1990 SCCR 175.
2 1991 SCCR 571.
3 *McLaren v McLeod* 1994 SLT 1281,1994 SCCR 493.
4 [1993] AC 319, [1992], 4 All ER 865, [1993] RTR 58.
5 1985 SCCR 412.
6 1993 SLT 782, 1993 SCCR 178.
7 1993 JC 110, 1993 SLT 155, 1993 SCCR 402.

accused was not subject to improper pressure, and the constable did not act in bad faith[1]. However, if the police go further and exert pressure on the accused which results in him being forced to make a choice, a conviction is not thereafter competent on the basis of the specimen of blood or urine thus produced[2].

If the lower of the two breath specimens is also below the level at which the Crown Office has indicated that proceedings will not in practice be taken, it would appear to be incompetent for this alternative procedure to be adopted[3].

4.16:4 Insufficiency of specimen

Where the Crown claims that an alternative specimen provided by the accused is insufficient to allow proper analysis to be carried out, this is normally established by expert evidence[4]. Once it is established that such a specimen is not capable of analysis, the Crown may revert to the lower of the two original breath specimen readings[5].

Where an accused was asked to give a urine specimen, which proved to be insufficient to divide into two parts, it was held that while the sufficiency of a specimen for analysis was a matter for an analyst, the police officers who required the specimen might be in the best position to decide whether the specimen was divisible[6].

---

1 *Woodburn v McLeod* 1986 JC 56, 1986 SLT 325, 1986 SCCR 107.
2 *Green v Lockhart* 1986 SLT 11, 1985 SCCR 257.
3 *Benton v Cardle* 1986 SLT 310, 1987 SCCR 738; *McConnachie v Scott* 1988 SLT 480, 1988 SCCR 176; see also 3.15 above.
4 *Carmichael v Gillooly* 1982 SCCR 119.
5 *Bain v Tudhope* 1985 SCCR 412.
6 *MacDougall v MacPhail* 1991 SLT 801, 1991 SCCR 358; 4.13:2 above.

Chapter Five

Use of specimens and evidence in proceedings under the Road Traffic Act 1988, sections 3A, 4 and 5

5.1   THE ROAD TRAFFIC OFFENDERS ACT 1988, s 15

Sections 15 and 16 of the Road Traffic Offenders Act 1988 provide important evidential considerations in prosecutions under ss 3A, 4 and 5 of the Road Traffic Act 1988. In the previous legislation, the general provisions now in ss 15 and 16 of the Road Traffic Offenders Act 1988 were found in ss 8(6) and 10 of the Road Traffic Act 1972[1].

Section 15 of the Road Traffic Offenders Act 1988[2] reads in full as follows:

'(1) This section and section 16 of this Act apply in respect of proceedings for an offence under section 3A, 4 or 5 of the Road Traffic Act 1988 (driving offences connected with drink or drugs) and expressions used in this section and section 16 of this Act have the same meaning as in sections 3A to 10 of that Act.

(2) Evidence of the proportion of alcohol or any drug in a specimen of breath, blood or urine provided by the accused shall, in all cases (including cases where the specimen was not provided in connection with the alleged offence), be taken into account and, subject to subsection (3) below, it shall be assumed that the proportion of alcohol in the accused's breath, blood or urine at the time of the alleged offence was not less than in the specimen.

(3) That assumption shall not be made if the accused proves –
   (a) that he consumed alcohol before he provided the specimen and –
      (i) in relation to an offence under section 3A, after the time of the alleged offence, and
      (ii) otherwise, after he had ceased to drive, attempt to drive or be in charge of a vehicle on a road or other public place, and
   (b) that had he not done so the proportion of alcohol in his breath, blood or urine would not have exceeded the prescribed limit and, if it is alleged that he was unfit to drive through drink, would not have been such as to impair his ability to drive properly.

---

1 As amended by the Transport Act 1981, s 25(3) and Schedule 8.
2 As amended by the Road Traffic Act 1991, Sch 4, para 87.

(4) A specimen of blood shall be disregarded unless it was taken from the accused with his consent by a medical practitioner.

(5) Where, at the time a specimen of blood or urine was provided by the accused, he asked to be provided with such a specimen, evidence of the proportion of alcohol or any drug found in the specimen is not admissible on behalf of the prosecution unless –

    (a) the specimen in which the alcohol or drug was found is one of two parts into which the specimen provided by the accused was divided at the time it was provided, and

    (b) the other part was supplied to the accused.'

Section 15(1) repeats and amplifies s 10(1) of the Road Traffic Act 1972 (as amended); s 15(2) reflects the terms of the first part of s 10(2) of the 1972 Act; s 15(3) repeats the statutory defence formerly found in the second half of s 10(2) of the 1972 Act; s 15(4) restates the first part of s 10(4) of the earlier Act; and s 15(5) repeats the provisions relating to the supply of part of a specimen of blood or urine to the accused previously found in s 10(6) of the 1972 Act.

5.2 THE ROAD TRAFFIC OFFENDERS ACT 1988, S 15(1)

Section 15(1)[1] reads as follows:

'This section and section 16 of this Act apply in respect of proceedings for an offence under section 3A, 4 or 5 of the Road Traffic Act 1988 (driving offences connected with drink or drugs) and expressions used in this section and section 16 of this Act have the same meaning as in sections 3A to 10 of that Act.'

The terms of this section are self-evident and simply make it clear that the same evidential considerations apply in terms of this and the following section to s 3A, 4 and 5 prosecutions.

5.3 EVIDENCE OF SPECIMEN TO BE TAKEN INTO ACCOUNT IN ALL CASES, S 15(2)

5.3:1 General

Section 15(2) of the Road Traffic Offenders Act 1988[2] provides:

1 As amended by the Road Traffic Act 1991, Sch 4, para 87(2).
2 As amended by the Road Traffic Act 1991, Sch 4, para 87(3).

'Evidence of the proportion of alcohol or any drug in a specimen of breath, blood or urine provided by the accused shall, in all cases (including cases where the specimen was not provided in connection with the alleged offence), be taken into account and, subject to subsection (3) below, it shall be assumed that the proportion of alcohol in the accused's breath, blood or urine at the time of the alleged offence was not less than in the specimen.'

This subsection is clearly designed to diminish the importance of formal or procedural requirements. In particular, notwithstanding the circumstances under which such specimens have been taken, the Act appears to provide that the evidence of the proportion of alcohol or drug in such specimens must be taken into account 'in all cases'. It is, however, not yet entirely clear what the effect of this will be in the variety of situations that will arise in practice. It has been suggested that the effect of this provision will be to render admissible in evidence even specimens which have been unlawfully obtained. However, it is submitted that the effect of this section can only at best cure procedural or technical requirements imposed by other parts of the legislation. Firstly, the Act provides specifically in s 15(4) that a specimen of blood is to be disregarded unless it was taken from the accused with his consent by a medical practitioner. Further, s 11(4) of the Road Traffic Act 1988 makes it clear that a specimen of blood is provided only if the accused consents to it being taken, and it is taken by a medical practitioner. Clearly, therefore, a specimen of blood taken without the accused's consent, or by someone other than a medical practitioner, cannot be admissible in evidence and cannot be used in any way or under any circumstances in proceedings under s 4 or 5 of the Road Traffic Act 1988. The additional removal of restriction by the amendment to s 15(2) provided by the Road Traffic Act 1991, Sch 4, para 87(3) apparently allows the Crown to use specimens provided for other purposes. This is more fully discussed at 3.9:1 above. If this is so, it is submitted that nonetheless any specimens always have to be taken in accordance with the other provisions of the Act. Reference is made to the following paragraphs.

5.3:2   Interpretation of section 15(2)

The only direct authority on this matter to date is to be found obiter in the judgment of Lord Fraser in *R v Fox*[1]. In that case the

---

1   [1985] RTR 337, [1985] 1 WLR 1126.

accused was the driver of a motor vehicle involved in an accident. No other vehicle was involved. The accused left the scene and went home. The police, who had no knowledge of his physical condition, went to his house and got no answer to their knock on the door, although they heard voices inside. The police therefore entered the premises and required the driver to give a specimen of breath (the roadside test), which he refused. He was then arrested and taken to a police station where he provided a breath specimen for analysis which exceeded the statutory limit.

It was held that, under English law, the police officers were trespassing at the time they made the first requirement for a breath specimen, and when they purported to arrest the accused.[1] In these circumstances it was held that neither the provision of a preliminary breath specimen nor the arrest were necessary preconditions of the procedure for the provision of specimens under the equivalent of s 7 of the Road Traffic Act 1988, and that the accused could accordingly be convicted on the basis of these specimens. It was explained that although the police, who were acting in good faith, may have exceeded their common law powers in their alleged arrest of the accused, the evidence subsequently obtained of an offence committed prior to the arrest was admissible and not tainted by the illegality of the arrest itself.

In discussing the terms of the equivalent of s 15(2) of the Road Traffic Offenders Act 1988, that the proportion of alcohol in a specimen of breath, blood or urine shall 'in all cases' be taken into account (a matter which was not necessary for the decision), Lord Fraser said[2]: 'As at present advised, I do not think those words can make evidence admissible if it would not be admissible under the general law. I am inclined to read them as referring only to a specimen "provided pursuant to the provisions of this Act."' The effect therefore of the terms of s 15(2), it is submitted, is to allow any sample to be considered in evidence even although procedural requirements have not been followed, or some other illegal or improper act is associated with the procedure which does not, however, contravene the provisions of the Act. It is thought, therefore, that failure to observe the following provisions will not render the results of the analysis of the specimen inadmissible.

1 It should be noted that in Scotland this conclusion would not have been reached – see *Cairns v Keane* 1983 SCCR 277.
2 At [1985] RTR 343.

5.3:3   Circumstances where failure does not render a specimen inadmissible

1. Section 4(6) of the Road Traffic Act 1988 empowers a constable to arrest, without warrant, a person whom he suspects of committing an offence under that section. If no arrest in fact takes place, it is clear that this has no bearing on the legality of the proceedings. The power of arrest is enabling only and does not have to be a prerequisite of the provision of a specimen (unlike earlier legislation). See, for example, *Orr v Urquhart*[1] and *Carmichael v Wilson*[2]. A police constable has the right to enter any premises in the course of an investigation[3].

A constable must have 'reasonable cause' to suspect that a person is or has been committing an offence under s 4 in order to arrest a motorist. If it is established that the constable does not have reasonable cause for his suspicion, any power of arrest exercised in terms of this section will be invalid, but any subsequent specimen given by the accused will not thereby become inadmissible in evidence (See 3.11 and 4.2:2 above).

2. Section 6(5) of the Road Traffic Act 1988 empowers a constable to arrest a person without warrant if, following a roadside breath test in terms of that section, he has reason to suspect that the accused's proportion of alcohol in his breath or blood exceeds the prescribed limit, or where the accused has failed to supply a breath specimen and the constable has reasonable cause to suspect that he has consumed alcohol. Again, a failure to arrest, or an improper arrest, will not invalidate the subsequent provision of a specimen for analysis (unless the person arrested is at hospital as a patient).

3. Section 6 (the preliminary or roadside test). None of the provisions of this section are required to have been implemented before a specimen of breath, blood or urine is given in terms of s 7(1)(a) or (b). Again this is different from the requirements of earlier law. The principal purpose of this section is procedural only; in other words, a constable does not have to administer a breath test before requiring a specimen of breath, blood or urine. Even if a breath test is negative, it would appear to be still open to the constable to require a specimen for analysis. For example, when there was no evidence that the constable who required the

---

1 1993 SLT 406, 1992 SCCR 295.
2 1993 JC 83, 1993 SCCR 290.
3 *Cairns v Keane* 1983 SCCR 277.

roadside test was in uniform this did not invalidate the resulting Camic procedure[1]. However, the provisions of s 6 are of course relevant in themselves if for any reason the outcome of the breath test procedure is to be used in any subsequent proceedings, for example if the driver fails to provide such a test contrary to s 6(4) (See 4.5:1 and 4.5:2 above). Further, in certain circumstances, the evidence produced as a result of such a test may have evidential significance[2]. In these latter cases, the other provisions of s 6 (including s 6(3)) will have to be observed if the requirement to provide a breath test, or the provision of the test and its result, has to be established in evidence.

5.3:4   Circumstances where failure will render a subsequent specimen inadmissible

On the other hand, it is submitted that the requirements of the following sections do have to be observed if the specimen is subsequently to be admissible in evidence.

1. Section 7 of the Road Traffic Act 1988. This section, which allows for the provision of specimens for analysis, contains within its terms a number of requirements which, it is submitted, must be observed before the specimen can be regarded as competent evidence. For example, in terms of s 7(1) and (2) a breath specimen can only be given into an approved device at a police station. Section 7(3) details in specific terms the circumstances in which a blood or urine specimen is to be taken rather than a breath specimen. Section 7(4) stipulates inter alia that if a medical practitioner is of the opinion that for medical reasons a blood specimen should not be taken then the specimen shall be one of urine. Section 7(5) defines how a specimen of urine should be given. It is submitted that if any of these specific provisions within s 7 is not observed, then any specimen taken in terms of this section should not be admissible in evidence.

Section 7(7) requires that a constable must warn any person required to give a specimen in terms of this section that failure to provide such a specimen may result in prosecution. Again it is submitted that this requirement is mandatory, and failure to give the warning will invalidate any subsequent proceedings under s 7(6).

---

1 *Orr v Urquhart* 1993 SLT 406, 1992 SCCR 295.
2 *Gallagher v McKinnon* 1987 SLT 531, 1986 SCCR 704.

2. Section 8 of the Road Traffic Act 1988. The various requirements of this section as described therein clearly have to be
observed before the specimens can be admitted into evidence.

3. Section 9 of the Road Traffic Act 1988. The provisions for the
protection of hospital patients require to be observed and failure
to do so will render any subsequent specimen inadmissible in
evidence.

4. Section 11(4) of the Road Traffic Act 1988 and s 15(4) of the
Road Traffic Offenders Act 1988. The requirement that a blood
sample can only be taken with the accused's consent and by a
medical practitioner is plainly a prerequisite of allowing that
specimen to be admitted in evidence.

5. Section 15(5) of the Road Traffic Offenders Act 1988. The
requirement to provide part of the specimen to the accused in
terms of this section, if the accused so claims, must also, it is
submitted, be observed before the results of the specimen can be
admitted. It would appear that the motorist must expressly indicate that he wishes to take the divided specimen at the time it is
offered to him[1]. Reference should also be made to 5.7 below.

5.3:5   Circumstances where admissibility is a matter of discretion

If the evidence of a specimen in terms of the foregoing paragraphs
would normally be admissible, it is submitted that there may still
be a residual power to exclude the evidence if the court considered
that the specimen had been obtained by fraud or deceit, or if the
police had behaved oppressively to the motorist in obtaining the
specimen. Reference should again be made to the opinion of Lord
Fraser in *R v Fox*[2]. Section 78(1) of the Police and Criminal Evidence
Act 1984 gives courts in England a wide discretion to exclude
evidence in any case which might cause unfairness. It is submitted
that the same consideration applies in Scotland at common law. It
should be underlined, however, that none of the matters in this and
the previous two paragraphs have yet been authoritatively settled
in Scotland; however, reference might usefully be made to *Douglas
v Stevenson*[3]; *Woodburn v McLeod*[4]; and *Green v Lockhart*[5].

1 *Aitchison v Johnstone* 1987 SCCR 225.
2 [1985] RTR 337, [1985] 1 WLR 1126.
3 1986 SCCR 519.
4 1986 JC 56, 1986 SLT 325, 1986 SCCR 107.
5 1986 SLT 11, 1985 SCCR 257.

5.4 LEVEL OF ALCOHOL HIGHER THAN READING

The way in which s 15(2) of the Road Traffic Offenders Act 1988 is phrased indicates that it is open to the Crown to attempt to prove that the proportion of alcohol in an accused's breath, blood or urine was, at the time he was driving or in charge of his vehicle, higher than that provided in the specimen. The assumption provided in the subsection is that the level of alcohol in the accused's body at the time of the alleged offence is to be not less than the proportion indicated in the specimens taken. In other words, the Crown is not precluded from proving that the proportion of alcohol in the accused's breath, blood or urine at the time of the alleged offence was greater than shown in the subsequently taken specimen. It is therefore possible for the Crown to secure a conviction even although the levels demonstrated to be present in the specimen were lower than the legal limit. This subject, sometimes called back calculation, is more fully described at 3.9:3 above.

5.5 THE STATUTORY DEFENCE (s 15(3))

5.5:1 Section 15(3)

Section 15(3) of the Road Traffic Offenders Act 1988[1] provides as follows:

'That assumption shall not be made if the accused proves –
(a) that he consumed alcohol before he provided the specimen and –
  (i) in relation to an offence under section 3A, after the time of the alleged offence, and
  (ii) otherwise, after he had ceased to drive, attempt to drive or be in charge of a vehicle on a road or other public place, and
(b) that had he not done so the proportion of alcohol in his breath, blood or urine would not have exceeded the prescribed limit and, if it is alleged that he was unfit to drive through drink, would not have been such as to impair his ability to drive properly.'

The assumption referred to is that contained in s 15(2) of the Road Traffic Offenders Act 1988.

---

1 As amended by the Road Traffic Act 1991, Sch 4, para 87(4).

5.5:2   Onus and standard of proof

The onus is on the accused to establish this defence. The standard of proof which is required is on the balance of probabilities[1]. However, if the circumstances are such that the evidence casts a reasonable doubt on the prosecution case, the accused will be entitled to the benefit of such doubt. In practice, however, this situation is unlikely to occur; the evidence of post-incident drinking has by its nature to be clearly distinguished from what was consumed prior to the driver ceasing to drive, attempt to drive or be in charge of his vehicle, and in most cases it will be for the accused to remove any doubt about the quantity of alcohol consumed before and after the material time. The accused will have to establish each part of his defence. Accordingly, he will in normal circumstances require to establish when it was that he stopped driving, attempting to drive or being in charge of the vehicle. He will then require to establish the amount of alcohol which he has consumed after that time. Thereafter, the accused will require to show that, but for the consumption of the alcohol, he as an individual would have provided a specimen at the time he ceased to drive, attempt to drive or be in charge which would have been lower than the maximum permitted level prescribed in s 11(2). The technical steps in the defence case are usually spoken to in practice by the evidence of an expert analyst.

This defence can be established by the evidence of a single witness[2].

This subject is more fully discussed at 3.9 and 3.17:2 above.

5.6   TAKING OF BLOOD SPECIMENS: S 15(4)

Section 15(4) of the Road Traffic Offenders Act 1988 provides as follows:

'A specimen of blood shall be disregarded unless it was taken from the accused with his consent by a medical practitioner.'[3]

Failure to observe the provisions of s 15(4) will make the evidence of the blood specimen and any analysis thereof inadmissible in

---

1 *Neish v Stevenson* 1969 SLT 229, overruling *Thaw v Segar* 1962 SLT (Sh Ct) 63.
2 *King v Lees* 1993 SLT 1184, 1993 SCCR 28.
3 See also the Road Traffic Act 1988, s 11(4).

evidence, notwithstanding the terms of s 15(2). Accordingly, if the specimen is not taken by a medical practitioner, or if it is taken without the accused's consent, the specimen will not be allowed in evidence[1].

5.7 PART OF SPECIMEN TO BE SUPPLIED TO ACCUSED: s 15(5)

Section 15(5) of the Road Traffic Offenders Act 1988 provides as follows:

'Where, at the time a specimen of blood or urine was provided by the accused, he asked to be provided with such a specimen, evidence of the proportion of alcohol or any drug found in the specimen is not admissible on behalf of the prosecution unless –
(a) the specimen in which the alcohol or drug was found is one of two parts into which the specimen provided by the accused was divided at the time it was provided, and
(b) the other part was supplied to the accused.'

This section repeats and replaces the terms of s 10(6) of the Road Traffic Act 1972[2].

The intention of s 15(5) is to allow the accused the right to part of the specimen of blood or urine he has provided in terms of s 7(1)(b) of the Road Traffic Act 1988 in order to allow him to have it independently analysed. Failure to observe the terms of this subsection will mean that the court cannot consider the results of any such analysis, notwithstanding the terms of s 15(2) of the Road Traffic Offenders Act 1988 as amended. Further, if the police do anything which frustrates the purpose of the section a conviction will not follow[3].

The purpose of this subsection is achieved in practice by dividing the specimen of blood or urine into two and handing one of the two parts to the accused. It is submitted that, in particular, having regard to the terms of s 11(3) of the Road Traffic Act 1988, each of the two parts of the divided specimen must be sufficient to allow proper analysis to be carried out. In *Gallagher v McKinnon*[4], it

---

1 *Friel v Dickson* 1992 SLT 1086, 1992 SCCR 513; 5.3:2ff above.
2 As amended by the Transport Act 1981, s 25(3) and Sch 8, which, by virtue of SI 1983/576, came into force on 6 May 1983.
3 *Perry v McGovern* [1986] RTR 240.
4 1987 SLT 531, 1986 SCCR 704.

was held that where the analysis of the specimen retained by the police differs from the analysis of the specimen handed to the accused, the court could look at extraneous evidence (but not the readings from the breath analyser device) in deciding which of the two results was accurate. Reference in this respect should also be made to *Jordan v Russell*[1] and *Campbell-Birkett v Vannett*[2]. Whether or not the accused has requested part of the specimen he has provided and such specimen has been given to him are questions of fact. It would appear from the terms of the subsection that the motorist must take the initiative in asking for his part of the specimen[3].

The part of the specimen given to the accused must be capable of being analysed within a reasonable time. In *Ellis v Cruikshank*[4] the specimen was found to be incapable of analysis some three months after its provision. It was held that any such specimen must be capable of analysis within a reasonable time at the point when it is delivered to the accused.

The supply of part of the specimen to the accused must be unconditional; where a police officer was only prepared to give the accused the specimen on condition that the motorist signed a receipt, this was held to invalidate the prosecution[5].

5.8   DOCUMENTARY EVIDENCE OF SPECIMENS (S 16)

5.8:1   Section 16

Section 16 of the Road Traffic Offenders Act 1988 reads in full as follows:

'(1) Evidence of the proportion of alcohol or a drug in a specimen of breath, blood or urine may, subject to subsections (3) and (4) below and to section 15(5) of this Act, be given by the production of a document or documents purporting to be whichever of the following is appropriate, that is to say –
(a) a statement automatically produced by the device by which the proportion of alcohol in a specimen of breath was measured and a certificate signed by a constable (which may but need not be

---

1 1995 JC 78, 1995 SLT 1301, 1995 SCCR 423.
2 1999 SLT 865.
3 See also *Aitchison v Johnstone* 1987 SCCR 225.
4 1973 SCCR Supp 49.
5 *Smith v Skeen* 1974 SCCR Supp 64.

contained in the same document as the statement) that the statement relates to a specimen provided by the accused at the date and time shown in the statement, and

(b) a certificate signed by an authorised analyst as to the proportion of alcohol or any drug found in a specimen of blood or urine identified in the certificate.

(2) Subject to subsections (3) and (4) below, evidence that a specimen of blood was taken from the accused with his consent by a medical practitioner may be given by the production of a document purporting to certify that fact and to be signed by a medical practitioner.

(3) Subject to subsection (4) below –

(a) a document purporting to be such a statement or such a certificate (or both such a statement and such a certificate) as is mentioned in subsection (1)(a) above is admissible in evidence on behalf of the prosecution in pursuance of this section only if a copy of it either has been handed to the accused when the document was produced or has been served on him not later than seven days before the hearing, and

(b) any other document is so admissible only if a copy of it has been served on the accused not later than seven days before the hearing.

(4) A document purporting to be a certificate (or so much of a document as purports to be a certificate) is not so admissible if the accused, not later than three days before the hearing or within such further time as the court may in special circumstances allow, has served notice on the prosecutor requiring the attendance at the hearing of the person by whom the document purports to be signed.

(5) In Scotland –

(a) a document produced in evidence on behalf of the prosecution in pursuance of subsection (1) or (2) above and, where the person by whom the document was signed is called as a witness, the evidence of that person, shall be sufficient evidence of the facts stated in the document, and

(b) a written execution purporting to be signed by the person who handed to or served on the accused or the prosecutor a copy of the document or of the notice in terms of subsection (3) or (4) above, together with, where appropriate, a post office receipt for the registered or recorded delivery letter shall be sufficient evidence of the handing or service of such a copy or notice.

(6) A copy of a certificate required by this section to be served on the accused or a notice required by this section to be served on the prosecutor may be served personally or sent by registered post or recorded delivery service.

(7) In this section "authorised analyst" means –

(a) any person possessing the qualifications prescribed by regulations made under section 76 of the Food Act 1984 or section 27 of the Food and Drugs (Scotland) Act 1956 as qualifying persons for appointment as public analysts under those Acts, and

(b) any other persons authorised by the Secretary of State to make analyses for the purposes of this section.'

Section 16 replaces the provisions of s 10(3), (4), (5), (7), (8) and (9) of the Road Traffic Act 1972[1]. The section, in general terms, provides that the evidence of the proportion of alcohol in a breath test under s 7(1)(a) of the Road Traffic Act 1988 may be proved by a statement produced automatically by an authorised breath analyser device, and evidence of the amount of alcohol in a specimen of blood or urine provided in terms of s 7(1)(b) of that Act may be given by a certificate signed by a certified analyst. There has been a substantial number of cases dealing with the certificates automatically produced by the Camic Breath Analyser Device (an approved device in operation for a number of years in Scotland) and these are reported in this chapter. However, since 1 January 2000 the Camic Breath Analyser is no longer an approved device. The Intoximeter EC/IR device is now widely used. A description of these two devices is found in Appendix C. The section also describes the proof of the taking of a blood specimen[2], and the requirements of service in respect of the service of the certificates described in the section[3]. A definition of the term 'certified analyst' is also provided[4].

5.8:2   Statement produced by a breath analyser device (s 16(1)(a))

Section 16(1)(a) of the Road Traffic Offenders Act 1988 reads as follows:

'Evidence of the proportion of alcohol or a drug in a specimen of breath, blood or urine may, subject to subsections (3) and (4) below and to section 15(5) of this Act, be given by the production of a document or documents purporting to be whichever of the following is appropriate, that is to say –
(a) a statement automatically produced by the device by which the proportion of alcohol in a specimen of breath was measured and a certificate signed by a constable (which may but need not be

---

1 As amended by the Transport Act 1981, s 25(3) and Sch 8 which, by virtue of SI 1983/576, came into force on 6 May 1983.
2 Road Traffic Offenders Act 1988, s 16(2).
3 RTOA 1988, s 16(3), (4), (5) and (6).
4 RTOA 1988, s 16(7).

contained in the same document as the statement) that the statement relates to a specimen provided by the accused at the date and time shown in the statement . . .'.

5.8:3 Approved breath analyser device

By virtue of the Breath Analysis Devices (Scotland) Approval Order 1998 which came into force on 31 July 1998, three devices are approved by the Secretary of State for use in Scotland. These are the Camic Datamaster, the Lion Intoxilyser 6000 UK and the Intoximeter EC/IR. The device commonly in use in Scotland for many years was the Camic Breath Analyser, but that device is now no longer approved as from 1 January 2000. It is assumed, however, that most, if not all of the case law concerned with the Camic device will apply *mutatis mutandis* to the devices now approved.

An approved device is not currently available in every police station in Scotland; in particular, a number of small and rural stations do not yet have one installed. In terms of s 7(3) of the Road Traffic Act 1988 only specimens of blood or urine can be required of motorists at police stations which do not have an approved device.

The prosecution are presumably entitled to a presumption that each of the breath analysers described above is an approved device within the meaning of the section[1]. It is unnecessary for the relevant Approval Order to be produced[2]. Further, when the device has in practice done what it should have done if it was in proper working order, then it is to be presumed that the machine is in proper working order and has been correctly maintained[3]. The court is entitled to use its knowledge of how the device operates (See 5.8:4 above).

5.8:4 Operation of approved devices

Essentially, any approved device must be in operational condition and maintained in accordance with the manufacturer's

---

1 *Davidson v Aitchison* 1986 SLT 402, 1985 SCCR 415; *Valentine v Macphail* 1986 JC 131, 1986 SLT 598, 1986 SCCR 321.
2 *Lee v Smith* 1982 SLT 200, 1981 SCCR 267.
3 *Tudhope v McAllister* 1984 SLT 395, 1984 SCCR 182.

directions. It should be operated only by a police officer who has been authorised to do so by the Chief Constable. In order to comply with the requirements of the legislation the devices have certain common operational features. The Camic Breath Analyser device in general terms operates as follows. Firstly, the device must be in an operational condition and maintained in accordance with the manufacturer's directions. It should be operated only by a police officer who has been authorised to do so by the Chief Constable and who has been trained in the proper working of the device. The device has a visual display unit which at the outset of the test should indicate the time. The machine is then tested and must indicate that it is purged of alcohol. The accused is then instructed to give a first breath specimen into the machine. In particular, the accused in terms of s 11(3) of the Road Traffic Act 1988 must provide a specimen of breath in such a way that the specimen is sufficient to enable the test or analysis to be carried out and be provided in such a way as to enable the objective of the test or analysis to be satisfactorily achieved. At that point the machine should be capable of producing on the visual display a reading which indicates the result of the analysis of the breath specimen which has just been provided. Thereafter, the machine should be satisfactorily purged of alcohol and the machine should indicate that this has been done. The accused is then invited to provide a second specimen of breath in circumstances similar to that provided in the first instance. When the breath specimen has been supplied, the machine should again indicate that it is working normally. Thereafter, the device automatically produces a statement indicating the results of the whole test. The statement also contains a form of certificate which is signed by one of the police officers who has witnessed the test. This document is known as a print-out and is considered to contain both a statement and a certificate which is described in the Road Traffic Offenders Act 1988 s 16(3)(a) and s 16(5) and as such will be admissible in evidence so long as the other provisions of the Act are complied with. The evidence of the officer who signed the certificate is not essential if there is sufficient evidence from other officers of the conduct of the test and its result[1].

Judicial knowledge extends to the operation of the Camic Breath Analyser (and, it is submitted, should also extend to other approved devices) and the fact that it produces an automatic

1 *Donoghue v Allan* 1985 SCCR 93.

print-out, and the prosecution does not have to prove that the print-out and its contents qualify as including both a statement and a certificate as above described[1].

The Intoximeter EC/IR in many respects operates in a similar fashion to the Camic Breath Analyser device which is now obsolete. Breath samples are given into the machine which are analysed, and the details of the test are displayed on a display unit. The machine also produces a print-out containing the relevant information and results of the test. However, the technology used in the Intoximeter machine is different. It is operated by an attached standard PC keyboard, which is used for data entry. Once the relevant information has been entered into the machine by way of the keyboard (after the machine has automatically purged itself of alcohol), a mouthpiece is fitted into the breath tube on the machine. The motorist is instructed to take a deep breath and blow into the mouthpiece as steadily and for as long as possible. The breath flowrate is indicated in the display by asterisks. The machine then evaluates the sample and again automatically purges itself of alcohol. If the motorist does not submit a valid breath sample, the unit displays 'specimen incomplete'.

Three minutes are allowed for a valid sample to be provided, failing which the test is aborted. The same procedure is operated for the second test. An example of the print-out produced is in Appendix C. The operator manual suggests that the machine should not be used in environments with heavy alcohol vapour, cigarette smoke, high levels of radio frequencies, magnetic interference or new paint. It is said that these conditions will not interfere with the results of the test but may affect the useful lifespan of various components. Further details of these devices are found in Appendix C.

It is open to the defence to establish any failure to comply with the manufacturer's instructions, and to argue that such failure should lead to acquittal[2]. Reference should also be made to *Kelly v MacKinnon*[3] and *Fleming v Tudhope*[4], and to Appendix C).

---

1 *Annan v Mitchell* 1984 SCCR 32; *Aitchison v Matheson* 1984 SCCR 83.
2 *Jeffrey v MacNeill* 1976 JC 54; *Sloan v Smith* 1978 SLT (Notes) 27; *Hogg v Smith* 1978 CO Circulars A/37 (all cases involving the roadside breathalyser device); *Allan v Miller* 1986 SLT 3, 1985 SCCR 227; *Fraser v McLeod* 1987 SCCR 294 (cases where observation of the manufacturer's instructions were not required).
3 1985 SLT 487, 1985 SCCR 97.
4 1987 CO Circulars A/16.

5.8:5   Informalities in print-out

There has been a number of cases concerned with informalities connected with the documents automatically produced by the breath analyser devices. The subsection does not indicate any particular formality in respect of the information produced by the machine in the statement or certificate; all that is required is that the statement and certificate should evidence the information required by the Road Traffic Act 1988[1]. Further, apparent defects in the statements are curable by parole evidence from a police officer present at the time the test was taken[2]. For example, when the statement did not indicate the name of the driver, or when the certificate was not signed by the constable supervising the taking of the specimen, the Crown may produce verbal evidence to show that the statement and certificate relate to the accused and the test which he has taken[3].

In *Allan v Miller*[4] it was held that where the device appeared to be performing its functions as it was supposed to there was no need to produce specialist evidence that the machine was working properly. There must always be evidence that the print-out relates to the accused[5].

When the statement gives information which is patently incorrect, then the prosecution may not be able to rely on the evidential presumptions created by this subsection. Nonetheless, it may still be open for the prosecution to establish the results of the test by other evidence, such as testimony from police officers present at the time, of what readings were produced on the visual display when the test was taken[6].

If the informalities or defects in the print-out are so fundamental as to indicate that the machine's analytical function is unreliable, the police may turn to the alternative procedure of requiring a specimen of blood or urine.

Informalities in the certificates relating to blood or urine specimens are dealt with at 5.8:7 below.

---

1 *Jones v McPhail* 1984 JC 67, 1984 SLT 396, 1984 SCCR 168; see also *Aitchison v Matheson* 1984 SCCR 83.
2 *Aitchison v Matheson* 1984 SCCR 83.
3 *NcNamee v Tudhope* 1985 SLT 322, 1984 SCCR 423.
4 1986 SLT 3, 1985 SCCR 227.
5 See *O'Brien v Ferguson* 1986 JC 82, 1987 SLT 96, 1986 SCCR 155 (a case involving a blood specimen) and 5.8:7 below.
6 *Smith v MacDonald, Smith v Davie* 1984 SLT 398, 1984 SCCR 190; see also *McLeary v Douglas* 1978 JC 57, 1978 SLT 140; *Gunn v Brown* 1987 SLT 94, 1986 SCCR 179.

5.8:6 Defects in print-out: reliability of device

In terms of s 7(3)(b) of the Road Traffic Act 1988, the provision of a specimen of breath for analysis must be made into a reliable device. The question of what is meant by a device being at the police station, or what is meant by it being for any other reason not practicable to use it there, is dealt with at 4.11:4 above. If the device is not reliable, then the alternative requirement of a blood or urine specimen must be made. The device may be properly considered unreliable if for some technical reason it is not working or functioning properly. However, in terms of the reported cases, the circumstances in which the reliability or otherwise of the device has been considered usually relate to the information contained within the statement or print-out automatically produced by the device.

As indicated in the foregoing paragraph (5.8:5) certain informalities or apparent defects may be cured by parole evidence. However, certain defects may be so fundamental that they must be regarded as indicating that the machine is unreliable. In *Tudhope v Quinn*[1] it was held that what the Crown had to prove was that the analytical or measuring function of the device was unreliable if the primary requirement of a breath specimen was to be set aside and a blood or urine specimen used instead. Although it is good practice to produce the print-out in evidence where the alternative procedure is employed, it is not necessary to do so[2].

The primary or best evidence that the machine is unreliable comes from the police officers who administered the test, and it has been said that the test of reliability is subjective to the officer carrying out the test; the police are entitled to go to the alternative procedure if they conclude on reasonable grounds that the device was unreliable, even if in the event it is proved to be working properly[3].

In *Aitchison v Meldrum*[4] and *Tudhope v Craig*[4] relatively minor defects in the operation of the machine evidenced in the print-out were held not to invalidate the results contained in the print-out.

---

1 1984 SCCR 255.
2 *Houston v McLeod* 1986 JC 96, 1986 SCCR 219.
3 *Burnett v Smith* 1990 JC 119, 1990 SLT 537, 1989 SCCR 628; *Whigham v Howdle* 1996 SLT 1175; *Miller v Dick* 2000 JC 71, 1999 SCCR 919.
4 1984 SLT 437, 1984 SCCR 241.
5 1985 SCCR 214.

In *Gilligan v Tudhope*[1] the device produced a print-out which gave nonsensical times and dates for the test, but there appeared to be nothing wrong with the analytical function of the machine. It was held that in these circumstances the machine was not unreliable, and that the alternative procedure of the provision of a sample of blood or urine was not open. Presumably the defects described in this case could have been cured by parole evidence from the police officers who administered the test. In *Ross v Allan*[2], the device gave a reading of 75 microgrammes in 100 millilitres of breath in respect of the first specimen of breath, and a reading of zero for the second. It was held that these readings clearly showed that the analytical function of the machine was not operating properly, that the device should therefore be regarded as unreliable, and that the Crown did not have to provide expert evidence on the question of the unreliability of the machine. In *Lunney v Cardle*[3] the machine gave readings of 92 and 14 microgrammes respectively, and the extent of the discrepancy was held to be sufficient to justify the conclusion that the device was unreliable. In *Carson v Orr*[4] the two readings were 87 and 58 microgrammes; it was there considered reasonable for the police officers to decide that the machine was reliable.

In *Hodgkins v Carmichael*[5], the Camic device calibrated properly but the tape inside was twisted and did not produce a print-out. This was discovered an hour later and the print-out recovered and successfully used, although the machine had been declared at the earlier stage to be unreliable. In *Burnett v Smith*[6] a driver gave a specimen into the Camic device and the print-out gave readings of 39 and 55 microgrammes. The supervising officer considered the readings and also that at an appropriate point in the proceedings a green light flashed on the device, and concluded that the device was unreliable, and turned to the alternative procedure. The appeal court decided that the belief of the supervising officer that the device was unreliable was in fact wrong, but reasonable, and refused to fault the procedure. Further, it was specifically determined in that case that the test of the reliability of the device had to be a subjective one at the instance of the officers conducting the procedure, and in effect the appeal court

1 1986 JC 34, 1986 SLT 299, 1985 SCCR 434.
2 1986 JC 49, 1986 SLT 349, 1986 SCCR 100.
3 1988 SLT 440, 1988 SCCR 104.
4 1992 SCCR 260.
5 1989 SLT 514, 1989 SCCR 69.
6 1990 JC 119, 1990 SLT 537, 1989 SCCR 628.

concluded that the courts should support the conclusions of the supervising officers so long as these were reasonably reached. In *Miller v Dick*[1] it was enough for the prosecution that police officers reasonably believed that the Camic device was faulty because another officer has mistakenly informed them to that effect.

In *Currie v MacDougal*[2] it was decided that a Camic device which was not regularly maintained and was used as a training device was properly regarded as unreliable. However, the Crown will normally have to show that if a device is regarded as unreliable there is no other available and reliable device within the police station[3]. The fact that there is no other such device available may be inferred from the evidence of the procedure[4]. If there is no reliable device at the station where the requirement is made, the accused can be taken to another station where a reliable device is available[5].

The test of whether the machine is reliable is determined at the time the requirement is made[6]. In *Wilson v Webster*[7] the clock on the Camic was faulty, so police officers took a blood sample instead, which proved insufficient for analysis. They went back to the Camic and obtained a reading. This was held to be in order because the analytical function was accurate at the time the request was made, even although the clock was wrong. The blood sample, if insufficient, would therefore have been inadmissible.

If the accused wishes to claim that the device is unreliable, in the face of prosecution evidence that it is reliable, the onus is on him to establish his defence on the balance of probabilities[8].

In summary, if the Crown seeks to rely on the fact that the machine is unreliable in requiring the alternative procedure of a blood or urine specimen, it must be demonstrated from the print-out that the analytical function of the device is not operating correctly or satisfactorily. If there are other defects in the print-out which do not relate to the analytical function of the device, such defects may be curable by parole evidence. If the print-out is

---

1 2000 JC 71, 1999 SCCR 919.
2 1988 SLT 632, 1988 SCCR 266.
3 *Houston v McLeod* 1986 JC 96, 1986 SCCR 219; *Walker v Walkingshaw* 1991 SCCR 695.
4 *Welsh v McGlennan* 1992 SCCR 379.
5 *Tudhope v Fulton* 1987 SLT 419, 1986 SCCR 567.
6 *Ramage v Walkingshaw* 1992 SCCR 82.
7 1999 SCCR 747.
8 *Aitchison v Matheson* 1984 SCCR 83.

defective and inadmissible in evidence the Crown may rely on the visual testimony of the test from the supervising officers[1].

It must be remembered in considering all the foregoing cases that they involved the Camic Breath Analyser device which is no longer approved, and care may have to be taken in applying these authorities to other devices. However, as all such devices must have common operational features, most if not all of the cases cited will be directly applicable to any other breath analysis device.

5.8:7   Analyst's certificate (s 16(1)(b))

Under this part of the subsection, evidence of the proportion of alcohol in a specimen of blood or urine may, subject again to the provisions of s 16(3)–(6) of the Road Traffic Offenders Act 1988, be given by a document purporting to be 'a certificate signed by an authorised analyst as to the proportion of alcohol or any drug found in a specimen of blood or urine identified in the certificate'.

An 'authorised analyst' is defined in s 16(7).

As before, the prosecution have to prove that the specimen was taken from the accused and transmitted to the analyst[2]. However, the fact that the specimen has been sent for analysis may be inferred[3].

In *O'Brien v Ferguson*[4] a specimen taken at the county hospital was wrongly labelled as having been taken at the police station. There was contradictory parole evidence as to whether the specimen was transmitted to a laboratory for analysis. It was held that there was insufficient evidence to link the specimen taken with the specimen analysed, and the driver was acquitted.

In *McKinnon v Westwater*[5] a specimen taken at Tain was wrongly marked as having been taken at Evanton; parole evidence was allowed which linked the specimen to the accused. This was followed in *McPherson v McNaughton*[6] when there was a discrepancy between the motorist's name on the specimen and on the certificate.

---

1 *Smith v MacDonald, Smith v Davie* 1984 JC 73, 1984 SLT 398 at 401, 1984 SCCR 190.
2 *O'Brien v Ferguson* 1987 SLT 96, 1986 SCCR 155.
3 *McLeary v Douglas* 1978 SLT 140; *Tudhope v Corrigall* 1982 SCCR 558.
4 1987 SLT 96, 1986 SCCR 155.
5 1987 SCCR 730.
6 1992 SLT 600, 1992 SCCR 434.

The certificate must state that the signatories have themselves carried out the relevant examination, unless the evidence is agreed[1].

In a case where an analyst was cited to give evidence and had no recollection of the particular analysis in question but refreshed his memory from a register of print-outs which were possibly still extant but which were not produced, it was held that the analyst's evidence was competent and did not breach the best evidence rule[2].

In a case decided under earlier legislation[3], it was held that the certificate was intended to vouch the analyst's conclusion and not the provenance of the specimen; accordingly factual errors in the certificate did not make the analyst's conclusions contained therein inadmissible[4].

5.8:8   Taking of blood specimens (s 16(2))

Section 16(2) of the Road Traffic Offenders Act 1988 provides as follows:

'Subject to subsections (3) and (4) below, evidence that a specimen of blood was taken from the accused with his consent by a medical practitioner may be given by the production of a document purporting to certify that fact and to be signed by a medical practitioner.'

Subsections (3) and (4) are concerned with the requirements of service of certificates. What constitutes a 'medical practitioner' is discussed at 4.11:6 above. Section 16(5) of the Act also applies for the purposes of this subsection.

Section 11(4) of the Road Traffic Act 1988 also provides that a person provides a specimen of blood if, and only if, he consents to its being taken by a medical practitioner, and it is so taken.

Accordingly, failure to observe the provisions of s 16(2) will be fatal to any prosecution based on a specimen of blood, notwithstanding the terms of s 15(2) (as amended) of the Road Traffic Offenders Act 1988. If the specimen is not taken by a medical

---

1 *Normand v Wotherspoon* 1993 JC 248, 1994 SLT 487, 1993 SCCR 912; *Donnelly v Schrikel* 1995 SLT 537.
2 *McLeod v Fraser* 1987 SLT 142, 1986 SCCR 271.
3 Road Safety Act 1967, s 3(8).
4 *Lawrie v Stevenson* 1968 JC 71, 1968 SLT 342.

practitioner, or if the specimen is taken without the accused's consent, the specimen will not be allowed in evidence and evidence of the analysis of the specimen will be inadmissible. The court must be satisfied that full and proper consent has been given by the accused to the taking of the specimen[1].

Reference should be made to 5.3:2ff above.

5.8:9   Service of statement or certificate (s 16(3))

Section 16(3) of the Road Traffic Offenders Act 1988 reads as follows:

'Subject to subsection (4) below –
(a) a document purporting to be such a statement or such a certificate (or both such a statement and such a certificate as is mentioned in subsection (1)(a) above) is admissible in evidence on behalf of the prosecution in pursuance of this section only if a copy of it either has been handed to the accused when the document was produced or has been served on him not later than seven days before the hearing, and
(b) any other document is so admissible only if a copy of it has been served on the accused not later than seven days before the hearing.'

This subsection has to be read along with the following subsection (s 16(4)); and also along with s 16(5) and (6).

Section 16(3) provides for the requirements of service in respect of both kinds of certificate described in s 16(1). In particular, s 16(3)(a) refers to the statement and certificate comprised in the print-out automatically produced by the breath analysis device. Service of this statement and certificate can be effected on the accused at the time the device produces the print-out. It is submitted that this means that the document or documents must be given to the accused in the course of the procedure involved in the taking of the specimen, and that, for example, handing the document to the accused after he has left the police station does not comply with the requirement of service. Alternatively, in accordance with the second part of s 16(3)(a), where the accused has not been handed a copy of the document at the time it was produced, service of the document must be made on him not later than seven days before the trial diet. By virtue of s 16(3)(b), the requirement of service is satisfied in the case of an analyst's

---

1 *Friel v Dickson* 1992 SLT 1086, 1992 SCCR 513.

certificate (in terms of s 16(1)(b) of the Act), or a doctor's certificate (in terms of s 16(2) of the Act), by service of such certificates on the accused not later than seven days before the trial diet.[1]

If service of documents or certificates is not effected by either of the methods described in s 16(3), then the documents or certificates are inadmissible in evidence, and the prosecution cannot rely on the evidence contained within the documents or certificates to secure a conviction[2]. However, in the event that the certificate and statement automatically produced by a breath analyser device are not handed to the accused at the time and were not subsequently served on the accused, and thus became inadmissible in evidence, it is still open to the Crown to secure a conviction on the basis of parole evidence from the police officers who administered the test of the readings they observed on the visual display unit of the breath analyser device[3].

Even if the accused declines to take the copy of the print-out at the time when it is produced by the breath analyser device, in terms of the first part of the subsection, then service of the copy must still be made in terms of the second part of the subsection[4]. If service in terms of this subsection has not been effected, objection to the production of the principal (which must be lodged) normally requires to be taken before the close of the Crown case[5].

The fact that certificates were served with a complaint which was dropped and substituted by a fresh complaint which was not accompanied by further certificates does not invalidate the initial service of the certificates, which remain valid for the purposes of the second complaint[6].

It is not necessary for the prosecution, in a case based on a blood or urine specimen, to produce the specimen on which the certificate is based[7].

---

1 All reference to 'days' in this and the following subsection means clear and full days (*McMillan v HM Advocate* 1983 SLT 24, 1982 SCCR 309).
2 *McLeary v Douglas* 1978 JC 57, 1978 SLT 140.
3 *Gunn v Brown* 1987 SLT 94, 1986 SCCR 179.
4 *Annan v Crawford* 1984 SCCR 382; *McDerment v O'Brien* 1985 SLT 485, 1985 SCCR 50.
5 *Skeen v Murphy* 1978 SLT (Notes) 2; however, reference should also be made to *McLeary v Douglas* 1978 JC 57, 1978 SLT 140 and *Macauley v Wilson* 1995 SLT 1070.
6 *Buonaccorsi v Tudhope* 1982 SLT 528, 1982 SCCR 249.
7 *Williamson v Aitchison* 1982 SLT 399, 1982 SCCR 102.

5.8:10   Certificate not admissible in evidence (s 16(4))

Section 16(4) of the Road Traffic Offenders Act 1988 provides:

'A document purporting to be a certificate (or so much of a document as purports to be a certificate) is not so admissible if the accused, not later than three days before the hearing or within such further time as the court may in special circumstances allow, has served notice on the prosecutor requiring the attendance at the hearing of the person by whom the document purports to be signed.'

This subsection applies not only to the documents automatically produced by a breath analyser device in terms of s 16(1)(a) and s 16(3)(a), but also to certificates supplied by analysts or doctors in terms of s 16(1)(b) and s 16(2) respectively. If the defence wish to avoid the evidential consequences of s 16(3), then notice must be served on the Crown to this effect not later than three clear days before the trial diet. The court has the discretion to allow later intimation by the accused, but will normally only exercise this discretion on cause shown. The effect of such intimation by the accused is to require the police officer who signs the certificate on the print-out to attend the trial diet to give evidence to the effect that he did so; or more commonly in practice, to require the presence of the authorised analyst who has examined the blood or urine specimen to speak to his findings, usually with a view to establishing one of the statutory defences.

If the accused wishes to challenge the contents of the print-out or the operation of the machine, he must do so by giving notice in terms of this subsection; otherwise the print-out, its contents, and the operation of the device cannot be challenged[1].

5.8:11   Sufficiency of evidence (s 16(5))

Section 16(5) of the Road Traffic Offenders Act 1988 provides:

'(5) In Scotland –
  (a) a document produced in evidence on behalf of the prosecution in pursuance of subsection (1) or (2) above and, where the person by whom the document was signed is called as a witness, the evidence of that person, shall be sufficient evidence of the facts stated in the document, and

---

1 *Annan v Mitchell* 1984 SCCR 32.

(b) a written execution purporting to be signed by the person who handed to or served on the accused or the prosecutor a copy of the document or of the notice in terms of subsection (3) or (4) above, together with, where approporiate, a post office receipt for the registered or recorded delivery letter shall be sufficient evidence of the handing or service of such a copy or notice.'

The effect of similar provisions under previous legislation was considered in *MacNeill v Perrie*[1].

5.8:12 Definition

'Purporting to be signed' – see *Donlon v MacKinnon*[2].

5.8:13 Evidence

In *Donoghue v Allan*[3] the police officer who signed the certificate part of the print-out was not called as a witness, but it was held that this did not preclude a conviction if there was adequate other evidence vouching the document. In *McLeod v Fraser*[4] the analyst's certificate was not referred to in evidence (although it was a production) but the analyst himself gave evidence. It was held that notwithstanding the terms of this subsection the analyst's testimony could be regarded as satisfying the best evidence rule.

The question of errors and defects in the certificates is discussed at 5.8:5 and 5.8:6 above.

5.8:14 Methods of service (s 16(6))

Section 16(6) of the Road Traffic Offenders Act 1988 provides:

'A copy of a certificate required by this section to be served on the accused or a notice required by this section to be served on the prosecutor may be served personally or sent by registered post or recorded delivery service.'

1 1978 CO Circulars A/13.
2 1981 SCCR 219.
3 1985 SCCR 93.
4 1987 SLT 142, 1986 SCCR 271.

This subsection prescribes the methods of service of the certificates, statements and notices referred to elsewhere in the section.

It is submitted that, in Scotland, personal service means that the documents in question must be handed personally to the accused, or to the procurator fiscal or a member of his staff, although in England effective service was held to have taken place where the documents were given to the accused's agent[1] and even, in one case, to the accused's counsel[2]. It is considered doubtful that these last two cases would be followed in Scotland; see *Geddes v Hamilton*[3].

5.8:15   Qualified analyst (s 16(7))

Section 16(7) of the Road Traffic Offenders Act 1988 provides:

'In this section "authorised analyst" means –
(a) any person possessing the qualifications prescribed by regulations made under section 76 of the Food Act 1984 or section 27 of the Food and Drugs (Scotland) Act 1956 as qualifying persons for appointment as public analysts under those Acts, and
(b) any other person authorised by the Secretary of State to make analyses for the purposes of this section.'

This subsection provides the definition of the term 'authorised analyst' referred to in s 16(1)(b) (see 5.8:7 above).

---

1 *Anderton v Kinnaird* [1986] RTR 11.
2 *Penman v Parker* [1986] RTR 403.
3 1986 SLT 536, 1986 SCCR 165.

Chapter Six

Miscellaneous; hospital patients; detention and interpretation

6.1 PROTECTION FOR HOSPITAL PATIENTS

6.1:1 Section 9

Section 9 of the Road Traffic Act 1988 provides:

'(1) While a person is at hospital as a patient he shall not be required to provide a specimen of breath for a breath test or to provide a specimen for a laboratory test unless the medical practitioner in immediate charge of his case has been notified of the proposal to make the requirement; and –
   (a) if the requirement is then made, it shall be for the provision of a specimen at the hospital, but
   (b) if the medical practitioner objects on the ground specified in subsection (2) below, the requirement shall not be made.
(2) The ground on which the medical practitioner may object is that the requirement or the provision of a specimen or, in the case of a specimen of blood or urine, the warning required under section 7(7) of this Act, would be prejudicial to the proper care and treatment of the patient.'

6.1:2 Definitions

'While a person is at hospital as a patient.' – This phrase is to be strictly construed, and does not, for example, include a person in an ambulance waiting to go to hospital. Such a person will not qualify for the protection conferred by this section[1]. The term 'hospital' is defined in s 11 (see 6.3:1 below).

'Provision of a specimen.' – The specimens referred to are a specimen of breath for a breath test in terms of s 6 of the Road Traffic Act 1988, or a specimen of blood or urine in terms of s 7(1) (b). The section does not refer to a specimen of breath for analysis in terms of s 7(1)(a) which can only be required at a police station[2].

'Medical practitioner' – see 4.11:6 above.

6.1:3 General application

It should be noted that the constable must seek out the medical practitioner's opinion before he can require a specimen of a person who is in hospital as a patient. In particular, it is clear that in terms of subsection (2), the constable must obtain the medical practitioner's opinion not only as to whether the patient can provide a sample of breath into the breathalyser or a specimen of blood or urine but, as a quite separate issue, whether the requirement or request for a specimen, or the warning which must be given in terms of s 7(7) of the Road Traffic Act 1988, to the effect that a failure to provide a blood or urine specimen may render the driver liable to prosecution, would be prejudicial to the proper care and treatment of the patient.

Failure to observe the requirements imposed by this section will render the specimen inadmissible (see 5.3:2ff above). It has not been decided whether a requirement made by a police officer, in the face of an objection by the medical practitioner in charge, will constitute a reasonable excuse for failing to provide a specimen in terms of s 8(7), but this point is probably academic. By virtue of s 15(4) of the Road Traffic Offenders Act 1988, and s 11(4) of the Road Traffic Act 1988, any specimen of blood has to be taken by a medical practitioner with the accused's consent.

---

1 *Manz v Miln* 1977 JC 78; see also *MacNeill v England* 1971 SLT 103; and *Watt v MacNeill* 1980 SLT 178.
2 Road Traffic Act 1988, s 7(2).

What should happen when a doctor at a hospital has advised that a driver should not give a breath specimen was raised, but not settled, in *Anderson v McClory*[1].

6.2 POWER TO DETAIN PERSONS AFFECTED BY ALCOHOL OR DRUGS

6.2:1 Section 10

Section 10 of the Road Traffic Act 1988 (as amended by the Road Traffic Act 1991, Sch 4, para 43) provides:

'(1) Subject to subsections (2) and (3) below, a person required to provide a specimen of breath, blood or urine may afterwards be detained at a police station until it appears to the constable that, were the person then driving or attempting to drive a mechanically propelled vehicle on a road, he would not be committing an offence under section 4 or 5 of this Act.

(2) A person shall not be detained in pursuance of this section if it appears to a constable that there is no likelihood of his driving or attempting to drive a mechanically propelled vehicle whilst his ability to drive properly is impaired or whilst the proportion of alcohol in his breath or urine exceeds the prescribed limit.

(3) A constable must consult a medical practitioner on any question arising under this section whether a person's ability to drive properly is or might be impaired through drugs, and must act on the medical practitioner's advice.'

This section in effect allows a police officer to detain any motorist who has been required to provide a specimen of breath, blood or urine at the police station until he is satisfied either that, in his opinion, the level of alcohol in the accused's body is such that were he to drive he would no longer be committing an offence or that there is no likelihood of him driving. The decision in these matters is left entirely to the constable in question, and there is no sanction provided by the section in respect of any abuse of power in respect thereof other than by making a complaint in the normal way. However, if the accused's condition arises from the consumption of drugs, the constable is required to seek out a medical practitioner's advice on the question of whether the

[1] 1991 SCCR 571.

accused's ability to drive is impaired and, having done so, the constable must act on the advice given.

6.3 INTERPRETATION (S 11)

Section 11 (as amended) of the Road Traffic Act 1988 provides:

'(1) The following provisions apply for the interpretation of sections 3A to 10 of this Act.
(2) In those sections –
    "breath test" means a preliminary test for the purpose of obtaining, by means of a device of a type approved by the Secretary of State, an indication whether the proportion of alcohol in a person's breath or blood is likely to exceed the prescribed limit,
    "drug" includes any intoxicant other than alcohol,
    "fail" includes refuse,
    "hospital" means an institution which provides medical or surgical treatment for in-patients or out-patients,
    "the prescribed limit" means, as the case may require –
        (a) 35 microgrammes of alcohol in 100 millilitres of breath,
        (b) 80 milligrammes of alcohol in 100 millilitres of blood, or
        (c) 107 milligrammes of alcohol in 100 millilitres of urine, or such other proportions as may be prescribed by regulations made by the Secretary of State.
(3) A person does not provide a specimen of breath for a breath test or for analysis unless the specimen –
    (a) is sufficient to enable the test or the analysis to be carried out, and
    (b) is provided in such a way as to enable the objective of the test or analysis to be satisfactorily achieved.
(4) A person provides a specimen of blood if and only if he consents to its being taken by a medical practitioner and it is so taken.'

The effect of the interpretation section has been referred to *passim* in the preceding chapters on sections 3A–10 of the Road Traffic Act 1988 and ss 15 and 16 of the Road Traffic Offenders Act 1988.

Chapter Seven

Other road traffic offences

7.1   GENERAL: HIGHWAY CODE

In addition to the offences covered by ss 1–11 of the Road Traffic
Act 1988 and described in the preceding chapters, there are a very

large number of further offences, directions and regulations contained in the extensive legislative instruments concerned with road traffic. The Highway Code does not create offences as such; rather it contains a series of directions for the guidance of persons using roads. Although, in terms of s 38(1) of the Road Traffic Act 1988, the Highway Code continues to have effect, a failure *per se* on the part of anyone using the road to observe the provisions of the code does not make that person guilty of a criminal offence. Section 38(7) of the Act provides:

'A failure on the part of a person to observe a provision of the Highway Code shall not of itself render that person liable to criminal proceedings of any kind but any such failure may in any proceedings (whether civil or criminal, and including proceedings for an offence under the Traffic Acts, the Public Passenger Vehicles Act 1981 or sections 18 to 23 of the Transport Act 1985) be relied upon by any party to the proceedings as tending to establish or negative any liability which is in question in those proceedings.'

Accordingly, the provisions of the Highway Code may provide useful guidance in determining whether a civil wrong, or an offence in terms of any of the principal Acts described, has or has not been committed[1]. The Secretary of State has the responsibility for issuing the Highway Code and has the power to revise it from time to time as the need arises, although in terms of s 38(5) of the Act he is obliged to consult such representative organisations as he thinks fit. Further, the Secretary of State and local authorities have powers and responsibilities to furnish road safety training and information, in terms of ss 39 and 40. The Highway Code is published by The Stationery Office, and is available from its own and some other bookshops, as are other Department of Transport motoring publications. There follows a description of some of the principal traffic offences contained in the legislation, although it must be remembered that there are a very large number of other provisions which do not often feature in practice. The penalties for offences under the Road Traffic Act 1988 (as amended by the Road Traffic Act 1991) are contained in Schedule 2 to the Road Traffic Offenders Act 1988 (as amended by Schedule 2 to the Road Traffic Act 1991), which also includes penalties in respect of other offences such as those described in the Road Traffic Regulation Act 1984 and contraventions of the Construction and Use regulations in terms of s 42 of the Road Traffic Act 1988 (as amended by

1 *McCrone v Normand* 1989 SLT 332.

s 8 of the Road Traffic Act 1991). Penalties in respect of offences under other Acts and regulations are normally found within the body of such legislation.

7.2   RACES AND TRIALS

7.2:1   Section 12

Section 12 of the Road Traffic Act 1988 (as amended) provides:

'(1) A person who promotes or takes part in a race or trial of speed between motor vehicles on a highway is guilty of an offence.

(2) In this section "highway" means, in England and Wales, a public highway and, in Scotland, a public road.'

7.2:2   Definitions

'*Motor vehicle*': see 1.2:1 above.

'*Public road*': see 1.8:1 and 1.8:2 above.

7.2:3   General application

For an offence to be committed under this section, it is not necessary that the race or trial of speed should have been pre-arranged. In *Ferrari v McNaughton*[1] the evidence indicated that two vehicles engaged upon a race or trial of speed quite spontaneously. In these circumstances, the appeal court held that a contravention of s 12 of the Road Traffic Act 1988 had occurred. No definition exists within the legislation of what constitutes a race or trial of speed and whether such an event has taken place will depend on the facts and circumstances in each case.

Competitions or trials may be permitted to take place on the road, provided that they are properly authorised and conducted in accordance with the relevant regulations[2].

1 1979 SLT (Notes) 62, 1979 CO Circulars A/13.
2 Road Traffic Act 1988, s 13; reference must also be made to s 13A, added by the Road Traffic Act 1991, s 5.

Similar provisions regulating cycle racing on public roads are found in s 31[1].

7.3   SEATBELTS AND PROTECTIVE HEADGEAR

Primary seatbelt legislation is found in ss 14, 15 and 15A of the Road Traffic Act 1988. Section 15A was introduced by the Motor Vehicles (Safety Equipment for Children) Act 1991. In particular, the requirement to wear a seatbelt imposed on the driver and adult front passenger is found in s 14, and further described in the Motor Vehicles (Wearing of Seat Belts) Regulations 1993[2]. These regulations have to be read along with regulations 46, 47 and 48 of the Road Vehicles (Construction and Use) Regulations 1986[3] which define the relevant terms and vehicle exemptions. Use exemptions are found in regulation 6 of the 1993 Regulations. These exemptions apply chiefly to those driving a vehicle constructed or adapted for the delivery or collection of goods or mail to consumers or addresses for the purpose of making local rounds or collections; drivers performing a manoeuvre, including reversing; the holder of a certificate in the prescribed form signed by a medical practitioner that it is inadvisable on medical grounds for the driver to wear a seatbelt; a constable or similar person protecting or escorting another person; firemen; taxi drivers; disabled persons wearing seatbelts; certain processions; and those testing a vehicle under trade plates. It is also an offence to wear a seatbelt which does not comply with the regulations; that in itself, however, may constitute a further offence.

Failing to wear a seatbelt by an adult in the front and rear of a motor car is covered by regulation 5, and the description of seat belts to be worn by children in the rear of a vehicle are covered by regulation 8. Seat belts to be worn by children in the front of a vehicle are described in the Motor Vehicle (Wearing of Seat Belts by Children in Front Seats) Regulations 1993[4]. The vehicles which require to have seatbelts fitted are described in regulations 46 and 47 (as amended, above) of the Road Vehicles (Construction and Use) Regulations 1986.

1 As amended by RTA 1991, Sch 4, para 49.
2 SI 1993/176.
3 SI 1986/1078 (as amended by SI 1987/1133; SI 1989/1478; and SI 1991/2003).
4 SI 1993/31.

The driver is guilty of an offence if he or any child is not wearing a seatbelt; the driver is not guilty of any offence if a seatbelt fails to be worn by an adult passenger[1]. These offences fall under the fixed penalty procedure.

Protective headgear for motor cyclists is governed by ss 16, 17 and 18 of the Road Traffic Act 1988, and the Motor Cycles (Protective Helmets) Regulations 1998[2].

7.4   TRAFFIC DIRECTIONS: CONSTABLE'S DIRECTIONS (S 35)

7.4:1   General

By virtue of s 35(1) of the Road Traffic Act 1988, where a constable is engaged in the regulation of traffic in a road, a person who, while driving or propelling a vehicle, neglects or refuses to stop the vehicle or make it proceed in or keep to a particular line of traffic when directed to do so by the constable in the execution of his duty shall be guilty of an offence. Section 35(2) gives similar powers to a constable to enable a traffic survey to be carried out. Any vehicle is covered by this section.

Whether an offence under this section has taken place is a matter of fact. A police officer does not have to be specially authorised to regulate traffic; however the Crown must show that the officer was acting in the execution of his duty. The section, however, does not specify that the constable must be in uniform. It is important to note that, in terms of s 21(3) of the Road Traffic Offenders Act 1988, the Crown can secure a conviction under this section on the evidence of only one witness[3].

It would appear to be a possible defence to a charge of this kind that the constable was acting capriciously[4]. In *Keane v McSkimming*[5], it was observed that it was sufficient for the prosecution to show that the signal given by the police officer was obvious; it is not necessary for a conviction that it is established in evidence that the driver in fact saw the signal. However, it is also

---

1 Road Traffic Act 1988, s 14(3).
2 SI 1998/1807.
3 See also *Sutherland v Aitchison* 1970 SLT (Notes) 48.
4 *Beard v Wood* [1980] RTR 454, [1980] Crim LR 384.
5 1983 SCCR 220.

clear from this case that the fact that the driver did not see the signal may in appropriate circumstances be a good defence to the charge.

7.4:2 Traffic signs (s 36)

It is an offence in terms of s 36 of the Road Traffic Act 1988 for a person driving or propelling a vehicle not to comply with a traffic sign of the prescribed size, colour and type or as otherwise authorised by the provisions of the Road Traffic Regulation Act 1984. The sign must indicate a statutory prohibition, restriction or requirement, and must also be properly established in terms of the legislation[1]. However, any traffic sign placed at or near a road is presumed to be properly authorised and lawfully placed unless the contrary is proved[2]. At the same time, any traffic sign must conform exactly to the description of that sign given in the appropriate regulations[3]. In *Skeen v Smith*[4] a sign displayed on a pole at a road junction was erected properly, but the corresponding 'stop' sign marked on the road was not entirely clear. It was held that this did not entitle the driver to ignore the sign on the pole. If lights are showing green in one direction, and there is evidence that the system is working properly, the court may assume that the counter lights are at red[5], provided that there is some evidence to support that conclusions such as that the lights are working correctly[6].

Part V of the Road Traffic Regulation Act 1984 gives general provisions as to traffic signs, and allows the Secretary of State to delegate the responsibility for placing such signs to the local authority. The principal regulations are the Traffic Signs Regulations and General Directions 1994[7].

As in s 35, in terms of s 21(3) of the Road Traffic Offenders Act 1988, a conviction for an offence under s 36 may follow from the evidence of one witness only[8].

---

1 Road Traffic Act 1988, s 35(2).
2 *Spiers v Normand* 1995 JC 147, 1996 SLT 78; RTA 1988, s 36(3).
3 *Davies v Heatley* [1971] RTR 145.
4 1979 SLT 295.
5 *Pacitti v Copeland* 1963 SLT (Notes) 52.
6 *Inwar v Normand* 1997 SCCR 6.
7 SI 1994/1519.
8 See also *Sutherland v Aitchison* 1970 SLT (Notes) 48.

For the prosecution of traffic light offences using photographic evidence, see 7.8:3 below.

7.4:3   Directions to pedestrians (s 37)

A pedestrian proceeding across or along a carriageway in contravention of a direction to stop given by a constable engaged in regulating traffic in the execution of his duty, is guilty of an offence[1]. The constable must be in uniform. Unlike the two preceding sections, s 21(3) of the Road Traffic Offenders Act 1988 does not apply to this offence, and the prosecution must offer full corroborative evidence to secure a conviction.

A constable may also require a person committing an offence under s 37 of the Road Traffic Act 1988 to give his name and address, and if that person refuses to do so, his refusal constitutes a further offence[2].

For possible defences to a charge under s 37, reference should be made to 7.4:1 above.

7.5   POWERS OF POLICE OFFICERS TO STOP VEHICLES AND REQUIRE INFORMATION (S 163)

7.5:1   General

By virtue of s 163 of the Road Traffic Act 1988[3], a person driving a mechanically propelled vehicle on a road, or riding a cycle on a road, must stop on being required to do so by a police constable in uniform. Failure so to stop is an offence. It is sufficient for a conviction that the Crown proves that the policeman's signal was obvious; it does not have to be proved that the driver saw the signal[4]. This offence is not one provable by the evidence of one witness only in terms of s 21 of the Road Traffic Offenders Act 1988; full corroborated evidence is required for conviction.

---

1 Road Traffic Act 1988, s 37.
2 RTA 1988, s 169.
3 As amended by the Road Traffic Act 1991, Sch 4, para 67.
4 *Keane v McSkimming* 1983 SCCR 220.

7.5:2 Duty to give information and documents (s 164)

By virtue of s 164 of the Road Traffic Act 1988[1], a police constable or vehicle examiner may require certain classes of person to produce their driving licence. The express purpose of this production of the licence is to enable the constable to ascertain the name and address of the holder of the licence, and its date and authority of issue. The classes of person of whom this requirement can be made are: a person driving a motor vehicle on a road; a person whom a constable has reasonable cause to believe was driving a motor vehicle on a road when it was involved in an accident or who has committed a motor vehicle offence; a person who is supervising a provisional licence holder, or who was supervising a provisional driver when an accident or a suspected offence occurred. If the driver is not able to produce his licence at the material time when he is required to do so, he can escape conviction in terms of subsections (7) and (8). Subsection (7) arises when a driver has previously surrendered his licence to a police officer or other authorised person in terms of the fixed penalty procedure and s 56 of the Road Traffic Offenders Act 1988. Subsection (8) covers the normal situation where a driver does not have his licence with him at the time the requirement was made. In those circumstances, the driver can escape conviction if (a) he produces his licence personally within seven days at a nominated police station, or (b) if he produces it at the police station as soon as reasonably practicable, or if he proves that it was not reasonably practicable for him to produce it to the police station before the day on which proceedings were commenced by the service of the complaint. In association with the requirement to produce a licence at a nominated police station, the police officer will normally issue a standard form (HORT 1) to the driver.

It should be noted that in certain circumstances the officer may seize a licence produced to him[2].

7.5:3 Duty to give name and address and certain documents (s 165)

By virtue of s 165 of the Road Traffic Act 1988[3], broadly the same categories of person as are described in s 164 (apart from the

1 As amended by the Road Traffic Act 1991, Sch 4, para 68.
2 Road Traffic Act 1988, s 164(3) and (5).
3 As amended by the Road Traffic Act 1991, Sch 4, para 69.

drivers of invalid carriages) may also be required by a constable to give their name and address, and the name and address of the owner of the vehicle. In addition, holders of a full licence may be required to produce certain documents relevant to the vehicle for examination, namely the insurance certificate, the MOT certificate and any relevant goods vehicle test certificate. There may be further duties to provide information in terms of s 171 (see 7.5:9 below). Again, it is a defence to a charge under this section if the driver produces the document or any other required evidence to a nominated police station within seven days, or as soon as reasonably practicable, or if he proves that it was not reasonably practicable for him to have presented the necessary information to the police station before the day on which any complaint was served.

7.5:4   Duty to give name and address in dangerous and careless driving (s 168)

By virtue of s 168 of the Road Traffic Act 1988[1], the driver of a vehicle who is alleged to have committed an offence under s 2 or 3 of the Act (dangerous or careless driving) must give his name and address to any person (not just a police officer) having reasonable grounds for requiring that information. Failure so to give the name and address, or the giving of a false name and address, is an offence. What constitutes reasonable grounds for making the requirement is a matter of fact in each case. The same requirement can be made in a case of dangerous or careless cycling in terms of ss 28 and 29 of the Act. Any person who fails to give his name and address or to produce his licence in these circumstances may be arrested without warrant[2]. In a prosecution under s 167, evidence identifying a driver who claimed he did not know who was driving at the material time is admissible[3].

7.5:5   Duty on pedestrian to give name and address (s 169)

A constable may require a person who is committing an offence under s 37 of the Road Traffic Act 1988 (failure by a pedestrian to

---

1 As amended by the Road Traffic Act 1991, Sch 4, para 71.
2 Road Traffic Act 1988, s 167.
3 *Clark v Allan* 1988 SLT 274, 1987 SCCR 333.

comply with a direction to stop given by a constable) to give his name and address, and failure to do so will constitute a further offence[1] (see 7.4:3 above).

7.5:6 Duty to give information as to identity of driver (s 172)

Section 172 of the Road Traffic Act 1988[2], requires the keeper or driver of a vehicle, or any other person, to give information to a duly authorised police officer as to the identity of the driver of the vehicle at any time the driver is alleged to have been guilty of most road traffic offences. The section is frequently used in the course of police investigations and reads in full as follows:

'(1) This section applies –
    (a) to any offence under the preceding provisions of this Act except–
        (i) an offence under Part V, or
        (ii) an offence under section 13, 16, 51(2), 61(4), 67(9), 68(4), 96 or 120,
    and to an offence under section 178 of this Act,
    (b) to any offence under sections 25, 26 or 27 of the Road Traffic Offenders Act 1988,
    (c) to any offence against any other enactment relating to the use of vehicles on roads, except an offence under paragraph 8 of Schedule 1 to the Road Traffic (Driver Licensing and Information Systems) Act 1989, and
    (d) to manslaughter, or in Scotland culpable homicide, by the driver of a motor vehicle.
(2) Where the driver of a vehicle is alleged to be guilty of an offence to which this section applies –
    (a) the person keeping the vehicle shall give such information as to the identity of the driver as he may be required to give by or on behalf of a chief officer of police, and
    (b) any other person shall if required as stated above give any information which it is in his power to give and may lead to identification of the driver.
In this subsection references to the driver of a vehicle include references to the person riding a cycle.
(3) Subject to the following provisions, a person who fails to comply with a requirement under subsection (2) above shall be guilty of an offence.

1 Road Traffic Act 1988, s 169.
2 As amended by the Road Traffic Act 1991, s 21 and the Vehicle Excise and Regulation Act 1994, s 63 and Sch 2.

(4) A person shall not be guilty of an offence by virtue of paragraph (a) of subsection (2) above if he shows that he did not know and could not with reasonable diligence have ascertained who the driver of the vehicle was.

(5) Where a body corporate is guilty of an offence under this section and the offence is proved to have been committed with the consent or connivance of, or to be attributable to neglect on the part of, a director, manager, secretary or other similar officer of the body corporate, or a person who was purporting to act in any such capacity, he, as well as the body corporate, is guilty of that offence and liable to be proceeded against and punished accordingly.

(6) Where the alleged offender is a body corporate, or in Scotland a partnership or an unincorporated association, or the proceedings are brought against him by virtue of subsection (5) above or subsection (11) below, subsection (4) above shall not apply unless, in addition to the matters there mentioned, the alleged offender shows that no record was kept of the persons who drove the vehicle and that the failure to keep a record was reasonable.

(7) A requirement under subsection (2) may be made by written notice served by post; and where it is so made –
    (a) it shall have effect as a requirement to give the information within the period of 28 days beginning with the day on which the notice is served, and
    (b) the person on whom the notice is served shall not be guilty of an offence under this section if he shows either that he gave the information as soon as reasonably practicable after the end of that period or that it has not been reasonably practicable for him to give it.

(8) Where the person on whom a notice under subsection (7) above is to be served is a body corporate, the notice is duly served if it is served on the secretary or clerk of that body.

(9) For the purposes of section 7 of the Interpretation Act 1978 as it applies for the purposes of this section the proper address of any person in relation to the service on him of a notice under subsection (7) above is –
    (a) in the case of the secretary or clerk of a body corporate, that of the registered or principal office of that body or (if the body corporate is the registered keeper of the vehicle concerned) the registered address, and
    (b) in any other case, his last known address at the time of service.

(10) In this section –
    "registered address", in relation to the registered keeper of a vehicle, means the address recorded in the record kept under the Vehicle Excise and Registration Act 1994 with respect to that vehicle as being that person's address, and
    "registered keeper", in relation to a vehicle, means the person in whose name the vehicle is registered under that Act;
and references to the driver of a vehicle include references to the rider of a cycle.

(11) Where, in Scotland, an offence under this section is committed by a partnership or by an unincorporated association other than a partnership and is proved to have been committed with the consent or connivance or in consequence of the negligence of a partner in the partnership or, as the case may be, a person concerned in the management or control of the association, he (as well as the partnership or association) shall be guilty of the offence.'

7.5:7 Definitions (s 172)

'*Keeper of the vehicle.*' This phrase is intended to refer to the person in whose custody the vehicle is, at the time of making the requirement. It is submitted that the keeper of any vehicle is not necessarily confined to the person who is the registered owner. The various parts of the section appear to draw a distinction between the registered keeper and the person keeping the vehicle.

'*Any other person.*' This phrase includes the driver himself[1]. Thus, where a police officer is investigating an alleged offence in terms of s 172(1) of the Road Traffic Act 1988, he is entitled to ask the person who is said to have been driving at the material time to confirm whether or not he was driving at the time the alleged offence is said to have been committed.

'*By or on behalf of a chief officer of police.*' This phrase includes any police officer whom the Chief Constable of the area has authorised to make the requirement on his behalf. The Chief Constable may, but does not have to, make a specific authorisation to each individual officer; a general authorisation may be given to particular officers to exercise this power[2]. A police officer who has not been duly authorised in terms of this section cannot ask the driver or any other person to confirm the driver's identity at the material time in terms of this section[3].

7.5:8 General application (s 172)

The provisions of s 172 of the Road Traffic Act 1988, as amended by the Road Traffic Act 1991, are significantly widened, and are

---

1 *Foster v Farrell* 1963 SLT 182.
2 *Gray v Farrell* 1969 SLT 250.
3 *Foster v Farrell* 1963 SLT 182.

specifically framed for the purpose of giving police officers the power to carry out the new procedures involved in the automatic detection of road traffic offences. Section 172(2) makes it clear that the requirement to provide information can be made of the keeper of the vehicle or anyone else. In particular the requirement can be made of officers of a company; this is to allow the identification of the drivers of fleet or hire vehicles. A requirement to furnish the police with the name of the driver is not a breach of the European Convention on Human Rights[1]. At present it is, however, incompetent to use this information to convict an accused driver on the view that it is a contravention of his human rights, but this decision is under appeal to the Privy Council[2].

It is a defence to an offence charged under this section that the person required to provide the information can demonstrate to the satisfaction of the court that he did not know and could not with reasonable diligence have ascertained who the driver of the vehicle was[3]. This defence is not available to a body corporate, partnership or unincorporated association unless in addition to the matters referred to in s 172(4) the accused shows that no record was kept of the person who drove the vehicle and that the failure to keep a record was reasonable[4]. The powers contained in this section are crucial to the operation of the automatic detection of offences which is described at 7.8:3 below.

By virtue of the Road Traffic Act 1991, Sch 2, para 30, which amends Schedule 2 to the Road Traffic Offenders Act 1988, the offence of failing to give information carries obligatory endorsement and three penalty points and discretionary disqualification. These penalties do not, however, apply to officers of bodies corporate charged in terms of s 172(5)–(11).

The offence of failing to give the required information under s 172 can be proved by the evidence of a single witness[5].

It is a defence to an offence alleged under this section that the person required to provide the information can demonstrate to the satisfaction of the court that he did not know and could not have ascertained with reasonable diligence who was the driver of the vehicle at the material time[6]. In requiring information under

---

1 *Jardine v Crowe* 1992 SCCR 52.
2 *Brown v Stott* 2000 SLT 379.
3 Road Traffic Act 1988, s 172(4).
4 RTA 1988, s 172(6).
5 Road Traffic Offenders Act 1988, s 21(3), as amended by the Road Traffic Act 1991, Sch 4, para 89.
6 RTA 1988, s 172(3).

this section, the police officer in making the requirement does not have to indicate that the person who was driving the vehicle at the material time is alleged to have been guilty of a particular offence[1]. A statement made by a driver in response to a requirement in terms of this section is admissible in evidence in any subsequent prosecution[2]. The officer should explain that failure to answer is an offence[3]. The police are entitled to make this requirement of any person if they have information to support an allegation against the driver that he has committed a relevant offence[4].

7.5:9   Duty of owner of vehicle to give insurance information (s 171)

The chief purpose of this section is to allow a police officer to require the owner of a vehicle to give such information as is necessary to determine whether a driver was driving without insurance on any occasion when the driver has been asked to produce a certificate of insurance under ss 165(1) or 170 of the Road Traffic Act 1988.

7.6   DUTIES ON DRIVER IN CASE OF ACCIDENT (S 170)

7.6:1   General

Section 170 of the Road Traffic Act 1988[5] reads in full as follows:

'(1) This section applies in a case where, owing to the presence of a mechanically propelled vehicle on a road, an accident occurs by which –
   (a) personal injury is caused to a person other than the driver of that motor vehicle, or
   (b) damage is caused –
       (i) to a vehicle other than that motor vehicle or a trailer drawn by that motor vehicle, or

---

1 *McNaughton v Buchan* 1980 SLT (Notes) 100; *McMahon v Cardle* 1988 SCCR 556; *Duncan v McGillivray* 1989 SLT 48, 1988 SCCR 488.
2 See *Foster v Farrell* 1963 SLT 182; *Gray v Farrell* 1969 SLT 250; *Galt v Goodsir* 1982 JC 4, 1982 SLT 94, 1981 SCCR 225; and *Clark v Allan* 1988 SLT 274.
3 *Duncan v McGillivay* 1989 SLT 48, 1988 SCCR 488.
4 *Galt v Goodsir* 1982 JC 4, 1982 SLT 94, 1981 SCCR 225; *McMahon v Cardle* 1988 SCCR 556; *Hingston v Pollock* 1990 SLT 770, 1989 SCCR 697.
5 As amended by the Road Traffic Act 1991, Sch 4, para 72.

(ii) to an animal other than an animal in or on that motor vehicle or a trailer drawn by that motor vehicle, or

(iii) to any other property constructed on, fixed to, growing in or otherwise forming part of the land on which the road in question is situated or land adjacent to such land.

(2) The driver of a mechanically propelled vehicle must stop and, if required to do so by any person having reasonable grounds for so requiring, give his name and address and also the name and address of the owner and the identification marks of the vehicle.

(3) If for any reason the driver of the mechanically propelled vehicle does not give his name and address under subsection (2) above, he must report the accident.

(4) A person who fails to comply with subsection (2) or (3) above is guilty of an offence.

(5) If, in a case where this section applies by virtue of subsection (1)(a) above, the driver of a motor vehicle does not at the time of the accident produce such a certificate of insurance or security, or other evidence, as is mentioned in s 165(2) of this Act –

   (a) to a constable, or

   (b) to some person who, having reasonable grounds for so doing, has required him to produce it,

the driver must report the accident and produce such a certificate or other evidence.

   This subsection does not apply to the driver of an invalid carriage.

(6) To comply with a duty under this section to report an accident or to produce such a certificate of insurance or security, or other evidence, as is mentioned in s 165(2)(a) of this Act, the driver –

   (a) must do so at a police station or to a constable, and

   (b) must do so as soon as is reasonably practicable and, in any case, within twenty-four hours of the occurrence of the accident.

(7) A person who fails to comply with a duty under subsection (5) above is guilty of an offence, but he shall not be convicted by reason only of a failure to produce a certificate or other evidence if, within seven days after the occurrence of the accident, the certificate or other evidence is produced at a police station that was specified by him at the time when the accident was reported.

(8) In this section "animal" means horse, cattle, ass, mule, sheep, pig, goat or dog.'

7.6:2   Definitions (s 170)

'Mechanically propelled vehicle' – see 1.2:1 above.

'A road' – see 1.8:1, 1.8:2 and 1.8:3 above.

'Accident' – see 1.9:1 above.

'*Personal injury*'. It is submitted that the meaning of this phrase is not confined to physical injury, but could include shock or even emotional distress.

'*Stop*'. The Act does not provide a definition of this word, nor a description of the period over which the duty to stop must be exercised. However it is clear that the driver must stop at, or as near as reasonably practicable, to the *locus* of the accident, and further that he must remain there for such time, as in the circumstances, gives persons entitled to have the particulars described in the section sufficient opportunity to require them of the driver personally[1].

'*Animal*'. For the purposes of this section, 'animal' means a horse, cattle, ass, mule, sheep, pig, goat or dog[2]. Accordingly, no duty to stop is imposed if damage is caused to fowl, deer, or any other wild or domestic animal.

7.6:3   General application (s 170)

The circumstances in which a duty under this section can arise are extremely wide. If an accident which is covered by any of the situations described in subsections 1(a) and (b) can be attributed in any way to the presence of a motor vehicle on a road, then the driver of that motor vehicle is under an immediate duty to stop. As indicated in the preceding paragraph, the driver must stop as near as is practicable to where the accident occurred. It will also be noted that the offending vehicle need not necessarily be being driven at the material time; if, for example, an accident happens as a result of a vehicle being dangerously parked, the duty to stop imposed upon the driver of that vehicle by this section will still arise. Even although the driver complies with all other parts of s 170 of the Road Traffic Act 1988, a failure to stop at the material time will nonetheless contravene the provisions of the first part of s 170(2).

In addition to the duty imposed on a driver to stop following such an accident, in terms of the first part of s 170(2), the same section imposes an additional and quite separate duty on the

---

1 *Campbell v Copeland* 1972 JC 24; *Singh v McLeod* 1987 SLT 550, 1986 SCCR 656; *Hynd v O'Brien* 1990 JC 252, 1990 SCCR 129; *Percy v Lees* 1992 SCCR 234; *Cunningham v Crowe* 1994 SCCR 330; *Souter v Lees* 1995 SCCR 33.
2 Road Traffic Act 1988, s 170(8).

driver in these circumstances to provide his name and address, and the name and address of the owner of the vehicle and the identifying marks of the vehicle, to any person who requires that information from him and who has reasonable grounds for making that requirement. Whether such a person has reasonable grounds for requiring this information will depend on the facts and circumstances of each case. The duty to furnish the required information is personal to the driver and may not be delegated[1]. Again, an offence can be committed under this part of s 170(2) even where all other parts of s 170 are complied with by the offending driver. On the other hand, in the case of *Adair v Fleming*[2], it was held that where a vehicle had collided with another vehicle and the driver of the offending vehicle had given his name and address to the driver of the other vehicle, the driver of the offending vehicle was not, in the circumstances, thereafter under a duty to report the accident to the police in terms of s 170(3).

If the circumstances of an incident of driving are such that a driver had, or should have had, reasonable cause to suppose that he might have been involved in an accident, then he has a duty in terms of this section to stop and satisfy himself about what had happened. In *Sutherland v Aitchison*[3], a driver on a single track road mounted the verge in order to pass a vehicle coming in the opposite direction. As he did so he heard a noise which he thought might have been his exhaust hitting a stone, but which was in fact a collision between the two vehicles. It was held that in these circumstances the driver, having heard some noise, was under a duty to stop and see if he had been involved in an accident. Accordingly, a driver would appear to have a duty to satisfy himself that he has not been involved in an accident, if the circumstances suggest that he might have been. Section 170(2) does not qualify in any way the time limits within which the duty conferred by the section must be discharged and accordingly it is submitted that the duty to stop or to furnish information if properly required to do so, must be discharged as soon as reasonably practicable after the duty has arisen.

Section 170(3) and (6) makes provision for an offence which is quite separate and distinct from the offence described in s 170(2). It is therefore possible, and not unusual, for a driver to contravene

---

1 *Campbell v Copeland* 1972 JC 24.
2 1932 JC 51, 1932 SLT 263.
3 1975 JC 1.

both subsections. The duty incumbent upon a driver in terms of s 170(3) and (6) arises in particular if he has failed in any way to discharge his duties under s 170(2). Thus, if a driver has failed to stop at an accident, or has declined to give his name and address to someone having reasonable grounds to require this information, or has not given his name and address because there was no one at the scene of the accident, or no one who had reasonable grounds for requiring the information, then he must discharge the obligation described in s 170(6). It should be emphasised that a driver does not have any kind of discretion to report the matter to the police within the 24 hours following the accident. Rather, he is under an absolute duty to report the matter to the police as soon as reasonably practicable, and in any event within the period of 24 hours. On the other hand, however, a driver who fulfils all of the duties incumbent on him in terms of s 170(2) is under no duty to report an accident to the police in terms of s 170(3) and (6)[1].

In *Wood v McLean*[2], it was held that it was sufficient for a conviction under an earlier version of the offence described in s 170(3) and (6) for the prosecution to show firstly that the driver's name and address were not given to anyone at the *locus* of the accident, and secondly that the accident was not duly reported to the police. It was also suggested in that case that if the accused sought out a person with an interest in the matter and reported the incident within 24 hours, this might provide a defence. However, it is submitted that such a defence could only be successfully pled in only the most exceptional of circumstances.

In effect the prosecution has to prove a negative, and it has been held that, for example, the court may infer from the fact that the police were still making inquiries into an accident a month afterwards that the driver had not complied with the subsection[3]

Any direct link between the presence of the vehicle on the road and the accident which occurs as a result, such as a passenger falling off the platform of a bus, imposes the duties described in s 170[4].

Where the accident involves personal injury in terms of s 170(1)(a), the driver must produce a certificate of insurance at the time of the accident, to a constable or to a person who has

---

1 *Adair v Fleming* 1932 JC 51, 1932 SLT 263.
2 1947 JC 18, 1947 SLT 22.
3 *Walton v Crowe* 1993 SCCR 885, following *Milne v Whaley* 1975 SLT (Notes) 75; see also *Brittan v Mackenzie* 1985 SCCR 114 and *Hornall v Scott* 1993 SLT 1140, 1993 SCCR 65.
4 *Quelch v Phipps* [1955] 2 QB 107.

reasonable grounds for requiring him to produce it. If he does not, he must report the accident to the police as soon as reasonably practicable and in any event within 24 hours, and produce the certificate of insurance within 7 days[1].

In *Martin v Hamilton*[2] a solicitor advised a client not to report an accident. He was charged with counselling another to commit an offence under s 176 of the Road Traffic Act 1972. It was held that in the absence of an averment that by the time the advice had been given it would still have been reasonably practicable for the motorist to have reported the accident, the charge was not relevant.

When an accused said that he had not stopped because he thought that he might be over the drink-driving limits, the court could legitimately consider this as an aggravation of the offence[3].

7.6:4   Accident inquiries

The Secretary of State may direct that inquiry be made into the cause of any accident which arises out of the presence of a mechanically propelled vehicle on a road[4]. The inquiry may be public. Such an inquiry, which normally takes place if the accident involves the death of a person who was at the material time in the course of his employment, has the power to inspect any vehicle in connection with that inquiry, but any report made to or by the Secretary of State following such inquiry may not be used in any subsequent legal proceedings.

7.7   TAKING AND DRIVING AWAY (S 178)

7.7:1   Section 178

Section 178 of the Road Traffic Act 1988 provides:

'(1) A person who in Scotland –
  (a) takes and drives away a motor vehicle without having either the consent of the owner of the vehicle or other lawful authority, or

---

1 Road Traffic Act 1988, s 170(5), (6) and (7), as amended.
2 1989 SCCR 292.
3 *Williams v Vannet* 1996 SCCR 16.
4 Road Traffic Act 1988, s 181.

(b) knowing that a motor vehicle has been so taken, drives it or allows himself to be carried in or on it without such consent or authority,

is subject to subsection (2) below, guilty of an offence.

(2) If –

(a) the jury, on proceedings under this section on indictment, or

(b) the court, on summary proceedings under this section,

is satisfied that the accused acted in the reasonable belief that he had lawful authority, or in the reasonable belief that the owner would, in the circumstances of the case, have given consent if he had been asked for it, the accused shall not be liable to be convicted of the offence.

(3) A constable may arrest without warrant a person reasonably suspected by him of having committed or of attempting to commit an offence under this section.'

In terms of s 23 of the Road Traffic Offenders Act 1988[1], if an accused on indictment is charged with stealing a car, a jury is entitled to bring an alternative verdict under this section.

7.7:2 Definitions

'*Drives*' – see 1.7:1 and 3.3:2 above.

'*Motor vehicle*' – see 1.2:1 above.

7.7:3 General application

The offence described in this section was originally created to deal with the offence of joy-riding, which occurs when a vehicle is taken without the permission of its rightful owner for the purposes of a single trip or for a short period, and where the taker of the vehicle does not necessarily have the intention of depriving the owner of his property on a permanent basis. Such cases may cover a variety of situations in practice, and formerly were charged simply as theft. However, because it could be argued in such cases that the intention permanently to deprive the owner of his property (a necessary ingredient of a common law charge of theft) might well be absent, it was considered appropriate to provide a special statutory offence. It is competent to charge an

---

1 As amended by the Road Traffic Act 1991, Sch 4, para 90.

accused with the alternative of a common law charge of theft and an offence in terms of s 178 of the Road Traffic Act 1988.

For a conviction under s 178(1)(a), the prosecution must prove that the accused both took and drove away the vehicle, and that he did so without the owner's permission. In particular, if the owner's permission is only given for a particular journey, but the driver then embarks on a wholly unauthorised journey, an offence may be committed under this section[1].

For a conviction under s 178(1)(b), the prosecution must show that the accused knew that the vehicle had been stolen[2]. Other cases on this last point are *Hipson v Tudhope*[3]; *Rowley & Davie v Hamilton*[4]. A statutory defence is available in terms of s 178(2), which is sometimes overlooked.

7.7:4   Penalties

The penalties under s 178 of the Road Traffic Act 1988 are found in Schedule 2, Part 1 to the Road Traffic Offenders Act 1988[5]. They include inprisonment, fines (which are not defined) and discretionary disqualification. The power of the court to impose penalty points and order endorsement of the driver's licence has been removed[6]. Similarly, while discretionary disqualification is available to the court for the offence of stealing or attempting to steal a motor car[7], the same provisions in the 1991 Act also remove the power to impose endorsement and penalty points previously available. The net effect of these provisions is that while the court may disqualify a driver for stealing or attempting to steal a vehicle, or for an offence under s 178, in neither instance can the court order penalty points or any endorsement of the driver's licence.

In terms of s 23(3) of the Road Traffic Offenders Act 1988 a jury may find an accused originally charged with stealing a motor vehicle guilty of an offence under this section in appropriate circumstances.

Endorsement and penalty points are no longer imposed in s 178 cases.

1 *Barclay v Douglas* 1983 SCCR 224.
2 See e g, *Ashcroft's Curator Bonis v Stewart* 1988 SLT 163.
3 1983 SLT (Notes) 659, 1983 SCCR 247.
4 1989 SCCR 211.
5 As amended by the Road Traffic Act 1991, Sch 2, para 31.
6 Road Traffic Act 1991, s 83 and Sch 8.
7 Road Traffic Offenders Act 1988, Sch 2, Pt II.

7.8 SPEED LIMITS

7.8:1 General

By virtue of the Road Traffic Regulation Act 1984, ss 81(1) and 89, it is an offence for anyone to drive a motor vehicle on a restricted road at a speed in excess of 30 mph. A restricted road is defined in s 82 of the Act[1] as a system of carriageway lighting furnished by means of lamps placed not more than 185 metres apart. Speed limits on roads other than restricted roads are provided for in s 84 of the Act, and the responsibility for erecting the necessary speed restriction signs are dealt with under s 85. This allows for the imposition of variable speed limits. The detailed description of the signs themselves is found in the Traffic Signs Regulations and General Directions 1994[2]. Failure by the relevant authority to observe these directions in any material respect may preclude a driver being found guilty of a speeding offence[3].

Further speed limits may be imposed by the Secretary of State on a temporary basis, and failure to observe these limits is also an offence[4]. Regulations made under this section, and at present continued indefinitely, are the 70 miles per hour, 60 miles per hour, and 50 miles per hour (Temporary Speed Limit) (Continuation) Order 1978[5].

Temporary speed restrictions can be imposed inter alia in respect of road works, cleaning works or any danger to the public on the road in terms of ss 14-16E of the Road Traffic Regulation Act 1984, as amended by the Road Traffic (Temporary Restrictions) Act 1991.

Finally, it is an offence for any person to drive a motor vehicle of any class on a road at a speed greater than the maximum speed specified for the vehicle of that class[6]. The various speeds specified for various classes of vehicle are set out in Schedule 6 to the Road Traffic Regulation Act 1984.

Fire brigade, ambulance and police vehicles being used for those purposes, are exempt from speed limits if their observance

---

1 As amended by the New Roads and Street Works Act 1991, s 168(1) and Sch 8, para 59.
2 SI 1994/1519.
3 *Smith v Rankin* 1977 SLT (Notes) 12.
4 Road Traffic Regulation Act 1984, s 88.
5 SI 1978/1548.
6 RTRA 1984, s 86.

would hinder those purposes[1]. However the ordinary rules of driving other than that still apply to emergency vehicles, and drivers of such vehicles can be found guilty of any other offence under the Road Traffic Acts, including dangerous and careless driving, in exactly the same way as ordinary drivers, although the fact that they are driving in emergency circumstances may afford significant mitigation in any sentence imposed.

7.8:2   Evidence

In the prosecution of any person for a speeding offence, evidence of the measurement of speed produced by a prescribed device is sufficient to establish that the offence has been committed[2]. In particular the section allows for the provision of a record produced by a prescribed device, and a certificate of the circumstances in which the record was produced duly signed. The production of the certificate does not exclude other competent evidence[3].

Any device so used must be approved by the Secretary of State; this is done by the passing of an Approval Order. In its original form s 20 of the Road Traffic Offenders Act 1988 was specifically concerned with the measurement of speed by radar. The amendment provided by s 23 of the Road Traffic Act 1991 extended the ambit of the devices covered by the section to other approved equipment, and in addition traffic light and bus lane offences[4] are also now included under this section. There are now various types of device approved by the Secretary of State available in Scotland for the detection of offences, including radar speed measuring devices, photographic or other image recording devices, and devices activated by sensors, cables or light beams. Not all of these devices are currently in use.

There has to be some way by which the court can be satisfied that the relevant order, and therefore the particular device in question, has been approved by the Secretary of State. In *Valentine v MacPhail*[5] it was held that the Camic device was sufficiently notorious for it to be regarded as within judicial knowledge that

---

1 RTRA 1984, s 87.
2 Road Traffic Offenders Act 1988, s 20, as amended by the Road Traffic Act 1991, s 23.
3 *Straker v Orr* 1994 SCCR 251.
4 See Criminal Procedure and Investigations Act 1996, s 47 and Sch 1, para 38.
5 1986 JC 131, 1986 SLT 321.

the device had been approved. In *Mackie v Scott*[1] police officers said in evidence that they had been trained in the operation of the speed detection device which they had used, and it was therefore held that the court could infer that the device was approved. However in *Pickland v Carmichael*[2] there was no such evidence, and therefore no grounds from which the court could draw the necessary conclusions. The orders currently in force are given at 7.8:3 below.

Section 26(1) of the Criminal Justice (Scotland) Act 1980[3] remains in force and allows certificate evidence to vouch the accuracy of speedometers fitted to police traffic patrol cars and other apparatus for measuring speed, time and distance, such as the Vascar device. Such certificates may be covered by the rule that certificates must state that the appropriate examination has been carried out by those who have signed the certificate[4]. The Vascar equipment is not a radar device but a machine fitted to a police vehicle which allows officers to record the time which an observed vehicle takes to cover a known distance and thus arrive at its speed.

In *Westwater v Scott*[5] it was held that a driver was not prejudiced and could properly be convicted when an inexperienced police officer failed to keep the offending speed on the visual display of the Muniquip gun for inspection.

In *Morrison v McCowan*[6] the distance covered in a speeding charge was held to be calculated with sufficient accuracy by a measuring device and an Ordnance Survey map. Convictions for speeding can theoretically be secured by hand-held stop watches and other observations. In *Morrison v McCowan*[7] a speeding offence was proved by the time taken for a particular journey as measured on a map; see also *Gillespie v Macmillan*[8]; *Houston v Leslie*[9]; and *Farrell v Simpson*[10]. Significantly, these are all now somewhat elderly authorities, and it is extremely unlikely that such procedures are in current use.

---

1 1992 SCCR 614.
2 1995 SLT 675, 1995 SCCR 76.
3 See also Criminal Procedure (Scotland) Act 1995, s 280 and Sch 9.
4 *Normand v Wotherspoon* 1993 JC 248, 1994 SLT 487, 1993 SCCR 912; *Donnelly v Schrikel* 1995 SLT 537.
5 1980 SLT (Sh Ct) 63 (and see also *Scott v MacPhail* 1992 SLT 907, 1991 SCCR 760).
6 1939 SLT 422.
7 1939 JC 45, 1939 SLT 422.
8 1957 JC 31, 1957 SLT 283.
9 1958 JC 8, 1958 SLT 109.
10 1959 SLT (Sh Ct) 23.

The reading produced by a device does not have to be corroborated, for example by the opinion of the police officers as to the speed of the vehicle, but other matters such as the identity of the driver do require to be established by corroborative evidence[1].

7.8:3   Orders and identification in speeding and traffic light offences

The Road Traffic Offenders (Prescribed Devices) Order 1992[2] approves devices designed or adapted for measuring the speed of a motor vehicle by radar. The Road Traffic Offenders (Prescribed Devices) (No 2) Order 1992[3] approves a device designed or adapted for recording by photographs or other image recording means the position of motor vehicles in relation to traffic lights. The Road Traffic Offenders (Prescribed Devices) Order 1993[4] (speed measuring devices triggered by sensors, cables or light beams), Road Traffic Offenders (Additional Offences and Prescribed Devices) Order 1997[5] (cameras to detect other vehicles on bus lanes) and the Road Traffic Offenders (Prescribed Devices) Order 1999[6] (image catching devices) have also been made.

This certificate evidence referred to at 7.8:2 above demonstrates only that an offence has been committed; the prosecution has also to prove who committed the offence (See 7.8:2 above). Because of the nature of the various radar devices previously available, police officers were usually able to stop, and thus identify, the accused at the time the offence was committed. Such devices will continue to be used in this way. However, it is not proposed that a photographic device will be used in such a way that will involve the driver being stopped at the time of the offence. To surmount the consequent problem of identification, the Road Traffic Act 1991, Sch 4, para 85 attempted to provide a further and particularly Scottish power to s 12 of the Road Traffic Offenders Act 1988, which had previously only applied to England and Wales. Put briefly, a written statement, purporting to be signed by the accused in response to a requirement under s 172(2) (as amended)

---

1 *Scott v MacPhail* 1992 SLT 907, 1992 SCCR 760; see also *Barbour v Normand* 1992 SCCR 331.
2 SI 1992/1209.
3 SI 1992/2843.
4 SI 1993/1698.
5 SI 1997/384.
6 SI 1999/162.

of the Road Traffic Act 1988, admitting that he was the driver at the material time, will be sufficient evidence of identification. Section 172 is described at 7.5:8 above.

It is envisaged that the police will require the information as to who was driving at the material time in the first instance from the registered keeper. If the keeper names another person as the driver, that person can also be made the subject of a requirement under s 172. Regrettably, paragraph 85 of Schedule 4 of the Road Traffic Act 1991 contains a wrong statutory reference and is therefore invalid. This has been cured by paragraph 5 of Schedule 5 to the Prisoners and Criminal Proceedings (Scotland) Act 1993. This will mean that the statutory procedure allows devices such as cameras to record the offences and an admission under s 172 to identify the accused. The prosecutions based on these procedures are to be carried out by the fixed penalty procedures (See 8.13 below).

In practice, once police officers have retrieved a piece of film showing the offending driving from their cameras the registered keeper will be asked by letter if he was the driver at the material time. If he replies with a signed statement that he was, the evidential ingredients of the offence are complete. If the registered keeper denies that he was the driver, he must indicate if he knows who was. If he does so, the police will then make the conditional offer of a fixed penalty to the named driver. If anyone fails to identify the driver at the material time and cannot rely on the defences provided (see 7.5:8 above) he is liable to a fine, discretionary disqualification and endorsement of his licence with three penalty points.

7.9   PARKING

7.9:1   General

The local roads authority[1] has the power to provide off-street parking, and parking on roads without payment, in terms of s 32ff of the Road Traffic Regulation Act 1984. Parking may also be authorised on the road for payment of a charge, and by the provision of parking meters[2]. Section 52 deals with offences relating to

1 See the Roads (Scotland) Act 1984, s 151.
2 Road Traffic Regulation Act 1984, ss 45–49.

interference with parking devices and the incorrect display of tickets. Excess parking charges are the responsibility of the owner of the vehicle[1]. The power to provide parking places extends to the provision, on roads, or elsewhere, of stands and racks for bicycles[2]. The Secretary of State has power to make regulations in respect of the removal of vehicles illegally, obstructively or dangerously parked, or abandoned, or broken down[3]. A police officer has the power in general terms to fix an immobilisation device to a vehicle illegally parked[4]; however the necessary regulations have not been made introducing this power to Scotland (see 7.9:3 below).

The power to exempt vehicles with Disabled Persons badges from parking restrictions is found in the Local Authorities' Traffic Orders (Exemptions for Disabled Persons) (Scotland) Regulations 1982[5]; see also s 21 of the Chronically Sick and Disabled Persons Act 1970.

The local roads authority may also make such orders as it considers expedient for the regulation of traffic[6]. However, once such an order is made, it only becomes effective when the authority has erected the appropriate signs[7]. Such signs (e g 'No Waiting' signs) may be made subject to exemptions (e g for loading).

7.9:2   Statutory provisions

Section 19 of the Road Traffic Act 1988 provides specifically that a heavy commercial vehicle[8] (see 1.6:4 above) cannot be parked wholly or partly on the verge of a road, on any land situated between two carriageways, or on a footway. Exemption is provided in cases where the driver proves that the parking was done with the permission of a uniformed police officer, or took

---

1 RTRA 1984, s 107; but see also ss 108–111.
2 RTRA 1984, s 63.
3 RTRA 1984, ss 99, 101, 102 and 104; see also Refuse Disposal (Amenity) Act 1978, s 2.
4 RTRA 1984, ss 104–106.
5 SI 1982/1740.
6 RTRA 1984, s 1ff.
7 Local Authorities Traffic Orders (Procedure) (Scotland) Regulations 1987, SI 1987/2245; *MacLeod v Hamilton* 1965 SLT 305; *Macmillan v Gibson* 1966 SLT (Sh Ct) 84.
8 Which is described in the Road Traffic Act 1988, s 20.

place in an emergency, or that it was engaged in loading or unloading in circumstances described in the section.

Section 22 (as amended) makes it an offence for a person in charge of a vehicle or a trailer to leave it in such a position or in such a condition or in such circumstances as to involve a danger of injury to others using the road. The word 'vehicle' is not qualified in any way in the section (e g by the word 'motor') and no exemptions or defences are indicated.

Regulation 101 of the Road Vehicles (Construction and Use) Regulations 1986 imposes general restrictions, subject to certain exceptions, on parking on roads during the hours of darkness.

7.9:3   Wheel clamping

The immobilisation of vehicles illegally parked is dealt with in ss 104–106 of the Road Traffic Regulation Act 1984. Private clamping may amount to theft but not to extortion[1].

7.10   PEDESTRIAN CROSSINGS

The local roads authority has the power to establish, alter or remove pedestrian crossings on any roads within its area[2]. Any pedestrian crossings on trunk roads are the responsibility of the Secretary of State[3]. The purpose of pedestrian crossings is to afford precedence in certain circumstances to pedestrians using a road over other road users. The power to make regulations in respect of such crossings is contained in s 25 of the Road Traffic Regulation Act 1984.

The current regulations made under this section are the Zebra, Pelican and Puffin Pedestrian Crossing Regulations and General Directions 1997[4], which provide in detail for the physical characteristics and markings for such crossings, including road markings, stud and globes, and in particular provides an absolute right of precedence in the circumstances therein described to pedestrians within the limits of such crossings. The regulations also provide for prohibitions against the waiting of vehicles and

1 *Black v Carmichael* 1992 SLT 897, 1992 SCCR 709.
2 Road Traffic Regulation Act 1984, s 23(1), as amended.
3 RTRA 1984, s 24 as amended.
4 SI 1997/2400.

pedestrians on a crossing and against vehicles overtaking within the area of a crossing. Cases involving this kind of crossings as reported are *McKerrell v Robertson*[1] and *Wishart v McDonald*[2].

7.11 SCHOOL CROSSINGS AND PLAYGROUNDS

In terms of s 26 of the Road Traffic Regulation Act 1984, as amended, local authorities are empowered to make arrangements for the patrolling of school crossings. A properly appointed school crossing patrol is entitled to require vehicles to stop at places where children are crossing a road on or from their way to school. It is an offence for any person driving a vehicle to fail to comply with such a requirement[3]. Sections 29 and 31 of the Road Traffic Regulation Act 1984 allow a local roads authority to make orders prohibiting the use of traffic on roads which are to be used as playgrounds.

7.12 CONSTRUCTION AND USE (S 41)

7.12:1 General

There are a very large number of provisions, normally introduced by statutory instrument, which regulate the construction, maintenance, use, weight and equipment of motor vehicles and trailers on the roads. A considerable number of these statutory provisions reflect the terms of the European Economic Communities' directives and regulations. A detailed examination of these regulations is outwith the scope of this book; many of the regulations specify what the statutory requirements are in very considerable detail. It is therefore proposed to deal with this subject in broad outline. Section 41 of the Road Traffic Act 1988[4], and in particular subsections (2)–(4), indicates the general headings under which the various regulations are issued. Section 41(1)–(4) reads as follows:

'(1) The Secretary of State may make regulations generally as to the use of motor vehicles and trailers on roads, their construction and equipment and the conditions under which they may be so used.

---

1 1956 JC 50, 1956 SLT 290.
2 1962 SLT (Sh Ct) 29, (1962) 78 Sh Ct Rep 3.
3 Road Traffic Regulation Act 1984, s 28.
4 As amended by inter alia the Road Traffic Act 1991, Sch 4, para 50).

Subsections (2) to (4) below do not affect the generality of this subsection.

(2) In particular, the regulations may make provision with respect to any of the following matters –

(a) the width, height and length of motor vehicles and trailers and the load carried by them, the diameter of wheels, and the width, nature and condition of tyres, of motor vehicles and trailers,

(b) the emission or consumption of smoke, fumes or vapour and the emission of sparks, ashes and grit,

(c) noise,

(d) the maximum weight unladen of heavy locomotives and heavy motor cars, and the maximum weight laden of motor vehicles and trailers, and the maximum weight to be transmitted to the road or any specified area of the road by a motor vehicle or trailer of any class or by any part or parts of such a vehicle or trailer in contact with the road, and the conditions under which the weights may be required to be tested,

(e) the particulars to be marked on motor vehicles and trailers (by means of the fixing of plates or otherwise) and the circumstances in which they are to be marked,

(f) the towing of or drawing of vehicles by motor vehicles,

(g) the number and nature of brakes, and for securing that brakes, silencers and steering gear are efficient and kept in proper working order,

(h) lighting equipment and reflectors,

(j) the testing and inspection, by persons authorised by or under the regulations, of the brakes, silencers, steering gear, tyres, lighting equipment and reflectors of motor vehicles and trailers on any premises where they are (if the owner of the premises consents),

(jj) speed limiters,

(k) the appliances to be fitted for –
   (i) signalling the approach of a motor vehicle, or
   (ii) enabling the driver of a motor vehicle to become aware of the approach of another vehicle from the rear, or
   (iii) intimating any intended change of speed or direction of a motor vehicle,
   and the use of any such appliance, and for securing that any such appliance is efficient and kept in proper working order,

(l) for prohibiting the use of appliances fitted to motor vehicles for signalling their approach, being appliances for signalling by sound, at any times, or on or in any roads or localities, specified in the regulations.

(3) The Secretary of State may, as respects goods vehicles, make regulations under this section –

(a) prescribing other descriptions of weight which are not to be exceeded in the case of such vehicles,

(b) providing for the marking on such vehicles of weights of any description or other particulars by means of plates (of any material) fixed to them,

(c) providing for the circumstances in which any particulars which are to be marked on such vehicles are to be so marked,

(d) providing that weights of any description or other particulars which are to be marked on particular goods vehicles may be determined in accordance with regulations under s 49 of this Act.

(4) Regulations under this section with respect to lighting equipment and reflectors –

(a) may require that lamps be kept lit at such times and in such circumstances as may be specified in the regulations, and

(b) may extend, in like manner as to motor vehicles and trailers, to vehicles of any description used on roads, whether or not they are mechanically propelled.

(4A) Regulations under this section with respect of speed limiters may include provision –

(a) as to the checking and sealing of speed limiters by persons authorised in accordance with the regulations and the making of changes by them,

(b) imposing or providing for the imposition of conditions to be complied with by authorised persons,

(c) as to the withdrawal of authorisation.'

7.12:2   Construction and use offences

The offences under the regulations are created by ss 40A, 41A, 41B and 42 of the Road Traffic Act 1988, all as introduced by s 8 of the Road Traffic Act 1991. These sections reflect the broad groupings under which construction and use topics are considered in the legislation, and this arrangement is reflected in other consequential adjustments introduced by the 1991 Act.

Section 40A creates an offence where a vehicle is used in a dangerous condition, for example where its condition, purpose of use, number of passengers, or the weight, position or distribution of its load, or the way in which the load is secured, involves a risk of injury to any person. Section 41A creates an offence where there is a contravention of the regulations involving brakes, steering, gear or tyres. Section 41B creates an offence where there is a breach of the requirements as to weight in respect of both goods and passenger vehicles. Section 41B indicates the defences which may be available in charges of overloading or excess weight, and these are discussed at 7.12:7. Section 42 covers other construction and use contraventions. The penalties for such offences are set out in Schedule 2, Part 1 to the Road Traffic

Offenders Act 1988, as amended by the Road Traffic Act 1991, Sch 2, para 17.

Section 43 provides for temporary exemption from the regulations, and s 44[1] for authorisation of use on roads of special vehicles which do not comply with the regulations.

Section 48 of the Road Traffic Offenders Act 1988[2] provides a statutory exemption from disqualification and endorsement following conviction of these offences if the accused shows that he did not know, nor had he reasonable cause to suspect, that the facts of the case were such that the offence would be committed. A case illustrating some of the considerations relevant to such a defence is *Forrest v Annan*[3].

In *Morrison v Mackenzie*[4], a case involving bald tyres, the appeal court held that where no prejudice existed, it was unreasonable to expect the tyres to be produced, and oral evidence of their condition was accepted. Obvious defects can be spoken of in evidence by persons other than authorised examiners[5].

7.12:3   Statutory instruments

The principal secondary legislation dealing with ss 40–42 offences is the Road Vehicles (Construction and Use) Regulations 1986[6]. These regulations apply to both wheeled vehicles and track-laying vehicles. The definition section of these regulations (reg 3) is particularly comprehensive. Also of importance are the Road Vehicles Lighting Regulations 1989[7] (see 7.12:6 below). In addition there are a huge number of regulations dealing with a variety of subjects and all of these are subject to a continuous stream of amendments. In practical terms, the only method of keeping up to date with the details of this secondary legislation is by recourse to one of the specialist road traffic 'encyclopedias' which are issued regularly on a loose-leaf system, and which seek to present the current state of all aspects of road traffic legislation.

---

1 As amended by Road Traffic Act 1991, Sch 2, para 51.
2 As amended by RTA 1991, Sch 4, para 101.
3 1992 SLT 510, 1990 SCCR 619.
4 1990 JC 185.
5 *Mowbray v Valentine* 1992 SLT 416, 1991 SCCR 494.
6 SI 1986/1078.
7 SI 1989/1796.

7.12:4   Type approval schemes

Certain of the construction and use requirements have, however, been superseded by type approval schemes. It is part of the European Economic Communities' overall plan to harmonise road traffic law, and eventually it is hoped that a universal and comprehensive series of schemes covering the manufacture of vehicles and parts will be introduced. In terms of such schemes, the manufacturer of a vehicle or of a vehicle part produces to the Secretary of State a type vehicle or part for inspection. If approval is given, the manufacturer is provided with a type approval certificate and is then enabled to produce vehicles or parts, of identical construction, as long as he issues certificates indicating that these further vehicles or parts conform exactly with the approval certificate. These are known as certificates of conformity. This scheme has been introduced to avoid the necessity of all vehicles and parts being individually inspected at the instance of the government. At present, some of these provisions are optional and some dealing mainly with certain kinds of passenger vehicles are obligatory. Reference to these schemes is made in ss 54–65A of the Road Traffic Act 1988, as amended; the principal regulations are the Motor Vehicles (Type Approval) (Great Britain) Regulations 1984[1], although there are a number of other relevant statutory instruments.

7.12:5   Maximum lengths

The Road Vehicles (Construction and Use) Regulations 1986, regulation 7 provides that, subject to certain exceptions, the overall length of certain vehicles or combination of vehicles, including articulated vehicles and trailers must not exceed prescribed overall maximum lengths. Regulation 8 gives certain prescribed overall width dimensions which must not be exceeded principally in commercial vehicles. Regulation 9 provides for certain maximum heights in the case of buses (4.57 metres) and articulated lorries. Regulation 10 provides further requirements in respect of the height of vehicles and in particular the indications required in respect of special vehicles and overall travelling height. Regulation 10A-C 1997[2] requires warning devices to be

1 SI 1984/981.
2 As amended by the Road Vehicles (Construction and Use) (Amendment) Regulations 1997 (SI 1997/530).

fitted where certain high level equipment is fitted to a vehicle. The maximum overhang permitted and the exceptions to the general provisions are provided in regulation 11. Regulation 12 provides details of the minimum ground clearance in respect of various vehicles. Regulations 13 and 14 apply to the turning circles, and connecting sections and direction–holding of articulated buses first used on or after 1 April 1982.

Detailed definitions of overall length, overall width, and over-hang, together with definition of the various classes of vehicle are provided in the definition section (reg 3). Two cases in which these matters have been considered are *Guest Scottish Carriers Ltd v Trend*[1]; *Hawkins v Russett*[2].

All the foregoing regulations have been amended in detail since 1986, by various Road Vehicle (Construction and Use) (Amendment) Regulations.

7.12:6 Weight

The regulations governing the weight of various vehicles are of particular importance. As has been indicated above, in terms of s 41 (as amended) of the Road Traffic Act 1988, the Secretary of State has the power to make regulations in respect of the maximum laden and unladen weight of vehicles, and the maximum weight to be transmitted to the road by any vehicle, the conditions under which such weights may be required to be tested, and the particulars to be marked on vehicles and trailers.

The Road Traffic Act 1988, s 190 provides the method of calculating the unladen weight of vehicles and trailers; for cases on this section see *McCowan v Stewart*[3]; and *Blaikie v Morrison*[4]. Regulation 23 of the 1986 Regulations provides that certain multi-wheel vehicles must have a compensating arrangement to ensure that under the most adverse conditions every wheel will remain in contact with the road and will not be subject to abnormal variations of load.

There are detailed and technical provisions in respect of the maximum permitted laden weights of various kinds of vehicles. These are of particular significance to heavy commercial vehicles.

1 [1967] 3 All ER 52.
2 [1983] RTR 406.
3 1936 JC 36, 1936 SLT 370.
4 1957 JC 46, 1957 SLT 290.

The restrictions apply not only to the total laden weights, but also, as a separate matter, to the weight transmitted to the road by one or more wheels and axles. It is therefore possible for a vehicle to commit an overloading offence in respect of the maximum permitted wheel or axle weight even where the total permitted laden weight is not exceeded. The provisions are set out in tabulated form in regulations 75–80 of the Road Vehicles (Construction and Use) Regulations 1986, as amended, and are to be read with the definition section (reg 3). In any prosecution of a vehicle or trailer for overloading, the prosecution must adduce evidence that the weighbridge is accurate[1]. Section 17(1) of the Road Traffic Offenders Act 1988 affords a presumption that the plated weight is the weight of the vehicle and s 17(4) provides that in any proceedings in Scotland for a traffic offence where the weight of the vehicle is an issue, a certificate pertaining to be signed by an inspector of weights and measures certifying that the weighbridge or other machine is accurate in sufficient evidence of that fact. Regulations 81–82 and 83–90 provide restrictions on the use of vehicles carrying wide or long loads or appliances, and on the number of trailers to be drawn by particular vehicles, the distance between motor vehicles and trailers, provisions in respect of unbraked trailers, the use of bridging plates between motor vehicles and trailers, requirements on leaving trailers at rest, and on passengers in trailers. Regulation 83 in particular provides for the number of trailers that may be drawn by various classes of vehicle.

Many of the foregoing regulations have been amended in detail since 1986.

7.12:7   Weight offences: defences

In prosecutions in respect of offences under s 41B of the Road Traffic Act 1988[2] where it is alleged that any of the weight regulations described in the preceding paragraph have been contravened, s 41B(2) provides two statutory defences. First, it is a defence if the vehicle is being used on the road at a time when it was proceeding to a weighbridge which was the nearest available one to the place where the loading of the vehicle was completed for the purpose of being weighed or was proceeding from a

---

1 *Grierson v Clark* 1958 JC 22, 1958 SLT 112.
2 As amended by the Road Traffic Act 1991, s 8.

weighbridge after being weighed to the nearest point at which it was reasonably practicable to reduce the weight to the relevant limit without causing an obstruction on any road. However, this defence is to be strictly applied; courts have in practice been reluctant to sustain such a defence if the vehicle has diverted in any way from what, in the circumstances, can be reasonably described as a direct route between the loading point and the weighbridge. Further, it would not appear to be a sustainable defence to argue that there was no such weighbridge available or open.

Secondly, in cases where the limit of weight has not been exceeded by more than five per cent (and only in such cases), it is a defence to prove that the limit was not exceeded at the time the loading of the vehicle was originally completed, and since that time no person has made any addition to the load. This second statutory defence is designed to cater for the situation where a load can be shown to have increased in weight since the start of its journey. This can happen, for example, where a load such as timber increases in weight through the absorption of snow or rain water. Alternatively, the defence may be relevant where the load can be shown to have shifted during the journey, and the driver is charged with excess weight on a single axle. Again however, the courts have tended to impose a strict construction on such defences. Apart from the two defences allowed by statute, overloading of any sort is an absolute offence. In particular, any consequence or effect brought about by the circumstances or condition of a particular road is irrelevant in computing the laden weight on a particular vehicle.

If it appears to an authorised police officer or other authorised official that a vehicle is overloaded, the further use of that vehicle on the road may be prohibited. Alternatively, the vehicle may be used subject to such directions as the authorised official thinks fit[1].

7.12:8 Plated weights and other plated particulars

The Secretary of State is empowered to make regulations providing for the marking of certain particulars, including weight, applicable to certain classes of goods vehicles[2]. The terms

---

1 See generally the Road Traffic Act 1988, ss 70–72, as amended by RTA 1991, ss 9–15.
2 Road Traffic Act 1988, s 41(2) and (3) (as amended by the Road Traffic Act 1991, Sch 4, para 50.

used are 'plated particulars' and 'plated weight', and these are defined in s 41(7) of the Road Traffic Act 1988. These details must be shown on a plate which is securely attached to the vehicle in a conspicuous and readily accessible position[1]. This latter regulation also contains a table which gives general descriptions of various classes of vehicles, including trailers, to which the legislation applies, and also lists the kinds of vehicles exempted from the requirements. Schedule 8 to the Regulations provides in detail what particulars must be shown on the plate. Part III of Schedule 8 to the regulations makes general provisions in respect of power to weight ratios and also determines the relevant weights to be shown on plates in accordance with regulation 66. The plated weight of any particular vehicle therefore is the weight which must be stamped on the plate of the particular vehicle in terms of regulation 66 and Schedule 8. It should be noted that the plated weight (or, where appropriate, the train weight) is not necessarily the same as the design weight. In terms of the Road Traffic Act 1988, s 41(6), the Secretary of State has to make sure that the plated weight or train weight of any vehicle is fixed having regard to the design weight of that vehicle, and does not exceed that weight. Further, every goods vehicle to which the Testing and Plating Regulations apply, must have a Ministry Plate[2].

Speed limiters must be fitted to certain passenger and commercial vehicles and must show plates which indicate that such devices are fitted[3].

Plates which must be attached to motor cycles are covered in regulation 69 and Schedule 9.

The phrases 'design weight' and 'train weight' are defined in regulation 3.

Tests relating to the satisfactory condition of certain classes of goods vehicles and the determination of plated weights are dealt with in ss 49–53 of the Road Traffic Act 1988[4]. Provisions dealing with the testing of vehicles on the road by vehicle examiners or police officers, and of their maintenance and loading, together with considerations relevant to the prohibition of unfit or over-

---

1 Road Vehicles (Construction and Use) Regulations 1986, reg 66.
2 1986 Regulations, reg 70, as amended by the Road Vehicles (Construction and Use) (Amendment) (No 7) Regulations 1998 (SI 1998/3112) and Schs 10 and 10A, introduced by amendment regulations 1987 (SI 1987/676).
3 1986 Regulations, regs 36A, 36B and 70, (all of which have been further amended).
4 As amended by the Road Traffic Act 1991, Sch 4, paras 54 and 55).

loaded vehicles, are found in the Road Traffic Act 1988, ss 67–73, as amended by the Road Traffic Act 1991, ss 9–15.

As indicated at 7.12:6 above, the maximum permitted laden weights of various classes of vehicles are furnished in detail in regulations 75–80, which should be consulted in detail in respect of any particular case. Reference should also be made to Schedule 11 which gives measurements in respect of these regulations.

7.12:9 Brakes

The detailed technical regulations concerning brakes are extensive and complex. The principal provisions in respect of brakes are contained in regulations 15 and 16 of the Road Vehicles (Construction and Use) Regulations 1986, as amended. These regulations refer in turn to Community Directive 79/489, which amends Council Directive 71/320 on the approximation of braking devices, and Community Directive 85/647.

Regulation 17, however, provides that every motor vehicle which is equipped with a braking system which embodies a vacuum or pressure reservoir is to be equipped with a device readily visible to the driver which is capable of indicating any pending failure of, or deficiency in, the vacuum or pressure system. The section contains certain limited exceptions to this requirement. In *Hamilton v MacKenzie*[1] it was held that there had been a breach of this requirement when the warning device, although installed, was found to be not working properly.

Regulation 18 provides that every part of every braking system and the means of operating thereof must be maintained in good and sufficient working order and be properly adjusted.

In general terms most vehicles require to have bridging systems, namely a service braking system (which is the principal means by which a vehicle is brought to a halt) and a secondary or parking brake system. Both brake systems require to be maintained to certain levels of efficiency, which are expressed in terms of a percentage of a total braking efficiency of which the brakes should be capable. The phrase 'braking efficiency' and other relevant phrases are defined in the definition regulation 3. Regulation 18 contains tables which describes the efficiencies of the respective braking systems which are required for various kinds of

---

1 1968 SLT 166, 1968 SLT (Notes) 36.

vehicle. This section provides an absolute offence and for example both a driver and his employers may be found guilty of using a vehicle with inadequately maintained brakes[1]. As the regulation contains an absolute offence, it is therefore not a defence to a charge under these regulations that a regular system of inspection was enforced by the owners of the vehicle[2].

In *Watson v Muir*[3] it was held that although it was desirable that the owner or user of any vehicle should be present while the braking system of any vehicle was being tested, such attendance was not essential and evidence of any such examination conducted in the absence of the owner or user was admissible in evidence.

The foregoing regulations have been severally amended in detail since 1986.

7.12:10   Wheels and tyres

Tyres are also subject to detailed provisions and requirements in terms of regulation 24 of the Road Vehicles (Construction and Use) Regulations 1986, which gives a full description of the classes of vehicles and the types of tyres which must be used. The phrases 'pneumatic tyre', 're-cut pneumatic tyre', 'retreaded tyre' and 'resilient tyre' are all defined in the definition section (reg 3). Regulation 25[4] makes provision for tyre loads and speed ratings in such a way as to ensure that the tyres are able to bear the maximum axle weight. The prohibition against the mixing of different kinds of pneumatic tyres on the same vehicle is provided in regulation 26. The regulation contains the necessary additional definitions of the different kinds of tyre involved. Regulation 27 provides for the condition and maintenance of tyres and in particular contains the detailed provisions which can form the basis of a prosecution for driving with a worn or defective tyre.

In these circumstances it is an offence to use or cause or permit to be used a vehicle on the road with such defects. The customary definitions apply and in particular it is plain that using includes parking the vehicle on a public road and is not confined to the vehicle being in motion.

---

1 *James & Son Ltd v Smee; Green v Burnett* [1955] 1 QB 78.
2 *Hawkins v Holmes* [1974] RTR 436.
3 1938 JC 181, 1939 SLT 14.
4 As introduced by SI 1990/1981.

Further, if the vehicle in question is the subject of a hire agreement, then the person who is 'using' the vehicle at the material time is the hirer and not the hire firm; see *Farrell v Moggach*[1]; *Mackay Brothers & Co v Gibb*[2].

These regulations have also been amended in detail since 1986.

7.12:11   Vision and glass

The regulations also provide that each motor vehicle is to be designed and constructed so that the driver has at all times a full view of the road ahead[3]. All glass or other transparent material fitted to a motor vehicle is to be maintained in such a condition that it does not obscure vision of the driver while the vehicle is being driven on a road[4]. There is also provision as to the kind of glass which must be fitted to certain vehicles in certain circumstances and in particular regulations 31 and 32 make provision for the fitting of safety glass.

Regulation 33 provides comprehensive details on the provision of mirrors to vehicles, and regulation 34 provides for windscreen wipers and washers.

7.12:12   Instruments and equipment

Regulation 35 provides that every vehicle shall be fitted with a speedometer capable of indicating speed in both miles per hour and kilometres per hour and regulation 36 provides that speedometers should be properly maintained at all material times. Further, regulation 37 provides that every vehicle subject to the included exceptions shall be fitted with a horn which is not a reversing alarm or a two-tone horn. Apart from such instruments designed to inform members of the public that goods are on a vehicle for sale, it is a specific condition that the sound omitted by any horn other than a reversing alarm or two-tone horn shall be continuous, uniform and not strident. Exceptions are granted to motor vehicles used for fire brigade, ambulance or police

---

1 1976 SLT (Sh Ct) 8.
2 1969 JC 26, 1969 SLT 216.
3 Road Vehicles (Construction and Use) Regulations 1986, reg 30.
4 1986 Regulations, reg 30(3).

purposes and other vehicles in the public or social service. Regulation 39 covers the construction and maintenance of petrol tanks.

Regulation 36A[1] provides that every coach first used on or after 1 April 1974 must have a speed limiter, set to restrict the speed of the vehicles to 70 mph.

7.12:13   Protective systems

Seatbelt anchorage points and seatbelts are the subject of the Road Vehicles (Construction and Use) Regulations 1986, regs 46–47, and their maintenance is governed by regulation 48; the requirements in respect of their use are described at 7.3 above. Requirements for fitting minibuses and coaches with additional seats is provided by reg 48A, which was introduced by the Road Vehicles (Construction and Use) (Amendment No 2) Regulations 1996[2]. Certain vehicles must have rear under-run protection and side-guards; see regulations 49–52. Single-decked coaches must comply with certain requirements in respect of their superstructure[3]; and double-decked coaches must have two staircases or the means on the top deck to break the windows in an emergency[4].

Every vehicle propelled by an external combustion engine must be fitted with an exhaust system including a silencer and the exhaust gases from the engine are not allowed to escape into the atmosphere without first passing through the silencer[5]. All exhaust systems and silencers must be properly maintained and certain noise limits are applied to various vehicles[6]. Regulation 61, which has been copiously amended over the years, provides comprehensive provision in respect of the emission of smoke vapour, gases and oily substances from vehicles. Regulation 60 requires that all vehicles should comply with the EEC regulations on radio interference suppression.

---

1 Introduced by the Road Vehicles (Construction and Use) (Amendment) (No 3) Regulations 1993, SI 1993/3048.
2 SI 1996/163.
3 Road Vehicles (Construction and Use) Regulations 1986, reg 53A, introduced by SI 1987/1133, and amended by SI 1989/2630.
4 1986 Regulations, reg 53B, as similarly introduced.
5 1986 Regulations, reg 54.
6 See 1986 Regulations, reg 55–59, as amended by amendment regulations SI 1994/14 and SI 1996/16 and 2329.

Again, these regulations have been subject to amendment in detail since 1986.

7.12:14 Control of noise

In terms of regulation 97 of the Road Vehicles (Construction and Use) Regulations 1986, no motor vehicle is to be used on a road in such a manner as to cause excessive noises which could have been avoided by the exercise of reasonable care on the part of the driver. There is further a general duty in terms of regulation 98, as amended by the amendment regulations[1] to stop the engine when a vehicle is stationary apart from the necessities of traffic for the purpose of preventing noise or exhaust emissions. The use of audible warning instruments is regulated in detail by regulation 99.

7.12:15 Avoidance of danger

The Road Vehicles (Construction and Use) Regulations 1986 make a number of provisions in respect of the safe use of vehicles. Regulation 100(1) requires that every motor vehicle and trailer drawn thereby and all parts and accessories of such vehicles and trailers shall at all times be in such condition, and the number of any passengers carried by such vehicles or trailers shall be such, that the weight, distribution and adjustment of the load of such a vehicle or trailer shall at all times provide that no danger is caused or is likely to be caused to any person in or on the vehicle or trailer or on the road. It should be noted that this is different from the restrictions on overloading. Regulation 100(2) requires that the load carried by a vehicle or trailer shall at all times be so secured and be in such a position that neither danger nor nuisance is likely to be caused to any person or property by reason of the load or any part of it falling or being blown from the vehicle or by reason of any other movement of the load or part thereof in relation to the vehicle[2]. Regulation 100(3) provides that no motor vehicle or trailer shall be used for any purpose for which it is so unsuitable as to cause or be likely to cause danger or nuisance to any person

1 SI 1998/1.
2 See, e g, *Wells v Guild* 1988 SCCR 438.

in or on the vehicle or trailer or on a road. These provisions are designed to secure the proper conduct of a vehicle on the road and in particular to avoid items falling from a vehicle onto the road. However, it should be noted that it is not necessary for part of the load actually to fall on a road or off a lorry, for an offence to be committed under this section. In particular, in terms of regulation 100(2), it is possible for an accused person to be convicted in circumstances where he was not aware of the defects in the load which caused the contravention of the subsection[1]. Regulation 100(1) therefore requires that the condition of the vehicle shall be at all times safe; that the number of passengers carried by a vehicle is, at all times, not excessive; and that weight distribution and packing of the load is at all times safe. Regulation 100(2) contains an offence of unlawful loading in circumstances where the load has been secured but there is still danger or nuisance or both to the public. Regulation 100(3) is restricted to offences related to the use of a vehicle for a purpose for which it is unsuitable.

Regulation 101 makes specific provision for the parking of motor vehicles in darkness and regulation 103 prohibits any person in charge of a motor vehicle or trailer to cause or permit the vehicle to stand on a road so as to cause any unnecessary obstruction. Accordingly, where the accused parked his car in a bus bay for five minutes but the prosecution did not establish that any bus was in fact obstructed, then an offence was not committed under this regulation[2]. The Crown must also show that the obstruction was unnecessary[3]. Regulation 104 makes it an offence to drive or cause or permit any other person to drive a motor vehicle on a road if proper control of the vehicle and a full view of the road and traffic ahead is not available to the driver. Regulation 105 makes it an offence to open a door of a vehicle on a road so as to injure or endanger any person; this regulation is sometimes used as the foundation of prosecutions particularly where a person in a parked vehicle has opened a door so that it comes into contact with a passing vehicle. Regulation 106 requires that no person shall drive or cause or permit a motor vehicle to be driven backwards on a road further than is necessary. Regulation 107 makes it an offence to leave a vehicle unattended with the engine running or the parking brake not properly set.

---

1 *MacNeill v Wilson* 1981 SLT (Notes) 109, 1981 SCCR 80; see also *Wells v Guild* 1988 SCCR 438.
2 *Brown v Cardle* 1983 SLT 218, 1982 SCCR 495.
3 *McDonald v Annan* 1979 CO Circulars A/22.

In addition to these provisions in the construction and use regulations, s 40A of the Road Traffic Act 1988[1] makes it an offence to use a vehicle on a road when its condition, the purpose for which it is used, the number of passengers or the manner in which they are carried, or the nature of the load is such that it involves a danger of injury to any person. Offences are charged summarily, and the penalties are found in the Road Traffic Act 1991, Sch 2, para 17.

7.12:16 Lighting

There are again numerous and complex provisions dealing with the lighting requirements of vehicles. These are contained not in the Road Vehicles (Construction and Use) Regulations 1986 but in the Road Vehicles Lighting Regulations 1989[2]. In general terms it is an offence to use, or to cause or to permit to be used on a road, any specified vehicle unless that vehicle is equipped with the prescribed lamps, reflectors, rear markings and devices. Regulation 3 contains a comprehensive list of relevant definitions.

Regulation 11 gives detailed provision for the colour of lights to be shown by lamps and reflectors, and regulation 12 qualifies the movement of such items. Regulation 13 provides that lamps must show a steady light except in the case of a direction indicator, warning beacons or special warning lamps and the like. Regulation 16 provides that no vehicle, other than an emergency vehicle, shall be fitted with a blue warning beacon or special warning lamp, or a device which resembles either of these. This, like other similar prohibitions, is an absolute offence[3].

Regulation 17 requires slow-moving vehicles such as agricultural tractors and trailers to carry warning beacons. The regulations and relative schedules provide in considerable detail the specification of obligatory or optional lamps and other equipment of all kinds and in all circumstances. It is an offence not to have obligatory lamps, reflectors, rear markings or devices even where they are not at the material time required. Regulation 17A[4] requires buses carrying children to fit certain prescribed signs.

In *Johnston v Cruickshank*[5], it was held that where a tractor unit

---

1 Introduced by the Road Traffic Act 1991, s 8.
2 SI 1989/1796.
3 *Brown v McGlennan* 1995 SCCR 724.
4 Introduced by SI 1994/2280, reg 6.
5 1963 JC 5, 1962 SLT 409.

draws a trailer, the motor vehicle for the purposes of these regulations is the driving unit and not the whole vehicle.

Certain exemptions are granted to these general requirements by virtue of regulations 4–9. Regulation 18, by reference to Schedule 1, makes detailed provision for obligatory lamps, reflectors, rear markings and devices. Regulations 19 and 20 specify certain restrictions on the obscuration of lamps and reflectors and the regulation of optional lamps and reflectors.

In terms of regulations 21 and 22 provision is made for the lighting of projecting trailers and vehicles carrying overhanging or projecting loads or equipment and additional side marker lamps.

All such lamps and reflectors, rear markings and devices must be properly maintained and kept clean and in good working order[1]. There are requirements about the use of headlamps and front fog lamps in certain situations, such as during the hours of darkness and in reduced visibility[2]. In general, a vehicle must be used with dipped beam headlamps during the hours of darkness, except on a road restricted for the purposes of s 71 of the Road Traffic Regulation Act 1967 by virtue of a system of street lighting when it is lit; and in seriously reduced visibility. There are also specific restrictions on the use of headlamps and front and rear fog lamps, reversing lamps, hazard warning signal devices and warning beacons and work lamps provided in regulation 27.

7.13   TESTING AND INSPECTION

The Road Traffic Act 1991, ss 9–15 provides new ss 66A–72 of the Road Traffic Act 1988 and thereby furnishes wide-ranging powers for the inspection of vehicles. Under earlier legislation, powers of inspection and testing were given to, among others, certifying officers, public service vehicle examiners, and examiners of goods vehicles. By virtue of s 66A there is now simply one class of vehicle examiner authorised by the Secretary of State, which will cover all the functions of the former different sorts of examiner.

In general the powers of inspection under the Road Traffic Act 1991 are much wider than was available under previous legisla-

---

1 Road Vehicles Lighting Regulations 1989, reg 23.
2 1989 Regulations, reg 25.

tion, and include the right to test and inspect not only passenger carrying vehicles (PCVs), which were formerly known as passenger service vehicles (PSVs), and large goods vehicles (LGVs), formerly known as heavy goods vehicles (HGVs), but also private cars. Section 11 of the Road Traffic Act 1991 deletes s 8(1) and (2) of the Public Passengers Act 1981 (which dealt with the inspection of public service vehicles) and substitutes a new s 68 of the Road Traffic Act 1988, and in doing so allows a vehicle examiner to inspect public passenger vehicles and goods vehicles at any time, to detain the vehicle, to enter premises, to test drive the vehicle, and to require the person in charge to drive the vehicle not more than five miles to a place of inspection. Section 12 of the 1991 Act provides a new s 69 of the Road Traffic Act 1988, giving vehicle examiners powers to prohibit the driving of unfit vehicles (of any description); and s 70 of the 1988 Act, which affords the power to prohibit the driving of overloaded vehicles, is amended by s 13 of the 1991 Act. The offence section (s 71 of the 1988 Act) is substituted by s 14 of the 1991 Act. The removal of prohibitions is covered by s 72 of the 1988 Act as substituted by s 15 of the 1991 Act.

Section 67 of the Road Traffic Act 1988[1] allows an authorised examiner to test a vehicle on a road to ascertain whether the construction and use requirements, and the requirement that the vehicle should not be in a dangerous condition, are being observed. The examiner may require the driver to comply with his reasonable instructions, and may also drive the vehicle himself. The motorist has the right to ask for deferment of such a test[2], but can be convicted of an offence revealed by the examination even although he has not had the opportunity to elect for such a deferment[3]. In *Watson v Muir*[4] it was held that although it was desirable that the owner or user of the vehicle should be present at any test, this is not essential. It should be noted that the examiner's powers refer to the driver rather than the owner. Obvious defects can be spoken to in evidence by persons other than authorised examiners[5].

By virtue of s 75 of the Road Traffic Act 1988[6] it is an offence to sell a vehicle which is in an unroadworthy condition; s 76 of the

1 As amended by the Road Traffic Act 1991, s 10.
2 Road Traffic Act 1988, s 67(6).
3 *Brown v McIndoe* 1963 SLT 233.
4 1938 JC 181, 1939 SLT 14.
5 *Mowbray v Valentine* 1992 SLT 416, 1991 SCCR 494.
6 As amended by RTA 1991, s 16.

1988 Act as amended by the Road Traffic Act 1991, Sch 4, para 58 makes it an offence to fit or supply defective, unsuitable or dangerous vehicle parts. Section 77 of the 1988 Act allows examiners to inspect used vehicles in showrooms. For further discussion on vehicle examiners see ch 9.

Chapter Eight

Licences, disqualification, endorsement and fixed penalties

227

8.1   DRIVERS' LICENCES

8.1:1   General

Section 87 of the Road Traffic Act 1988[1] provides:

'(1) It is an offence for a person to drive on a road a motor vehicle of any class otherwise than in accordance with a licence authorising him to drive a motor vehicle of that class.

(2) It is an offence for a person to cause or permit another person to drive on a road a motor vehicle of any class otherwise than in accordance with a licence authorising that other person to drive a motor vehicle of that class.'

The way in which this section is now phrased emphasises that the offence created is not simply that of driving without a licence of any sort, but can and will occur where a person drives a vehicle of a class not authorised by his licence. This reflects the decision in *Ogilvie v O'Donnell*[2] which held that a licence is only valid when used in accordance with its conditions of issue. The classes of

---

1 As amended by the Road Traffic Act 1991, s 17.
2 1983 SCCR 257.

vehicle authorised by a licence are shown on the licence itself. Licences are issued at the instance of the Secretary of State through the Driver and Vehicle Licensing Authority (DVLA) Swansea, which is responsible for keeping details of all licences, including disqualifications and endorsements. A new universal European Community form of licence is now issued which is valid for all member states, and which covers all of the driver's driving entitlements in its authorised classes, including those for commercial and passenger vehicles. HGV licences are now issued separately. Existing old-style licences remain valid until replaced. Duplication of licences is prohibited[1]. Records kept by the Secretary of State in respect of this part of the Act are admissible as copies in evidence, and are sufficient evidence of the facts contained therein[2].

One significant consequence of the way in which s 87 is now phrased is that all prosecutions based on the failure of the driver to have the appropriate licence (apart from driving while disqualified by order of court which remains an offence under s 103) are now taken under s 87(1). Accordingly, offences involving driving without being the holder of a licence, driving a vehicle otherwise than in accordance with the terms of the licence, driving while disqualified by reason of age, and driving as a provisional licence holder without supervision or L plates, or unauthorised driving with a passenger on a motor cycle are currently prosecuted under s 87. Certain limited exceptions to the absolute requirement of holding a licence are found in the Road Traffic Act 1988, s 88.

Prescribed classes of driver who are normally resident outside the United Kingdom and who do not hold a European Community licence may drive on licences held by them for a period of one year[3]. Community licence holders are entitled to drive in this country[4].

Any change in the name or address of the licence holder must be intimated to DVLA forthwith[5]. Relevant considerations in respect of the issue of licences are to be found in the Motor Vehicle (Driving Licences) Regulations 1996[6]. In particular, the various

---

1 Road Traffic Act 1988, s 102.
2 Road Traffic Offenders Act 1988, s 13, as amended by the Civil Evidence Act 1995, s 15(1), Sch 1, para 15.
3 Motor Vehicles (International Circulation) Order 1975, SI 1975/1208.
4 RTA 1988, s 99A and subsequent sections introduced by the Driving Licences (Community Driving Licence) Regulations 1996 (SI 1996/1974) and 1998 (SI 1998/1420).
5 RTA 1988, s 99(4)).
6 (SI 1996/2824).

classes of vehicle which may be authorised on a licence are described in Schedule 2 and include categories in respect of heavy goods and passenger carrying vehicles.

In a charge of driving otherwise than in accordance with the conditions of a licence in contravention of s 87(1), once the Crown has shown prima facie that a driver has no licence, the responsibility for proving that he has a licence rests on the accused[1].

Sections 97 and 98 of the Road Traffic Act 1988 as amended cover the granting and form of licences. It should be noted that s 17 of the Road Traffic Act 1991 deletes ss 97(7) and 98(5) of the 1988 Act; s 100 allows an appeal to the sheriff against a refusal to grant a licence, but a further appeal to the sheriff principal is incompetent[2].

8.1:2 Definitions and penalties

'Drives' – see 1.7:1 above.

'Road' – see 1.8:1, 1.8:2 and 1.8:3 above.

'Motor vehicle' – see 1.2:1ff above.

'Causing or permitting' – see 1.10:3 above.

Penalties for such an offence are found in Schedule 2, Part I of the Road Traffic Offenders Act 1988[3], and normally involve discretionary disqualification and obligatory endorsement. If disqualification is not ordered, three to six penalty points must be endorsed on the licence.

8.1:3 Test of competence to drive

A driving licence will not be issued unless a test of competence to drive has been passed[4]. Various exceptions are allowed[5] and other alternative provisions are found in s 89A[6]. In addition to the

---

1 *Milne v Whaley* 1975 SLT (Notes) 75.
2 *Hopkin v Ayr Local Taxation Office* 1964 SLT (Sh Ct) 60.
3 As amended by the Road Traffic Act 1991, Sch 2, para 19.
4 Road Traffic Act 1988, s 89, as amended.
5 RTA 1988, s 88.
6 Introduced by the Road Traffic Driver Licensing and Information Systems Act 1989, ss 4(1) and 4(4).

requirements of Part III of the Road Traffic Act 1988, further provision on categories of entitlement, application for licences, provisional licences, the nature and conduct of the driving test and special regulations in respect of licences to drive goods and passenger carrying vehicles are found in the Motor Vehicles (Driving Licences) Regulations 1996[1].

Section 90 allows for a review that the test was properly conducted in accordance with the regulations by way of application to the sheriff. However, such an appeal is not intended to be a review of the test; to succeed the appellant must demonstrate that the test was not conducted properly, and that there has been for example, malice or oppression or unfair conduct in the way in which the test was conducted[2]. A further appeal to the sheriff principal is incompetent[3].

8.1:4   Physical fitness

An applicant for a driving licence must furnish a declaration as to whether he is suffering from any relevant or prospective disability which may make his driving a source of danger to the public[4]. Certain prescribed disabilities are given in the Motor Vehicles (Driving Licences) Regulations 1996[5]. A licence may be revoked if the Secretary of State is at any time satisfied on inquiry that the licence holder is suffering from a relevant or prospective disability[6]. This section may be invoked in practice where a court becomes aware during a road traffic prosecution that the accused may be suffering from such a disability, and intimates this to the Secretary of State in terms of s 22 of the Road Traffic Offenders Act 1988. Section 22 provides that the court must notify the Secretary of State of these disabilities if they become evident, irrespective of the outcome of the prosecution. If a licence holder becomes aware that he is suffering from a relevant or prospective disability during the currency of his licence, he must likewise

---

1 SI 1996/2824.
2 *Corrigan v Fox* 1966 SLT (Sh Ct) 79.
3 *Hopkin v Ayr Local Taxation Officer* 1964 SLT (Sh Ct) 60.
4 Road Traffic Act 1988, s 92 as amended inter alia by the Road Traffic Act 1991 s 18, which also amends s 94, and introduces a new s 94A. Penalties are amended by paragraphs 21–23 of Schedule 2 to the 1991 Act.
5 SI 1996/2824, regs 66–69.
6 RTA 1988, s 93.

intimate this[1]; and he must also intimate the refusal by any authorised insurer to provide him with statutory insurance cover on
health grounds[2]. It is an offence to drive with defective eyesight[3].

An appeal against a refusal by the Secretary of State to grant a
licence is available to the sheriff[4] but not to the sheriff principal[5].
In *McFarlane v Secretary of State for Scotland*[6] the principal consideration was whether the appellant was suffering from a relevant
disability likely to cause the driving of a vehicle to be a source of
danger to the public.

8.1:5 Duration and form of licences

The earliest ages at which persons may hold licences are specified
in s 101 of the Road Traffic Act 1988 (as amended) (see 8.2:1
below). Thereafter, full driving licences are issued and in normal
course remain valid until the holder's seventieth birthday, after
which they have to be renewed at three-year intervals[7].

Section 98 requires that the licence should indicate the classes of
vehicle that the driver is entitled to drive and any restrictions on
the driving of such vehicles. Classes of vehicles are detailed in
Schedule 2 to the Motor Vehicles (Driving Licences) Regulations
1996[8]; see also reg 17. Special conditions attaching to the grant of
licences authorising the holder to drive large goods vehicles and
passenger carrying vehicles are found in Chapter 9, Part IV of the
Road Traffic Act 1988, and Part IV of the above regulations.

8.1:6 Provisional licences

Provisional licences are granted for the purpose of enabling the
applicant to pass a test of competence to drive[9].This section, and

---

1 RTA 1988, s 94.
2 RTA 1988, s 95.
3 RTA 1988, s 96.
4 RTA 1988, s 100.
5 *Hopkin v Ayr Local Taxation Office* 1964 SLT (Sh Ct) 60.
6 1988 SCLR (Sh Ct) 623.
7 Road Traffic Act 1988, s 99.
8 SI 1996/2824.
9 Road Traffic Act 1988, s 97(2)–(6).

regulations 13–17 of the Motor Vehicles (Driving Licences) Regulations 1996[1], provide for the conditions and duration of such licences. In particular these regulations provide that a learner driver can only drive on the road while supervised by a qualified driver who must be over 21 years of age and have held a licence for over three years[2].

8.1:7   Driving instruction

No instruction in the driving of motor vehicles for payment can be undertaken by any person who is not on the register of approved instructors, and who is not licensed to undertake such instruction. Driving instruction is dealt with in Part V of the Road Traffic Act 1988. The relevant regulations are the Motor Cars (Driving Instruction) Regulations 1989[3]. The Road Traffic Offenders Act 1988, s 18, provides that a certificate from the Registrar relating to the status of any person on the register is sufficient proof of the facts stated therein.

8.2   DISQUALIFICATION BY REASON OF AGE: OBTAINING LICENCE OR DRIVING WHILE DISQUALIFIED

8.2:1   General

Section 101(1) of the Road Traffic Act 1988[4] provides:

'A person is disqualified for holding or obtaining a licence to drive a motor vehicle of a class specified in the following Table if he is under the age specified in relation to it in the second column of the Table.

---

1 SI 1996/2824.
2 SI 1996/2824, reg 13A, as amended by SI 1999/617.
3 SI 1989/2057.
4 As amended by the Driving Licences (Community Driving Licence) Regulations 1996, SI 1996/1974.

TABLE

Class of motor vehicle	Age (in years)
1. Invalid carriage	16
2. Moped	16
3. Motor bicycle	17
4. Agricultural or Forestry Tractor	17
5. Small vehicle	17
6. Medium-sized goods vehicle	18
7. Other motor vehicles	21'

Section 32 of the Act disqualifies persons under 14 years of age from driving an electrically assisted pedal cycle.

Regulations under this section are the Motor Vehicles (Driving Licences) Regulations 1996[1].

8.2:2   Obtaining licence or driving while disqualified

Section 103 of the Road Traffic Act 1988[2] provides:

'(1) A person is guilty of an offence if, while disqualified for holding or obtaining a licence, he –
   (a) obtains a licence, or
   (b) drives a motor vehicle on a road.

(2) A licence obtained by a person who is disqualified is of no effect (or, where the disqualification relates only to vehicles of a particular class, is of no effect in relation to vehicles of that class).

(3) A constable in uniform may arrest without warrant any person driving a motor vehicle on a road whom he has reasonable cause to suspect of being disqualified.

(4) Subsections (1) and (3) above do not apply in relation to disqualification by virtue of section 101 of this Act.

(5) Subsections (1)(b) and (3) above do not apply in relation to disqualification by virtue of section 102 of this Act.

(6) In the application of subsections (1) and (3) above to a person whose disqualification is limited to the driving of motor vehicles of a particular class by virtue of –
   (a) section 102 or 117A of this Act, or
   (b) subsection (9) of section 36 of the Road Traffic Offenders Act 1988 (disqualification until test is passed),
   the references to disqualification for holding or obtaining a licence and driving motor vehicles are references to disqualification for holding or obtaining a licence to drive and driving motor vehicles of that class.'

1 SI 1996/2824.
2 As amended inter alia by the Road Traffic Act 1991, s 19.

This is an absolute offence and there can be no room for a defence of mistake or ignorance. However, a defence of necessity or duress may be available[1]; reference should also be made to 2.5 above. A licence only entitles the holder to drive vehicles of categories specified in the licence. Failure to observe these categories will result in an offence under this section[2]. Duplication of licences is prohibited[3].

8.2:3   Definitions and penalties

'Drives' – see 1.7:1 above.

'Road' – see 1.8:1, 1.8:2 and 1.8:3 above.

'Motor Vehicle' – see 1.2:1 above.

The penalties for an offence under s 103 (1)(b) of the Road Traffic Act 1988 are found in Schedule 2, Part I to the Road Traffic Offenders Act 1988[4], and normally involve discretionary disqualification and obligatory endorsement. If disqualification is not imposed, six penalty points are endorsed on the licence. Proceedings may be summary or on indictment; the maximum prison sentences are six months and 12 months respectively. An offence under s 103 (1)(a) has no consequence for the licence.

8.3   EVIDENCE

In order to obtain a conviction under s 103 of the Road Traffic Act 1988, the prosecution must adduce sufficient evidence that the accused has been disqualified[5]. If the prosecution attempt to prove the disqualification by reference to a schedule of previous convictions in any form, and that schedule reveals that the accused has previous convictions other than that which imposed the period of disqualification, any subsequent conviction under

---

1 *Moss v Howdle* 1997 JC 123, 1997 SLT 782, 1997 SCR 215.
2 *Ogilvie v O'Donnell* 1983 SCCR 257.
3 Road Traffic Act 1988, s 102.
4 As amended by the Road Traffic Act 1991, Sch 2, para 25.
5 *Herron v Nelson* 1976 SLT (Sh Ct) 42; *Andrews v McLeod* 1982 SLT 456, 1982 SCCR 254.

this section will be quashed[1]. However, reference should also be made to *Moffat v Smith*[2]; *Johnston v Allan*[3]; *Kerr v Jessop*[4], *Harkin v H M Advocate*[5] and *MacLean v Buchanan*[6]. The rule may be less strictly observed in summary cases, and where no real prejudice results.

The statutory provisions which prohibit the disclosure of previous convictions prior to any finding of guilt are found in the Criminal Procedure (Scotland) Act 1995, s 101 (solemn) and s 166 (summary).

In terms of s 19 of the Road Traffic Offenders Act 1988, in any proceedings for an offence under s 103(1)(b) of the Road Traffic Act 1988 (driving while disqualified) a conviction or extract conviction of which a copy has been served on the accused not less than 14 days before his trial, which purports to be signed by the clerk of court, and which shows that the person named in it is disqualified, is to be sufficient evidence of the application of that disqualification to the accused, unless the accused serves notice on the prosecutor, not less than six days before his trial, that he denies that the conviction applies to him. Proof of previous convictions generally is provided for in ss 285 and 286 of the Criminal Procedure (Scotland) Act 1995.

A person who is charged under this section with driving while disqualified by virtue of age is regarded as being in a special capacity in terms of the Criminal Procedure (Scotland) Act 1995, s 255[7], that is to say, that the fact that he is so disqualified is to be held as admitted unless this is challenged by a preliminary objection before his plea is recorded[8].

Even where the accused has not disputed the special capacity, the prosecution can lead evidence of a disqualification previous conviction[9].

---

1 *Herron v Nelson* 1976 SLT (Sh ct) 42; *Mitchell v Dean* 1979 SLT (Notes) 12; *Boustead v McLeod* 1979 JC 70, 1979 SLT (Notes) 48; *Robertson v Aitchison* 1981 SLT (Notes) 127, 1981 SCCR 149.
2 1983 SCCR 392.
3 1984 SLT 261, 1983 SCCR 500.
4 1991 JC 1.
5 1996 SLT 1004, 1996 SCCR 5.
6 1997 SLT 91.
7 See also *Paton v Lees* 1992 SCCR 212.
8 *Smith v Allan* 1985 SLT 565, 1985 SCCR 190.
9 *Campbell v HM Advocate* 1999 JC 147, 1999 SLT 399.

8.4   DISQUALIFICATION FOLLOWING OFFENCE

8.4:1   General

Apart from considerations of disability or age described earlier in this chapter, disqualification of a driver by removal of his licence usually occurs as a consequence of penalties imposed for road traffic offences. In general terms, disqualification may follow in three sets of circumstances; firstly, when the legislation provides that disqualification is obligatory following a particular offence[1]; secondly, when the legislation provides that disqualification is discretionary following a particular offence and the court elects to exercise its discretion in favour of disqualification[2]; and thirdly, where the offence committed involves disqualification for repeated offences or the application of what is known as the totting-up procedure[3]. Whether a particular offence carries obligatory or discretionary disqualification is noted in Schedule 2, Part I to the Road Traffic Offenders Act 1988[4].

However, there are further categories of disqualification. Section 36 of the Road Traffic Offenders Act 1988 (as amended) provides for disqualification until a test of competence to drive is passed (see 8.11:1 below); disqualification may be imposed where a vehicle has been used to commit an offence (see 8.11:4 below); s 248 of the Criminal Procedure (Scotland) Act 1995 allows disqualification where a vehicle has been used for the purpose of committing an offence; s 248A of the same Act, as amended by s 15(1) of the Crime and Punishment (Scotland) Act 1997, allows disqualification for offences other than those connected with road traffic (see 8.11:5 below), and s 248B (again, as similarly introduced) allows the court to disqualify fine defaulters from driving (see 8.11:8 below). Special provisions concerning newly qualified drivers are dealt with at 8.11:7 below. Section 26 of the Road Traffic Offenders Act 1988[5] provides for a system of interim disqualification (see 8.4:3 below). Special consideration is also given to short periods of disqualification (see 8.4:2 below).

Where an accused has committed a number of offences which involve disqualification, the correct procedure is for the court to

---

1 Road Traffic Offenders Act 1988, s 34(1).
2 RTOA 1988, s 34(2) as amended by the Road Traffic Act 1991, s 29(2).
3 RTOA 1988, s 35, as amended by RTA 1991, Sch 4, para 95.
4 As amended by RTA 1991, Sch 2.
5 As amended by RTA 1991, s 25.

consider what is the appropriate period of disqualification for each offence, and not to take account of the accused's behaviour as a whole in order to increase the cumulative period of disqualification[1].

The appeal court has often indicated that anyone who is to be disqualified for any reason should normally be given the opportunity to appear and proffer any special reasons why he should not be.

8.4:2   Short periods of disqualification

Section 37(1A) of the Road Traffic Offenders Act 1988[2] provides that where disqualification is imposed by a court for a fixed period shorter than 56 days in respect of an offence involving obligatory endorsement or where interim disqualification is imposed (see 8.4:3 below), the licence is not revoked in terms of s 37(1) of the Road Traffic Act 1988, as is normally the case following disqualification, but simply continues to have effect at the end of the short period of disqualification or interim disqualification. In practice this means that, unlike the normal situation following disqualification where the licence is revoked and the motorist has to apply to DVLA for the issue of a fresh licence, in these cases the licence is in effect suspended and revives at the end of the period of disqualification. The normal practice contemplated for this procedure is that the licence is to be surrendered to the court, and the clerk of court becomes responsible for endorsing the licence with the details of the disqualification and returning it at the end of the disqualification period to the holder.

The purpose of these provisions reflects the desire of the legislature that courts should more frequently disqualify drivers for short periods.

8.4:3   Interim disqualification

Section 26 (particularly subsections (3), (4), (5) and (6)) of the Road Traffic Offenders Act 1988[3] allows a court to impose interim

---

1 *McMurrich v Cardle* 1988 SCCR 20.
2 As introduced by the Road Traffic Act 1991, s 33.
3 As amended by the Road Traffic Act 1991, s 25.

disqualification after conviction where sentence has been deferred for reports or for good behaviour, or where the accused has been remitted to the High Court for sentence. Specific provision[1] is made for such interim disqualification to be imposed for periods in excess of six months. In general terms, a court can impose an order for interim disqualification in cases where obligatory or discretionary disqualification is available and sentence is deferred for reports on other inquiries, where sentence is simply deferred for a period, or for good behaviour, or where the accused is remitted for sentence to the High Court. Orders can only be made on one occasion[2], but can be continued at subsequent hearings[3]. The period of interim disqualification should not have any effect on the period subsequently selected by the court at disposal[4], but in terms of s 26 (12) the final disqualification is deemed to be reduced by the time served under any relevant interim disqualification. This does not apply if the driver has been forbidden to drive under a bail order. Such an order can be appealed by virtue of the Road Traffic Offenders Act 1988, s 38(2) (see 8.11:2 below).

8.4:4   Consequences of disqualification

In every case where disqualification is obligatory or discretionary, and in every case where penalty points are to be imposed, details of the convictions, and where appropriate the number of penalty points, must be endorsed on the accused's licence[5]. However the court cannot impose disqualification and penalty points for separate offences at the same time[6].

Following disqualification (either obligatory or discretionary), the court may order the driver to give details of his date of birth and other information[7]; and on conviction of an offence involving obligatory endorsement, the court must order the licence to be produced[8]. Where the licence is produced, the court may take into

---

1   Road Traffic Act 1988, s 26(5).
2   RTA 1988, s 26 (6).
3   *Edwards v Whelan* 1999 SLT 917, 1998 SCCR 689.
4   *Wilson v Heywood* 1999 SLT 915, 1998 SCCR 686.
5   Road Traffic Offenders Act 1988, s 44.
6   *Ahmed v McLeod* 1999 SLT 762, 1998 SCCR 486.
7   Road Traffic Offenders Act 1988, s 25.
8   RTOA 1988, s 27, as amended by RTA 1991, Sch 4, para 91.

account any existing endorsements[1]. Where the licence is not produced, a document purporting to be information from the Secretary of State's records[2] may likewise be considered, provided that the accused admits the accuracy of the record as it applies to him[3]. Reference should also be made to 8.10:4 below.

Where a person fails to comply with a court order to produce his licence to the court in terms of s 27, a police constable may require the production of the licence and seize it[4].

8.4:5 Duration of disqualification

By virtue of s 37(1) of the Road Traffic Offenders Act 1988, any period of disqualification commences from the moment it is imposed by the court; there is no provision for back-dating or post-dating such an order.

In cases of obligatory or discretionary disqualification not involving the application of the totting-up procedure, a period of disqualification may not be imposed on a consecutive basis[5]. The court is allowed to look at any other period of disqualification being served by the accused, and any other offence which is being considered at the same time for which disqualification is liable to be imposed, in considering the appropriate length of the disqualification order[6]. Also the court may consider a current prison sentence in deferring the length of any ban[7]. By the nature of the procedure, consecutive disqualification cannot apply in totting-up cases. Any period of disqualification must be for a fixed term; however, in appropriate circumstances a driver may be banned for life.

Where a person is convicted of an offence involving obligatory disqualification, the minimum period of disqualification is 12 months, unless the court considers that special reasons exist for restricting the period of disqualification, or for not imposing disqualification at all[8]. There are several exceptions to this rule.

---

1 RTOA 1988, s 31, as amended by RTA 1991, Sch 4, para 93.
2 Known as a DVLA print-out.
3 RTOA 1988, s 32 as amended by RTA 1991, Sch 4, para 94.
4 Road Traffic Act 1988, s 164(5), as amended by RTA 1991, Sch 4, para 68.
5 *Williamson v McMillan* 1962 SLT 63.
6 *Allan v Crowe* 1994 SCCR 596; *Wishart v Miller* 1998 SCCR 21.
7 *Riddich v Normand* 1996 SCCR 56.
8 Road Traffic Offenders Act 1988, s 34(1).

Firstly, where a driver is convicted of culpable homicide, causing death by dangerous driving[1], or causing death by careless driving while under the influence of drink or drugs[2], the minimum period of disqualification is two years[3]. Further, a minimum period of two years' disqualification is to be imposed in relation to a person on whom more than one disqualification for a fixed period of 56 days or more has been imposed within the three years immediately preceding the commission of the offence[4]. In this latter respect, disqualification imposed as a result of an offence committed by using a vehicle[5] or of taking a vehicle in terms of the Road Traffic Act 1988, s 178 is to be disregarded[6]. Finally, where a driver is convicted within ten years of a second offence involving (i) s 3A of the Road Traffic Act 1988 (causing death by careless driving when under the influence of drink or drugs), (ii) s 4(1) (driving or attempting to drive while unfit through drink or drugs), (iii) s 5(1)(a) (driving or attempting to drive with excess alcohol), or (iv) s 7(6) (failing to provide a specimen where that offence, because it relates to a specimen for analysis rather than for the roadside breathalyser test, involves obligatory disqualification) then the second offence carries a minimum period of disqualification of three years[7]. It is clear that any of these disqualifying offences, if repeated or committed in addition to either of the other disqualifying offences mentioned, causes the three-year minimum period to be introduced; the rule is not restricted to cases where two similar offences under any one of the nominated sections, occur within the prescribed period. However, it should be noted that neither an offence under s 5(1)(b) of the Road Traffic Act 1988 (being in charge of a vehicle with excess alcohol) nor an offence under s 6(4) (failure to provide a road-side test) is included in the list of offences which trigger the three-year minimum period. The ten-year period mentioned in s 34(3) runs from the date of conviction of the initiating offence to the date of the commission of the second offence.

Where conviction follows an offence involving discretionary disqualification, there is no minimum period; the disqualification is for such period as the court thinks fit[8].

1 Road Traffic Act 1988, s 1.
2 RTA 1988, s 3A.
3 RTOA 1988, s 34(4), as amended by the Road Traffic Act 1991, s 29(4)(a).
4 RTOA 1988, s 34(4), as amended by RTA 1991, s 29(4)(b).
5 Criminal Procedure (Scotland) Act 1995 s 248.
6 RTOA 1988, s 34(4A), as introduced by RTA 1991, s 29(4).
7 RTOA 1988, s 34(3) as amended by RTA 1991, s 29(3).
8 RTOA 1988, s 34(2) as amended by RTA 1991, s 29(2).

In cases under the totting-up procedure, the minimum period, in the absence of special reasons, is six months unless there is one or more periods of disqualification within the preceding three years when the minimum periods of disqualification are one and two years respectively[1].

If disqualification is suspended by virtue of s 41 pending an appeal in terms of s 38, the period of suspension is not included in calculating the period of disqualification[2]. The only ways in which a period of disqualification can be reduced are by the attendance and completion by the accused driver of an approved course[3] (see also 8.11:3 below), or by a petition for restoration of the licence before the end of the period of disqualification (see 8.11:8 and 8.11:9 below), or by a successful appeal (see 8.11:2 below).

8.5 OBLIGATORY DISQUALIFICATION

8.5:1 General

By virtue of s 34 of and Schedule 2, Part I to the Road Traffic Offenders Act 1988[4], certain offences carry obligatory disqualification. These are contraventions of s 1 of the Road Traffic Act 1988 (causing death by dangerous driving); s 2 (dangerous driving); s 3A (causing death by careless driving when under the influence of drink or drugs); s 4(1) (driving or attempting to drive while unfit through drink or drugs); s 5(1)(a) (driving or attempting to drive with excess alcohol in breath, blood or urine); s 7 (failing to provide specimen for analysis or laboratory test where the specimen was required to ascertain the ability to drive or the proportion of alcohol at the time the accused was driving or attempting to drive); and s 12 (motor racing and speed trials on public roads). Culpable homicide by the driver of a motor vehicle also attracts compulsory disqualification[5]. In all of these instances, disqualification can only be avoided if the offending motorist successfully pleads that there are special reasons for him not being disqualified (see 8.5:2ff below).

---

1 RTOA 1988, s 35 as amended by RTA 1991, Sch 4, para 95.
2 RTOA 1988, s 43.
3 RTOA 1988, ss 34A, 34B and 34C, as introduced by RTA 1991, s 30.
4 As amended by the Road Traffic Act 1991, Sch 2.
5 Road Traffic Act 1988, Sch 2, Pt II, as amended by RTA 1991, Sch 2, para 32.

Disqualification is also obligatory in certain circumstances where the motorist has been guilty of repeated offences within a three-year period (the 'totting-up' procedure: see 8.8 below). Such disqualification may also be avoided on specific grounds provided by statute (see 8.10:5 below).

8.5:2   Special reasons: general

A court may only refrain from disqualifying a driver for the minimum period as described at 8.4:5 above for the offences referred to at 8.5:1 above, where it is satisfied that special reasons exist for not imposing such disqualification, or for reducing the period of disqualification to one shorter than the minimum period specified above. In *Kempsell v MacDonald*[1] the appeal court indicated that where disqualification was a possible consequence of a road traffic offence, the notice of penalties should indicate that disqualification may be avoided if there are special reasons for so doing. In that case, the appeal court remitted the case back to the sheriff to see whether such special reasons existed.

Special reasons can be defined as mitigating or extenuating circumstances relating to the offence itself, which do not amount to a defence to the charge which results in the obligatory disqualification, but which may justify the court in imposing either no disqualification at all or alternatively a lesser period than the minimum prescribed. A principal consideration in deciding whether such reasons qualify as being special or not is that they must relate to the nature of the offence itself and cannot under any circumstances refer to the personal circumstances of the driver[2]. A further essential condition is that special reasons must as a prime consideration be governed by the overall interests of public safety[3]. Accordingly, special reasons are a question of law and are not purely a matter of discretion for the court.

It is important to remember that in all cases of obligatory disqualification, the number of penalty points to be entered on a licence, if for any reason disqualification is not imposed, is

---

1 1956 SLT 114.
2 *Adair v Munn* 1940 JC 69, 1940 SLT 414.
3 *Adair v Munn* 1940 JC 69, 1940 SLT 414; *Fairlie v Hill* 1944 JC 53, 1944 SLT 224; *Carnegie v Clark* 1947 JC 74, 1947 SLT 218.

within a range of 3 to 11[1]. Parliament has clearly intended that a driver with any relevant points on his licence who escapes disqualification as a result of establishing special reasons should have a further hurdle to clear if he wishes to retain his licence. Should there be any existing points on the licence, the maximum number of points available if disqualification is not imposed (namely 11) will inevitably bring in the totting-up procedure. It may be thought that if special reasons are established, then a low number of penalty points will be imposed, but this is not necessarily the case. Accordingly, in every case where special reasons are established, the successful pleader will then have to address the question of how many penalty points in the range of 3 to 11 the court should cause to be entered on the accused's licence.

In situations not covered by the cases described below, some guidance may, in certain circumstances, be obtained from the cases relating to reasonable excuse for failing to provide a specimen (see 4.14:7 above) although it must be remembered that the nature of the substantive defence to s 7(6) of the Road Traffic Act 1988 is essentially different from a special reasons submission, which is a plea in mitigation following a finding of guilt.

Different considerations will apply to cases when the accused has been found guilty of driving offences on the one hand, and of failing to provide a specimen on the other. Most of the examples which follow relate to special reasons in relation to driving offences. In *Scott v Hamilton*[2] the appeal court observed that it was difficult to imagine circumstances which would justify a refusal to furnish a specimen when required to do so.

Cases where the evidence falls short of providing a full defence of coercion or duress may provide grounds for establishing special reasons[3] (see also 8.5:4 below).

Special reasons can always be established by uncorroborated evidence[4]. However the court may question the absence of apparently available confirmatory evidence.

---

1 Road Traffic Offenders Act 1988, Sch 2, as amended by the Road Traffic Act 1991, Sch 2.
2 1988 SCCR 262.
3 Eg *McLeod v McDougall* 1989 SLT 151, 1988 SCCR 519.
4 *Watson v Adam* 1996 JC 104, 1996 SLT 459, 1996 SCCR 382.

8.5:3   Not special reasons

As indicated above, considerations other than those which apply to the offence itself cannot under any circumstances constitute special reasons. Secondly, the major consideration to be taken into account is the question of danger or risk or potential danger or risk to public safety. The courts have explored various circumstances and concluded that in the following situations, special reasons were not established.

A. Triviality of offence

The comparative triviality of an offence cannot justify a court considering that special reasons exist for not imposing disqualification, if the legislation provides for obligatory disqualification. For example, if a particular driver has exceeded the statutory alcohol limits in terms of s 5(1)(a) of the Road Traffic Act 1988 by a small margin, this cannot justify a claim that special reasons exist for imposing anything less than the statutory minimum period of disqualification[1].

B. Personal hardship

As indicated above, special reasons must relate to the quality and nature of the offence and not the circumstances of the offender. Thus in cases involving obligatory disqualification, even exceptional hardship will not justify the court in mitigating or refraining from disqualification. In *Carnegie v Clark*[2], it was held that where disqualification might result in a medical student being expelled from university, this did not entitle the court not to disqualify the driver.

In *Adair v Munn*[3] and *Muir v McPherson*[4], it was made clear that loss of livelihood and consequent hardship following therefrom to the driver's family could not amount to special reasons. Even a disabled driver who requires his licence to remain mobile cannot argue that his condition amounts to special reasons for not disqualifying[5].

---

1 *Herron v Sharif* 1974 SLT (Notes) 63.
2 1947 JC 74, 1947 SLT 218.
3 1940 JC 69, 1940 SLT 414.
4 1953 SLT 307.
5 *Copeland v Pollock* 1976 CO Circulars 1428.

C. Previous character

It has long been established that the fact that a driver has a clean driving record for a long number of years cannot amount to special reasons for not endorsing the licence[1].

D. Ability of driver to meet consequences

In a case where the accused was convicted of driving without insurance, the fact that he was financially able to meet any claims made against him arising out of his driving did not justify the court in finding special reasons for not disqualifying[2].

E. Consequences to public interest

The fact that a period of disqualification may have particularly serious consequences for the public interest where the driver has significant public duties to perform, which he cannot do without his licence, again does not amount in normal circumstances to special reasons for refraining from disqualification. In *Murray v Macmillan*[3], a driver was not disqualified in circumstances which related to his war time duties; but in the subsequent cases of *Fairlie v Hill*[4], *McFadyean v Burton*[5] and *Robertson v McGinn*[6], it was made very clear that *Murray* was an exceptional case and not to be followed.

F. Special reasons unrelated to the offence

In *MacDonald v MacKenzie*[7], a motorist agreed to give a blood sample from his arm; this was found to be impossible and he declined to give any further samples. The court held that in these circumstances, special reasons did not exist.

In *Smith v Peaston*[8] a vehicle was stopped by police officers purportedly acting under the equivalent of s 163 of the Road Traffic Act 1988. On the subsequent conviction of the driver for a drink-driving offence it was held that an allegation that the police officers had no justification for exercising these powers, even if correct, would not amount to special reasons for not imposing disqualification.

---

1 *Muir v Sutherland* 1940 JC 66, 1940 SLT 403.
2 *Robertson v McGinn* 1955 JC 57.
3 1942 JC 10.
4 1944 JC 53, 1944 SLT 224.
5 1954 JC 18, 1953 SLT 301.
6 1955 JC 57.
7 1975 SLT 190.
8 1977 JC 81.

In cases under s 7(6) of the Road Traffic Act 1988 (refusal to provide specimen for analysis), it is well recognised that the special reasons must relate to the refusal, and not to other circumstances which might amount to special reasons in another situation. In *Smith v Nixon*[1] an accused was driving in an emergency to join his mountain rescue team which had been called out in circumstances where the lives of others might be in danger. While it is possible in certain circumstances that such a consideration might amount to special reasons for not disqualifying if the accused had been convicted of a drink-driving offence, it was held that special reasons had not been established in respect of the refusal to provide a specimen. In *McNicol v Peters*[2] it was decided that the fact that the driver had not been drinking did not justify his refusal to give a specimen.

In *Tudhope v O'Kane*[3] a refusal to provide a specimen because the accused was a teetotaller was held, exceptionally, to amount to special reasons. However, it is not a special reason where the accused maintains that he had only taken alcohol after driving had ceased[4].

G. Shortness of distance

The fact that a motorist has embarked on only a short journey will not in normal circumstances amount to special reasons[5]. However, the position is not entirely straightforward. In *Mackay v MacPhail*[6], a driver who had been drinking moved his car a short distance in a car park and came into minor collision with another vehicle; in these circumstances it was held on appeal that special reasons did not exist. On the other hand, where a car was moved only a short distance on the public road, special reasons were held to have been established without apparent reference to the above authorities[7]. In view of the fact that one of the principal considerations is the interest of public safety (see 8.5:4 below), the fact that a minimal distance was driven may be a relevant consideration in certain circumstances. In England, the fact that the journey undertaken is of very short duration is a matter which may be taken into account (see 8.5:4G below).

---

1 1985 SLT 192, 1984 SCCR 373.
2 1969 SLT 261.
3 1986 SCCR 538.
4 *Emms v Lockhart* 1988 SLT 222, 1987 SCCR 622.
5 *Skeen v Irvine* 1980 SCCR Supp 259; *Lamb v Heywood* 1988 SLT 728, 1988 SCCR 42.
6 1989 SCCR 622.
7 *Lowe v Mulligan* 1991 SCCR 551.

H. Impairment of ability to drive

A claim, even if established in evidence, that the accused driver's ability to drive was not impaired, for example in terms of s 4(1) of the Road Traffic Act 1988, will not, it is submitted, establish that there are special reasons for not disqualifying in a charge under s 5(1)(a). Nor will the erroneous belief by the accused that he had waited a sufficient time to allow the level of alcohol in his system to fall below the permitted level[1].

I. Medical condition

In *Scott v Hamilton*[2] a lady motorist pled guilty to failing to provide a specimen for analysis, but claimed that she had been suffering from pre-menstrual tension and was not amenable to reason. It was held that this was not a special reason for not disqualifying.

8.5:4 Circumstances which may justify special reasons

As indicated above, the case of *Adair v Munn*[3], is authority for the view that special reasons are a question of law and not of discretion, and that prime consideration must be given to the interest of public safety. Further, special reasons must relate to the offence, rather than to the accused. If special reasons are established, the court has the discretion to reduce the normal obligatory period of disqualification, or to refrain from imposing disqualification completely. The onus is generally on the accused to establish special reasons on the balance of probabilities[4]. The courts have held that special reasons may exist in the following circumstances.

A. Medical emergency

Where a driver is compelled to drive by an unforeseen medical emergency and circumstances where he assured he would not have otherwise driven, special reasons may exist[5]. However,

---

1 *Normand v Cameron* 1992 SCCR 390.
2 1988 SCCR 262.
3 1940 JC 69, 1940 SLT 414.
4 *Skinner v Ayton* 1977 SLT (Sh Ct) 48.
5 *Copeland v Sweeney* 1977 SLT (Sh Ct) 28; *Graham v Annan* 1980 SLT 28; *Watson v Hamilton* 1988 SLT 316, 1988 SCCR 13.

failure to use another reasonably available method of undertaking the journey will exclude the establishment of special
reasons[1].

B. Other emergencies

In *Ortewell v Allan*[2] a disqualified driver pushed a broken-down
car off a busy main road and then got into the driving seat and
was pushed or free-wheeled into a car park where it collided with
another vehicle. In these circumstances, the appeal court held that
there were grounds for restricting the period of disqualification.
Where the accused extricated a car from a snow drift when the
driver was unable to do so, and then reversed some distance
down the road to allow other cars to get by, it was held that the
accused need not be disqualified[3]. Necessity or duress may constitute a defence to any driving offence (see 2.5 above). However,
where the circumstances do not justify such a defence, they may
nonetheless form the basis of a special reasons submission.
Similarly, the drivers of emergency service vehicles are under the
same duties of care on the road as other drivers apart from the
observance of speed limits[4], but the situation may indicate that
special reasons exist. In *Connorton v Annan*[5] a driver claimed he
was driving under duress. The appeal court rejected this but
considered that the circumstances justified reducing a discretionary period of disqualification. See also *Morrison v Valentine*[6]
and *McLeod v McDougall*[7].

C. Laced drinks

Where a driver consumes alcohol unknown to himself because
his drink has been interfered with, by the addition of an alcoholic beverage by a third party, special reasons for not disqualifying may exist. However, if the accused shows that his drinks
were interfered with without his knowledge in such a way that
he totally lost control of his actions he may have a complete substantive defence to any drink-driving charge[8] (see 2.5 above). If

---

1 *Copeland v Sweeney* 1977 SLT (Sh Ct) 28.
2 1984 SCCR 208.
3 *Riddell v MacNeill* 1983 SCCR 26.
4 Road Traffic Regulation Act 1984, s 87.
5 1981 SCCR 307.
6 1991 SLT 413, 1990 SCCR 692.
7 1989 SLT 151, 1988 SCCR 519.
8 *Ross v HM Advocate* 1991 SLT 546, 1991 SCCR 823.

for any reason this defence cannot be made out (where, for example, there is insufficient evidence as to the nature of the substance introduced into the drink consumed by the accused, or of its effect) it may still be possible to argue after conviction that special reasons exist for not disqualifying. In *Skinner v Ayton*[1] it was held that special reasons could only be found in these circumstances if the accused establishes in evidence that his drink was in fact laced, that he did not know or have reasonable cause to suspect that this had happened, and that the alcohol level in the accused's blood would not have exceeded the legal limit but for the lacing of the drink. In *Watson v Adam*[2] a motorist drove in circumstances where he realised that he had taken alcoholic instead of non-alcoholic liquor, but wrongly believed he was fit to drive. It was held that this did not amount to special reasons. It is submitted that in presenting an argument that special reasons exist in these circumstances, the same overall approach should be taken as in the case of post-accident drinking defences (see 3.9 and 3.17:1 above). In particular, it is submitted that in establishing that the alcohol level in the accused's blood would not have exceeded the legal limit but for the fact that further alcohol had been introduced unknown to him into his system, evidence (by an analyst or suitably qualified doctor) relating to the effect that such addition of alcohol would have had on his system should normally be adduced where possible. In *McLeod v Napier*[3] the appeal court held that there should be evidence as to the effect of the particular substance introduced into the drink on the human metablolism.

Whether the accused should plead not guilty or rely on special reason submissions in these circumstances is a matter of judgment, although there is nothing to stop an accused pleading not guilty, and if that is not successful, going on to argue for special reasons.

Reference should also be made to Appendix E.

D. Driving when instructed by police

In *Farrell v Moir*[4] a driver was ordered to drive his vehicle by a police officer in order that it should cease being an obstruction to

---

1 1977 SLT (Sh Ct) 48.
2 1996 JC 104, 1996 SLT 459, 1996 SCR 382.
3 1993 SCCR 303.
4 1974 SLT (Sh Ct) 89.

other traffic. In these circumstances, because it was demonstrated that the driver would not otherwise have been driving but for the direction of the police officer, it was held that there were special reasons for not imposing a period of disqualification.

E. Reasons unconnected with offence

Where a driver refused to give a specimen for analysis on the ground that he was a teetotaller, this was held to amount to a special reason[1]. This is perhaps a somewhat exceptional case.

F. Public interest

As indicated earlier, in *Murray v McMillan*[2], it was held that where very special and significant damage might be caused to the public interest by the disqualification of an offender (as in the case of a doctor who had to carry out essential tasks during the time of war), special reasons for not disqualifying were established. However, it has been repeatedly said in other cases[3] that such a situation was entirely remarkable and it is extremely unlikely that it would be followed in any circumstances.

G. General directions in English cases

In England the appeal court in the case of *Chatters v Burke*[4] laid down a number of considerations which should be looked at in coming to the conclusion that special reasons exist. These matters are as follows: firstly, how far the vehicle was driven; secondly, in what manner it was driven; thirdly, the state of the vehicle; fourthly, whether it was the intention of the driver to go further; fifthly, an assessment of the conditions of the road and traffic travelling at the time; sixthly whether there was a possibility of danger of the driver coming into contact with other road users or pedestrians; and finally, the reasons for the driving of the vehicle. The appeal court made it clear that the sixth of these considerations was by far the most important.

---

1 *Tudhope v O'Kane* 1986 SCCR 538.
2 1942 JC 10.
3 Eg in *Fairlie v Hill* 1944 JC 53, 1944 SLT 224; *McFadyean v Burton* 1954 JC 18, 1953 SLT 301; *Robertson v McGinn* 1955 JC 57.
4 [1986] RTR 396, DC.

8.6 PROCEDURE IN SPECIAL REASON SUBMISSIONS

8.6:1 General

It is for the accused to raise the question of special reasons at the time of sentence. The court is not entitled to conclude that special reasons exist for not imposing disqualification from the submissions made to him without the matter having been specifically argued by the accused. Reference should be made to *McLeod v Scoular*[1]; *Tudhope v Birbeck*[2] and *McNab v Feeney*[3]. The facts relied on may have become sufficiently clear from the evidence if the matter has gone to trial. If, however, the accused pleads guilty the appropriate procedure is for the accused or his solicitor to indicate, at the time of pleading guilty, that the plea is qualified by the submission that special reasons exist for not imposing disqualification. It is considered good practice for the defence agent to indicate this intention in advance of the date of sentence to the procurator fiscal in order to allow the fiscal suitable opportunity for considering the nature of the special reasons. If, on hearing the nature of the special reasons at the time of sentence, the procurator fiscal requires further time to examine the reasons so adduced, the court will normally grant a continuation for that purpose. It should be emphasised that if a form of motion is not made at the time of sentence to the effect that special reasons exist for not disqualifying, the accused will not be permitted to raise the question of special reasons thereafter unless the circumstances are exceptional[4].

It is proper practice for evidence to be led in support of the special reasons that are to be established rather than simply to rely on *ex parte* statements by the accused's solicitor. However, it is open for the prosecutor to accept *ex parte* statements as correct in appropriate circumstances[5]. If the Crown does not accept what is said by the accused, then the onus of proof is on the accused and the standard of proof that must be reached is the balance of probabilities[6].

---

1 1974 JC 28, 1974 SLT (Notes) 44.
2 1979 SLT (Notes) 47.
3 1980 SLT (Notes) 52.
4 *Hynd v Clark* 1954 SLT 85, distinguishing *Trotter v Burnett* 1947 JC 151.
5 *McLeod v Scoular* 1974 JC 28, 1974 SLT (Notes) 74.
6 *Farrell v Moir* 1974 SLT (Sh Ct) 89; *Skinner v Ayton* 1977 SLT (Sh Ct) 48; see also *Irvine v Pollock* 1952 JC 51, 1952 SLT 185 and *MacFadyean v Burton* 1954 JC 18, 1953 SLT 301.

In particular, in *McLeod v Scoular*[1], the High Court laid down the rules relating to the onus and standard of proof and the procedure to be followed in cases where special reasons are argued. Firstly, the prosecutor may agree that what is said by the accused is true, in which case the court may deal with the submissions in the absence of evidence. It is of course always open to the court to continue the case for further information if required. Secondly, if the accused has been found guilty following a trial, the court may be satisfied from the evidence heard as to whether special reasons have been established or not without further inquiry. Thirdly, where the Crown disputes the statement by the defence, the court should order a further hearing to allow the defence to lead evidence in support of its case and the opportunity of leading evidence to contradict the defence case. This procedure should also be adopted in cases where the procurator fiscal can neither admit nor deny what is said by the accused. The proper procedure in all circumstances where special reasons are to be put forward is that the accused or his solicitor should at the time of tendering the plea of guilty when sentence is to be imposed intimate that special reasons are to be advanced and give a general outline of the facts on which these reasons are to be based. Thereafter, the procurator fiscal should be asked whether he is in a position to accept what is said or whether he either denies the accused's version of events or is in a position neither to confirm or deny that version. If the procurator fiscal is in a position to confirm the submissions made by the defence, the matter can then be dealt with. However, in all other circumstances, it is submitted that the proper course is to defer sentence for the purpose of fixing a hearing on the special reasons.

If the accused does not appear personally and is not represented by a solicitor, but pleads guilty by letter, the responsibility still remains on the accused to raise the question of special reasons. If he does not do so in the course of his letter, then the mandatory period of disqualification or endorsement, as appropriate, must be imposed. However, the appeal court has made it clear that where an accused pleads guilty by letter, the court should normally continue the matter to allow for the personal appearance of the accused. If therefore the accused states in his letter that special reasons do or might exist for not imposing disqualification, then in general terms the same procedure should be followed as in the preceding paragraph. In other words, if the

1 1974 JC 28, 1974 SLT (Notes) 44.

procurator fiscal is in a position to agree expressly with what is said in the letter for the purposes of considering special reasons, it may be possible for the court to dispose of the case on that basis. However, in all other circumstances, a continuation should be granted in order to allow a hearing to be fixed on the question of special reasons and the accused given an opportunity to attend. Further details about the procedure to be adopted in this situation were given in the case of *Keane v Perrie*[1].

Where an accused is abroad, and cannot attend court, his case may be dealt with in his absence, even if obligatory disqualification is involved[2].

The appeal court is normally reluctant to listen to reasons not raised in the lower court[3].

8.7 DISCRETIONARY DISQUALIFICATION

8.7:1 Discretionary disqualification: statutory offences

Discretionary disqualification is available in a significant number of offences, which are detailed in the tables forming Parts I and II of Schedule 2 to the Road Traffic Offenders Act 1988[4]. Discretionary disqualification is always a matter for the court[5]. The court must take into account all facts and circumstances which are relevant in reaching its decision. However, the accused should always be given an opportunity of leading before the court any reasons why he should not be disqualified in such cases[6]. The reason for disqualifying must properly relate to the offence[7].

8.7:2 Discretionary disqualification: vehicle used in offence

Discretionary disqualification is also available to the court where (except in charges which are triable only summarily) a person is

---

1 1983 SLT 63, 1982 SCCR 377.
2 *Imrie v McGlennan* 1990 SCCR 218.
3 *Stewart v Carnegie* 1988 SCCR 431.
4 As amended by the Road Traffic Act 1991, Sch 2.
5 RTOA 1988, s 34(2), as amended by RTA 1991, s 29(2).
6 *MacDonald v McGillivray* 1986 SCCR 28; but see also *Imrie v McGlennan* 1990 SCCR 218.
7 *Henderson v McNaughtan* 1992 SCCR 767.

convicted of an offence and the court which passes sentence is satisfied that a motor vehicle was used for the purpose of committing or facilitating the commission of that offence[1]. It appears from the terms of these sections that persons so disqualified need not have been driving, or indeed in, the vehicle at the material time.

This form of disqualification is unusual in that it is not associated with endorsement of the licence or the alternative imposition of penalty points, but exists, and is to be imposed, as a separate and individual penalty.

8.8   DISQUALIFICATION FOR REPEATED OFFENCES

In addition to offences which carry obligatory or discretionary disqualification, disqualification will also follow in certain circumstances where a driver has been guilty of repeated offences within a three-year period, by virtue of s 35 of the Road Traffic Offenders Act 1988[2]. Generally, in addition to other penalties, a number of offences under the legislation carry penalty points which on conviction are endorsed on the licence by the court or DVLA Swansea. In the event of a motorist acquiring 12 or more such points within a three-year period, the court must order disqualification for specified minimum periods, unless there are grounds for not doing so. The three year period is computed *de die in diem* and the day of the later or last offence is not included in the reckoning; so that an offence committed on 25 July 2003 falls one day outwith the three-year period following an offence committed on 25 July 2000[3].

In respect of some offences, a set number of penalty points must be endorsed on the driver's licence; in respect of others, the court must select a number of penalty points from a range provided. The offences to which penalty points relate are found in the Road Traffic Regulation Act 1984 and the Road Traffic Act 1988. The penalty points themselves are detailed against the appropriate offences in Schedule 2, Parts I and II of the Road Traffic Offenders Act 1988[4]. However, disqualification under the totting-up proce-

---

1 Criminal Procedure (Scotland) Act 1995, s 248.
2 As amended by the Road Traffic Act 1991, Sch 4, para 95.
3 *Keenan v Carmichael* 1992 SLT 814, 1991 SCCR 680.
4 As amended by RTA 1991, Sch 2.

dure cannot be imposed consecutively on other periods of disqualification given at the same time[1].

The general purpose of what has become known as the totting-up procedure is to penalise, by disqualification, drivers who repeatedly commit relatively minor offences, as opposed to the imposition of obligatory disqualification for the more serious offences. However, the use of penalty points to accelerate the penalty of disqualification has been employed in two ways by the Road Traffic Act 1991. Firstly, as indicated at 8.5:2 above, the introduction of a range of penalty points of between 3 and 11 in all cases of obligatory disqualification, where such disqualification is in the event not imposed (as, for example, where special reasons are established or where mention of disqualification is omitted from the notice of penalties), is intended to restrict the opportunity for the motorist to escape disqualification, by making totting-up more readily available. Secondly, in terms of the amendments to the totting-up legislation introduced by the Road Traffic Act 1991, the court may in certain circumstances aggregate penalty points where more than one offence has been committed on the same occasion (see 8.10:2 below).

8.9 NOTICE OF PENALTIES

Following the passing of the Criminal Procedure (Scotland) Act 1995 the Crown no longer has to serve a notice of penalties on the accused.

8.10 TOTTING-UP AND PENALTY POINTS: STATUTORY PROVISIONS

8.10:1 General operation

For the practitioner, the principal subsections of s 28 of the Road Traffic Offenders Act 1988[2], are as follows:

'(1) Where a person is convicted of an offence involving obligatory endorsement, then, subject to the following provisions of this section, the number of penalty points to be attributed to the offence is –

1 *Middleton v Tudhope* 1986 JC 101, 1986 SCCR 241.
2 As amended by the Road Traffic Act 1991, s 27.

(a) the number shown in relation to the offence in the last column of Part I or Part II of Schedule 2 to this Act, or

(b) where a range of numbers is shown, a number within that range.

(2) Where a person is convicted of an offence committed by aiding, abetting, counselling or procuring, or inciting to the commission of, an offence involving obligatory disqualification, then, subject to the following provisions of this section, the number of penalty points to be attributed to the offence is ten.

. . .

(4) Where a person is convicted (whether on the same occasion or not) of two or more offences committed on the same occasion and involving obligatory endorsement, the total number of penalty points to be attributed to them is the number or highest number that would be attributed on a conviction of one of them (so that if the convictions are on different occasions the number of penalty points to be attributed to the offences on the later occasion or occasions shall be restricted accordingly).

(5) In a case where (apart from this subsection) subsection (4) above would apply to two or more offences, the court may if it thinks fit determine that that subsection shall not apply to the offences (or, where three or more offences are concerned, to any one or more of them).

(6) Where a court makes a determination it shall state its reasons in open court and, if it is a magistrates' court, or in Scotland a court of summary jurisdiction, shall cause them to be entered in the register (in Scotland, record) of its proceedings.'

Where Schedule 2 to the Road Traffic Offenders Act 1988[1] provides a fixed number of penalty points, the court has no option on conviction but to impose that number of points on the licence. Where a range of penalty points is available, the procedure that the court must adopt is to consider what number of points within the specified range is appropriate to the particular offence, having regard to all the circumstances of the offence and the offender[2].

In normal circumstances, in the event of the accused person being convicted of two or more offences which carry penalty points and which were committed on the same occasion, the proper procedure for the court is to consider the appropriate number of points to be imposed in respect of each offence, and order that the higher or highest of these numbers is to be the number of penalty points to be endorsed on the licence. Subsection (4) does not require that the court must impose the

---

1 As amended by RTA 1991, Sch 2.
2 *Briggs v Guild* 1987 SCCR 141.

highest possible number of points available for any of the relevant charges. For example, an accused may face a charge under s 3 of the Road Traffic Act 1988 (careless driving) which carries 3 to 9 points, and a further charge under s 143 (driving without insurance) which carries 6 to 8 points. If the court considers that the appropriate number of points for the careless driving charge is 7, and for the insurance charge is 6, then 7 penalty points will be endorsed on the careless driving charge. If the court considers that the careless driving charge should carry 6 points, and the insurance charge 8, then the latter number of points will be endorsed against the insurance offence.

Subsection (4) applies to offences committed 'on the same occasion'. What is meant by this phrase is that the offences must be committed during the same incident of driving, or during a series of closely related incidents, and further that the offences themselves must be related. Thus, illegal parking and a subsequent refusal to take a breath test were held in the circumstances to be unrelated and thus not committed on the same occasion and two sets of penalties were imposed[1]. What is not yet clear is whether a series of offences committed over an extended period of driving, such as overtaking a number of vehicles on the inside on a motorway (which is normally regarded as careless driving) would result in a number of charges which were committed 'on the same occasion'.

It will also be noted that, so long as the offences charged were committed on the same occasion, the rule contained in subsection (4) applies even when the charges are split up and brought against the accused on different occasions. It would seem that if a charge brought on a later occasion has a higher pointage, the court may have to instruct that the higher points are endorsed on the licence, and the lesser ones removed. It is not thought that this should prove to be a course to which DVLA Swansea would object. The situation is not likely to arise where a motorist is charged with two offences, one of which is taken under the fixed penalty procedure, and one which is prosecuted (under a different time scale) by summary complaint[2].

---

1 *Cameron v Brown* 1997 SLT 914, 1996 SCCR 675; see also *Robertson v McNaughtan* 1993 SLT 1143, 1993 SCCR 526; *McDonald v Hingston* 1994 SCCR 268; and *McKeever v Walkinshaw* 1996 SCCR 189.
2 See *Green v O'Donnell* 1997 SCCR 315, overturning *Reith v Thomson* 1994 SCCR 577.

8.10:2   Aggregation

Section 28(5) of the Road Traffic Offenders Act 1988, introduced by s 27 of the Road Traffic Act 1991, however, provides an important exception to the foregoing general rule. In effect, s 28(5) allows a court, if it sees fit, not to bind itself to the restrictions imposed by s 28(4). The apparent purpose of s 28(5) is to let the court choose, where it is dealing with two or more offences, to impose penalty points on more than one, or indeed all, of such offences, and thus in effect aggregate points on all the charges, so that totting-up disqualification may become instantly available. It would seem from the way in which s 28(4) and (5) is framed that aggregation of penalty points is meant to be an exceptional procedure, but the Act does not specifically say so, nor does it give any indication of the circumstances under which aggregation should be used.

It is submitted that the court should only use the powers of aggregation in exceptional circumstances. For example, it would be wrong to aggregate penalty points to punish what the court considered to be a particularly serious offence of its sort. A motorist charged with no insurance and two unrelated construction and use offences may have caused considerable damage and loss; however, as the other offences are unconnected, the legislation appears not to contemplate that the serious nature of the insurance charge should justify aggregating its penalty points with those of the other offences to achieve instant disqualification. It appears that aggregation should only occur when the particular combination of offences demonstrates, by virtue of that combination alone, that a serious danger to road safety is thereby created. Should the court choose to make such a determination in terms of s 28(5), the reasons must be stated in open court and marked on the complaint[1].

Cases where aggregation has been considered are *Robertson v McNaughtan*[2] and *McDonald v Hingston*[3].

8.10:3   Statutory provisions (s 29): penalty points to be taken into account

Section 29 of the Road Traffic Offenders Act 1988[4] provides:

---

1 Road Traffic Offenders Act 1988, s 28(6).
2 1993 SLT 1143, 1993 SCCR 526.
3 1994 SCCR 268.
4 As amended by the Road Traffic Act 1991, s 28.

'(1) Where a person is convicted of an offence involving obligatory endorsement, the penalty points to be taken into account on that occasion are (subject to subsection (2) below) –
  (a) any that are to be attributed to the offence or offences of which he is convicted, disregarding any offence in respect of which an order under section 34 of this Act is made, and
  (b) any that were on a previous occasion ordered to be endorsed on the counterpart of any licence held by him, unless the offender has since that occasion and before the conviction been disqualified under section 35 of this Act.
(2) If any of the offences was committed more than three years before another, the penalty points in respect of that offence shall not be added to those in respect of the other.
(3) In relation to licences which came into force before 1st June 1990, the reference in subsection (1) above to the counterpart of a licence shall be construed as a reference to the licence itself.'

The critical starting date in the calculation of the number of penalty points on a licence is the date of the commission of the offences, rather than the date of the conviction. Any penalty points imposed on a licence outwith the three-year period from the date of commission of the starting offence to the date of commission (not the date of conviction) of the offence or offences currently under consideration fall to be disregarded. However, this means that any penalty points endorsed on a licence following a conviction which is prior in time to the offences being considered, where the commission of the offence relative thereto is after the date of the commission of the offence under consideration, have also to be taken into account. In other words, penalty points for any offences committed after, but dealt with before, the current offence are included in the calculation. The section also makes it clear that any period of disqualification imposed under s 34 of the Act (for offences involving obligatory or discretionary disqualification), does not have the effect of cancelling out all penalty points within the three-year period prior to the disqualification. This amended provision reverses the previous position in respect of any order of obligatory or discretionary disqualification. However, an order of totting-up disqualification continues to have the effect of wiping out previous penalty points. The three-year period is computed *de die in diem* and the day of the later or last offence is not included in the reckoning[1].

---

1 *Keenan v Carmichael* 1992 SLT 814, 1991 SCCR 680.

8.10:4   Statutory provisions: production of licence

In terms of s 27 of the Road Traffic Offenders Act 1988[1], where a person who is the holder of a licence is convicted of an offence involving obligatory or discretionary disqualification the court must require the licence to be produced to it before it can make any order involving such endorsement. Conversely, s 7 of the Road Traffic Offenders Act 1988[2] imposes a duty on every accused prosecuted for an offence involving obligatory disqualification to produce his licence for the hearing.

Section 31[3] and the Criminal Procedure (Consequential Provisions) (Scotland) Act 1995, s 5 and Sch 4, para 71(4), then provides:

'(1) Where a person is convicted of an offence involving obligatory or discretionary disqualification and his licence is produced to the court –
  (a) any existing endorsement on his licence is prima facie evidence of the matters endorsed, and
  (b) the court may, in determining what order to make in pursuance of the conviction, take those matters into consideration.
(2) This section has effect notwithstanding anything in s 166 (1) to (6) of the Criminal Procedure (Scotland) Act 1995 (requirements as to notices of penalties and previous convictions).'

This section is self-explanatory but must be read along with the terms of s 29, which for totting-up purposes, restricts consideration of such previous endorsements to the preceding three years.

Where the licence is not available for production to the court (for example where it is lost or destroyed, or has been sent to DVLA Swansea for alteration) then it is open to the court to consider a DVLA print-out (normally produced by the prosecution), if the accused agrees that the particulars therein are accurate and relate to himself[4]. The terms of s 32 (as amended by the Road Traffic Act 1991, Sch 4, para 94) and the Criminal Procedure (Consequential Provisions) (Scotland) Act 1995[5] are as follows:

'(1) Subsections (2) or (5) below apply where a person is convicted in Scotland of an offence involving obligatory or discretionary disqualification but his licence is not produced to the court.

---

1 As amended by the Road Traffic Act 1991, Sch 4, para 91.
2 As amended by RTA 1991, Sch 4, para 83.
3 As amended by RTA 1991, Sch 4, para 93.
4 See also *McCallum v Scott* 1987 SLT 491.
5 s 5 and Sch 4, para 71(4).

(2) The court may, in determining what order to make in pursuance of the conviction, take into consideration (subject to subsection (3) below) –
    (a) particulars of any previous conviction or disqualification pertaining to him, and
    (b) any penalty points ordered to be endorsed on any licence held by him which are to be taken into account under s 29 of this Act,
    which are specified in a document purporting to be a note of information contained in the records maintained by the Secretary of State in connection with his functions under Part III of the Road Traffic Act 1988.
(3) If the prosecutor lays before the court such a document as is mentioned in subsection (2) above, the court or the clerk of court must ask the accused if he admits the accuracy of the particulars relating to him contained in the document.
(4) Where the accused admits the accuracy of any particulars, the prosecutor need not adduce evidence in proof of those particulars, and the admission must be entered in the record of the proceedings.
(5) Where the accused does not admit the accuracy of any particulars the prosecutor must, unless he withdraws those particulars, adduce evidence in proof of them, either then or at any other diet.
(6) This section has effect notwithstanding anything in sections 166(1) and (6) of the Criminal Procedure (Scotland) Act 1995 (requirements as to notices of penalties and previous convictions).'

Again this section is self-explanatory; it is submitted that the procedure for establishing the accuracy of the particulars contained in the print-out should be strictly observed. If no licence or print-out is properly before the court, the Crown must serve a schedule of previous convictions[1].

In terms of s 201 of the Criminal Procedure (Scotland) Act 1995 a deferment of sentence or inter alia the production of a DVLA print-out cannot exceed three weeks if the accused is in custody; otherwise the period is four weeks, or eight weeks on cause shown[2].

The DVLA code used in noting convictions on licences is given in Appendix D.

8.10:5 Statutory provisions (s 35): mitigating circumstances

Section 35 of the Road Traffic Offenders Act 1988[3] provides:

---

1 *Anderson v Allan* 1985 SCCR 262.
2 *Wilson v Donald* 1993 SLT 31, *Holburn v Lees* 1993 SCCR 426; *Burns v Wilson* 1993 SCCR 418; *McCulloch v Scott* 1993 SLT 901; *Douglas v Jamieson* 1993 SLT 816 and; *Douglas v Peddie* 1993 SCCR 717 which are all cases under the previous statutory provisions.
3 As amended by the Road Traffic Act 1991, Sch 4, para 95.

'(1) Where –
- (a) a person is convicted of an offence to which this subsection applies, and
- (b) the penalty points to be taken into account on that occasion number twelve or more,

the court must order him to be disqualified for not less than the minimum period unless the court is satisfied, having regard to all the circumstances, that there are grounds for mitigating the normal consequences of the conviction and thinks fit to order him to be disqualified for a shorter period or not to order him to be disqualified.

(1A) Subsection (1) above applies to –

- (a) any offence involving discretionary disqualification and obligatory endorsement, and
- (b) an offence involving obligatory disqualification in respect of which no order is made under s 34 of this Act.

(2) The minimum period referred to in subsection (1) above is –
- (a) six months if no previous disqualification imposed on the offender is to be taken into account, and
- (b) one year if one, and two years if more than one, such disqualification is to be taken into account;

and a previous disqualification imposed on an offender is to be taken into account if it was for a fixed period of 56 days or more and was imposed within the three years immediately preceding the commission of the latest offence in respect of which penalty points are taken into account under s 29 of this Act.

(3) Where an offender is convicted on the same occasion of more than one offence to which subsection (1) above applies –
- (a) not more than one disqualification shall be imposed on him under subsection (1) above,
- (b) in determining the period of the disqualification the court must take into account all the offences, and
- (c) for the purposes of any appeal any disqualification imposed under subsection (1) above shall be treated as an order made on the conviction of each of the offences.

(4) No account is to be taken under subsection (1) above of any of the following circumstances –
- (a) any circumstances that are alleged to make the offence or any of the offences not a serious one,
- (b) hardship, other than exceptional hardship, or
- (c) any circumstances which, within the three years immediately preceding the conviction, have been taken into account under that subsection in ordering the offender to be disqualified for a shorter period or not ordering him to be disqualified.

(5) References in this section to disqualification do not include a disqualification imposed under section 26 of this Act or section 44 of the Powers of Criminal Courts Act 1973 or sections 223A or 436A of the Criminal Procedure (Scotland) Act 1975 (offences committed by

using vehicles) or a disqualification imposed in respect of an offence
of stealing a motor vehicle, an offence under sections 12 or 25 of the
Theft Act 1968, an offence under section 178 of the Road Traffic Act
1988, or an attempt to commit such an offence.

(5A) The preceding provisions of this section shall apply in relation to a
conviction of an offence committed by aiding, abetting, counselling,
procuring or inciting to the commission of an offence involving
obligatory disqualification as if the offence were an offence involving
discretionary disqualification.

(6) In relation to Scotland, references in this section to the court include
the district court.

(7) This section is subject to section 48 of this Act.'

It is clear from the terms of s 35(1) that it does not matter on
how many occasions during the three-year period that endorsement has taken place. Once 12 penalty points have been accumulated on a driver's licence within that period, then the totting-up
procedure automatically comes into effect. It is therefore possible
that the procedure will operate following a second endorsement.
Immediately 12 points are accumulated on a licence then the court
has no option but to impose the minimum period of disqualification as described in subsection (2), unless there are mitigating
circumstances. Indeed, a motorist may be disqualified under the
totting-up provisions on his first court appearance if the court
chooses to use its powers of aggregation (see 8.10:2 above).

Section 35(1) provides the basic requirement that a court must
impose disqualification if the totting-up procedure applies, unless
mitigating circumstances exist. Subsection (1A)(a) suggests that
where discretionary disqualification is available, the totting-up
procedure should nonetheless be adopted, although it is
submitted that in such circumstances the court can always impose
a period of disqualification in excess of the minimum of six
months. Subsection (1A)(b) emphasises that totting-up may apply
if penalty points are imposed on the licence in an offence
involving obligatory disqualification where special reasons have
been established.

Section 35(2) provides certain minimum periods of disqualification; six months in the ordinary case, and one year and two years
where one or two previous disqualifications respectively have to
be considered. A previous disqualification is to be considered if it
was within the three-year period preceding the commission (not
the conviction) of the latest offence for which penalty points are to
be taken into account, so long as the previous disqualification was
for more than 56 days.

Section 35(3) deals with the situation where more than one

offence involving obligatory or discretionary disqualification is dealt with on the same occasion. It may be that the offences were committed on different dates; the important consideration in this subsection is that such offences are dealt with on the same occasion. The subsection provides that only one period of disqualification under the totting-up procedure is to be imposed in such circumstances. However, the court is entitled to take into account all the offences in determining the length of that period of disqualification. It will also be noted that while s 35(2) provides certain minimum periods of disqualification in certain circumstances, no upper ceiling is given.

Section 35(4) imposes significant qualification on what may be adduced as mitigating circumstances in an effort to avoid disqualification under s 35(1). However, it is clear that the standard required to establish mitigating circumstances is not so exacting or high as that which applies in the establishment of special reasons for avoiding obligatory disqualification. In particular, the circumstances which can be considered in determining whether or not mitigating circumstances exist are not confined to the nature of the offence as in the case of special reasons. Both the circumstances of the offence and of the offender may be relevantly considered. Accordingly, the court can take into account such matters as the fact that the accused has a previously unblemished personal character.

Although in general terms the discretion open to the court in considering mitigating circumstances is far wider than is the case in special reasons, s 35(4)(a) emphasises that the triviality of the particular offence for which the accused has been convicted is not a mitigating circumstance[1]. Nor is the court entitled to take into account that there is a significant period between the current offence and the earlier offences which contributed to the accumulation of 12 penalty points[2]. However, as a matter to be weighed in the balance, it is possible for the accused to submit that consideration should be given to the relative triviality of the other offences which go to make up the 12 points. It should also be borne in mind that in these circumstances there may be special reasons for not endorsing the licence in the first place, which obviously does away with the need to consider mitigating circumstances[3].

---

1 However, see *North v Tudhope* 1985 SCCR 161 at 163 where it was said that the nature of the offence could be taken into account once special hardship had been established.
2 See *Smith v Baker* 1979 SLT (Notes) 19; *Macnab v Smith* 1977 CO Circulars A/30.
3 *Scott v Ross* 1994 SLT 945, 1994 SCCR 538; *Gordon v Russell* 1999 SLT 897.

In terms of s 35(1), the court is entitled to have regard to all the circumstances of the offence (under reference to what is referred to in s 35(4)); accordingly when an accused genuinely believed that he was covered by insurance when in fact he was not, the court was entitled not to disqualify under the totting-up procedure[1].

Section 35(4)(b) makes it clear that any hardship caused by the disqualification must be exceptional to qualify as mitigating circumstances. A series of authorities, culminating in *Allan v Barclay*[2], has held that the fact that the accused is likely to lose his employment is not in itself exceptional hardship, but that if the ensuing hardship is extended to others it may in suitable circumstances be described as exceptional. The appeal court has further examined what is exceptional hardship in a number of subsequent cases. Exceptional hardships need not always involve hardship to others. Also, loss of employment or difficult financial consequences are not the only grounds for establishing exceptional hardship. A driver who had to drive a sick child regularly to hospital, a previous child having died[3], and a single parent who had to drive disabled children[4] both established that they would experience exceptional hardship. Other cases referred to are *Railton v Houston*[5]; *Miller v Ingram*[6]; *Robinson v Aitkenson*[7]; *McFadyen v Tudhope*[8]; *Briggs v Guild*[9]; *Gray v Jessop*[10]; *Mowbray v Guild*[11]; *Bibby v McDougall*[12]; *Clumpas v Ingram*[13]; *McLaughlin v Docherty*[14]; *Marshall v McDougall*[15]; *Ewan v Orr*[16]; *Howdle v Davidson*[17]; *Brennan v McKay*[18] and; *Findlay v Walkingshaw*[19]. The

1 *Carmichael v Shevlin* 1992 SLT 113, 1992 SCCR 247.
2 1986 SCCR 111.
3 *Edmonds v Buchanan* 1993 SCCR 1048.
4 *Colgan v McDonald* 1999 SCCR 901.
5 1986 SCCR 428.
6 1986 SCCR 437.
7 1986 SCCR 511.
8 1986 SCCR 712.
9 1987 SCCR 141.
10 1988 SCCR 71.
11 1989 SCCR 535.
12 1990 SCCR 121.
13 1991 SCCR 223.
14 1991 SCCR 227.
15 1991 SCCR 231.
16 1993 SCCR 1015.
17 1994 SCCR 751.
18 1997 SLT 603.
19 1998 SCCR 181.

foregoing cases only provide guidelines; there are no hard and fast rules as to what circumstances will or will not justify exceptional hardship. Success in such applications often reflects in significant measure the care and skill exercised in their presentation, as well as on the particular circumstances.

The correct procedure for the court to adopt is firstly to decide what is the appropriate number of penalty points which should be applied to the offence, and thereafter go on to see whether totting-up applies[1]. The court should not proceed by determining the number of penalty points needed to bring the totting-up procedure into operation as the first consideration.

Section 35(4)(c) provides that an accused person can argue that a particular set of mitigating circumstances exists and so avoid totting-up disqualification only once within any three-year period. If an accused successfully argues that he should not be disqualified for given reasons under the totting-up procedure, then he is disallowed from presenting similar arguments for a similar purpose in any court in the United Kingdom within three years of the conviction following which he avoided disqualification. It would seem to be open for an accused to argue that exceptional hardship or other mitigating circumstances exist for quite separate reasons on a second occasion.

Section 35(5) does not seem to have been updated to change the reference to the Criminal Procedure (Scotland) Act 1975 s 223A or 436A to the Criminal Procedure (Scotland) Act 1995, s 248. The rest of the subsection is self-explanatory.

8.10:6   Procedure in mitigating circumstances submissions

The procedure in dealing with pleas of guilty to offences which do not involve obligatory or discretionary disqualification but which do involve disqualification under the totting-up procedure is broadly the same as in the case of letter pleas and special reasons cases (see 8.6:1 above). It should be emphasised that if the accused is to be disqualified, then it is proper practice for him to be given every opportunity to put forward reasons why he should not be disqualified. The appeal court has made it clear that it regards it as a 'sensible practice' for the accused to be required to appear personally if disqualification is a possibility[2].

---

1 *Briggs v Guild* 1987 SCCR 141.
2 *Stephens v Gibb* 1984 SCCR 195 and *MacDonald v McGillivray* 1986 SCCR 28.

8.10:7 Procedural consequences

If a period of disqualification (either obligatory or under the totting-up procedure) is avoided because of special reasons or mitigating circumstances, the court must give the reasons for its decision in open court, and cause these reasons to be entered on the record of proceedings[1]. If the court does not order disqualification, the appropriate number of penalty points must be endorsed on the licence[2]. Where endorsement is ordered the court may, and where disqualification for more than 56 days is ordered it must, send the licence to DVLA, Swansea[3].

Following the expiry of a period of disqualification, a person may not drive until he has applied for and received the return of his licence[4].

8.11 ADDITIONAL AND FURTHER CONSEQUENCES OF DISQUALIFICATION

8.11:1 Disqualification until test is passed

Section 36 of the Road Traffic Offenders Act 1988[5] provides:

'(1) Where this subsection applies to a person the court must order him to be disqualified until he passes the appropriate driving test.
(2) Subsection (1) above applies to a person who is disqualified under section 34 of this Act on conviction of –
   (a) manslaughter, or in Scotland culpable homicide, by the driver of a motor vehicle, or
   (b) an offence under section 1 (causing death by dangerous driving) or section 2 (dangerous driving) of the Road Traffic Act 1988.
(3) Subsection (1) above also applies –
   (a) to a person who is disqualified under section 34 or 35 of this Act in such circumstances or for such period as the Secretary of State may by order prescribe, or
   (b) to such other persons convicted of such offences involving obligatory endorsement as may be so prescribed.

1 Road Traffic Offenders Act 1988, s 47(1).
2 RTOA 1988, s 44.
3 RTOA 1988, s 47(2), as amended by the Road Traffic Act 1991, Sch 4, para 100.
4 *Stewart v Paterson* 1959 SLT (Sh Ct) 66.
5 As amended inter alia by the Road Traffic Act 1991, s 32.

(4) Where a person to whom subsection (1) above does not apply is convicted of an offence involving obligatory endorsement, the court may order him to be disqualified until he passes the appropriate driving test (whether or not he has previously passed any test).

(5) In this section –
'appropriate driving test' means –
   (a) an extended driving test, where a person is convicted of an offence involving obligatory disqualification or is disqualified under section 35 of this Act,
   (b) a test of competence to drive, other than an extended driving test, in any other case,
'extended driving test' means a test of competence to drive prescribed for the purposes of this section, and
'test of competence to drive' means a test prescribed by virtue of section 89(3) of the Road Traffic Act 1988.

(6) In determining whether to make an order under subsection (4) above, the court shall have regard to the safety of road users.

(7) Where a person is disqualified until he passes the extended driving test –
   (a) any earlier order under this section shall cease to have effect, and
   (b) a court shall not make a further order under this section while he is so disqualified.

(8) Subject to subsection (9) below, a disqualification by virtue of an order under this section shall be deemed to have expired on production to the Secretary of State of evidence, in such form as may be prescribed by regulations under section 105 of the Road Traffic Act 1988, that the person disqualified has passed the test in question since the order was made.

(9) A disqualification shall be deemed to have expired only in relation to vehicles of such classes as may be prescribed in relation to the test passed by regulations under that section.

(10) Where there is issued to a person a licence on the counterpart of which are endorsed particulars of a disqualification under this section, there shall also be endorsed the particulars of any test of competence to drive that he has passed since the order of disqualification was made.

(11) For the purposes of an order under this section, a person shall be treated as having passed a test of competence to drive other than an extended driving test if he passes a corresponding test conducted—
   (a) under the law of Northern Ireland, the Isle of Man, any of the Channel Islands, another EEA State, Gibraltar or a designated country or territory, or
   (b) for the purposes of obtaining a British Forces licence (as defined by section 88(8) of that Act);
and accordingly subsections (8) to (10) above shall apply in relation to such a test as they apply in relation to a test prescribed by virtue of section 89(3) of that Act.

(11a) For the purpose of subsection (11) above, "designated country or territory" means a country or territory designated by order under section 108(2) of the Road Traffic Act 1988 but a test conducted under the law of such a country or territory shall not be regarded as a corresponding test unless a person passing such a test would be entitled to an exchangeable licence as defined in section 108(1) of that Act.

(12) This section is subject to section 48 of this Act.

(13) The power to make an order under subsection (3) above shall be exercisable by statutory instrument; and no such order shall be made unless a draft of it has been laid before and approved by resolution of each House of Parliament.

(14) The Secretary of State shall not make an order under subsection (3) above after the end of 2001 if he has not previously made such an order.'

In terms of s 36 as originally enacted under the Road Traffic Offenders Act 1988, the court had the discretionary power to order a driver to be disqualified until he passed a driving test on the expiry of the period of disqualification in any case where obligatory or discretionary disqualification was competent. The courts held that this discretionary requirement should not be exercised to provide an additional punishment to the sentences imposed on a driver in a particular case. Such an order could only be imposed where the circumstances of the offence, or the driver's previous convictions for road traffic offences, indicated that it was in the public interest that the driver's ability and skill should be checked before he was allowed to resume driving following his period of disqualification[1]. In particular, a token period of disqualification should not be imposed where the purpose of so doing was simply to make the driver resit a driving test[2]; nor should such a requirement be made automatically in cases where a long period of disqualification was imposed[3]. These considerations will continue to apply to those cases where statute does not require a driving test be re-taken, but the court is considering its discretionary power in this respect in terms of s 36(4).

Under the provisions of s 36, as now amended inter alia by s 32 of the Road Traffic Act 1991, the test of when this requirement should be imposed is significantly altered. The requirement to resit an appropriate driving test is now obligatory where an accused is disqualified for an offence of culpable homicide, or s 1 or s 2 of the Road Traffic Act 1988[4]. The section also provides that

---

1 See *Sweeney v Cardle* 1982 SLT 312, 1982 SCCR 10.
2 *McLean v Annan* 1986 SCCR 52.
3 *Sweeney v Cardle* 1982 SLT 312, 1982 SCCR 10.
4 Road Traffic Offenders Act 1988, s 36(1).

this obligatory requirement may be extended by the Secretary of State if he decides to make the appropriate order covering (1) cases involving obligatory, discretionary or totting-up disqualification[1] or (2) cases simply involving obligatory endorsement[2]. The Secretary of State has not yet made an order under 36(3) in respect of either of these two provisions, which means that a driver with a totting-up disqualification regains his licence in the normal way. Section 36(14) contains a sunset provision, which restricts the Secretary of State's power to make such an order to the end of 2001.

The appropriate driving test is therefore to be an extended driving test in cases of obligatory disqualification and will be when the relevant order is made in cases of totting-up disqualification[3]. The ordinary driving test is to be passed in all other cases (in other words where disqualification is discretionary). The extended test is about twice the length of the ordinary test. The motorist can only take the test once his period of disqualification has expired. Section 37(3) allows a driver to obtain a provisional licence in order to pass his test[4]. The provisions in respect of driving tests are found in the Motor Vehicles (Driving Licences) Regulations 1996[5].

Accordingly, the current position is that the extended driving test must be taken at the end of a period of disqualification following conviction on a charge of culpable homicide; s 1 or s 2[6]. The Secretary of State has the power to extend this requirement to disqualifications inter alia under the totting-up procedure in terms of s 36(5) but has not yet done so. The court continues to have the discretionary power to require a driver in other circumstances to resit a driving test[7]. However, the test in this respect was significantly changed by s 36(6) of the Act; in determining whether to make such an order the court shall simply have regard to the safety of road users. This change is thought to reflect the desire of the legislature to make the requirement to resit the test of competence to drive more widely used by the courts. This test will remain for all cases of discretionary disqualification irrespective of what future alterations are made to the system of obligatory disqualification.

---

1 RTOA 1988, s 36(3)(a).
2 RTOA 1988, s 36(3)(b).
3 RTOA 1988, s 36(5)(a).
4 See also *Stewart v Paterson* 1959 SLT (Sh Ct) 66.
5 SI 1996/2824.
6 RTOA 1988, s 36(3).
7 RTOA 1988, s 36(4).

8.11:2 Appeal against disqualification and requirement to resit test

Section 38(2) of the Road Traffic Offenders Act 1988 provides:

'A person disqualified by an order of a court in Scotland may appeal against the order in the same manner as against sentence.'

The form of such an appeal is therefore the same as in an appeal against sentence. The appellant may apply for an interim suspension of the disqualification to the court which made the order[1] or, which failing, to the High Court of Justiciary[2]. Suspension is also available where a person makes an application under section 34B (see 8.11:3 below) for a drink-driving course, pending the outcome of the determination[3]. In the latter case, the application may be to a single judge. Any period of interim suspension is not included in the period of disqualification[4]. Because the requirement to resit a test is formally part of an order of disqualification, any appeal against the imposition of the requirement is taken under this section. There appears to be no grounds for appealing against the mandatory requirements to resit and pass a driving test[5] but discretionary orders are available under other sections of the Act and can be appealed.

The question of ordering the accused to be disqualified until a driving test was passed was considered in *Smith v Wilson*[6]; *Neill v Annan*[7]; and *Fraser v Lockhart*[8]. In *Harper v Lockhart*[9] the fact that a driver was 81 years of age was held not to be a reason by itself for imposing a period of disqualification with a condition that a driving test be thereafter passed.

8.11:3 Courses for drink-drive offenders

Section 34A, 34B and 34C of the Road Traffic Act 1988[10], and s 31 of the 1991 Act, make provision for a scheme whereby a driver

1 Road Traffic Offenders Act 1988, s 39(2).
2 RTOA 1988, s 41.
3 RTOA 1988, s 41A, as introduced by the Road Traffic Act 1991, s 48 and Sch 4, para 97.
4 RTOA 1988, s 43.
5 Eg under the Road Traffic Act 1988, ss 1 and 2.
6 1989 SCCR 395.
7 1990 SCCR 454.
8 1992 SCCR 275.
9 1992 SCCR 429.
10 As introduced by the Road Traffic Act 1991, s 30.

convicted of an offence under ss 3A, 4, 5 or 7 of the Road Traffic Act 1988 may have his period of disqualification reduced if he satisfactorily completes an approved course prescribed by the Secretary of State. The opportunity to take such a course only arises when the court at the time of imposing the disqualification also makes an order that the period of disqualification may be reduced if the offender satisfactorily completes the course. The reduction will only apply in cases of 12 months' disqualification or more, and will amount to a period between 3 months and one quarter of the total period of disqualification. This scheme is now introduced throughout Scotland but is not always available. It should not be confused with schemes for drivers convicted of an offence, which are run by local authority social work departments and can form part of a probation order. The relevant orders are SI 1992/3013 and SI 1997/949 but, as indicated above, are not yet universally on offer. The applicant has to pay a fee for attendance at such a course.

8.11:4 Disqualification where vehicle used to commit offence

Section 248 of the Criminal Procedure (Scotland) Act 1995 provides:

'(1) Where a person is convicted of an offence (other than one triable only summarily) and the court which passes sentence is satisfied that a motor vehicle was used for the purpose of committing, or facilitating the commission of that offence, the court may order him to be disqualified for such period as the court thinks fit from holding or obtaining a licence to drive a motor vehicle granted under Part III of the Road Traffic Act 1988.
(2) A court which makes an order under this section disqualifying a person from holding or obtaining a licence shall require him to produce any such licence held by him and its counterpart.
(3) Any reference in this section to facilitating the commission of an offence shall include a reference to the taking of any steps after it has been committed for the purpose of disposing of any property to which it relates or of avoiding apprehension or detection.
(4) In relation to licences which came into force before 1st June 1990, the reference in subsection (2) above to the counterpart of a licence shall be disregarded.'

The power to disqualify under this section may only be exercised in cases other than those which can only be tried on summary complaint. Disqualification may be imposed on any person involved in the offence, even if that person was not driving, or even in, the vehicle at any time.

8.11:5   Forfeiture of vehicle following offence

Section 33A of the Road Traffic Offenders Act 1988, as introduced by s 5 of and Schedule 4, para 71(6) to the Criminal Procedure (Consequential Provisions) (Scotland) Act 1995, provides:

'(1) Where a person commits an offence to which this subsection applies by –
  (a) driving, attempting to drive or being in charge of a vehicle, or
  (b) failing to comply with a requirement made under section 7 of the Road Traffic Act 1988 (failure to provide a specimen for analysis or laboratory test) in the course of an investigation into whether the offender had committed an offence while driving, attempting to drive or being in charge of a vehicle, or
  (c) failing, as the driver of a vehicle, to comply with subsections (2) and (3) of section 170 of the Road Traffic Act 1988 (duty to stop and give information or report an accident)
the court may, on an application under this subsection, make an order forfeiting the vehicle concerned, and any vehicle forfeited under this subsection shall be disposed of as the court may direct.'

This section therefore allows the court to forfeit vehicles where a road traffic offence punishable by imprisonment has been committed, and also in cases of culpable homicide[1]. Applications may be made before proceedings commence where powers of search and seizure are sought prior to sentence[2].

Forfeiture should not be regarded as automatic[3]. Forfeiture is possible even where the vehicle has been disposed of, although the original owner may still have a right of relief[4]. It is inappropriate to consider the level of fine that might be imposed and the value of the car in deciding whether to order forfeiture[5]. The power to forfeit is arbitrary[6].

---

1 Road Traffic Offenders Act 1988, s 33A(2)–(6).
2 RTOA 1988, s 33A(3)–(5).
3 *Carron v Russell* 1994 SCCR 681; *Donald, Petitioner* 1996 JC 22, 1996 SLT 505, 1996 SCCR 321.
4 *Lloyds and Scottish Finance v HM Advocate* 1974 JC 24, 1974 SLT 3; *Woods, Petitioner* 1993 SCCR 105.
5 *Wilson v Hamilton* 1996 SCCR 193.
6 *Purdie v MacDonald* 1997 SLT 483.

Forfeiture has been ordered where a wife did not do enough to stop her disqualified husband from driving her car[1], and where a very drunk driver drove dangerously after being warned by the police not to take to the road[2].

Suspended forfeiture orders are available to the court on conviction in respect of any property including vehicles[3]. The property must, at the time of the accused's apprehension, be in his ownership or possession or under his control and must have been used to commit the offence. Before conviction the property may be seized on warrant[4]. Search warrants in respect of forfeiture are empowered by s 254 of the Criminal Procedure (Scotland) Act 1995.

8.11:6 Disqualification of newly qualified drivers

The Road Traffic (New Drivers) Act 1995 (c.13) makes provision in respect of offences committed by drivers who thereby acquire six or more penalty points within a period of two years of passing their driving test. The court must in these circumstances send a notice of the relevant information to the Secretary of State[5]; the Secretary of State then serves a notice on the driver revoking his licence[6]. The driver then reverts to the status of a learner. Provisions to prevent further consequences of the disqualification to the driver are found in s 7, and the licence is restored by virtue of s 7 in the event of a successful appeal.

8.11:7 Disqualification of general offenders and fine defaulters

Section 248A of the Criminal Procedure (Scotland) Act 1995, introduced by s 15 of the Crime and Punishment (Scotland) Act 1997[7] allows the court to disqualify an offender even where a vehicle is not involved in the offence. Section 248B applies the same power

---

1 *Donaldson v Hamilton* 1996 JC 22, 1996 SCCR 68.
2 *Craigie v Heywood* 1996 SCCR 654.
3 Proceeds of Crime (Scotland) Act 1995, s 21(2).
4 *Shaw v Conley* 1998 SLT 17.
5 Road Traffic (New Drivers) Act 1995, s 2.
6 RT(ND)A 1995, s 30.
7 Which came into effect by virtue of SI 1997/2323.

to fine defaulters. No guidelines are available as to how these powers should be used or how the orders should be recorded. It is to be assumed that the normal powers of appeal will be available. The experience of the operation of these provisions in pilot courts suggest that the use of these powers may not be widespread, but restricted to particularly deserving cases. An example of the use of such powers is found in *Patterson v Gilchrist*[1].

8.11:8   Removal of disqualification

Section 42 of the Road Traffic Offenders Act 1988[2] provides:

'(1) subject to the provisions of this section, a person who by an order of a court is disqualified may apply to the court by which the order was made to remove the disqualification.
(2) On any such application the court may, as it thinks proper having regard to –
   (a) the character of the person disqualified and his conduct subsequent to the order
   (b) the nature of the offence, and
   (c) any other circumstance of the case,
either by order remove the disqualification as from such date as may be specified in the order or refuse the application.
(3) No application shall be made under subsection (1) above for the removal of the disqualification before the expiration of whichever is relevant of the following periods from the date of the order by which the disqualification was imposed, that is –
   (a) two years, if the disqualification is for less than four years,
   (b) one half of the period of disqualification, if it for less than ten years but not less than four years,
   (c) five years in any other case;
and in determining the expiration of the period after which under this subsection a person may apply for the removal of a disqualification, any time after the conviction during which the disqualification was suspended or he was not disqualified shall be disregarded.
(4) Where an application under subsection (1) above is refused, a further application under that subsection shall not be entertained if made within three months after the date of the refusal.
(5) If under this section a court orders a disqualification to be removed, the court –
   (a) must cause particulars of the order to be endorsed on the licence, if any, previously held by the applicant, and

---

1 1999 SCCR 419.
2 As amended by the Road Traffic Act 1991, s 48 and Sch 4, para 98.

(b) may in any case order the applicant to pay the whole or any part of the costs of the application.

(5A) Subsection (5)(a) above shall apply only where the disqualification was imposed in respect of an offence involving obligatory endorsement, and in any other case the court must send notice of the order made under this section to the Secretary of State.

(5B) A notice under subsection (5A) above must be sent in such a manner and to such address, and must contain such particulars, as the Secretary of State may determine.

(6) The preceding provisions of this section shall not apply where the disqualification was imposed by order under section 36(1) of this Act.'

This section is self-explanatory. Apart from the restrictions in subsections (3) and (4), there is no limit on the number of such applications that may be made during the period of disqualification. It is clear from the terms of the section that the application is to be made to the court where the disqualification was imposed. If an accused person has received periods of disqualification in more than one court, it follows that an order in one court lifting the disqualification imposed there will not in any way affect the disqualifications imposed in other courts. The section affords no power to reduce the disqualification; an application must be either refused or granted *simpliciter*.

8.11:9   Removal of disqualification: procedure

Whether the application is made in the sheriff court or the High Court of Justiciary, it is presented in the form of a petition. Although there is no specific provision governing the procedures to be observed, it is normal and proper practice for the applicant to serve a copy of the petition on the procurator fiscal or the Crown Agent, depending on whether the application is in the sheriff court or the High Court of Justiciary. Service should be made in sufficient time to allow the Crown to instruct its own report (normally from a local police officer) on the merits of the petition. A separate petition is required for each indictment or complaint in respect of which disqualification was imposed. In terms of this section it is suggested that the court should have regard to the character of the person disqualified and his conduct subsequent to the order, the nature of the offence committed which caused the disqualification and any other circumstances of the case.

In presenting the application to the court, it is submitted that the applicant should be prepared to lead evidence in support of his application rather than rely on *ex parte* statements. However, if the circumstances are sufficiently clear, and the police report is favourable, and if in addition, the Crown does not dispute the salient facts put up by the petitioner, there appears to be no bar to such an application proceeding entirely on the basis of statements made by the accused or his solicitor. Such applications should be presented with considerable care. It is normal for such applications to be granted only where the applicant can demonstrate clearly that his behaviour since the commission of the offence is such as to indicate that it is unlikely that he will commit such offences again. In addition, pressing reasons must be adduced to demonstrate why the appellant should have his licence restored. These can include the avoidance of hardship, for example by indicating that the restoration of the licence will allow the applicant to resume employment, or by demonstrating that the lack of a licence causes the applicant serious personal difficulty or hardship to his family. Any such claims, however, should be properly vouched and supported where appropriate by evidence. It is also normal for such applicants to provide testimonials of good conduct which will satisfy the court that the applicant can safely have his licence restored to him.

There is no appeal from the decision of the court to which the application is made[1].

The appeal is to the court of original jurisdiction and not necessarily the same judge[2].

8.11:10 Compensation orders

On conviction of any offence, including those under the Road Traffic Acts, the court may make an order requiring the convicted person to pay compensation for any personal injury loss or damage caused, whether directly or indirectly by the acts which constituted the offence[3].

The section specifies the kind of situation where a compensation order cannot be made, but in case of unlawful taking and using of a property, or a contravention of s 178(1) of the Road

---

1 *McLeod v Levitt* 1969 JC 16, 1969 SLT 286.
2 *McIntyre v Henderson* 1911 JC 73.
3 Criminal Procedure (Scotland) Act 1995, s 249.

Traffic Act 1988, any damage caused while out of the owner's possession can be the subject of a compensation order[1].

Section 249 (4) provides:–

'No compensation order shall be made in respect of
    (a) loss suffered in consequence of the death of any person
    (b) injury, loss or damage due to an accident arising out of the presence of a motor vehicle on a road, except such damage as is treated by virtue of subsection (3) above, as having been caused by the convicted person's acts.'

Although the terms of this subsection are perhaps not wholly clear, it would appear that there must be actual loss, injury or damage. However, in *Stewart v HM Advocate*[2] compensation was ordered for inconvenience. In *Ely v Donnelly*[3] it was held not to matter that the victim was insured.

Section 250 deals with supplementary provisions, including that the order is a sentence and therefore can be appealed in the normal way. Section 251 is concerned with review of orders, section 252 deals with enforcement, and section 253 provides for the effect of a compensation order or subsequent awards of damages in civil proceedings.

Other cases on compensation orders in other areas that may be of interest are *Goodhall v Carmichael*[4]; *Carmichael v Siddique*[5]; *Brown v Normand*[6]; *Smillie v Wilson*[7]; *Collins v Lowe*[8]; and *Robertson v Lees*[9].

8.12   ENDORSEMENT OF LICENCES

8.12:1   General

Section 44 of the Road Traffic Offenders Act 1988, as amended, provides:

---

1 CP(S) Act 1995, s 249 (3).
2 1982 SCCR 203.
3 1996 SCCR 537.
4 1984 SCCR 247.
5 1985 SCCR 145.
6 1988 SCCR 229.
7 1990 SCCR 133.
8 1990 SCCR 605.
9 1992 SCCR 545.

'(1) Where a person is convicted of an offence involving obligatory endorsement, the court must order there to be endorsed on the counterpart of any licence held by him particulars of the conviction and also –
   (a) if the court orders him to be disqualified, particulars of the disqualification, or
   (b) if the court does not order him to be disqualified –
      (i) particulars of the offence, including the date when it was committed, and
      (ii) the penalty points to be attributed to the offence.
(2) Where the court does not order the person convicted to be disqualified, it need not make an order under subsection (1) above if for special reasons it thinks fit not to do so.
(3) In relation to Scotland, references in this section to the court include the district court.
(4) This section is subject to section 48 of this Act.'

Endorsement is not a penalty as such, rather it is a direction that certain matters must be marked or noted on the accused's licence. These matters are details of any period of disqualification, or if no disqualification is imposed, details of the offence and the number of penalty points attributed by the court thereto. Details of offences which require endorsement, and the number of penalty points for such offences are found in the Road Traffic Offenders Act 1988, Sch 2, as amended by the Road Traffic Act 1991, Sch 2.

These details are normally endorsed on the licence by DVLA, Swansea. Where disqualification for a period of 56 days or more is ordered, the court must send the licence with the details of the disqualification to DVLA; where endorsement is ordered, the court may (and usually does) do likewise[1]. However, simple endorsement of the licence or disqualification for a period of less than 56 days, may be done by the clerk of court. In practice, details of the date of the offence, the date of conviction, the nature of the offence, and the disposal including penalty points and disqualification period are physically marked on the licence. The nature of the offence is indicated by a code, which is reproduced as Appendix D at the end of this book. Any endorsements on a licence are prima facie evidence of the matters so endorsed[2]. The effect of endorsement and the periods for which various endorsements remain live and the procedure for having spent

1 Road Traffic Offenders Act 1988, s 47(2), as amended by the Road Traffic Act 1991, Sch 4, para 100.
2 RTOA 1988, s 31, as amended by RTA 1991, Sch 2, para 93.

endorsements removed and a clean licence issued are described in the Road Traffic Offenders Act 1988, s 45, as amended by the Road Traffic Act 1991, Sch 2, para 99.

It is not possible to enforce disqualification and penalty points at the same time, irrespective of when the separate offences were committed[1].

8.12:2   Special reasons for not endorsing licence

Section 44(2) of the Road Traffic Offenders Act 1988 allows a court to refrain from endorsing a licence if there are special reasons for doing so. As in the case of special reasons for not disqualifying, a special reason for not endorsing is a matter of law, and not at large for the discretion of the court[2]. Triviality of the offence is not a ground for not endorsing[3], particularly since the introduction of the penalty points system. In addition, *Stephens v Gibb*[4], and *Holden v MacPhail*[5] make it clear that endorsement should normally follow on the appropriate conviction. It is for the accused to raise the question of special reasons[6]. A useful general rule of reference is whether the special reasons explain why the offence was committed in circumstances where it would otherwise not have been.

The procedure for putting forward and considering special reasons submissions are described in *McLeod v Scoular*[7], *McNab v Feeney*[8] and *Keane v Perrie*[9]. The court may not refrain from endorsement unless special reasons are spoken to by or on behalf of the accused at the time. The fiscal is always entitled to be heard. If the court finds that special reasons exist for not endorsing the licence, these reasons must be given in open court and marked on the record (complaint) by the clerk of court[10].

---

1 *Ahmed v McLeod* 1999 SLT 762, 1998 SCCR 486.
2 *Muir v Sutherland* 1940 JC 66, 1940 SLT 403.
3 *Tudhope v Birbeck* 1979 SLT (Notes) 47, not following *Smith v Henderson* 1950 JC 48, 1950 SLT 182.
4 1984 SCCR 195.
5 1986 SCCR 486.
6 *McLeod v Scoular* 1974 JC 28, 1974 SLT (Notes) 44; *Heywood v O'Connor* 1994 SLT 254, 1993 SCCR 471.
7 1974 JC 28, 1974 SLT (Notes) 44.
8 1980 SLT (Notes) 52.
9 1983 SLT 63, 1982 SCCR 377.
10 Road Traffic Offenders Act 1988, s 47(1); see also *MacNab v MacPherson* 1978 JC 21.

In *McDade v Jessop*[1] it was observed that factors which constitute special reasons for not disqualifying might not carry the same
weight in relation to endorsement; and the fact that the penalty
points available where the accused had failed to provide a specimen were in excess of what would have been imposed if the
accused had been driving was not a special reason for not
ordering endorsement.

Where a driver was genuinely unaware for legitimate reasons
that he was no longer qualified to drive, special reasons existed
for not endorsing penalty points[2]. This should be contrasted with
the slightly different situation in *Carmichael v Shevlin*[3] where a
motorist's belief that he was insured to drive founded mitigating
circumstances for not adopting the totting-up procedure.
Something which happens after the offence will not normally
justify a failure to order endorsement[4].

In *Heywood v O'Connor*[5] it was held in a case where a driver had
no insurance that it was not a special reason for refraining from
endorsement that the vehicle was not much used; and in *McDade
v Jessop*[6], the fact that the accused was not driving or intending to
drive when he refused to give a specimen was similarly unsuccessful.

If there is credible evidence from a single witness that he
believed that he was insured to drive, this may afford grounds for
non-endoresement[7].

Emergency vehicle drivers may in certain situations escape
endorsement[8]. Section 87 of the Road Traffic Regulation Act 1984
exempts fire brigade, ambulance and police vehicles from speed
limits if the limit is likely to hinder the use of the vehicle for the
purpose for which it is being used at the time.

8.12:3 Notice of penalties

Since the passing of the Criminal Procedure (Scotland) Act 1995 the
prosecution do not need to serve a notice of penalty on any accused.

1 1990 SCCR 156.
2 *Robertson v McNaughtan* 1993 SLT 1143, 1993 SCCR 526; see also *Gordon v Russell*
1999 SLT 897.
3 1992 SLT 1113, 1992 SCCR 247.
4 *Morton v Munro* 1998 SCCR 178.
5 1994 SLT 254, 1993 SCCR 471.
6 1990 SLT 800, 1990 SCCR 156.
7 *Marshall v McLeod* 1998 SLT 1199, 1998 SCCR 317.
8 *Husband v Russell* 1997 SCCR 592.

8.12:4   Connected offences

Where a number of offences occur at the same time, the prosecution of these may be separated, some being processed under the normal procedure of service of a complaint, others by the procedure of fixed penalty. The fixed penalty procedure covers offences to which a fixed number of penalty points applies. If, in dealing with such a case, the court becomes aware that a connected offence is to be, or has been considered by the fixed penalty procedure, the number of penalty points that will apply or has been applied must be deducted from the penalty points to be imposed by the court[1]. Reference should be made to *Green v O'Donnell*[2] and 8.10:1 above).

8.12:5   Exemption from disqualification and endorsement: construction and use

Where a person is convicted of an offence under ss 40A or 41A of the Road Traffic Act 1988 (which were introduced by the Road Traffic Act 1991, s 8 and which relates to using a vehicle in a dangerous condition and to contraventions of the construction and use regulations), the court must not order him to be disqualified or order his licence to be endorsed with or without penalty points if he proves that he did not know, and had no reasonable cause to suspect that the facts of the case were such that the offence would be committed (Road Traffic Offenders Act 1988, s 48, as amended by the Road Traffic Act 1991, Sch 4, para 101). It is submitted that the standard of proof required to establish this defence is on the balance of probabilities. A case which usefully illustrates some of the relevant features of such a defence is *Forrest v Annan*[3].

8.12:6   Offender escaping endorsement by deception

Where a person is convicted of an offence involving a deception which might have had a bearing on disqualification, the court

---

1 Road Traffic Offenders Act 1988, ss 28–30, as amended by the Road Traffic Act 1991, Sch 4, para 92.
2 1997 SCCR 315.
3 1992 SLT 510, 1990 SCCR 619.

dealing with the deception offence has the same powers of disqualification as the deceived court, and must take into account any orders actually imposed by that court[1].

8.13 FIXED PENALTIES AND CONDITIONAL OFFERS

In order to reduce the volume of road traffic cases going through the courts, a system of fixed penalties has been introduced which allows for the avoidance of prosecution by an offender by payment of a fixed penalty in respect of certain minor traffic offences. It is a feature of the general system that a number of these offences involve endorsement and penalty points being imposed on a licence without any order of court.

Practice can vary, but often the police issue a conditional offer of a fixed penalty which if accepted avoids the formal process of prosecution. If the offence is speeding or otherwise involves penalty points, the driver must submit his licence to the relevant clerk of court in order to have the relevant penalty points endorsed. The fixed penalty must be paid within 28 days[2]. If the licence holder is subject to disqualification the conditional offer procedure is not available. If the conditional offer is not accepted, the fiscal normally thereupon proceeds a prosecution, although he can also issue a further conditional offer.

The statutory procedure for the system is found in Part III of the Road Traffic Offenders Act 1998. Put briefly, where it appears that certain sorts of offences have been committed, the fiscal may make a conditional offer to the alleged offender to the effect that on payment of a fixed penalty any liability to conviction will be discharged. Where the offence involves obligatory endorsement, the alleged offender must deliver his licence to the relevant clerk of court, who endorses the particulars of the conviction on the licence. The fixed penalty must be paid within 28 days[3]. If the licence holder may be subject to disqualification, the conditional offer procedure is not available[4]. If the alleged offender declines the offer, prosecution for the offence will normally follow.

The offences in respect of which conditional offers may be made are listed in Schedule 3 to the Road Traffic Offenders Act 1988.

1 Road Traffic Offenders Act 1988, s 49.
2 Road Traffic Offenders Act 1988, s 75.
3 RTOA 1988, s 75.
4 RTOA 1988, s 75.

Where an offence does not involve obligatory endorsement, the notice of penalty may be fixed to the offending vehicle, rather than given at the time to the motorist[1]. The subsequent procedure is described in ss 63–65. Briefly, the police then serve a 'notice to owner' in terms of s 63(2). The owner can either pay the fixed penalty, or, if he does not, a prosecution will then be initiated by the service of a complaint. Alternatively, the motorist may deny that he was the driver of the vehicle at the material time, and provide a statutory statement of ownership, together with a signed request by the person purporting to be the driver to request a hearing (or in other words inviting a prosecution). It would seem that if the driver does not sign the statutory statement, the registered keeper will become liable for what is known as a registered fine, which amounts to one and a half times the fixed penalty. If the fixed penalty is ignored, it is, after the response period has expired, registered with the clerk of a court of summary jurisdiction (in effect the local district court) for the area in which the defaulter appears to reside as a fine amounting to one and a half times the fixed penalty. The clerk of court is then required to notify the defaulter of the registration. At this stage the defaulter can have the registration made invalid if he makes a statutory declaration within 21 days to the effect that either (a) he did not know of the fixed penalty until he received the notice of registration, or (b) that he was not the owner of the vehicle at the time of the alleged offence and that he has a reasonable excuse for failing to comply with the notice, or (c) that he gave notice requesting a hearing. It is not clear how a reasonable excuse is to be determined, nor in what form the statutory declaration is to proceed. It is however to be conclusively presumed that a person on whom the notice of fixed penalty was served was the driver of the vehicle at the material time, unless it is shown that the vehicle was in the possession of some other person without the consent of the accused[2]. Fixed penalty notices under s 62 may be fixed to vehicles by traffic wardens as well as by police officers[3]. Particular provision is made for hired vehicles by s 66.

The intended consequence of the present fixed penalty system is to put the onus on any accused motorist who wishes to dispute any charge to take the necessary statutory action, and failure to do so will mean that either the fixed penalty must be paid or, failing

---

1 RTOA 1988, s 62.
2 RTOA 1988, s 64(5) and (6).
3 RTOA 1988, s 86, as amended by the Road Traffic Act 1991, Sch 4, para 106.

such payment, an increased fine is registered against the motorist, subject to the safeguards described above.

The powers of the district court in this area are restricted[1].

8.14 INSURANCE

8.14:1 Section 143

Section 143 of the Road Traffic Act 1988 provides:

'(1) Subject to the provisions of this Part of this Act—
  (a) a person must not use a motor vehicle on a road unless there is in force in relation to the use of the vehicle by that person such a policy of insurance or such a security in respect of third party risks as complies with the requirements of this Part of this Act, and
  (b) a person must not cause or permit any other person to use a motor vehicle on a road unless there is in force in relation to the use of the vehicle by that other person such a policy of insurance or such a security in respect of third party risks as complies with the requirements of this Part of this Act.
(2 If a person acts in contravention of subsection (1) above he is guilty of an offence.
(3) A person charged with using a motor vehicle in contravention of this section shall not be convicted if he proves—
  (a) that the vehicle did not belong to him and was not in his possession under a contract of hiring or of loan,
  (b) that he was using the vehicle in the course of his employment, and
  (c) that he neither knew nor had reason to believe that there was not in force in relation to the vehicle such a policy of insurance or security as is mentioned in subsection (1) above.
(4) This Part of this Act does not apply to invalid carriages.'

8.14:2 Definitions

'Motor Vehicle' – see 1.2:1 above.

'Road' – see 1.8:1 above.

---

1 Road Traffic Offenders Act 1988, ss 10 and 50.

'*Policy of Insurance*' – the requirements in respect of a policy of insurance are provided by s 145 of the Road Traffic Act 1988. A policy of insurance includes a cover note[1].

'*Causing or permitting*' – see 1.10:3 above.

8.14:3   Insurance: general

From the terms of s 143 of the Road Traffic Act 1988, it is clear that the principle which underlies the requirement of compulsory insurance is that cover must be provided in respect of the use to which the vehicle is to be put, rather than in respect of the person who is using the vehicle. It therefore follows that anyone charged with a contravention of the section does not necessarily have to be the owner of the vehicle, and that a corporate body may competently be charged with such an offence. Whether insurance cover is effective in respect of any particular use is a matter of fact and law to be understood from the facts and circumstances of each case; the question to be determined is whether the material use is legally covered by the insurance contract[2].

The insurance contract normally stipulates the conditions under which insurance cover is to be effective. If these conditions are not observed in any material respect, the contract may be avoided and an offence will result. For example, most contracts of insurance require that the user of any vehicle is properly licensed. Accordingly, if a person drives a vehicle of a class not covered by his licence, he will in normal circumstances automatically also be guilty of an offence under this section.

The extent of the cover provided by an insurance document must be disclosed by the terms of the document. The principal sorts of cover are comprehensive (which covers damage to both the owner's vehicle and vehicles owned by third parties) and third party, fire and theft (which extends to damage caused to vehicles owned by third parties only, as well as loss caused by fire or the theft of the vehicle). The latter form of insurance is the minimum cover allowed (see 8.14:5 below).

No policy of insurance is valid or effective for this part of the Act unless and until a certificate of insurance is delivered by the insurer to the person by whom the policy is effected[3]. Even if all

1 Road Traffic Act 1988, s 161(1).
2 *Agnew v Robertson* 1956 SLT (Sh Ct) 90.
3 Road Traffic Act 1988, s 147(1).

the other requirements of drawing up a policy of insurance have been satisfied, it is an offence for a vehicle to be used on the road before the certificate of insurance is delivered. Once the certificate has been delivered, the fact that the person to whom it has been delivered subsequently becomes bankrupt, or the company to which it is delivered is wound up or goes into receivership does not affect claims by third parties[1]. If a contract of insurance is avoidable, the contract remains valid until it is in fact avoided[2]. A driver may not be covered before he pays the premium, if that is a condition of the policy even after delivery of the policy[3].

As an offence is constituted under s 143(1) by use of a vehicle on a road without being covered by insurance, prosecutions are not confined to instances where the vehicle is being driven at the material time. The section is also contravened if a vehicle is parked on a public road and is not covered; and this will apply even in cases where the vehicle cannot physically be moved[4]. Similarly, a vehicle being towed is in use and must be insured[5]. The owner is still using the vehicle when he gives it to another person to repair[6]. A motorist was deemed to be the user of his vehicle for insurance purposes as soon as it was returned to him after he had lent it to another[7].

8.14:4 Onus of proof

It has been held in both Scotland and England that the onus of proof that a particular use is covered by an appropriate policy of insurance rests on the person charged with using the vehicle at the material time, on the principle that whether insurance for such use at the material time was in force or not is a matter which should be within the user's knowledge[8]. It is of course open to any accused person in these circumstances to show that he was not using the vehicle at the material time.

---

1 RTA 1988, s 153; see also Third Parties (Rights Against Insurers) Act 1930.
2 *Goodbarne v Buck* [1940] 1 KB 77 but reference should also be made to *Barr v Carmichael* 1993 SLT 1030, 1993 SCCR 366.
3 *McCulloch v Heywood* 1995 SLT 1009, 1995 SCCR 221.
4 *Simpson v McDonald* 1960 SLT (Notes) 83; *Tudhope v Every* 1976 JC 42, 1977 SLT 2.
5 *Robb v McKechnie* 1936 JC 25, 1936 SLT 300.
6 *Dickson v Valentine* 1989 SLT 19, 1988 SCCR 325.
7 *McLaughlin v Friel* 1997 SLT 824.
8 *Philcox v Carberry* [1960] Crim LR 563; *Milne v Whalley* 1975 SLT (Notes) 75.

If a driver allows another to drive his vehicle so long as that other insures the vehicle, he is not deemed to have permitted its use if the other driver does not in fact get insurance[1].

Section 143(3) of the Road Traffic Act 1988 provides a statutory defence to persons who are driving a vehicle which they do not own and have not hired or leased, who are using the vehicle in the course of their employment, and who neither knew or had reason to believe that no policy of insurance was in force at the material time.

Section 143(1) does not apply to invalid carriages. Further exemptions are granted in s 144, as amended by the Road Traffic Act 1991, s 20, and in terms of s 183 the requirement for insurance does not apply to vehicles and persons who are at the material time in the service of the Crown. However, on the principle that it is the use of the vehicle that is important, there must be insurance cover in respect of any private use of Crown vehicles[2].

8.14:5   Requirements of insurance policies

To comply with the requirements of the Road Traffic Act 1988, an insurance policy must be issued by an authorised insurer[3]. The term 'authorised insurer' is defined in s 145(5) and it is a prerequisite of authorisation that the insurance company is a member of the Motor Insurers' Bureau[4]. The policy must insure specified persons or classes of persons in respect of any liability by the policy holder in respect of the death of, or bodily injury to, any person, or damage to property which may be caused by, or arise out of, the use of the vehicle on the road in Great Britain or in the states of the European Community[5]. This is generally known as third party insurance, and is the minimum required; additional or comprehensive insurance is also offered by insurance companies[6].

The policy must also insure against any liability for emergency treatment[7] in terms of ss 157–159; however, such payments must

---

1 *MacDonald v Howdle* 1995 SLT 779, 1995 SCCR 216.
2 *Salt v McKnight* 1947 JC 99, 1947 SLT 327.
3 Road Traffic Act 1988, s 145(1).
4 RTA 1988, s 145(5) and (6).
5 RTA 1988, s 145(3) and (4).
6 RTA 1988, s 145(3).
7 RTA 1988, s 145(3)(c).

be made 'under or in consequence of' the policy[1]. The policy is not required to cover liability for death or bodily injury of any person employed by the insured in respect of that person's employment[2].

There are restrictions on attempts by insurance companies to qualify the cover provided by a policy[3], and on private agreements to avoid liability[4]; and special provision in respect of car-sharing agreements[5].

8.14:6   Evidence, Procedure, Penalites

If an accused gives credible but uncorroborated evidence that, for example, he believed that he was properly covered by insurance at the material time, he is entitled to be acquitted[6]. Where a driver drove in circumstances where he believed he had permission, this may amount to special reasons for not imposing penalty points[7].

If a driver does not have his insurance with him at any material time he may require to produce his documents at a police station of his choice within seven days. Failure to do so is a separate offence[8].

The appeal court has confirmed that a straightforward first offence of having no insurance may well attract a penalty of disqualification[9]. Other penalties are found in Schedule 2, as amended, to the Road Traffic Offenders Act 1988.

8.14:7   Motor Insurers' Bureau

As indicated in the preceding paragraphs, an authorised insurer must be a member of the Motor Insurers' Bureau. By s 151 of the Road Traffic Act 1988[10], the insurers are required to satisfy any judgment against persons insured for third party risks. Such risks

---

1 *Glasgow Royal Infirmary v Municipal Mutual Insurance* (1953) 69 Sh Ct Rep 297.
2 RTA 1988, s 145(4).
3 RTA 1988, s 148.
4 RTA 1988, s 149.
5 RTA 1988, s 150.
6 *Marshall v McLeod* 1998 SLT 1199, 1998 SCCR 317.
7 *Gordon v Russell* 1999 SLT 897.
8 Road Traffic Act 1988, s 165(3).
9 *Docherty v Normand* 1995 SCCR 20.
10 Subject to the provisions of s 152, as amended by the Road Traffic Act 1991, Sch 4.

must of course be *ex facie* of the policy[1]. If such a judgment is not satisfied by the insurers, then the claim must be met by the Motor Insurers' Bureau, in terms of an agreement between the Bureau and the Ministry of Transport. A further agreement extends the obligation to judgments obtained against untraced drivers. The texts of these agreements are published by Her Majesty's Stationery Office. The address of the Bureau is Aldermary House, 10–15 Queen Street, London. It should be stressed that notice of the commencement of any action against an uninsured driver must be given to the Bureau within 21 days, and it is advisable to give such notice in any case where it is thought that the judgment might be unsatisfied.

Notwithstanding the Bureau's obligations the principal responsibility for meeting any claim rests with the insured[2], and the Bureau is not accountable for any unsatisfied judgment which proceeds on a liability which the Act does not require to be covered[3].

8.15   VEHICLES EXCISE AND REGISTRATION

8.15:1   General

These matters are consolidated for the first time in the Vehicle Excise and Registration Act 1994 (universally known as "VERA"). Section 1 provides:

'(1) A duty of excise ("vehicle excise duty") shall be charged in respect of every mechanically propelled vehicle which is used, or kept on a public road in the United Kingdom and shall be paid on a licence to be taken out by the person keeping the vehicle.
(2) A licence taken out for a vehicle in this Act is referred to as a "vehicle licence".'

An excise duty is therefore charged on every mechanically propelled vehicle used or kept on the public roads and this duty is paid in respect of a licence which must be taken out by the keeper of the vehicle.

---

1 *Robb v McKenzie* 1936 JC 25, 1936 SLT 300.
2 *Corfield v Groves* [1950] 1 All ER 488.
3 *Lees v Motor Insurers' Bureau* [1952] 2 All ER 511.

8.15:2   Definitions

'*Public road*' – see 1.8:1 and 1.8:2 above. The statutory definition is supplied by s 62(1) of the Road Traffic Act 1988 and has the same meaning as in the Roads (Scotland) Act 1984[1]

'*Mechanically propelled vehicle*' – see 1.2:1 above. The Act does not require any duty to be paid in respect of any vehicle which is not mechanically propelled. Section 185(1) of the Road Traffic Act 1988 provides a number of definitions of mechanically propelled vehicles, but this list of definitions is not exhaustive.

'*Used or kept*'. The section does not qualify the word 'used' in any way. Any kind of use will therefore require the vehicle to be licensed. Further, s 62(2) of the Act provides 'For the purposes of this Act and any other enactment relating to the keeping of vehicles on public roads, a person keeps a vehicle on a public road if he causes it to be on such a road for any period, however short, when it is not in use there.' Accordingly, it is clear that, in terms of this Act, Parliament intended that any vehicle which is mechanically propelled and which is on a public road in any circumstances whatsoever, irrespective of the time or the nature of the use involved, must be covered by an excise licence; see also 8.15:5 below.

The duty charged in terms of the Act is described in the Schedules to the Act.

8.15:3   Obtaining a licence

In terms of regulation 4 of the Road Vehicles (Registration and Licensing) Regulations 1971[2], the keeper of a mechanically propelled vehicle satisfies this statutory requirement by applying to the Secretary of State (through the Post Office) for an excise licence. In making such an application, the keeper must produce evidence of insurance or security[3]; an appropriate test certificate where the vehicle is over three years old[4]; and, where appropriate at the first licensing of a vehicle subject to the type approval regu-

---

1 See *Russell v Annan* 1993 SCCR 234 which is also a reference for whether the court can assume that a road is public when there is no evidence on the matter.
2 SI 1971/450.
3 Motor Vehicles (Third-party Risks) Regulations 1972, SI 1972/1217, reg 9.
4 Motor Vehicles (Production of Test Certificates) Regulations 1969, SI 1969/418.

lations, a suitable certificate or certificates in terms of the Motor Vehicles (Type Approval) (Great Britain) Regulations 1984[1]. In addition, the appropriate level of duty requires to be paid.

Different classes and weights of vehicle attract different rates of duty, and these are described in the Schedules to the Act. The annual rates of duty, the duration of the licence and the amount of duty are provided for in ss 2–4 of the Act.

8.15:4   Exemptions

There are certain exemptions from excise duty given principally to vehicles such as fire engines, ambulances, police vehicles, vehicles for disabled people, old vehicles (25 years) and vehicle testing operations (Schedule 2). However, although the excise duty is not chargeable the licence will still have to be displayed[2].

8.15:5   Using and keeping a vehicle without a licence

Offences in respect of using or keeping a vehicle on a public road are dealt with in Part III of the Road Traffic Act 1988, and in particular by sections 29–41. Section 29(1) contains the principle offence, and s 29(3) provides that the excise penalty is either level 3 in the standard scale or five times the excise duty chargeable in respect of the vehicle, whichever is greater.

Accordingly it is an offence to use or keep a mechanically propelled vehicle on a public road for any purpose whatsoever when a licence is not in force in respect of that vehicle[3].

An offence in terms of s 29(1) can be proved by the evidence of only one witness[4].

A broken-down vehicle or one which is not capable of being moved still may require to have a licence. The only qualification which the Act applies to the requirement is that the vehicle must be mechanically propelled. However, in *MacLean v Hall*[5], a van which had neither an engine nor a gear box and which was being

1 SI 1984/981, reg 14.
2 Road Traffic Act 1988, s 43A, as introduced by the Finance Act 1997, s 18, and Sch 3, para 5.
3 *MacNeill v Dunbar* 1965 SLT (Notes) 79.
4 Road Traffic Act 1988, s 54.
5 1962 SLT (Sh Ct) 30.

towed along a public road on its way to a scrap yard was held not to be a mechanically propelled vehicle within the meaning of the Act.

8.15:6 Vehicles excise: general provisions

Section 30 of the Road Traffic Act 1988 provides that a further liability may attach to the keeper of an unlicensed vehicle in respect of any unpaid excise duty.

This is calculated on a monthly basis. If the amount of unpaid duty is challenged by the keeper of the vehicle (who for example may claim that he has not been the keeper for the whole period of the unpaid duty) then what is called a back duty proof may have to be fixed. In *Peacock v Hamilton*[1] it was held that where a motorist was charged with using a vehicle it was therefore not competent to require her to pay back duty as keeper of the vehicle.

It is a separate offence to fail to exhibit a licence[2]. Even exempt vehicles must display a licence; the exemption only relates to the duty charged[3]. Offences under s 33 can be proved by the evidence of one witness[4]. The court should take the excise penalty into account when fixing the fine[5].

Sections 11–14 of the Act cover the issue and use of trade licences to be taken out by a motor trader or vehicle tester.

The vehicles covered by a trade licence are, in the case of a motor trader, all mechanically propelled vehicles which are from time to time temporarily in his possession in the course of his business as a motor trader, and all recovery vehicles kept by him for the purpose of dealing with disabled vehicles in the course of that business. Whether a vehicle is a recovery vehicle is a question of fact but the term includes vehicles which are equipped to tow or raise disabled vehicles. In the case of a vehicle tester, the licence covers all mechanically propelled vehicles which are from time to time submitted to him for testing in the course of his business as a vehicle tester; and in the case of a motor trader who is a manufacturer of mechanically propelled vehicles, the licence covers vehicles kept and used by him solely for research and development. In all these circumstances, however, only one vehicle may be used

---

1 1996 SLT 777.
2 Road Traffic Act 1988, s 33 as amended.
3 Road Traffic Act 1988, s 33(1A).
4 RTOA 1988, s 54.
5 *Walker v Ritchie* 1997 SCCR 486.

under a trade licence at any one time, and the vehicles so covered may not be kept on the road. In addition to the provisions of ss 11-14, reference must be made to regs 28–40 of the Road Vehicles (Registration and Licensing) Regulations 1971[1]. In particular it should be noticed that for a vehicle to be disabled, it must have broken down or in other words be incapable of movement because of some mechanical defect or as the result of an accident[2]. However, it has been held in *Smith v Holt*[3] that more than one disabled vehicle may be carried at any one time by a recovery vehicle, and thus the decision in *Lockhart v Ayrshire Commercial Spares*[4] no longer applies. A motor trader or vehicle tester who has had an application for a trade licence refused may require the Secretary of State to review the decision in terms of s 14 of the Act.

If a vehicle is registered in terms of a particular class of duty because of its nature and composition but thereafter its nature and composition is altered, this may bring the vehicle into another class of duty which the keeper is obliged to pay[5]. Sections 16 and 17 (as amended) provide exceptions. See also 8.15:11 below.

Section 66 of the Road Traffic Act 1988 allows the Secretary of State to make regulations prohibiting the grant of excise licences for certain vehicles except in compliance with certain conditions.

Section 10 of the Act and the Road Vehicles (Registration and Licensing) Regulations 1971[6] allows that a vehicle excise licence may be surrendered at any time, and on doing so the keeper is entitled to any appropriate refund on unexpired duty.

8.15:7 Registration and registration numbers

Part II of the Vehicle Excise and Registration Act provides for the registration of vehicles and the issue of registration marks and numbers. These numbers must be clearly fixed on a vehicle and legible, and be capable of being properly illuminated during the hours of darkness[7].

---

1 SI 1971/450, as amended by SI 1976/1680, SI 1986/2101 and SI 1987/2123.
2 See *MacNeill v Calligan* 1973 SLT (Sh Ct) 54; *Smith v Holt* 1986 SLT (Sh Ct) 49, 1983 SCCR 175.
3 1986 SLT (Sh Ct) 49, 1983 SCCR 175.
4 1983 SLT (Sh Ct) 74, 1982 SCCR 192.
5 RTOA 1988, s 15; *Blaikie v Morrison* 1957 JC 46; 1957 SLT 290 and *Blue Band Motors Ltd v Kyle* 1972 SLT 250.
6 SI 1791/450.
7 Road Vehicles Registration and Licensing Regulations 1971, SI 1971/450, regs 18–22, as amended by SI 1975/1089 and SI 1984/814.

8.15:8   Forgery or fraud

In terms of s 44 of the Vehicle Excise and Registration Act 1994, it is an offence to forge, or fraudulently to alter or use, or fraudulently lend or allow to be used by any other person any registration mark, trade plate or licence or registration document. In terms of s 45 it is an offence to make a false or misleading statement in respect of any application for a licence or registration mark, or in respect of a requirement to furnish particulars relating to a vehicle or the keeper thereof.

By virtue of s 46 and s 46A (as amended) of the Act any person who is the registered keeper of a vehicle or any other person in a position to do so, or the alleged user of an unlicensed vehicle, is obliged to give such information as he may be required on behalf of a Chief Officer of Police or the Secretary of State as to the identity of the person or persons involved in an alleged offence of using or keeping a motor vehicle on a road without a licence or in contravention of the requirements in respect of trade plates, or in respect of a vehicle alleged to have been altered so that a different rate of duty applies. It is an offence to fail to comply with any of these requirements. The institution and conduct of proceedings in Scotland relative to licensing matters is dealt with in s 48, including prosecution outwith the normal time limits, but when the prosecution was taken within six months of sufficient information coming to the notice of the person instituting proceedings.

8.15:9   Evidence

Section 52 of the Vehicle Excise and Registration Act 1994[1] provides for the admission of records as evidence.

The section states inter alia –

'(1) A statement to which this section applies is admissible in any proceedings as evidence (or, in Scotland, sufficient evidence) of any fact stated in it with respect to matters prescribed by regulations made by the Secretary of State to the same extent as oral evidence of that fact is admissible in the proceedings.

(2) This section applies in a statement in a document purporting to be:–
   (a) a part of the records maintained by the Secretary of State in connection with any functions exercisable by him under or in terms of this Act,

---

1 As amended by the Finance Act 1995, s 19 and Sch 4, para 38.

(b) a copy of a document forming part of those records, or
(c) a note of any information contained in those records, and to be authenticated by a person authorised to do so by the Secretary of State.
(3) In subsections (1) and (2) "statement" and "document"–
    . . .
    (c) in Scotland have the same meaning as Schedule 3 to the Prisoners and Criminal Proceedings (Scotland) Act 1993,
(4) In subsections (2) the reference to a copy of the document is to be constituted –
    . . .
    (c) in Scotland in accordance with Schedule 3 to the Prisoners and Criminal Proceedings (Scotland) Act 1993.'

The Vehicle and Driving Licences Records (Evidence) Regulations 1970[1] are made in terms of s 52 (1) of the Vehicle Excise and Registration Act 1994.

In *Cardle v Wilkinson*[2], a statement contained in a document as described in subsection 1 and authenticated by a rubber stamp signature was held to be admissible in evidence.

8.15:10   Change of ownership

In terms of the Road Vehicles (Registration and Licensing) Regulations 1971[3], regs 12, 12A and 15[4], when a mechanically propelled vehicle changes ownership, the former owner is under a duty to deliver the registration book and any current licence to the new owner and intimate to the Secretary of State in writing that the change has taken place. An offence occurs if this notification of change of ownership is not made 'as soon as possible'. What constitutes 'as soon as possible' will be a matter of fact and circumstances in each case; in *A & C McLellan (Blairgowrie) Ltd v McMillan*[5], a prosecution for failure to make proper notification failed because it had not been embarked upon within a six-month period after it could be reasonably said that the former owner had failed to make notification as soon as possible. Further, the owner of a vehicle must intimate any change of address on the registra-

1 SI 1970/1997.
2 1982 SLT 315, 1982 SCCR 33, 1982 CO Circulars A/3.
3 SI 1971/450.
4 As amended by SI 1997/401.
5 1964 SLT 2.

tion book or licence document and send it to the Secretary of State. In terms of regulation 14, the owner of a vehicle must notify the Secretary of State when a vehicle has been broken up and destroyed or sent permanently out of the country and in those circumstances the registration document must be surrendered.

A cherished number plate may be transferred from one vehicle to another on application to the Post Office and payment of the appropriate fee.

8.15:11 Alteration of vehicle

In terms of regulation 11 of the Road Vehicles (Registration and Licensing) Regulations 1971 and s 18 of the Road Traffic Act 1988, where a vehicle licence has been taken out for a vehicle at a rate of duty specified in the legislation and the vehicle is at any time used in an altered condition, or in a manner or for a purpose which brings it under the description of vehicle to which a higher rate of duty applies in accordance with s 18 of the Act, the owner of the vehicle is under a duty to furnish the prescribed particulars to the Secretary of State and must send those details to him together with the licence and the registration book and the additional duty chargeable[1].

8.15:12 Registration documents

In association with the issue of a licence in respect of a mechanically propelled vehicle, the Secretary of State also issued a registration document giving details of the vehicle and its owner, in terms of the Road Vehicles (Registration and Licensing) Regulations 1971[2], reg 8 (as amended). Although the document is associated with the vehicle rather than the driver, the owner must produce the document for inspection if he is required to do so by a police officer at any reasonable time or by anyone acting on behalf of the Secretary of State. Mutilation or alteration of the document except under the procedure provided for on a change of ownership is an offence.

1 *Blaikie v Morrison* 1957 JC 46, 1957 SLT 290; *Blue Band Motors Ltd v Kyle* 1972 SLT 250.
2 SI 1971/450.

8.16   TEST CERTIFICATES (MOT CERTIFICATES)

In terms of ss 45–48 of the Road Traffic Act 1988[1], any motor vehicle other than a goods vehicle used on the road must have a valid and current test certificate, unless exempted. The requirements for goods vehicles are dealt with in ch 9. It is an offence for a vehicle which must have a certificate not to have one. It is submitted that a vehicle which is parked on a road is normally being 'used' in terms of s 47; however in the case of *Tudhope v Every*[2] it was held that a vehicle which had been immobilised could not be 'used' in this sense of the word.

The requirement to have a test certificate applies to all vehicles not less than three years old (Road Traffic Act 1988, s 47). The three-year period follows on the date of the first registration of the vehicle. Small passenger coaches, taxis and ambulances need a certificate after one year[3]. The Motor Vehicles (Test) Regulations 1981[4], provide exemption for vehicles being taken to or being retrieved from a prearranged test[5]. The regulations made by the Secretary of State in respect of the requirements of construction and condition of such vehicles and for the issue of the relevant certificates in all matters relating thereto are provided for in the foregoing regulations as amended by numerous detailed amendment regulations from 1982 onwards.

The examination of vehicles for the purpose of issuing a test certificate has to be carried out by duly appointed inspectors who receive their commission from the Secretary of State, and further such tests must be carried out in approved stations with approved apparatus[6].

1 As amended by the Road Traffic Act 1991, Sch 4, paras 52 and 53.
2 1976 JC 42, 1977 SLT 2.
3 Road Traffic Act 1988, s 47(3)).
4 SI 1981/1694.
5 Reg 6(2).
6 RTA 1988, s 46.

Chapter Nine

Public service vehicles and carriage of goods by road

PART 1   PUBLIC SERVICE VEHICLES

9.1   TRAFFIC AREAS AND TRAFFIC COMMISSIONERS

The United Kingdom is split into various traffic areas and the Scottish traffic area serves as a single authority for the whole of Scotland[1]. There is a single traffic commissioner for each such area who is appointed by and acts under the general directions of the Secretary of State[2]. The traffic commissioners are obliged to publish information in respect of their activities in terms of regulations made under s 5 of the Public Passenger Vehicles Act 1981[3]. The traffic commissioner's office is a part of the Department of Transport. In practice, the traffic commissioner uses that title when dealing with passenger vehicle matters, and is known as the 'licensing authority' when dealing with matters concerning goods vehicles. The commissioners have widespread responsibilities in respect of the licensing of large goods vehicles and passenger carrying vehicle drivers, and also for operators' licences for public service and transport of goods operations. The commissioners also have duties in respect of the supervision of public service and

1 Public Passenger Vehicles Act 1981 (c14), s 3(1) as amended.
2 PPVA 1981, s 4(1) as amended by the Transport Act 1985, s 3(2).
3 As amended by the Transport Act 1985, s 3(2).

freight operations. A commissioner may hold an inquiry into any matter as he thinks fit in connection with the exercise of his functions[1]. Each Commissioner must report annually to the Secretary of State[2] and keep a record of all licences granted by his office[3].

The traffic commissioner discharges some of his responsibilities in practice through vehicle examiners appointed to his department. Like the police, examiners are entitled to carry out roadside tests and to require particular vehicles to undergo weight testing. In addition, the Vehicle Inspectorate, which is an executive agency within the Department of Transport, is the body which has day-to-day responsibility for the authorisation of MOT garages and mechanics; the testing and plating of goods vehicles; the licensing by certificates of initial fitness or certificates of conformity of public service vehicles and their annual testing; and the notifiable alterations for both public service vehicles and goods vehicles.

9.2 DEFINITIONS

9.2:1 Public service vehicle

In terms of s 1 of the Public Passenger Vehicles Act 1981 (and subject to the whole provisions of the section) 'a public service vehicle' means –

'... a motor vehicle (other than a tramcar) which –
(a) being a vehicle adapted to carry more than eight passengers, is used for carrying passengers for hire or reward; or
(b) being a vehicle not so adapted, is used for carrying passengers for hire or reward at separate fares in the course of a business of carrying passengers.'

9.2:2 General

The phrase 'for hire or reward' is defined in s 1(5) and (6) of the Public Passenger Vehicles Act 1981; see also *Hawthorn v Knight*[4].

---

1 PPVA 1981, s 54 (as amended by TA 1985, s 4).
2 PPVA 1981, s 55.
3 PPVA 1981, s 56, as amended.
4 1962 JC 31, 1962 SLT 69.

The phrase 'separate fares' means payment by individual passengers in respect of any journey or journeys, whether the payments are made in terms of a fixed tariff imposed by the operator or under an arrangement between the passenger and the carrier[1]. For the purposes of the Act, a vehicle is deemed to be in use until that use has been permanently discontinued[2]. Section 1(3) provides exceptions for vehicles carrying passengers at separate fares in the course of a business of carrying passengers, under certain circumstances described in Parts 1 and 3 of Schedule 1 to the Act, unless the vehicle is adapted to carry more than eight passengers. Further, in terms of s 1(4) private motorists are allowed to make car-share arrangements, for a fare or for a consideration. A 'fare' need not be paid only to the driver or owner of the vehicle[3].

9.3   PUBLIC PASSENGER SERVICE REQUIREMENTS

9.3:1   General

In respect of any such operation of public passenger service, there must be a certificate of fitness in respect of the public service vehicles which are used for the purpose of the service; the person or company who is the operator of the service must have a public service vehicles operator's licence; and the driver of the vehicle must have a public service vehicle driver's licence (See 9.5 below). In addition the drivers of certain kinds of passenger carrying vehicle are subject to the legislation on drivers' hours and records of work.

9.3:2   Deregulation

Under the previous system, a public passenger service operation required a road service licence for what were called stage carriage services, (in addition to an operator's licence), in terms of ss 2 and 30–37 of the Public Passenger Vehicles Act 1981. These sections were repealed by ss 1 and 139(3) of and Schedule 8 to the

---

1 *Aitken v Hamilton* 1964 SLT 125.
2 PPVA 1981, s 1(2).
3 *Hawthorn v Knight* 1962 JC 31, 1962 SLT 69.

Transport Act 1985 which came into force on 26 October 1986 in terms of the Transport Act 1985 (Commencement No 6) Order 1986[1]. As a result of the repeal of ss 30–37 of the 1981 Act, such services were deregulated. In the place of the former road service licences, additional conditions may now be imposed by the traffic commissioner on the licences issued to public service vehicle operators in respect of what are now termed local services and which are defined in s 2 of the Transport Act 1985. The commissioner's powers to impose these conditions in respect of registration and traffic regulation are found in ss 6–9 of the 1985 Act.

9.3:3   Certificates of fitness of public service vehicles

In terms of s 6 (as amended) of the Public Passenger Vehicles Act 1981, any public service vehicle adapted to carry more than eight passengers cannot be used on a road unless there is in force in respect of such a vehicle a certificate of initial fitness or its equivalent (which is a certificate of conformity under a type approval scheme: see 9.3:3 below). Such a certificate may not provide a defence to a civil claim based on a failure to supply employees with safe equipment[2]. Such certificates of fitness are issued by a vehicle examiner by virtue of s 9 of the Road Traffic Act 1991 which introduces a new s 66A of the Road Traffic Act 1988. The powers of inspection and testing available to such examiners are described at 7.13 above, and such officials have the right of inspection of all public vehicles by virtue of s 68 of the Road Traffic Act 1988[3].

A public service vehicle may not ply for hire generally[4]. Certain exemptions are given to school buses used in certain circumstances by a local education authority in terms of s 46(1) of the Public Passenger Vehicles Act 1981.

By virtue of s 6(1)(b) and (c) and s 10 of the Public Passenger Vehicles Act 1981, the approval by the Secretary of State of a vehicle as a type vehicle or a certificate of type of approval, may be treated as an equivalent to a certificate of fitness or as a certificate of initial fitness[5].

---

1 SI 1986/1794.
2 *Donnelly v Glasgow Corporation* 1953 SC 107, 1953 SLT 161; but see also *Sullivan v Gallagher and Craig* 1959 SC 243, 1960 SLT 70.
3 As amended by the Road Traffic Act 1991, s 12.
4 Transport Act 1985, s 30.
5 See also RTA 1988, s 54ff, and the relevant regulations.

9.4   PUBLIC SERVICE VEHICLE OPERATORS' LICENCES

9.4:1   General

In addition to certificates of fitness or equivalents relating to vehicles, the operator of any public service vehicle operation must have a licence granted to him in accordance with the relevant statutory provisions[1]. The term 'operator' is defined in s 81 of the Public Passenger Vehicles Act 1981. In terms of s 46, exemption may be granted to a school bus used by an education authority. The licence relates to the operator rather than the vehicle and is granted by the traffic commissioner for the relevant area in which are situated the operating centre or centres of the vehicles used in the operation[2]. The power of the traffic commissioners to grant licences is contained in s 4(3) and the procedure to be followed by the commissioner is dealt with in ss 14 and 14A[3]. The commissioner also regulates the fees in respect of the issue of licences and must report annually to the Secretary of State and keep records of all licences issued[4]. Only one public service vehicle licence can be held by any one person in a particular area but there is no restriction on such a person holding such licences in other traffic areas[5].

Licences can either be standard or restricted[6]. There is a limit imposed on the number of vehicles that may be used under a restricted licence[7]. In terms of s 14(1) of the 1981 Act, the commissioner must be satisfied that the applicant for a licence is of good repute, of appropriate financial standing and of the requisite professional competence. For a restricted licence the last of these qualifications is not required. Schedule 3 to the Act gives further details in respect of such applications. By virtue of s 14 the applicant must also demonstrate that he has sufficient facilities or arrangements for maintaining the vehicles which are to be operated in terms of the licences in a fit and serviceable condition and that he can provide suitably for observing the requirements of the legislation governing the driving and operation of such vehicles. Provisions in respect of the conditions that may be applied to such

1   Public Passenger Vehicles Act 1981, s 12, as amended by Transport Act 1985, Sch 1, para 4.
2   PPVA 1981, s 12(2).
3   Introduced by TA 1985, s 25.
4   PPVA 1981, s 56, as amended by TA 1985, s 3(5) and Sch 2, Pt II.
5   PPVA 1981, s 12(3).
6   PPVA 1981, s 13.
7   PPVA 1981, s 16 as amended by TA 1985.

licences are dealt with in ss 26 and 27 of the Transport Act 1985. The chief constable of the area or the local authority may object to the grant of such licences by virtue of s 14A[1]. The powers of the traffic commissioner to disqualify operators from holding a licence are described in s 28 of the 1985 Act.

The licence specifies the date it comes into force and, subject to its revocation or termination under any other statutory provision, continues indefinitely[2]. The previous duration of five years was dispensed with by the Deregulation and Contracting Out Act 1994, s 61. Further, the licence normally indicates the maximum number of vehicles which may be operated, together with further conditions where they are prescribed or otherwise[3]; the same section allows the commissioner to designate stops and include undertakings in the licence, and these can all be revoked or varied; and a description of the prescribed conditions to be attached to a licence is provided in the Public Service Vehicles (Operators Licences) Regulations 1995[4]. By virtue of s 17(1) and (5) of the Public Passenger Vehicles Act 1981 as amended and (5), the commissioner has the power to revoke, suspend or vary the conditions on a licence at any time. If the commissioner wishes to revoke a licence on the ground that the operator no longer satisfies the requirement of being of good repute or having the appropriate financial standing, or being professionally competent, a public hearing must first be held if the operator requires. The commissioner may appoint assessors in terms of s 17A[5].

By virtue of s 18[6], the operator has a duty to exhibit on each vehicle covered by the licence an appropriate disc issued by the commissioner. This disc gives particulars of the operator of the vehicle, his operator's licence and its date of expiry, but no details of the vehicle itself. Current regulations are the Public Service Vehicles (Operations Licences) Regulations 1995[7].

The operator must inform the Secretary of State of any relevant criminal convictions, or of any incident or damage relating to any of the vehicles covered by the licence, which might have a bearing on public safety[8].

---

1 Inserted by TA 1985, s 25.
2 PPVA 1981, s 15.
3 PPVA 1981, s 16.
4 SI 1995/2869.
5 Introduced by TA 1985, s 5.
6 As amended by the Deregulation and Contracting Out Act 1994, ss 63 and 68 and Sch 14, para 6.
7 SI 1995/2908.
8 PPVA 1981, ss 19 and 20, as amended by TA 1985, s 29.

Exemption from some of the foregoing requirements is available to local education authorities in respect of schoolbuses carrying fare-paying passengers[1]. Community bus services exempted from some operator and driver licensing requirements under a system of permits are dealt with under ss 22 and 23 of the Transport Act 1985 together with other regulations and in general, reference should be made to ss 18–23 of the Transport Act 1985 in respect of these exemptions.

By virtue of s 57 of the 1981 Act, an operator's licence is not assignable and ceases to be valid on the death, bankruptcy or mental incapacity of the holder, or in respect of any other event described in the licence by the commissioner. Deferment of termination may be granted in certain circumstances. The regulations covering the procedure for applications for such licences come in terms of s 59; current regulations are the Public Service Vehicle Operators (Qualifications) Regulation 1981[2] and the Public Service Vehicles (Operators' Licences) Regulations 1986[3]; reference should also be made to the Public Service Vehicles (Driver's Licences) Regulations 1985[4] and the Public Service Vehicles (Operators' Licences) Regulations 1995[5].

It is an offence to forge or alter any licence, disc, certificate or document, or to make a false statement in any application connected with an operator's licence[6]. The registered keeper of a public service vehicle has a duty to disclose the identity of the driver of that vehicle at any given time[7].

Section 74 of the Road Traffic Act 1988 imposes duties on the operator to inspect his vehicles and keep records of such inspections.

9.4:2   Appeals

In the event of a traffic commissioner refusing an application for a public service vehicle operator's licence, or if a condition is imported into the licence which has not been included in the

---

1 PPVA 1981, s 46.
2 SI 1981/266.
3 SI 1986/1668.
4 SI 1985/214.
5 SI 1995/2908.
6 PPVA 1981, ss 65 and 66, as amended.
7 PPVA 1981, s 70.

application, the appellant has the right to appeal to the Transport Tribunal[1]. Under previous legislation, the decision of the Secretary of State could be appealed on a point of law to the Court of Session[2]. Such an appeal is no longer specifically provided for but is not necessarily unavailable, for example by means of the process of judicial review.

Further, a person who has had an application for a certificate of initial fitness in terms of s 6 of the Public Passenger Vehicles Act 1981, or a type vehicle certificate in terms of s 10, refused, may appeal to the Secretary of State under s 51[3]. Section 49A[4] allows the commissioner to vary or revoke his own decisions.

9.5 PUBLIC SERVICE VEHICLES DRIVERS' LICENCES

Drivers of public service vehicles (now called passenger carrying vehicles or PCVs) and of heavy goods vehicles (now called large goods vehicles or LGVs) no longer require the issue of a separate licence. The licensing of PCV or LGV drivers is now incorporated in the ordinary driving licence, but the additional authorisations are under the control of the traffic commissioners. The legislation governing these matters is found in the Road Traffic (Driver Licensing and Information Systems) Act 1989, ss 1–5 and Sch 2, which extensively alters Part IV of the Road Traffic Act 1988 and in particular ss 110–121 thereof. Section 121 of the 1988 Act contains definitions of passenger carrying vehicles. The holder of a licence entitling the driver to drive a passenger carrying vehicle is therefore subject to the general rules that apply to the holder of a driving licence[5]; for example, it is an offence to cause or permit another to drive a passenger carrying vehicle without a licence allowing him to drive a vehicle of the class[6]. Appropriate provision is made for the earlier form of licence to remain in effect.

Regulations may be made to govern the conduct of drivers,

---

1 PPVA 1981, s 50, as amended by the Transport Act 1985, s 31 and the Deregulation and Contracting Out Act 1994.
2 See, for example, *Strathclyde Passenger Executive v McGill's Bus Service* 1984 SLT 377.
3 As amended by the Transport Act 1985, s 31 and the Road Traffic Act 1991, ss 48 and 83, Sch 4, para 16 and Sch 8.
4 Added by the Deregulation and Contracting Out Act 1994, s 65(1).
5 See the Road Traffic Act 1988, Ch 8 and Pt III.
6 RTA 1988, s 87(2).

conductors and inspectors of public service vehicles, and also to regulate the conduct of passengers, by virtue of ss 24 and 25 of the Public Passengers Vehicles Act 1981. The regulations currently in force are the Public Service Vehicles (Conduct of Drivers, Inspectors, Conductors and Passengers) Regulations 1990[1]. A special driving test requires to be taken (See 9.12:2 below). These regulations inter alia impose duties of care on the drivers of buses only in respect of persons entitled to board the bus and not in respect of anyone attempting to board while it is in motion[2]. These sections and regulations do not apply to tramcars and trolley buses, which are covered by the Stage Carriages Act 1832, s 48 (as amended).

The Motor Vehicle (Driving Licences) Regulations 1999[3] make detailed provision for categories of entitlement, age limits, licence applications, tests of competence to drive and other matters concerning goods and passenger carrying vehicles.

9.6   LOCAL AUTHORITY SERVICES

By virtue of s 101(1) of the Road Traffic Act 1930, as amended by the Transport Act 1968, ss 31 and 37, a local authority may run public service vehicles on any road inside or outside its district as part of any operation of tramways, light railways, trolley vehicles or omnibuses which it undertakes in terms of a local Act or order.

9.7   PASSENGER TRANSPORT AUTHORITIES AND EXECUTIVES

The function of passenger transport authorities is to make general policy in respect of any unmet demand for public transport service in the area. The function of the Passenger Transport Executive is to secure services which will comply with that policy. How this is achieved varies from area to area. The detailed provisions for these functions, and in respect of local authority bus operations, are found in Part IV of the Transport Act 1985. The consequent financial provisions including those relating to travel

---

1 SI 1990/1020.
2 *Reid v MacNicol* 1958 SLT 42.
3 SI 1999/2824.

concession schemes, are dealt with in Part V of the Act. Part V covers general miscellaneous matters including questions of competition law, travel concession schemes, the reconstitution of the Transport Tribunal, the provision by British Rail of substitution road services and the constitution of the Disabled Persons Transport Advisory Committee.

9.8   TRAVEL CONCESSIONS

The local authority may make travel concessions to certain qualified persons who travel on its vehicles, by introducing either free travel or reduced fares. Persons who qualify for these concessions may be men over 65 and women over 60 years of age; children under 16; persons between the minimum school leaving age and 18 who are undergoing full time education; blind persons; disabled persons; and members of the local authority. Those provisions are contained generally in the Transport Act 1985, ss 93ff.

9.9   INTERNATIONAL CARRIAGE OF PASSENGERS AND LUGGAGE BY ROAD

The convention on the above is given effect to by the Carriage of Passengers by Road Act 1974, which is yet to come into force.

PART 2   CARRIAGE OF GOODS BY ROAD

9.10   GOODS VEHICLES

The legislation imposes certain requirements on the operation of commercial goods vehicles and the carriage of goods on the roads for hire or reward. The principal considerations met with in practice are the requirement that anyone operating a goods vehicle should have an operator's licence, the need for the driver to have a licence authorising him to drive the vehicle in question, and the qualification of the amount of hours of work that a driver of a commercial vehicle is entitled to do and the records which he must keep in respect of that work.

9.11   GOODS VEHICLES OPERATORS' LICENCES

9.11:1   General

It is an offence to use a goods vehicle on a road for the carriage of goods for hire or reward, or for in connection with any trade or businesses carried on by the operator except under an operator's licence[1]. The licensing authority is the traffic commissioner[2]. A description of the phrase 'hire or reward' is given at 9.2:2 above. A vehicle is used for reward where a payment is made, even although there is no legal obligation on the payer to make such payment[3]. For further definitions of the phrase 'hire or reward', reference should be made to the cases of *Wurzel v Houghton Main Home Delivery Service Ltd*[4] and *Albert v Motor Insurers Bureau*[5].

Small goods vehicles are exempted from the licence requirements[6]. It should be noted that a small goods vehicle will be subject to all of these legislative provisions in respect of commercial vehicles if a trailer is added to the vehicle and the total weight of the vehicle and trailer exceeds the statutory minimum (which is currently 3.5 tonnes).

The licensing authority may specify in the operator's licence what vehicles the operator is authorised to use in terms of the licence[7]. Applications for licences, their issue and duration, their conditions, suspension, curtailment and variation, and the disqualification and revocation of licences are dealt with in ss 8–34 of the 1995 Act. Schedule 2 provides the qualifications expected of applicants for operators' licences. Reference should also be made to the Goods Vehicles (Licensing of Operators) Regulations 1995[8]. The power of traffic commissioners to hold inquiries (which are wide-ranging) and review and appeals procedure are provided for in ss 35–37. In order to secure that the

1 Goods Vehicles (Licensing of Operators) Act 1995, s 2.
2 GV(LO)A 1995, s 1.
3 *Aitken v Hamilton* 1964 SLT 125.
4 [1937] 1 KB 380.
5 [1972] AC 301.
6 GV(LO)A 1995, s 2(2)(a) and Sch 1.
7 GV(LO)A 1995, s 5 and 5(b).
8 SI 1995/2869.

conditions of an operator's licence are being observed, authorised examiners have powers of entry and inspection[1]. Operators' licences are not transferable[2]. All these sections have been subject to amendment in detail.

Operators' licences may be standard, which allow the vehicles to be used both for hire or reward, and in connection with the trade or business, and for international transport operations or national transport operations only. Alternatively licences may be restricted, which allows the vehicles covered by the licence to be used in respect of the operator's trade or business only. The nature of these licences, relevant conditions, exceptions and the qualifications which have to be met by an operator before a licence is granted to him are contained in the Goods Vehicles (Licensing of Operators) Regulations 1995[3]. Reference needs also to be made to the schedules of the Act. For more detailed and practical advice on the licensing of the operators of goods vehicles, the Traffic Commissioner's Office issues, in association with the Department of Transport, a number of useful booklets and guides on the subject.

9.11:2 Operators' licences: inspection and evidence

The operator of a goods vehicle has a duty to inspect the vehicle and a further duty to keep records of that inspection[4]. In any proceedings for a failure to observe regulations under s 74 of the Road Traffic Act 1988 or a failure to observe the construction and use regulations, such records are sufficient evidence of the matters stated therein[5].

9.12 GOODS VEHICLES DRIVERS' LICENCES

9.12:1 General

Drivers of heavy goods vehicles (now called large goods vehicles or LGVs) no longer need to obtain a separate licence. The entitle-

---

1 GV(LO)A 1995, s 40–42.
2 GV(LO)A 1995, s 48.
3 SI 1995/2869.
4 Road Traffic Act 1988, s 74, as amended by the Road Traffic Act 1991, Sch 4, para 57.
5 Road Traffic Offenders Act 1988, s 14, as amended by RTA 1991, Sch 4, para 86; see also Good Vehicles (Licensing of Operators) Act 1995, s 43.

ment to drive various classes of commercial vehicle is incorporated in the ordinary driving licence. The additional authorisations are under the control of the traffic commissioners. The legislation governing these matters is found in the Road Traffic (Driver Licensing and Information Systems) Act 1989, ss 1–5 and Sch 2, which extensively alters Part IV of the Road Traffic Act 1988 and in particular ss 110–121 thereof. The holder of a licence authorising the driver to drive a large goods vehicle is therefore subject to the general rules that apply to any other holder of a driving licence[1]. It is not only persons who have actual knowledge of the absence of an appropriate licence on the part of the driver who can be found guilty of causing or permitting the driver to commit an offence; constructive or imputed knowledge of the lack of such a licence may lead to conviction[2].

A large goods vehicle is defined in s 121 of the Road Traffic Act 1988 (as amended) as

'a motor vehicle (not being a medium sized vehicle within the meaning of Part III of this Act) which is constructed or adapted to carry or haul goods and the permissible maximum weight of which exceeds 7.5 tonnes'.

An appeal against the refusal by the Secretary of State to grant a licence is available in terms of 119 of the Road Traffic Act 1988[3]; (see also 9.12:2 below).

In terms of the definition of the term 'maximum permissible weight' contained in s 108 of the Road Traffic Act 1988, a rigid or articulated vehicle drawing a trailer may bring a vehicle into the category of LGV licensing if the total weight of the combination exceeds 7.5 tonnes.

9.12:2   Application for, and nature of, licence

An application for a licence is made to the traffic commissioner for the area in which the applicant resides[4]. Generally, the principal requirements and conditions of such licences are found in Part IV of the Act, but there are also a number of important statu-

---

1 See the Road Traffic Act 1988, Ch 8 and Pt III.
2 *MacPhail v Allan and Day* 1980 SLT (Sh Ct) 136.
3 Introduced by the Road Traffic (Driver Licensing and Information Systems) Act 1989, s 2(1).
4 Road Traffic Act 1988, s 111, as amended.

tory instruments[1]. Again, the traffic commissioner issues booklets in respect of applications for such licences. In particular an applicant must pass a special driving test[2]. Reference should also be made to the Motor Vehicles (Driving Licences) Regulations 1999[3].

The licensing authority has power to revoke or suspend a licence[4]. Considerations which may result in revocation and disqualification are the driver's conduct, his failure to keep records or a physical disability[5]. The disqualification may be indefinite or for such period as the licensing authority considers to be appropriate. The revocation of a licence by a traffic commissioner results in disqualification from driving the prescribed classes of vehicle[6].

If the test of competency to drive is alleged to have been unfairly conducted, or was not conducted properly in terms of the relevant regulations, the applicant may appeal by way of application to the sheriff for the area where he resides[7]. An appeal to the sheriff is also available in respect of any refusal, revocation or curtailment of a licence.

9.13 GOODS VEHICLES PLATING AND TESTING CERTIFICATES

9.13:1   General

Sections 45 and 49 of the Road Traffic Act 1988[8], and Part IV of that Act generally provide that all goods vehicles which are used on the roads must have both a plating certificate and a test certifi-

---

1 Eg, the Motor Vehicles (Driving Licences) (Heavy Goods and Public Service Vehicles) Regulations 1990, SI 1990/2611; the Motor Vehicles (Driving Licences) (Large Goods and Passenger-Carrying Vehicles) Regulations 1990, SI 1990/2612; the Driving Licences (Community Driving Licence) Regulations 1996, SI 1996/1974, and the Motor Vehicles (Driving Licences) Regulations 1999, SI 1999/2864.
2 Road Traffic Act 1988, ss 89 and 89A, as amended by the Road Traffic (Driver Licensing and Information System) Act 1989 etc.
3 SI 1999/2864.
4 RTA 1988, s 115, as amended.
5 See *Warrender v Scottish Traffic Area Licensing Authority* 1976 SLT (Sh Ct) 76.
6 RTA 1988, s 117.
7 RTA 1988, s 119, as amended; see, eg, *Crawford v Scottish Traffic Area Licensing Authority* 1974 SLT (Sh Ct) 11.
8 As amended by the Road Traffic Act 1991, Sch 4, paras 52 and 54.

cate, and provision is also made for the testing of goods vehicles. A plating certificate contains the plated particulars (including the plated weight) which are prescribed. The test certificate relates to requirements of construction and use. The Goods Vehicles (Plating and Testing) Regulations 1988[1] make provision in respect of both types of certificate. Reference should also be made to Part III of the Road Vehicles (Construction and Use) Regulations 1986[2], in respect of plating requirements, testing and inspection. Test certificates have to be renewed periodically.

9.13:2   Type approval schemes

The plating and testing certificates are required for all goods vehicles that are manufactured or produced and used. For practical reasons, they are implemented by means of type approval schemes. Manufacturers may submit to the Secretary of State a type vehicle for approval. The approval is intended to cover all matters of design, construction, equipment and marking. The Secretary of State then issues a type approval certificate, and this enables the manufacturer to provide other vehicles with a certificate of conformity to the effect that all such further vehicles conform to the type vehicle submitted to the Secretary of State. The plated particulars must be indicated on every vehicle. The principle of the scheme is extended to vehicle parts. There are a number of statutory instruments which implement the schemes in detail. A discussion of these details is not within the scope of this book.

9.13:3   Inspection

Authorised examiners have extensive powers of test and inspection of all kinds of motor vehicles. Sections 9–15 of the Road Traffic Act 1991 replace or amend various sections in the Public Passengers Vehicles Act 1981 and the Road Traffic Act 1988. In effect, the previous categories of certifying officers, examiners of goods vehicles and public service examiners are replaced by a single class of vehicle examiners. Such examiners are appointed

1 SI 1988/1478 (as amended).
2 SI 1986/1078.

and authorised by the Secretary of State. It is anticipated that most of such examiners will be members of the Vehicle Inspectorate (an independent agency operating within the Department of Transport), but there is provision for police officers also to be appointed and authorised.

By virtue of ss 9–15 the following provisions are made for vehicle examination. Section 66A of the Road Traffic Act 1988 allows the Secretary of State to appoint vehicle examiners. Section 67 of the Act provides that vehicles may be tested on roads to check that they comply with all aspects of the construction and use regulations (including lighting) and includes the power of the examiner to drive the vehicle in question, and to require the driver to comply with his instructions. Section 68 provides specifically for the inspection of public passenger vehicles and goods vehicles, and gives the examiner the power to drive the vehicle, as well as the power to enter premises to inspect the vehicle or detain it for the purpose of testing it. It is an offence intentionally to obstruct an examiner in his pursuit of any of these powers. Further, an examiner or a police officer in uniform may direct the driver to drive his vehicle to a testing station not more than five miles distant from where the vehicle is stopped. Section 69 gives the examiner the power to prohibit the driving of any unfit vehicle (not only PCVs or LGVs). Section 70 allows the prohibition of overloaded passenger or goods vehicles, and ss 71 and 72 create offences and allow for removal of prohibitions respectively. Section 74 imposes inspection duties on the operator.

Prosecution for overloading or dangerous vehicles is dealt with at 7.12:6, 7.12:7 and 7.12:15 above.

9.14 DRIVERS' HOURS AND RECORDS OF WORK

9.14:1 General

Section 95 of the Transport Act 1968 (as substantially amended) provides that drivers engaged in the road transport industry, whether engaged in the carriage of passengers or of goods, must observe certain restrictions in the hours worked. It should be noticed that the term 'working' used throughout this part of the legislation is not necessarily exclusively confined to 'driving'. The basic idea is that no driver of any vehicle engaged in the carriage of passengers or goods should drive for longer than certain periods[1], and such vehicles should have installed and use prescribed recording equipment ('the tachograph')[2]. Accordingly, the legislation makes provision for two sorts of offences: those concerned with maximum permitted driving hours and rest periods and breaks, and those concerned with the fitting and use of tachographs. It should be emphasised from the outset that this is a particularly complex field of law, and adequate coverage of the topic is not within the scope of this book.

The purpose of these restrictions and provisions is specifically described as a protection of the public against the risks which arise when drivers are suffering from fatigue. The Secretary of State has extensive power to make regulations in respect of these matters and in practice makes regulations to take account of any requirement imposed by the rules of the European Economic Community. Numerous regulations have been made in terms of s 95. Part VI of the Act outlines the general framework of the scheme. Broadly speaking, there are two kinds of rules: those which apply to national and international driving, and those which, exempted from the first category, apply to what is called domestic driving. The international and national rules apply to most goods vehicles over 3.5 tonnes maximum weight. There are various exceptions from these requirements provided for in the regulations.

Generally, the requirements of international and national driving are at present as follows. The rules apply to all goods vehicles which exceed 3.5 tonnes permissible maximum weight and to all passenger vehicles carrying more that nine persons including the driver (see 9.14:4 below).

The permitted hours of driving are complex and are contained in Council Regulation (EEC) 3820/85. A very approximate general survey of the rules now follows.

A driver must not drive for more than nine hours in a day. This may be extended to ten hours twice a week. After four and a half hours of driving a driver must take a break of at least forty-five minutes. Weekly rest periods must be taken after six consecutive daily driving periods. The total period of driving per fortnight must not exceed ninety hours. A driver must have a minimum daily rest of eleven consecutive hours which may be reduced in certain circumstances. These general rules are subject to extensive exceptions and revision. Vehicles not subject to these rules may be

---

1 Transport Act 1968, s 96(2).
2 TA 1968, s 97, as amended.

required to observe the requirements in Part VI of the Transport Act 1968, which contains other rules of a like kind. Statutory defences of both sets of regulation offences are found in s 96(11) and s 96(11B) of the 1968 Act[1].

Journeys to some European countries outside the Common Market are subject to an international agreement on drivers' hours. These agreements (the AETR Rules) may also have to be observed. Further, if a country is neither in the Common Market nor subject to the AETR Rules (eg Switzerland) the domestic rules of that country have to be observed.

Certain operations are exempted from the international and national drivers' hours and tachograph rules when they are engaged in specific operations. In such cases, drivers of goods vehicles which are so exempted are subject to certain domestic rules. These are that no driver may drive for more than ten hours in a day or be on duty for more than eleven hours on any working day. There are also special considerations given to mixed domestic and Common Market driving and there are certain exemptions even from the domestic rules. Drivers governed by domestic rules do not have to install and use the tachograph.

9.14:2   Offences

In respect of offences in terms of these regulations, returns tendered by drivers as correct which show that driving has occurred for longer than the permitted hours are in themselves sufficient, in the absence of any definite and further evidence, to constitute the offence[2]. However, evidence that the weekly rest period has not been taken has to be established by demonstrating the number of hours worked[3]. The onus is on the driver to show that he is entitled to any of the statutory exceptions[4]. In determining whether an offence has been committed, hours of driving outside the United Kingdom can properly be taken into account[5].

Tachographs must be kept regularly calibrated and periodic inspection every two and six years is required.

---

1 See also *Lees v Styles* 1997 SLT (Sh Ct) 11.
2 Transport Act 1968, s 97(B), as amended by Passenger and Goods Vehicles (Recording Equipment) Regulations 1979, SI 1979/1746; *Adair v Craighouse Cabinet Works Ltd* 1937 JC 89, 1937 SLT 499.
3 *Douglas v Glass* 1990 SCCR 445.
4 *Lees v Styles* 1997 SLT (Sh Ct) 11.
5 *Fox v Lawson* [1974] AC 803, [1974] 2 WLR 247.

There can be difficulties of jurisdiction in respect of offences libelled because of the terms of s 103(7) of the Transport Act 1968; and practitioners may encounter some difficulty in discovering what might be the appropriate penalties for some tachograph offences, particularly as the Crown no longer has to serve notices of penalty. Practitioners may also wish to note the provisions of s 244 of the Road Traffic Act 1960, which describes time ban provisions slightly different from those generally applied by the Criminal Procedure (Scotland) Act 1995. Section 244 has been amended by s 16(2) of and Schedule 2, paragraph 11 to the Vehicle and Driving Licences Act 1969, s 4 of and Schedule 3, paragraph 2(2) to the Road Traffic (Consequential Provisions) Act 1988 and s 60 of and Schedule 7, paragraph 2 to the Goods Vehicle (Licensing of Operators) Act 1995.

9.14:3   Keeping of records

There are numerous requirements relating to the keeping of records in terms of Part VI of the Transport Act 1968. Employers have a duty to provide their drivers with record charts of an approved type that can be used in the tachograph. The driver is obliged to enter certain information on the chart before inserting it into the tachograph. It is the driver's responsibility to see that recording by the tachograph takes place properly. Drivers are then obliged to return their charts to their employers who must keep them for a year. Only those drivers whose driving is governed by these EC Rules require to operate the tachograph; other drivers are merely constrained by the domestic driving rules. However, the provision of the tachograph requirements as indicated above is complex and there are a number of exceptions.

The basic regulations are the Drivers Hours (Goods Vehicles) (Keeping of Records) Regulations 1987[1].

Any entry on a record sheet made by a crew member can be sufficient evidence of the matters appearing therein[2]. However, in any prosecution the Crown must prove the number of hours worked when the driver was engaged in both regulated and unregulated driving[3]. It is recommended that practitioners

---

1 SI 1987/1421.
2 ss 97 and 97B, as amended by Passenger and Goods Vehicles (Recording Equipment) Regulations 1979, SI 1979/1746.
3 *Douglas v Glass* 1990 SCCR 445.

involved in this detailed and continually changing subject should consult a specialist work on the subject for further information on this matter.

9.14:4 Exemptions

Certain exemptions are granted in respect of both drivers' hours and the installation and use of the tachograph in respect of certain vehicles. For example, certain passenger and public authority vehicles; ambulances; breakdown vehicles; vehicles in restricted use in agricultural, forestry and fishing enterprises; vehicles carrying animal carcases and waste unfit for human consumption are exempted[1]. Also exempted are vehicles in respect of operations carried out by specialised vehicles[2]; this exemption applies to the operations which are carried out (such as door-to-door selling) rather than the vehicles themselves[3]. Police officers and other appropriate persons have an extensive power of inspection in respect of tachograph operations[4] and exemption from all these requirements is given to the police and fire brigade and to armed service vehicles, but not to vehicles in the public service of the Crown[5]. Reference should also be made to the Community Drivers' Hours and Recording Equipment Regulations 1986[6]; the Drivers' Hours (Harmonisation with Community Rules) Regulations 1986[7]; and the Drivers' Hours (Goods Vehicles) (Modifications) Order 1986[8].

---

1 See Council Regulations (EEC) 3820/85 and Community Drivers' Hours and Recording Equipment (Exemptions and Supplementary Provisions) Regulations 1986, SI 1986/1456, regs 2(1) and 4(1), as amended by the Community Drivers' Hours and Recording Equipment (Exemptions and Supplementary Provisions) Regulations 1987, SI 1987/805 and the Schedule thereto; see also *Ross-Taylor v Houston* 1986 SCCR 210 (exemption for transport of livestock to local markets or slaughterhouses); *Weir v Tudhope* 1987 SCCR 307 (exemption for specialised breakdown vehicles).
2 Paragraph 6 of the Schedule.
3 *Struthers (Lochwinnoch) v Tudhope* 1982 SLT 393, 1981 SCCR 329; *Stewart v Richmond* 1983 SLT 62, 1982 SCCR 383; *Baron Meats Ltd v Lockhart* 1993 SLT 279, 1991 SCCR 537; *Reith v Skinner* 1996 SCCR 506.
4 Transport Act 1968, s 99.
5 TA 1968, s 102, as amended by the Road Traffic (Consequential Provisions) Act 1988, Sch 3, para 6.
6 SI 1986/1456.
7 SI 1986/1458.
8 SI 1986/1459.

EC Regulations 3820/85 provides[1] for similar exemptions in the equivalent EC legislation. In particular, article 4(7) and (8) appear to extend the exemption to ambulance-type vehicles, while the UK regulations do not. It is suggested that ambulances are exempt in terms of regulation 2 of the Drivers' Hours (Goods Vehicles) (Exemptions) Regulations 1986[2].

9.15   FOREIGN GOODS VEHICLES AND PUBLIC SERVICE VEHICLES

9.15:1   General

By virtue of s 1 of the Road Traffic (Foreign Vehicles) Act 1972 (as amended), appointed examiners are entitled to inspect foreign goods vehicles and foreign public service vehicles, to satisfy themselves that the relevant provisions of domestic road traffic legislation are being observed.

9.15:2   International carriage of goods by road

Special authorisation is required in respect of journeys by goods vehicles to certain continental destinations[3].

The International Carriage of Perishable Foodstuffs Act 1976[4] provided for the international carriage of perishable foodstuffs[5].

The conditions governing contracts for the international carriage of goods by road between a number of European states are now standard, reflecting the agreement contained in the convention for the international carriage of goods by road (known as CNR) which was drawn up in 1956. The European Council Regulation (EEC) 881/92 of 26 March 1992 authorises goods vehicle access between member states and is implemented by the Goods Vehicle (Community Authorisations) Regulations 1992[6].

---

1 Art 4.
2 SI 1986/1492.
3 International Road Haulage Permits Act 1975, as amended, and the appropriate regulations (SI 1975/2234).
4 As amended by International Carriage of Perishable Foodstuffs Act 1976 (Amendment) Order 1983, SI 1983/1123.
5 See also International Carriage of Foodstuffs Regulations 1985, SI 1985/1071.
6 SI 1992/3077.

Tables

SHORTEST STOPPING DISTANCES IN OPTIMUM CONDITIONS FOR MOTOR CARS

Miles per hour	Thinking distance Feet	Thinking distance Metres	Braking distance Feet	Braking distance Metres	Total Feet	Total Metres
20	20	6	20	6	40	12
30	30	9	45	14	75	23
40	40	12	80	24	120	36
50	50	15	125	38	175	53
60	60	18	180	55	240	73
70	70	21	245	75	315	96
80	80	24	320	98	400	122
90	90	27	405	124	495	151
100	100	29	500	153	600	182

APPROXIMATE SPEED-DISTANCE TABLE

Miles per hour	Yards per second	Metres per minute
20	10	530
30	15	805
40	20	1 080
50	25	1 335
60	30	1 610
70	35	1 885
80	40	2 140
90	45	2 425
100	50	2 670

APPROXIMATE RATE OF ABSORPTION IN BREATH ANALYSIS CASES (AVERAGE OF 6.5µg PER 100ml PER HOUR)

Breath reading	30 min	60 min	90 min	120 min
30	29	23	20	17
35	32	28	25	22
40	37	33	30	27
45	42	38	35	32
50	47	43	40	37
60	57	53	50	47
70	67	63	60	57
80	77	73	70	67
90	87	83	80	77
100	97	93	90	87
110	107	103	100	97
120	117	113	110	107
130	127	123	120	117
140	137	133	130	127
150	147	143	140	137

APPROXIMATE RATE OF ABSORPTION IN BLOOD ANALYSIS CASES (AVERAGE OF 15µg PER 100ml PER HOUR)

Breath reading	30 min	60 min	90 min	120 min
80	72	65	57	50
90	82	75	67	60
100	92	85	77	70
110	102	95	87	80
120	112	105	97	90
130	122	115	107	100
140	132	125	117	110
150	142	135	127	120
160	152	145	137	130
170	162	155	147	140
180	172	165	157	150
190	182	175	167	160
200	192	185	177	170

Roadside Breathalyser Test Devices

The roadside breath test devices currently approved for use in Scotland are contained in the Breath Test Device (Scotland) Approval 1997, which came into force on 6 March 1997. Over the last few years, reports of devices in fact used appear to relate to the Lion Alcolmeter S-L2A, the Alcolyser and the Alcotest R 80A. In addition, some forces are looking to introduce the Lion Alcolmeter SL-400A, which possesses the same features as the Lion Alcolmeter S-L2A but which also gives the indication of the amount of alcohol in the breath of the person taking the test.

Both the Lion Alcolmeter S-L2A and the Alcolyser are produced by Lion Laboratories Limited, Ty Verlon Industrial Estate, Barry, South Wales, CF6 3BE, who have kindly given permission for the following descriptions of their products to be reproduced.

Another device, the Alco-Sensor IV, has been approved for use in England and Wales and it is believed is very shortly to be approved for use in Scotland. The device is produced by Intoximeters UK Ltd, The Alpha Centre, Babbage Road, Totnes, Devon, TQ9 5JA.

1. The Alcolmeter

The Lion Alcolmeter S-L2A is a breath alcohol screening device based on an electrochemical fuel cell which generates a voltage in proportional response to alcohol vapour concentration. The alcohol detector is unaffected by acetone, paint and glue fumes, foods, confectionery, methane and practically any other substance likely to be found in breath (apart from those which contain alcohol). No warm-up time is required for the device to be operated, and the temperature range is 0–40°C., although it is recommended that in very cold temperatures the device should be kept warmed in a coat pocket.

If the subject has consumed alcohol within the last twenty minutes, there may still be residual mouth alcohol which could give an inflated reading. Further, the operator must check that the fuel in the device is clear of alcohol from any previous test, and this is done by carrying out the 'Ready Check'. The procedure for conducting the 'Ready Check' is described in the manufacturer's handbook.

The subject should be instructed to fill his lungs, blow strongly into the mouthpiece to bring on the first breath sampling light (A), and continue to blow at that pressure until the second breath sampling light (B) comes on. If the driver fails to bring on one or both sampling lights, he will normally be deemed to have failed to provide a sample. The driver should also be instructed to keep his hands away from the sampling mechanism, as this may interfere with the reading.

A fresh mouthpiece must be removed from its wrapper and attached to the device for each test.

APPENDIX B(2)

1.2 Operator Controls: Alcolmeter S-L2A

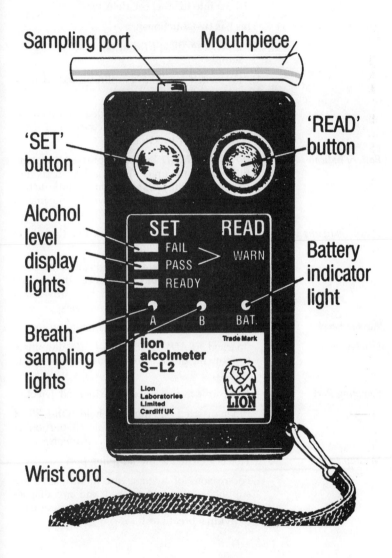

1.3   Description of Operator Controls

SET button	– This forms part of the sampling system. When fully depressed the button locks to set the instrument ready for sampling. When the button rises, the sample to be analysed is drawn into the fuel cell detector.
READ button	This has two functions:

1) to release the *SET* button – so taking the sample.

2) to switch on the amplifier and display system.

The button is spring loaded. Momentary depression will effect '1' but constant pressure is required for function '2'.

Battery Indicator Light	– When the *READ* button is pressed and held fully down, the green light marked '*BAT*' illuminates (with the *READY* light) to indicate that the battery has sufficient power for the instrument to operate.
Breath Sampling Lights	– Light '*A*' illuminates to indicate that the subject is blowing hard enough.

Light '*B*' illuminates to indicate when the *READ* button should be pressed. It will only illuminate when the subject has provided a suitable sample of breath for analysis.

Alcohol Level	– Three lights coloured green, amber and red
Display Lights	(marked *READY, PASS* and *FAIL*) illuminate to show the blood alcohol concentration of the subject.
Sampling Port	– This forms the entrance to the fuel cell detector.

When inserted into the small hole in the side of the mouthpiece it allows a small portion of breath to be drawn into the instruments.

Mouthpiece	– This is attached to the sampling port.

For reasons of hygiene the mouthpieces are supplied separately packed and are disposable. A new mouthpiece *must* be used for each individual breath test.

APPENDIX B(3)

2. The Alcolyser

The Alcolyser is a simple disposable device for measuring the alcohol content of a person's body by means of a breath analysis. The determination of blood alcohol concentration via expired breath is based on Widmark's principle; the alcohol in expired breath reacts with yellow crystals to change their colour to green. Expired breath (a mixture of tidal and deep-lung air) is blown through a tube into a 1 litre plastic bag in approximately 15 seconds. If the green stain in the tube containing the crystals extends beyond the red line at the centre of the tube then the alcohol level in the subject's blood exceeds the prescribed limit.

The instructions for use are simple; the assembly directions for the device must be correctly observed, and the driver must then be instructed to take a deep breath and blow steadily through the mouthpiece until the plastic bag is fully inflated (usually this takes between 10 and 20 seconds).

No test should be conducted if the driver has consumed alcohol within the previous twenty minutes.

3. The Alcotest R80A

The Alcotest R80A device operates in a similar fashion to the Alcolyser; it too has to be assembled in accordance with the manufacturer's instructions and the equipment has a 'use-by' date which must be observed. This device is produced by Drager Ltd, The Willows, Mark Road, Hemel Hempstead, Herts, HP2 7BW.

The Alcotest equipment is supplied in a box containing ten tubes, ten mouthpieces, and one plastic bag. Each tube has a yellow ring around its circumference; a blue arrow indicates the flow of breath through the tube, and the end marked with a green band is fitted to the plastic bag. Each bag may be used ten times, and so each box provides sufficient equipment for ten tests.

Before using the equipment, the operator must check the expiry date on the label attached to the box, and satisfy himself that the yellow crystals in the tube to be used are free from discolouration and cracks. The tube is shown in that condition to the motorist, and then broken open at each end. The green end of the tube is fixed into the collar of the plastic bag, and the other end is pushed into the mouthpiece, which has for this purpose been removed from its protective envelope. The mouthpiece should not be touched. The motorist is then asked to blow into the bag in one continuous breath of not less than ten seconds and not more than twenty seconds. Two exhalations have been allowed in an English case, but the manufacturers specifically advise that only one exhalation should be permitted to avoid the possibility of accumulation. If as a result, the yellow crystals in the tube turn green up to and beyond the centre line, the test is positive: up to the centre line is negative.

It should be noted that a false positive result will be obtained if the motorist has consumed alcohol within the twenty minutes which precede the test. Also, smoking immediately before the test should not be permitted, as tobacco smoke may cause the crystals in the tube to turn brown. A fresh mouthpiece must be used for each test.

4.   Alcosensor IV UK

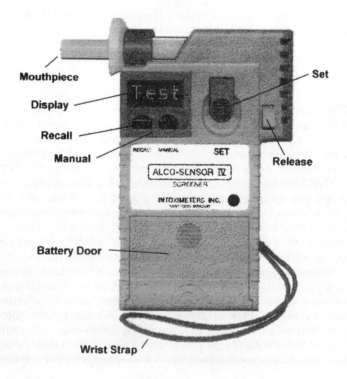

The Alcosensor IV UK is a microprocessor controlled breath alcohol screening device containing an advanced fuel cell sensor and an electronically controlled sampling system. An electronic flow sensor monitors the subject blowing into the instrument so that the sampling system operates while the subject is still blowing and when deep lung air is reached. A small, fixed volume sample of deep lung air is drawn into the fuel cell. Alcohol in a subject's breath is converted into an electrical signal by the fuel cell. It is then translated into a display of the breath alcohol concentration shown on the screen as ZERO, PASS, WARN or FAIL. The limits are factory set to coincide with current legislation and can be quickly and economically changed if the legal limit is changed. The Alconsensor IV UK is provided with an optional memory facility, data stored in memory can be uploaded to a suitable P.C. or printer.

The advanced fuel cell sensor, patented sampling system and analytical software used in the AS-IV are similar to those used in the Home Office approved evidential instrument the Intoximeter EC/IR. The fuel cell sensor is very specific to alcohol and unaffected by virtually all breath contaminants. It is powered by a single 9 volt Alkaline battery which should run at least 500 tests. The instrument is approved to be operated at temperatures between 5°C and 45°C.

Insertion of a mouthpiece switches the instrument on and then operation is automatic. The AS-IV mouthpiece has a non-return valve in it to ensure a correct sample is taken by preventing the subject from sucking back. The instrument checks the fuel cell sensor to ensure that there is no alcohol remaining in the system from a previous test. A flow sensor in the manifold monitors the breath flow and ensures sampling of deep lung air. A tone will be heard when the subject begins blowing in the mouthpiece and will continue until the instrument has monitored an adequate, continuous, breath flow and volume, at this time the sampling system operates and a sample will automatically be drawn into the fuel cell chamber for analysis. A single click will indicate that the sample has been taken. The result will then be displayed.

As with all breath alcohol testing devices, a period of 20 minutes should be allowed to elapse since the last consumption of alcohol (including breath sprays & mouthwashes). A new mouthpiece should always be used for any subject breath test sequence. On insertion of the mouthpiece, the display should be observed and when the word TEST is flashing, the subject should be instructed to take a deep breath, hold their breath for a brief moment and then blow steadily through the mouthpiece for as long as he/she can. A single click will indicate that the sample has been taken.

Description of Components and Functions

Mouthpiece	The mouthpiece contains a quick acting non-return valve, which permits only one-way airflow. It is also Home Office approved to be used with the Intoximeter EC/IR. On correct insertion of the mouthpiece, the Alconsensor IV UK is switched on.
Display	The display turns on when the mouthpiece is inserted. Various commands and symbols appear on the display to direct the operator through the testing protocol and to alert the operator to improper testing conditions detected by the system.
Set Button	The SET button cocks the sampling system when depressed. It is essential that the internal pump be cocked when the instrument is not in use. In this position instrument is ready for immediate use when the mouthpiece is inserted and the chance of contaminants entering the fuel cell chamber is eliminated.
Recall Button	The primary function of the RECALL button is to re-display the current test result. Once the mouthpiece is removed, the results of the previous test cannot be recalled.
Manual Button	The primary function of the MANUAL button is to allow an operator to take a sample manually during Calibration and Accuracy Check procedures.
Mouthpiece Release Button	When depressed, the red MOUTHPIECE RELEASE button releases the mouthpiece from the mount and ejects it from the chamber, switching off the instrument. This allows the instrument to be turned off and the mouthpiece removed without the operator having to handle a contaminated mouthpiece. The mouthpiece should never be pulled from the mouth without depressing the RELEASE button.

Breath analysis devices

The Breath Analysis Devices (Scotland) Approval Order 1998, which came into effect on 31 July 1998, provides details of the three machines currently approved for use in Scotland. These are the Camic Datamaster, the Lion Intoxilyser 6000 UK, manufactured by Lion Laboratories plc, and the Intoximeter EC/IR, manufactured by Intoximeters Inc of Saint Louis, Missouri.

Following the introduction of the terms of s 7(1)(a) of the Road Traffic Act 1988 the most commonly used apparatus was the Camic Breath Analyser Device. Its use featured in so many cases that its description is retained in this edition. The machine was manufactured by Camic Car & Medical Instrument Co Ltd, Camden Street, North Shields, Tyne and Wear NE30 1OG. The following description of their product is reproduced from their Operator's Manual with permission.

The Intoximeter EC/IR is now also widespread throughout Scotland, and a description of the operation of that device is also given.

CAMIC BREATH ANALYSER[1]

The Camic Breath Analyser is an instrument designed to analyse the alcohol content of a breath sample quickly and accurately.

Incorporated into the instrument is an automatic sequence to check the calibration of the instrument before and after each breath test. This allows the user to have full confidence in the final result.

The user operational controls of the instrument have been kept to the absolute minimum, with only one push button to initiate a full test sequence. After pressing the start button the analyser will run through its test sequence automatically with a lamp to tell the suspect when to provide a breath sample and a lamp to indicate when to stop blowing (normally set at 6 seconds).

---

1 This device is no longer approved. Its description is included because of its significance in many of the reported cases on incidents up to the end of 1999.

If the suspect fails to provide a suitable breath sample the instrument will indicate the fault and revert back to the start of the sequence.

At the end of the test the Breath Analyser will provide printed copies of the test results including the date, time, calibration check results and analysis of the breath samples.

The Camic Breath Analyser operates on the Non-Dispersive Infra Red principle, measuring the absorption of the Ethyl Alcohol vapour in breath at 3.4 microns. Narrow band Optical filters are used to provide very high discrimination against possible interference.

A short path length analysis cell has been designed to provide easy breath sample requirements and has the advantage of giving a linear relationship between alcohol concentration and electrical output.

The analysis cell is held at a constant temperature to provide immunity against ambient temperature changes and also to prevent condensation from the breath sample obscuring the optical path.

The pipework of the instrument has been kept simple and any part of the pipework which may be susceptible to condensation problems is heated and all lines are back purged between samples to remove any residual gas.

A bench fixing kit is available from Camic to allow the instrument to be securely screwed to the bench top to prevent accidental damage. ONLY the Camic kit must be used.

OPERATIONAL INSTRUCTIONS

Check that the analyser and simulator units are both switched on. If the analyser has been switched off for any reason allow a 30 minutes warm up period to elapse before taking any breath test.

TO START TEST SIMPLY PRESS TEST BUTTON

The instrument will now calibrate itself and after approximately one minute the green 'blow now' lamp will come on requesting the subject to blow.

A CONTINUOUS breath of at least six seconds is required to provide an accurate sample and bring on the 'stop blow' lamp.

The subject has a total of 3 minutes to provide a correct sample. The subject may make as many attempts as necessary to provide a six second continuous sample.

If, after providing a correct breath sample, the subject attempts to suck the gas back out of the breath pipe, the instrument will sense this and immediately reset and print out 'Breath Invalid'.

After the first breath test has been completed the instrument will request a second breath sample exactly as before.

After the second breath test the instrument will again check its calibration and if accurate then the results will be printed out, together with the date and time of test.

The instrument is set to calibrate at the reading of 35 Ug/100ml and a reading within the range 32–38 Ug/100ml will be accepted and allow the analyser to proceed with the test.

If the calibration check falls outside the 32–38 limits the analyser will print 'Calibration Out' and reset itself to the Ready for Test mode.

CAMIC BREATH ANALYSER OPERATIONAL MODE

1. Instrument Switched on.
2. Front Panel Switch flashes on and off until the instrument reaches its operational temperature, when the illuminated switch stays on.
3. Initiate Test by pressing illuminated switch – the light will go out to indicate the automatic test sequence has started.
4. The analysis cell is purged with clean, alcohol free air, for 30 seconds.
5. Calibration gas is injected into the analysis cell and the readout for the gas is indicated on the digital display.
   If the calibration is within the allowed limits the test sequence continues:
   if the calibration is outside the preset limits the instrument will reset itself to the start of the sequence and printout that the reading was outside the required limits.
6. After calibration the analysis cell is purged for 30 seconds.
7. The instrument is now ready to accept a breath sample, as indicated by the green 'BLOW NOW' lamp illuminating. A continuous 6 second breath sample must now be provided within the next 3 minutes to allow the sequence to proceed. After a 6 second blow the 'STOP BLOW' lamp will illuminate. If no breath sample is provided within 3 minutes the analyser

will print out 'BREATH INVALID' and reset itself to the start of the sequence.

If a suitable breath sample has been provided the alcohol level will be displayed on the Digital Display.

8. The instrument purges for 30 seconds.
9. The instrument will now accept a second breath sample as No. 7.
10. The instrument purges for 30 seconds.
11. The instrument will now re-check its calibration as No. 5.
12. All test results are printed out in sequence as shown overleaf with test time and date.

Sample Camic print-out

```
POLICE STATION

NAME OF SUBJECT

SUBJECTS'S SIGNATURE

OPERATOR

OPERATOR'S SIGNATURE
. . . . . . . . . . . . . . . . .

        · · RESULTS · ·

CAL CHECK NO.1
   037 UG/100ML
   · ZERO CHECK ·
   000 UG/100ML

BREATH TEST NO.1
   062 UG/100 ML
DATE   15/04/82
TIME   11:22 GMT.

BREATH TEST NO.2
   064 UG/100ML
DATE   15/04/82
TIME   11:23 GMT.

CAL. CHECK NO. 2
   035 UG/100ML

        · · · CAMIC · · ·
```

Note

In practice, most forces appear to issue set instructions to Camic operators for use in every case. These normally include the reading by the operator to the motorist (after agreement by the motorist to provide two breath specimens) of the sequence of the operation of the test, with the operator indicating the relevant parts of the machine as appropriate during the explanation. The explanation is generally along the following lines.

The procedure begins by pressing a button which carries out a calibration check which should produce a figure of between 32 and 38 on the visual display panel. If the figure is between 32 and 38, the motorist will then be required to provide two specimens of breath. If the figure is not within these two figures, the device is not to be used, and an alternative procedure will be adopted.

When the green light comes on, the motorist has three minutes within which he must blow continuously into the tube for at least six seconds until the red light comes on. If the attempt is unsuccessful, further attempts may be made within the three-minute period. Failure to provide a sufficient specimen within the three-minute period will result in the machine printing 'Breath Invalid'.

If a proper and sufficient first specimen is given, the visual display panel will show the analysis of the motorist's breath and then reset itself. When the green light comes on again, a second specimen will be required. Any attempt to suck air out of the tube at any time will produce a 'Breath Invalid' printout.

Following two proper and sufficient specimens being given, a further calibration check is carried, which should again indicate a figure between 32 and 38. If this is correct, the machine will automatically print out the results of the analysis, and a copy will be given to the motorist.

INTOXIMETER EC/IR

The Intoximeter EC/IR is a breath alcohol analyser which brings together two separately controlled sub-systems. The first is an analogue control system which controls all analytical functions of the instrument. The second is an input/output control system, which controls all aspects of the user interface as well as controlling various test sequences and protocols.

Further, the device employs two distinct analytical techniques to measure alcohol concentration. These are a fuel cell (ie an electro-chemical sensor) and a miniaturised non-dispersive infrared molecular absorption IR bench. The fuel cell sensor is specific to alcohol, while the IR sensor can be affected by several common breath constituents. In addition the fuel sensor is a linear sensing device, while the IR is non-linear. This means that the fuel cell sensor can be calibrated with a simple one-point calibration, ensuring calibration through the full range of its sensing capabilities. The IR sensor has several capacities that the fuel cell sensor does not possess. The most important of these is that the IR sensor is able to make continuous determinations of alcohol concentration, thus allowing the device to monitor a breath sample in real time. This helps determine the correct moment at which to take a sample of breath for fuel cell analysis.

In combination these two analytical systems provide all the necessary information to make precise and accurate determinations of breath alcohol concentration. The sample is one made up of alveolar breath and should not be tainted by alcohol from the upper respiratory tract of the subject. Further technical details may be available from the manufacturer, whose design is Intoximeters UK Ltd, The Alpha Centre, Babbage Road, Totnes, Devon, TQ9 5JA.

The machine shows a number of error messages on its display unit. The most significant of these are 'MOUTH ALCOHOL UNSATISFACTORY SPECIMEN' (which means that the instrument has detected the presence of mouth alcohol in the subject), 'BREATH DIFFERENCE' (which means that the instrument has detected an unacceptably large difference between the two breath samples), 'INTERFERING SUBSTANCE UNSATISFACTORY SPECIMEN' (which means that the instrument has detected a substance other than ethanol in the sample which gives rise to an elevated reading), 'SPECIMEN INCOMPLETE' (which means that the subject has failed to provide an adequate breath sample within the three-minute period available), 'HIGH BLANK' (which means alcohol or similar vapours have been detected in the room air) and 'SPECIMEN OUT OF RANGE' (which means that the breath sample was out of range of the instrument being over 220 µgs, resulting in the print-out reading 'OVER 220'). There are a number of other technical messages to do with the operation of the machine.

The Intoximeter EC/IR in many respects operates in a similar fashion to the Camic breath analyser device which is now obsolete. Breath samples are given into the machine which are analysed, and the details of the test are displayed on a display unit.

The machine also produces a print-out containing the relevant information and results of the test. However the technology used in the Intoximeter machine is different. It is operated by an attached PC keyboard, which is used for data entry. Once the relevant information has been entered into the machine by way of the keyboard (after the machine has automatically purged itself of alcohol), a mouthpiece is fitted into the breath tube on the machine. The motorist is instructed to take a deep breath and blow into the mouthpiece as steadily and for as long as possible. The breath flowrate is indicated on the display by asterisks. The machine then evaluates the sample and again automatically purges itself of alcohol. If the motorist does not submit a valid breath sample, the unit displays 'specimen incomplete'.

Three minutes are allowed for a valid sample to be provided, failing which the test is aborted. The same procedure is operated for the second test. An example of the print out produced is in Appendix C. The operator manual suggests that the machine should not be used in environments with heavy alcohol vapour, cigarette smoke, high levels of radio frequencies, magnetic interference or new paint. It is said that these conditions will not interfere with the results of the test but may effect useful lifespan of various components.

Sample Intoximeter EC/IR print-out

```
SUBJECT TEST
Intox EC/IR
SERIAL NUMBER:
03496

TEST NUMBER:
991218296
START DATE:
Sat 18 Dec 99
START TIME:
17:19 GMT
LOCATION:


NAME:


DATE OF BIRTH:
07:09:64
```

SUBJECT SIGNATURE:

	Value Ug/100ml	Time GMT
Blank	0	17:20
Simulator		
Check 1	35	17:21
Blank	0	17:22
Breath		
Specimen1	60	17:23
Blank	0	17:25
Breath		
Specimen2	57	17:26
Blank	0	17:27
Simulator		
Check 2	34	17:27

NO ERRORS

I CERTIFY THAT IN
THIS STATEMENT,
READING ONE RELATES
TO THE FIRST
SPECIMEN OF BREATH
PROVIDED BY THE
SUBJECT NAMED ABOVE
AND READING TWO TO
THE SECOND, AT THE
DATE AND TIME SHOWN
HEREIN.

OPERATOR:
4753
OPERATOR SIGNATURE

Appendix D

Endorsement Offence Codes

Aiding, Abetting, Counselling or Procuring
Offences as coded below, but with 0 changed to 2, eg UT10 becomes UT12.

Causing or Permitting
Offences as coded below, but with 0 changed to 4, eg PL10 becomes PL14.

Inciting
Offences as coded below, but with O changed to 6, eg DD30 becomes DD36.

Periods of Time
Periods of time are signified as follows: D = Days, M = Months, Y = Years. A consecutive period of disqualification is signified by an asterisk* against the period.

Code	Accident Offences
AC10	Failing to stop after an accident
AC20	Failing to give particulars or to report an accident within 24 hours
AC30	Undefined accident offence

	Disqualified Driver
BA10	Driving while disqualified by order of court
BA20	Driving while disqualified as under age
BA30	Attempting to drive while disqualified by order of court

	Careless Driving
CD10	Driving without due care and attention
CD20	Driving without reasonable consideration for other road users
CD30	Driving without due care and attention or without reasonable consideration for other road users
CD40	Causing death through careless driving when unfit through drink

Code	**Careless Driving**
CD50	Causing death by careless driving when unfit through drugs
CD60	Causing death by careless driving with alcohol level above the limit
CD70	Causing death by careless driving then failing to supply a specimen for analysis

	Construction and Use Offences
CU10	Using a vehicle with defective brakes
CU20	Causing or likely to cause danger by reason of use of unsuitable vehicle or using a vehicle with parts or accessories (excluding brakes, steering or tyres) in a dangerous condition
CU30	Using a vehicle with defective tyre(s)
CU40	Using a vehicle with defective steering
CU50	Causing or likely to cause danger by reason of load or passengers
CU60	Undefined failure to comply with Construction and Use Regulations

	Reckless/Dangerous Driving
DD30	Reckless driving (replaced by DD40 as from 1–12–91)
DD40	Dangerous driving
DD60	Manslaughter or culpable homicide while driving a vehicle
DD70	Causing death by reckless driving (replaced by DD80 as from 1–12–91)
DD80	Causing death by dangerous driving

	Drink or Drugs
DR10	Driving or attempting to drive with alcohol level above limit
DR20	Driving or attempting to drive while unfit through drink
DR30	Driving or attempting to drive then failing to supply a specimen for analysis
DR40	In charge of a vehicle while alcohol level above limit
DR50	In charge of a vehicle while unfit through drink
DR60	Failure to provide a specimen for analysis in circumstances other than driving or attempting to drive
DR70	Failing to provide specimen for breath test
DR80	Driving or attempting to drive when unfit through drugs

Code	Drink or Drugs
DR90	In charge of a vehicle when unfit through drugs

Insurance Offences

IN10	Using a vehicle uninsured against third party risks

Licence Offences

LC10	Driving without a licence (replaced by LC20 as from 1–12–91)
LC20	Driving otherwise than in accordance with a licence
LC30	Driving after making a false declaration about fitness when applying for a licence
LC40	Driving a vehicle having failed to notify a disability
LC50	Driving after a licence has been revoked or refused on medical grounds

Miscellaneous Offences

MS10	Leaving a vehicle in a dangerous position
MS20	Unlawful pillion riding
MS30	Playstreet offences
MS40	Driving with uncorrected defective eyesight or refusing to submit to a test
MS50	Motor racing on the highway
MS60	Offences not covered by other codes
MS70	Driving with uncorrected defective eyesight
MS80	Refusing to submit to an eyesight test
MS90	Failure to give information as to identity of driver etc

Motorway Offences

MW10	Contravention of Special Roads Regulations (excluding speed limits)

Pedestrian Crossings

PC10	Undefined contravention of Pedestrian Crossing Regulations
PC20	Contravention of Pedestrian Crossing Regulations with moving vehicle
PC30	Contravention of Pedestrian Crossing Regulations with stationary vehicle

Provisional Licence Offences

PL10	Driving without 'L' plates
PL20	Not accompanied by a qualified person
PL30	Carrying a person not qualified

Code	**Provisional Licence Offences**
PL40	Drawing an unauthorised trailer
PL50	Undefined failure to comply with conditions of a Provisional Licence

Speeding Offences

SP10	Exceeding goods vehicle speed limits
SP20	Exceeding speed limit for type of vehicle (excluding goods or passenger vehicles)
SP30	Exceeding statutory speed limit on a public road
SP40	Exceeding passenger vehicle speed limit
SP50	Exceeding speed limit on a motorway
SP60	Undefined speed limit offence

Traffic Directions and Signs

TS10	Failing to comply with traffic light signals
TS20	Failing to comply with double white lines
TS30	Failing to comply with a 'Stop' sign
TS40	Failing to comply with direction of a constable or traffic warden
TS50	Failing to comply with a traffic sign (excluding 'Stop' signs, traffic lights or double white lines)
TS60	Failing to comply with a school crossing patrol sign
TS70	Undefined failure to comply with a traffic direction or sign

Theft or Unauthorised Taking

UT10	Taking and driving away a vehicle without consent or an attempt thereat
UT20	Stealing or attempting to steal a vehicle
UT30	Going equipped for stealing or taking a vehicle
UT40	Taking or attempting to take a vehicle without consent; driving or attempting to drive a vehicle knowing it to have been taken without consent; allowing oneself to be carried in or on a vehicle knowing it to have been taken without consent

Special Codes

TT99	To signify a disqualification under 'totting-up' procedure

Appendix E

Expert Scientific Evidence in Statutory Defences and Special Reasons by Professor J K Mason*

There are three main situations in which 'scientific' evidence may be needed to satisfy a statutory defence. Firstly, there is the post-accident drinking defence, established by the Road Traffic Offenders Act 1988, s 15(3) to charges brought under Road Traffic Act 1988, s 3A(1)(b) or 5(1); the latter constitutes the most commonly invoked defence and provides the template for all the relevant calculations. Secondly, there is the defence provided in Road Traffic Act 1988, s 5(2) that a person accused of being in charge of a vehicle with a tissue alcohol level above the prescribed limit was not going to drive so long as his or her tissue level exceeded the limit; in contrast to the s 15 defence, there is nothing in s 5(2) that insists on substantiating 'scientific' evidence. The third situation is not, strictly speaking, a defence but is one in which the accused pleads 'special reasons' for non-disqualification; almost invariably this depends on the drinks having been 'laced' with excess alcohol but, occasionally, the accused may plead that he was served drinks having an alcoholic concentration different from that ordered. There is some suggestion – certainly in England – that expert evidence is not always required on this point[1]; the situation in Scotland is considered below.

The word 'scientific' has been apostrophised above. This is to emphasise that the calculations involved in these defences cannot be regarded as scientific in the sense that their accuracy satisfies scientific criteria. There are so many variables involved in a biological situation that any calculation is in the nature of an approximation. Since it is impossible to cover all these in a single equation, it is easier – and more honest – to use very simple data

---

* Regius Professor (Emeritus) of Forensic Medicine at the University of Edinburgh. The views expressed in Appendix E are those of the author and do not necessarily represent those of John Wheatley QC.

1 *Pugsley v Hunter* [1973] RTR 284; *DPP v Younas* [1990] RTR 22.

and, having admitted the limitations of the method, to make any necessary adjustments on an empirical basis. For these reasons, it is probably best to eschew the sophisticated and complex analyses that have appeared from time to time[1] and to rely instead on the Tables prepared by the British Medical Association in 1960[2]; these have not been challenged in court and have the merit of public judicial approval[3]. A resumé of the Tables, amended to include breath equivalents, is given in Annexe 1.

There are several major impediments to scientific accuracy in this field. The first lies in the individual's metabolic rate for alcohol (or the rate at which alcohol is broken down in the body) which is unknown and unknowable – for any later experimental assessment gives only the metabolic rate at the time of the experiment, not at the time of the offence. The rate of absorption of alcohol is a further complication. This is slowed by food in the upper gastrointestinal tract but the extent of this is variable; reasonable practice based on the majority of experimental protocols, is to allow 30 minutes before assuming that *some* alcohol is available in the blood stream for metabolism. More problematic is the time taken for *all* the alcohol ingested to have been absorbed and, here, it is only possible to say that liquid contents of the stomach are *likely* to have been absorbed in the upper small intestine within 2 hours but, clearly, it could be less and the total volume will be a major influence – indeed, the general empirical evidence is that the alcohol in beer is absorbed more slowly than is that in spirits or wine. The problem arises particularly when an impossible result is obtained (see p 285). Perhaps more importantly, a proportion of ingested alcohol is destroyed by the gastric enzyme alcohol dehydrogenase, the quantity and power of which is, again, a biological variable; the significance is, of course, that alcohol destroyed in this way will *never* reach the blood stream[4]. The final 'scientific' variable depends upon the body's weight and configuration; the significance of these is discussed below at p 286.

---

1 See for example, A W R Forrest 'The estimation of Widmark's factor' (1986) 26 *Journal of the Forensic Science Society* 249
2 British Medical Association *The Relation of Alcohol to Road Accidents* (1960) London: BMA, Appendix A.
3 *R v Somers* [1963] 3 All ER 808.
4 RJK Julkunen et al 'First pass metabolism of ethanol: an important determinant of blood levels after alcohol consumption' (1985) 2 Alcohol 437. For the same reason, a person who has had a gastrectomy is likely to have a higher tissue alcohol level than anticipated: J Caballeria, M Frezza, R Hernández-Muñoz et al 'Gastric origin of the first-pass metabolism of ethanol in humans: effect of gastrectomy' (1989) 97 Gastroenterology 1205.

Of the other, non-specific, imponderables, the accused's memory is likely to be of major importance. Here, it has to be noted that the s 15(3) defence is not, as it is frequently and pejoratively described in the English courts, a 'hip-flask' defence. The majority of cases arise from the accused not appreciating that he is likely to be breathalysed and legitimately taking a restorative drink in his home after a stressful experience. The man who can quantitate with great accuracy what alcohol he consumed in such circumstances is, possibly, less credible than one who has no more than a fair idea. In this connection, the decision in *Hassan*[1], which allows the court to accept a good approximation, is to be welcomed as a corrective of the earlier draconian decisions[2]. Even so, if the post-incident drinking has taken place at home, it is essential that a marked glass be produced for measurement; in practice, most people know the approximate size of drinks they pour for themselves and both the court and the expert witness are working in a vacuum without such an estimate. A further problem arose as to whether the accused's evidence must be corroborated in Scots law; it was determined in *King v Lees*[3] that this was not necessary – thereby eliminating a source of discrimination against the single person. Another complication that is often ignored in precognition is the effect of vomiting; in practice, this may be of great significance in limiting the amount of alcohol available for absorption.

THE SECTION 15(3) DEFENCE

The section is directed in sub-section (a) to credibility and in sub-section (b) to scientific corroboration; it is the latter with which we are concerned here. Theoretically, the method is simple. The gross 'value' of the post-incident drink is calculated from the Tables using a correction factor based on the formula 154/W where W is the person's weight in lbs. – the rationale of this is discussed below. Knowing both the time the person started drinking after the incident and the time of the definitive breathanalysis – and allowing 30 minutes for effective absorption to occur – the

1 *Hassan v Scott* 1989 SCCR 49.
2 Eg *Sutherland v Aitchison* 1979 SLT 37; *Ferns v Tudhope* 1979 SLT 23; *Campbell v Mackenzie* 1981 SCCR 341.
3 *King v Lees* 1993 JC 19. For discussion, see D Sheldon, 'Hip flasks and burdens' 1992 SLT 33.

amount metabolised prior to testing can be estimated on the assumption that the rate is 6.5 mg alcohol/100 ml breath/hour. This immediately introduces an uncertainty into the calculations because the *actual* metabolic rate, as discussed more fully under the s 5(2) defence below, can be taken to vary between 4.4 and 10.9 mg alcohol/100 ml breath/hour; since the precise value within this bracket is unknown, the only fair compromise is to use the most likely value[1]. Deducting this figure from the gross value gives the net value for the post-incident consumption (N). The defence under s 15(3)(b) is established if O [the observed value on the Intoximeter print-out] – N is less than 35 mg alcohol/100 ml breath.

To give an example: a man weighing 168 lbs. (12 stone), and who has not had any alcohol during the day, is involved in an incident; he, subsequently, drinks 8 fl oz whisky starting at 22:30 and, at 02:00, he provides a specimen of breath which contains 58 mg alcohol/100 ml. The calculated net post incident value (N) is then: (79 [Annexe 1] 154/168 [correction factor]) – (3 x 6.5 [metabolism]) = 53 mg alcohol/100 ml breath. Then 58 [O] – 53 [N] = 5 mg alcohol/100 ml breath which is below the prescribed limit. The difference (5 mg) between the calculated and the expected zero value is within the inherent limitations and uncertainties of the method – although, provided there is time for complete absorption, the shorter the period involved, the less can error be attributed, say, to variations in the metabolic rate. This problem is discussed further under 'the credibility factor'.

Such a simple calculation cannot obtain when there is some residual pre-incident alcohol in the body. In these circumstances, to attribute metabolism wholly to either the pre- or post-incident alcoholic component is not only physiologically incorrect; it is also likely to be disadvantageous to one side or the other.

In such circumstances, the only plausible procedure seems to be to attribute a proportional metabolism on the basis of the relative concentrations. Thus, if p is the concentration of the pre-incident drinking when the post-incident drinking started to influence the tissue value and q is the calculated post-incident value, the metabolism of the former is given by $p/(p + q)$ x b and, of the latter, by $q/(p + q)$ x b where b is the basic metabolic rate – normally accepted, as above, as 6.5 mg alcohol/100 ml breath/hour.

---

1 The figures, converted from blood levels are taken from *Gumbley v Cunningham* [1989] RTR 49. For background analysis, see M J Lewis 'Blood alcohol: The concentration-time curve and retrospective estimation of level' (1986) 26 *Journal of* the *Forensic Science Society* 95.

To give a further example: suppose the residual pre-incident value is 30 mg and the calculated post-incident value 60 mg. Then, the latter is being metabolised at a rate of $60/(30 + 60) \times 6.5 = 4.3$ mg alcohol/100 ml breath/hour and it is this figure which should be used when calculating the post-incident contribution to the Intoximeter read-out. In point of fact, it is only very rarely that this makes any significant difference to the conclusion; it may or may not be scientifically correct but it is a compromise that serves to forestall any objection put forward – quite reasonably – by either prosecution or defence.

The credibility factor

It is submitted that the wording of the Act is such that the *only* calculation needed for the defence is the value of O – N, and there is some English precedent which suggests that this interpretation is correct[1]. The matter has not been tested in the courts but it is probable that the Scottish preference would be to admit any evidence relevant to establishing the alcohol level at the time of driving[2]. It is clear from what has been said that 'back-calculation' is subject to considerable potential error and medical scientists have persistently advised that it should not be attempted[3]. Nonetheless, the mere existence of s 15(3)(b) indicates that the legislature anticipated its use and the expert must make the best of what is, admittedly, a bad job in assisting the court. Thus, in Scotland at least, the expert will almost certainly be asked to evaluate the contribution of any pre-incident drinking and, as a consequence, a credibility gap may well appear. To revert to the example given above: the calculated post-incident value certainly satisfies the subsection so long as the accused had no drink before. But, suppose he admitted to, say, 30 mg's 'worth' of pre-incident drinking? The difference between the calculated and anticipated results would now amount to $(30 – 5) = 25$ mg alcohol/100 ml breath which casts a different light on the end result – the expert evidence in subsection (3)(b) is, in essence, being used in the general context of subsection (3)(a). Practical experience indicates that the courts, in fact, quite rightly regard such variations as influential rather than determinant evidence.

1 *Millard v DPP* [1990] RTR 201.
2 *Tudhope v Williamson* 1976 JC 16.
3 And there are good reasons for supporting this view: J K Mason 'Conversion on the Road to Auchtermuchty' 1996 SLT 33.

Nonetheless, the problem is raised as to what constitutes an unreasonable discrepancy in the *expert's* mind – and this is impossible to answer. One can say that one 'likes to get within one drink' of the anticipated result but there are so many variables which alter with the circumstances that this can be no more than a rule of thumb. A specific area which needs clarification is the 'impossible' or 'minus' result which occurs when the supposed post-incident value exceeds the observed value. This can, often, impair credibility but, in many cases, the conditions are such as to cast serious doubt on whether the whole 'alcohol dose' was absorbed at the time of breathanalysis. Again, this is a biological variable which the expert should take into account but cannot quantitate with scientific accuracy; the proposition becomes increasingly tenable not only as the interval between the last drink and the test shortens but also as the amount of alcohol drunk within a short time of the Intoximeter test increases.

The effect of body weight

Once absorbed, the alcohol in the body should be distributed equally throughout the body water[1]. It has to be assumed that the body water represents a fixed proportion of the body weight – and this is allowed for in the Tables; accordingly, we can say that the tissue (or water) concentration will depend upon the total body weight which is a directly measurable variable. The Tables indicate that a further correction factor of 6/5 should be applied in the case of women, this being said to reflect the different fat/water content in men and women and hence, a differing body water/weight distribution. A moment's thought will show, however, that there is no such thing as a 'standard' man or woman – some are fat, some are thin, some are more muscular than others and it is wrong to generalise. Experience has shown, for example, that the correction factor applied to women often appears to exaggerate the tissue level calculated from a stated intake but, as would be expected, the degree of deviation varies considerably.

---

1 The water miscibility of alcohol explains the difference between blood and urine levels. Alcohol is not concentrated in the urine; the difference merely reflects the fact that, whereas urine is almost pure fluid, blood contains a considerable proportion of solid material. This results in relatively standard urine: blood alcohol ratio of 1.33:1.

The 'Widmark factor'

In an attempt to get round this problem, many laboratories apply the so-called Widmark equation when correlating alcoholic intake and distribution[1]. This is based on the simplified assumption a = bwr/100 where a = the amount of alcohol ingested measured in grams, b = the blood alcohol concentration in mg/100ml, w = the body weight in kg and r = the 'Widmark factor' which is, essentially, the ratio of the total body water to the blood water. Using this method, it is conventional to regard r = 0.6 for men and 0.5 for women

It is apparent that this introduces yet another uncertainty to the calculations. Whatever figure is chosen from whatever published results, it is bound to be an average which may be far removed from the individual's actual status[2] - and it will be seen that relatively minor deviations will have considerable effect on the end result. Many efforts have been made to overcome these, and related, difficulties, such as applying different distribution factors to differing body configurations but, at the end of the day, these involve idiosyncratic decisions which impart a sense of accuracy which may be spurious; they are better avoided.

Variations in alcohol content of liquors

It is clear that one cannot, nowadays, speak in terms of 'beer' or 'spirits'; there are wide variations in alcoholic concentration in all generic alcoholic drinks and these must be accommodated when making the necessary calculations.

The Tables are based on a 40% v/v alcoholic concentration for spirits but not all are of this strength. Most vodkas and baccardis are 37.5% strength and most British gin has now been reduced to a similar figure. By contrast, some vodkas and most 'duty free' spirits are stronger. Suitable correction factors must be used in each case. The alcohol content of wine generally varies between 8–12% v/v. It is convenient to convert the intake to fluid ounces and to use the tables for spirits with a correction factor of: x w/40 – where w is the alcoholic concentration of the wine drunk.

---

1 Based on the work of E M P Widmark, a German physiologist who published his findings in 1932.
2 The r factor is estimated as varying between 0.55 and 0.9 for men.

The Tables relate to beers of a strength of 3.2% alcohol v/v[1]. Normally, a correction factor of x b/3.2 would be used where b is the concentration v/v of alcohol in the beer or cider actually drunk and this holds for small amounts of such drinks. However, experience has, again shown that the tables do not allow for the fact that large volumes of fluid remain in the stomach longer than do, say, measures of spirits. As a consequence, gastric alcohol dehydrogenase has longer to operate and relatively less 'beer alcohol' is available for absorption by comparison with 'spirit alcohol'. Some authors allow for this by altering the r factor[2] (see above) but it is submitted that this is illogical – the body water distribution cannot alter with oral intake and the effect must alter with the quantity as well as the nature of the drink. This problem of gastric destruction of alcohol can be circumvented, somewhat empirically, by using a correction factor of b/4 for moderate quantities of beer (2–3 pints) and b/5 for larger amounts.

Some useful volumetric equivalents are given in Annexe 2 and the alcoholic strengths of some beers commonly drunk in Scotland are listed in Annexe 3.

DEFENCE TO CHARGES UNDER ROAD TRAFFIC ACT 1988, S 3A

The principles behind the defence to charges under s 3A are obviously similar to those under s 5(1)(a) save that s 3A(1)(a) specifically refers to the tissue alcohol concentration at the time of driving while s 3A(1)(c) allows for a compulsory test within 18 hours of that time. The result is to put the stamp of parliamentary approval on 'back calculation'. This introduces some additional problems.

It is difficult to see why the legislature specifically introduced an 18 hour limit. As an end-point, it is virtually meaningless. To show *any* alcohol in the breath at this point in time, the breath concentration at the time of the incident must have been in the region of 120 mg alcohol/100 ml – or a blood level of

---

1 Ie volume/volume. Ethanol has a specific gravity of 0.8; the strength of an alcoholic drink would, therefore, appear lower if expressed as weight/weight rather than as v/v.
2 Eg L A King 'Alcohol concentrations with quantity of alcohol consumed' (1993) 23 *Journal of the Forensic Science Society* 213.

270 mg/100 ml – at which point, it is at least unlikely that a person would have been capable of driving a car. In practice, the effect of the wide variation in individual metabolic rates becomes so great after 8 hours as to discredit any 'probability' of a *true* back-calculation. The best that could be done would be to provide theoretical limits based on the figures that were not disputed in *Gumbley v Cunningham* (see below).

Rather more concern lies in the terms of the constituting evidence in s 3A cases. It is at least arguable that a report based on back calculation can only be valid if the resulting figure is qualified by 'provided no further alcohol was drunk between the incident and the test'. That being so, it would follow that *any* alcohol taken would invalidate the evidence. A defence would be established under s 15(3)(a) of the Road Traffic Offenders Act 1988 (the 'credibility limb') without necessary recourse to the expert evidence required under ss 15(3)(b) – the situation would revert to that in England prior to *Rowlands v Hamilton*[1]. The proposition has not, however, been tested in the courts.

Finally, the question has to be asked whether the license to back calculate is particular to s 3A or whether it can be extrapolated to s 5(1) offences. The only apposite case still leaves the general question of back calculation in doubt[2].

THE SECTION 5(2) DEFENCE

There is no statutory requirement for expert evidence to sustain this defence but it is reasonably certain that the courts will seek such evidence unless the circumstances are absolutely clear[3]; the same considerations would apply as in 'laced drinks' cases (see below). On the other hand, since there can be virtually no opinion evidence in what is almost entirely a matter of mathematics, the expert's report cries out for a minute of admission. This generalisation is, however, subject to an interesting ethical point as to the presentation of the evidence. The relevant question can be put to the expert in two ways:

1 [1971] RTR 153.
2 *Hain v Ruxton* 1999 SCCR 243. For discussion, see J K Mason 'Back-calculation and the Crown Agents' letters' (2000) 5 SLPQ 25.
3 In England, a distinction is to be made between prosecutions under s 4(2) (unfit to drive) and s 5(1)(b) (exceeding the prescribed limit): *DPP v Frost* [1989] RTR 11. The latter requires expert evidence to establish a defence.

(a) At what time would the accused have been fit to drive? or

(b) Would the accused have been fit to drive at [a certain time]?

The former construction clearly allows for deception on the part of the accused – he can formulate his story according to the answer given; the latter, by contrast, limits the expert evidence to corroborating or disproving the accused's unbiased statement. It is suggested that the former may well be an improper formulation and the prosecution are entitled to elicit how the expert evidence was sought.

Such considerations aside, however, the 'scientific' defence *ought* to be simply established. Given a knowledge of how much was drunk from what time and of the time and reading of the Intoximeter test, the accused's *actual* metabolic rate (R) should be given by the formula $(V - C)/t$ where V is the 'value' of the drink taken, C is the Intoximeter reading and t is the time in hours between starting to drink (+ the arbitrary 30 minutes for effective absorption) and the Intoximeter test. It can then be said that he would be fit to drive in s 5(1) terms in $(C - 35)/R$ hours.

This deceptively simple calculation does not, however, always work out in practice. In the first place, there is no reason why those accused in this situation should know their consumption with any accuracy; secondly, and more pragmatically, it is hard to convince them that it is in their interests to be as truthful as possible. The majority greatly underestimate their intake and the result is an impossibly low calculated metabolic rate; this inevitably reacts against credibility – a particularly unfortunate matter as the defence, essentially, stands or falls on the question of credibility. The error may, however, be genuine and, for this reason, it is very much fairer to both sides to stay clear of the difficulties associated with the precise circumstances and to concentrate on the certainties offered by *Gumbley v Cunningham*[1].

In that case, the House of Lords did not dispute that the limits of metabolism of alcohol – converted from blood values – lay between 4.4 and 10.9 mg alcohol/100 ml breath/hour with a most likely value of 6.5 mg alcohol/100 ml breath/hour. Using these figures, we can assess the interval given by $(C - 35)/R$ at the slowest, fastest and most likely rates and can express the result as when the accused would certainly, might and would most probably have been fit to drive. The defence is made out if the accused's estimate falls within these parameters and it is open to the court to apply its own criteria of credibility.

1 [1989] AC 281.

SPECIAL REASONS FOR NON-DISQUALIFICATION

The fact that the accused drank alcohol unknowingly has been accepted as a special reason for non-disqualification in both Scotland[1] and England[2]. Although the courts tend to look on the plea with some scepticism, it is nevertheless frequently accepted. The conditions for acceptance have appeared, at times, to be very severe in England[3] but many of the recorded decisions are inconsistent; as one English judge put it: 'Cases in this particular branch of the law are not always easy to reconcile'[4]. Much of the problem may stem from the nature of the act. 'Lacing' drinks is dangerous and selfish – and the perpetrator is probably unable to appreciate that he is laying himself open to a charge of abetting a criminal offence[5]. Consequently, the main evidence as to credibility is likely to be of poor quality and, as a corollary, the scientific evidence must be founded on a doubtful basis. The very limited Scottish precedents indicate that expert evidence must be led unless the circumstances are clear and obvious to the court[6] (see paragraph 8.5:4C).

The method follows that for the s 15(3)(b) defence. The 'value' of the added alcohol is deducted from the Intoximeter reading and the conditions for acceptance of the plea are established if the resultant figure is less than 35 mg/100 ml breath. It will be apparent, however, that the effect of metabolism must be calculated on a proportional basis as described above unless the accused was an intended teetotaller. Aside from the court's almost inevitable suspicion of collusion, the plea commonly breaks down not so much on the calculations as on the anticipated effect on the target of the 'lacing' – 'surely', it will be said, 'he ought to have appreciated that something was wrong and he should not have driven?'

This is not an easy question to answer for the effects of alcohol depend almost as much on psychological as on pharmacological

---

1 *Skinner v Ayton* 1977 SLT (Sh Ct) 48.
2 *Pugsley v Hunter* at note 1 above; *Alexander v Latter* [1972] RTR 441; *R v Krebs* [1977] RTR 406.
3 *Adams v Bradley* [1975] RTR 233.
4 *Beauchamp-Thompson v DPP* [1989] RTR 54 per Hutchison J at 61.
5 In England, *Attorney General's Reference (No 1 of 1975)* [1975] QB 773; *DPP v Anderson* [1990] RTR 269.
6 See note 15 above. For England, see *DPP v O'Connor* and allied cases [1992] RTR 66.

factors. It is, for example, a nice point to decide whether a teeto-taller will be disproportionately affected because of a lack of habituation or whether he will be quite unable to understand his symptoms and to refer them to a substance of which he has no general or immediate knowledge. It is clear, however, that the higher the Intoximeter reading, the less likely is it that 'special reasons' will be accepted.

FURTHER POSSIBLE DEFENCES

It would be inappropriate here to try to detail the defences which might be founded on the presumption that the breath alcohol level was apparently, but falsely, raised. A few notes must suffice.

A defence that is commonly put forward is by the diabetic who maintains that the reading is due to acetone rather than alcohol in the breath. The Intoximeter provides a very high degree of discrimination against possible interference by substances other than ethanol. It seems likely that such a defence could be consid-ered only if the subject was so affected as to be close to diabetic coma – and, in that case, he would be unlikely to be driving a car or, indeed, to be out drinking. Even then, the concentration of acetone would be significant only as an additive around the important 'cut-off levels' – 35, 40 and 50 mg.

A number of defences have relied on accidental inhalation of the fumes of alcohol or other contaminating solvents when, say, at work. Experiments have shown that it is not possible to raise the tissue alcohol level significantly by inhaling alcohol[1] and expo-sure to industrial solvents would be unlikely to affect the analysis within the usual time parameters of testing[2].

A 'petrol defence' – generally involving a supposed remainder in the mouth following syphoning of petrol – has often been invoked but experimental data indicate that such a residue is eliminated within some 15–20 minutes. Instances of successful defences based on the application of, say, spirits of camphor to the

---

1 J K Mason, and D J Blackmore, 'Experimental inhalation of ethanol vapour' (1972) 12 *Medicine, Science and the Law* 205. See also M J Lewis, 'A theoretical treatment for the estimation of blood alcohol concentrations arising from inhala-tion of ethanol vapour' (1985) 25 *Journal of the Forensic Science Society* 11.
2 R C Denney, 'Solvent inhalation and "apparent" alcohol studies on the Lion Intoximeter 3000' (1990) 30 *Journal of the Forensic Science Society* 357.

lips have been reported; experimentation has shown that the alcohol in such preparations may give rise to a high reading but that this is dissipated within minutes.

A very similar defence is based on the presence of mouth alcohol following the normal ingestion of an alcoholic drink. It is important to appreciate that this does not involve a claim that the residual alcohol is, of itself, sufficient to raise the tissue alcohol. The rationale is that the mouth is acting as if it were a calibrating cell in the old Camic machine in which air was drawn over a standard solution of alcohol. Since the solution which will give a recording of 35 mg alcohol/100ml air consisted of .0893% alcohol, it is clear that the remains of a whisky can be diluted several hundred times in the saliva and still produce a positive result. Once again, however, any effect of mouth alcohol wears off within minutes[1] and, for this reason, it is standard practice for the police to delay testing for 20 minutes if the subject claims he has only recently had an alcoholic drink – something which, in practice, will apply only to the roadside test. In fact, the printout from the Intoximeter claims to be able to distinguish mouth alcohol; the validity of this assertion has yet to be tested in the courts.

The same reasoning applies to a plea that a gargle or mouthwash containing alcohol – of which there are a surprising number – was used before the test[2]. It has to be remembered that any such contamination must also have affected the roadside test if it is to constitute a valid defence – and, in the majority of cases, a double contamination of this type is likely to stretch credulity too far. To complete the picture, the frequent contention that the Intoximeter is faulty and is giving an impossibly high reading must be considered. Any mechanical apparatus is liable to breakdown; but, once again, it is difficult, if not impossible, to see how such a claim can be supported in the face of a positive roadside test and in the absence of any supporting evidence of malfunction. The English courts have allowed a defence along these lines but do not seem to have commented on this particular question[3].

The question of medication remains. Since alcohol is a central nervous depressant, a large number of medicines with similar properties will potentiate the *effects* of alcohol and are, therefore,

1   S D A Franklin and A Stephens 'Can wine tasting be used as a defence to a charge of excess alcohol?' (2000) 40 *Science and Justice* 39.
2   J G Modell, J P Taylor and J Y Lee 'Breath alcohol values following mouthwash use' (1993) 270 *Journal of the American Medical Association* 2955
3   *DPP v Spurrier* [2000] RTR 60. Interestingly, the court specifically rejected the need for supporting expert evidence.

important in respect of charges under s 4. They will not, however, affect the Intoximeter reading and are, thus, irrelevant in the great majority of s 5 prosecutions. An exception may, however, lie in the so-called H2 receptor antagonist group of drugs that are used in treatment of peptic ulceration and other intestinal complaints. Some work has indicated that these drugs, by inhibiting the action of gastric alcohol dehydrogenase, will lead to a higher tissue alcohol than would normally be achieved by a given intake[1]. The evidence is sufficient for the Danish authorities to have imposed the placing of a warning on containers of the drug cimetidine[2]. Experimental work, however, relates to relatively low alcoholic intake and it has to be said that the findings are not universally accepted – even so, the possibility remains. Were such an effect shown to be significant at social drinking levels, it would give rise to a plea of special reasons for non-disqualification rather than defence to a charge under s 5(1). It is of interest that there is no evidence of a similar reaction using the more modern drugs of the 'proton pump inhibitor' group.

It is inappropriate to include in this section a full discussion of defences based on physical incapacity to provide a specimen (ss 6(4) and 7(6)). These are multiple and range from an inability to activate the Intoximeter to a fear of needles. Whether or not the latter condition constitutes a 'reasonable excuse' is a matter of fact and outwith the province of the expert witness[3]

CONCLUSION

It is obvious that the expert will not agree to give evidence on behalf of the accused unless his calculations indicate that a defence is available; as many as 40% of cases may fall at this first hurdle. It is impossible to predict the outcome of a trial simply on the basis of the relevant figures. The inference must be that the courts are, in general, willing to accept the scientific element of the evidence once it is seen as providing a valid defence. But, at

---

1 C DiPadova, R Roine, M Frezza et al 'Effects of Ranitidine on blood alcohol levels after ethanol ingestion' (1992) 267 *Journal of the American Medical Association* 83.

2 M Andersen and J S Schou 'Are H2 receptor antagonists safe over-the-counter drugs?' (1994) 309 *British Medical Journal* 493.

3 *DPP v Warren* [1993] AC 319 as interpreted in *DPP v Jackson* (Failure to provide specimen) [1999] 1 AC 406.

the same time, it is appreciated that the expert is working only from information provided by the accused; whether or not a defence is successful then depends entirely on the court's assessment of the credibility of that information.

ANNEXE 1

TISSUE ALCOHOL EQUIVALENTS OF ALCOHOLIC DRINKS
(Based on the Tables prepared by the British Medical Association 'The Relationship of Alcohol to Road Accidents' (1960))

(a) Beers, lagers, ciders etc

Intake in pints	breath mg/100ml	blood mg/100ml	urine mg/100ml
.5	8	18	24
1	16	37	49
1.5	24	55	73
2	32	73	97
3	48	110	147
4	64	147	195
5	80	183	244
6	96	220	293
7	112	257	343
8	129	295	391
9	144	329	439
10	160	366	488

(b) Standard spirits

Intake in fl oz	Breath mg/100ml	Blood mg/100ml	Urine mg/100ml
1	9.63	22	30
2	20	45	60
3	29	67	90
4	39	90	120
5	49	112	150
6	59	135	180
7	69	157	210
8	79	180	240
9	88	202	270
10	98	225	300
13.3	131	300	400
26.7	262	600	800

Note 1. All figures are reduced to the nearest whole number – the accuracy of the method does not justify the use of decimal points.

Note 2. All values must be multiplied by 154/W where W is the weight of the man in lbs. The stated correction factor for women is 154/W 6/5. The rationale is discussed in the text.

Note 3. For spirits other than those of standard strength, the value must be multiplied by c/40 where c is the alcoholic concentration v/v. Thus, the correction factor for ordinary vodka is 0.94.

Note 4. Regulations now state that single measures will be dispensed in 25ml amounts.

ANNEXE 2

SOME USEFUL EQUIVALENTS

1 fluid ounce	=	28.4 ml
1 gill	=	5 fl oz
1 pint	=	568 ml
	=	20 fl oz
	=	4 gills
1 gallon	=	4.55 litres
1 litre	=	35.2 fl oz
	=	1.76 pints
Standard bottle of spirits	=	26.7 fl oz
	=	750 ml (approx.)

ANNEXE 3

ALCOHOLIC CONTENT (V/V) OF SOME BEERS, LAGERS AND CIDERS COMMONLY DRUNK IN SCOTLAND

Beers (%)		Lagers (%)	
Youngers Tartan	3.5	Tennent's lager	4.0
McEwan's Export	4.2	McEwan's lager	3.8
Tetley Bitter	3.6	Skol	3.6
Tennent's/McEwan's 70/-	3.5(d)	Harp	3.1
Tennent's/McEwan's 80/-	4.2(d)	Kestrel	3.3
Guinness (stout)	4.1(d)	Beck's Bier	5.0
Newcastle Brown	4.5	Castlemaine XXXX	4.8
Alloa Export	4.2(d)	Tennent's Superlager	9.0
Caledonian Deuchars IPA	3.8(d)	Red Stripe	4.8
Old Peculiar	5.6(d)	Carlsberg Export	4.8
Dryborough's Heavy	3.6(d)	Carlsberg Special Brew	8.5
Elephant	7.5	Holsten Pils	5.8
Tiger Bitter	4.0	Stella Artois	5.0

Ciders (%)	
Strongbow	5.3
Woodpecker	3.5
Scrumpy Jack	6.0
Diamond White	8.2

Note: There are minor variations according to whether the product is sold in cans, kegs or draught. The values above are for cans or bottles except were marked (d).

ANNEXE 4

MINIMUM REQUIREMENTS FOR DEFENCE CALCULATIONS

(a) RTOA, 1988 s 15(3)(b)

The following information will always be required:

(a) The time the accused started drinking (if applicable)
(b) How much was consumed before the accident/incident
(c) The time of the accident/incident
(d) The time the accused started drinking after the accident/incident
(e) The amount drunk between then and the Intoximeter test
(f) The time of the Intoximeter test
(g) The result of the Intoximeter test
(h) The accused's weight at the relevant time
(i) The *precise* type of beer, wine etc drunk

(b) RTA, 1988 s 5(2)

In most cases, the defence depends upon the accepted limits of metabolism. In this case, all that is needed is:

1   The time of the Intoximeter test
2   The result of the Intoximeter test
3   The expert *ought* to know the time when the accused intended to drive again (see text for discussion of this point)

It is, however, often desirable to work out the accused's actual metabolic rate – and the higher the Intoximeter reading, the more important this is. More information is then needed:

(a) The time the accused started to drink
(b) The amount drunk – accuracy is imperative here
(c) The specific type of alcohol drunk
(d) The time drinking stopped
(e) The time of the Intoximeter test
(f) The result of the Intoximeter test
(g) The accused's weight

(c) Plea of 'Special Reasons'

The essential information is:

(a) The time the 'lacing' started

(b) The precise quality and quantity of the 'lacing' material
(c) The time and result of the Intoximeter test
(d) The accused's weight at the time

These cases, however, depend a great deal on credibility, for which the following additional information will be needed:

(e) The time the accused thought he started drinking
(f) Precisely what he thought he was drinking
(g) How much he drank voluntarily

Appendix F

Drugged Driving by Professor A Busuttil*

Increasingly evidence is accumulating world-wide that drugs which have an effect on brain function, ie have psychoactive effect, may cause problems with the co-ordination of physical and mental activities that are required for safe and careful driving of mechanically propelled vehicles[1-9]. In 1999 the Pompidou Group of the European Council arranged a seminar on 'Road Traffic and Illicit Drugs', to highlight this aspect of driving. Drugs have been shown in both simulated and actual performance testing to alter reaction time, information processing, sustained attention, speed estimation, short-term memory, judgement, learning comprehension, decision-making, and the response to multiple stimuli[10,11].

---

* Regius Professor of Forensic Medicine at the University of Edinburgh. The views expressed in Appendix F are those of the author and do not necessarily represent those of John Wheatley QC.

1 Seppala T, Linnoila M, Mattila MJ: *Drugs, alcohol and driving*; Drugs 17: 389; 1979.
2 Cimbura G, Lucas DM, Bennet RC, Warren RA, Simpson HM: *Incidence and toxicological aspects of drugs detected in 484 fatally injured drivers and pedestrians in Ontario.* J Forensic Science 27: 855; 1982.
3 Crouch DJ, Birky MM, Gust SW et al: *The prevalence of drugs and alcohol in fatally injured truck drivers.* J Forensic Science 38: 1342; 1993.
4 Bjornboe A, Beulich KM, Christopherson AS et al: *Prevalence of alcohol and other intoxicants in blood samples from drivers involved in road traffic accidents.* Norsk Epi 6: 49; 1996 5; 1997.
5 Christopherson AS, Morland J: *Drugged driving; a review based on the experience in Norway.* Drug Alcohol Depend: 47: 12; 1997.
6 Albery IP, Gossop M, Strang J: *Illicit drugs and driving: a review of epidemiological and psychological correlates.* Journal of Substance Misuse 3: 140; 1998.
7 Barbone F, McMahon AD, Davey PG et al: *Association of road-traffic accidents with benzodiazepine use.* Lancet 352:1331; 1998.
8 Augusburger IP, Gossop M, Strang J: *Drugs and alcohol among suspected impaired drivers in Canton de Vaud.* Forensic Science International 85; 95; 1997.
9 Logan BK, Schwilke EW: *Drug and alcohol use in fatally injured drivers in Wasington State.:* J Forensic Science 41; 505; 1996.
10 Hindmarch I, Gudgeon AC: *The effects of clobazam and lorazepam on aspects of psychomotor performance and car handling ability.* British J Clin Pharmacology 26; 10: 45, 1980.
11 Hindmarch I, Kerr JS, Sherwood A: *The effects of alcohol and other drugs on psychomotor performance and cognitive function.* Alcohol Alcoholism 26; 71; 1991.

In Britain s 4 (1) of the Road Traffic Act 1988, as amended by s 4 of the Road Traffic Act 1991, makes it a criminal offence if it can be shown that while driving or attempting to drive, the person was unfit to drive through the taking of drugs.

Charges brought under this procedure have become much commoner owing to the higher and apparently increasing incidence of drug misuse in the population, the nation-wide public health policy of instituting harm-reduction policies for drug addicts in the community (which intrinsically involve the prescribing of antidepressants, tranquillisers and substitute opioid or opiate medication on a regular basis),[1] and the widespread use of similar types of medication in the population at large.

DRUNK DRIVING AND DRUGGED DRIVING

The relationship between alcohol and driving has been used as a model for drugged driving by some. This is not a good analogy, as when compared with ethanol even very small quantities of drugs within the body may lead to defective driving capacity. Unlike alcohol, drugs are not distributed evenly throughout the body water compartments but may be bound to fat and protein, and then gradually released therefrom.

TABLE 1

Drug	Time to peak in hours	Per cent protein binding	Elimination half-life in hours
Morphine	0.1–0.3	26–30 %	1.3–3.4
Methadone	4.0	60–87	18–97
Cocaine	0.75–1.5		0.75–1.25

Furthermore drugs, unlike alcohol, are not broken down by body ferments or enzymes, mostly located within the liver, to

---

1 Berghaus G, Friedel B: *Methadone-substitution und fahreignung (Methadone substitution and driving aptitude)*. Neue Z Wehrr 7: 377; 1994.

innocuous compounds, but their break-down products or metabolites may still be active per se and indeed may last longer in the body and will continue to effect driving capabilities for an inordinately lengthy period. This is usually referred to as the elimination half-life of the drug namely the amount of time which would be required for the body to lose or inactivate half the amount of the drug present in the body.

For example diazepam will be broken down to temazepam and desmethyldiazepam both of which are pharmacologically active metabolites; diazepam has an elimination half-life of 92 to 99 hours, desmethyldiazepam an elimination half-life of up to 98 hours.

Drugs may also have more than one (first) peak of action with an effect on driving soon after ingestion, and a second peak several minutes or hours after the drug enters the body. Thus with cannabis there is a peak of its psychotropic effects on the brain within twenty minutes, and another peak of less marked activity about one and a half to two hours later, when some of the drug, formerly bound to fat and lipids in the body, is released back into the main circulation.

As compared with alcohol, a level of a particular drug in blood or urine cannot usually be equated with a particular change of behaviour as may be the case, within certain broad parameters, for intoxication with alcohol; the relationship that exists between problems with driving and specific drug levels is a matter on which there has been little research.

It is also a well established fact that different individuals because of their genetic make-up or for other reasons, such as variations in liver function, hyperactive breakdown enzymes (due to so-called acceleration of activity ie induction thereof by other drugs, eg anticonvulsants), will produce a certain effect on a particular person on one occasion, and a slightly different effect on another person or on the same person on another occasion.

With drugs there is also with the passage of time and the continuous use of a particular compound, an element of habituation arises in the subject and there is a development of a decreased or altered effect from the taking of drugs resulting in larger doses being required by the addict to obtain the same effects therefrom. The latter phenomenon is often referred to as tolerance to a drug, and in some cases the effects derived from a large dose of a particular drug may be similar in a chronic addict to the effect of a much smaller quantity of the drug in a novice or naive user of the same drug.

DRUG INTERACTIONS

Drugs also interact with one another giving an addictive effect. This addictive effect may sometimes be synergistic, namely that the sum total of the effects of two drugs may be in excess of that would be expected from a summing up of the effects derived from the use of each drug individually and separately.

All drugs that may affect the brain may interact with alcohol, a depressant of the central nervous system even when this is concomitantly present in small doses within the body[1-4]. Thus a person who has consumed alcohol as well as such drugs may appear to a lay person much more inebriated than would be expected for a given amount of alcohol, simply because together with the alcohol he has also taken a drug which has an effect on the brain and the mind.

For these reasons it is often impossible to state how much of a particular drug was actually taken even when armed with a toxicological result; quantification of the amount of drug consumed is thus very much in the realms of guesswork.

Published series on drugs very often list so-called therapeutic levels for a particular drug in the blood (or urine); these are levels to be expected in a person taking the drug for medicinal purposes. *Toxic* levels indicate that the drug is associated with noxious and undesirable effects; *fatal* or *lethal* levels are those found in deaths from overdose. It cannot be stated that a drug prescribed in therapeutic doses will not have any adverse effects on driving if taken in the appropriate doses.

1 Kerr JS, Hindmarch I: *The effect of alcohol alone and in combination with other drugs on information processing, task performance and subjective responses.* Human Psychopharmacology 13: 1, 1998.
2 Morland J, Setchleiv J, Haffner JF et al: *Combined effects of diazepam and ethanol on mental and psychomotor functions.* Acta Pharmacologica Toxicologica (Copenhagen) 34: 5; 1974.
3 Manno JE, Kipinger GF, Scholz N, Forney RB: *The influence of alcohol and marihuana on motor and mental performance.* Clin Pharmacol Thera. 12: 202; 1971.
4 Linnoila M, Hakkinen S: *Effects of diazepam and codeine alone and in combination with ethanol, on simulated driving.* Clin Pharmacol Thera 15: 368; 1974.

The following table gives some examples of this:

TABLE 2

Drug concentration in blood plasma in mg per litres	Therapeutic level	Toxic level	Fatal level
Codeine	0.03–0.1	0.3–0.9	3.2–4.5
Diazepam	0.1–2.5	5.0–30.0	> 50.0
Paracetamol	10.0–25.0	30.0–300.0	> 350.0
Thioridazine	1.0	> 5.0	> 7.0

THE DOCTOR AND THE MEDICAL EXAMINATION

A medical practitioner is invariably asked to attend by the police in a so-called section 4 procedure. This procedure is laid out in step-by-step sequential forms that are available in policed offices, and should be followed to the letter by the arresting police officers. These forms take on board all the recommendations laid out in *Reid v Nixon; Dumigan v Brown* 1948 J C 68, 1948 SLT 295 as follows

1. Before being examined the person arrested should be cautioned in the usual manner before being asked to submit to a medical examination by a doctor who will be selected and called out by the police.
2. The person arrested should be formally informed of his right to summon a doctor of his own choosing and afforded facilities to do so, although the clinical examination by a police doctor need not be delayed until this second medical practitioner actually arrives.
3. If consent to a medical examination is not forthcoming, this fact is recorded; then even if a doctor is actually called out, he can only visually observe the person detained. This is done from a distance. No form of medical examination or testing can be carried out. The doctor can only make notes as to his appearance, demeanour, gait and speech which to some extent may reinforce the observations made by the police.
4. If a medical practitioner is called out, he should be briefed fully about the circumstances of the arrest. The actual examination normally proceeds outwith the physical presence and the earshot of police officers unless they are required as a

chaperone in an examination of a person of the opposite sex to that of the doctor or if the person to be examined appears to be showing violence towards the doctor.

5.   Any interviewing of this person in relation to recent events should be directed solely to testing his memory, coherence and orientation, and not directed towards obtaining information about his possible guilt. It is however legitimate to ask about prescribed medication.

If such procedures are not followed, it is possible that the evidence collected by the doctor may be deemed to be inadmissible.

Information about the taking of drugs or prescribed medication may already have been volunteered to the police by the persons arrested. The police may also have discovered powders, tablets or other substances within the vehicle or in the clothing, which suggest that the accused had recent access to drugs. It is also often the case that a so-called field test is carried out on such substances. Solvents and the paraphernalia used to inhale these, cannabis reefers or 'joints' and other objects may be found in the vehicle which may alert police to the possible use of such substances.

The detained driver will already have been asked at the roadside to provide a sample of breath for alcohol analysis, and if this roadside test is positive samples of breath for testing in the static, legally approved device for assaying breath alcohol would also have been asked for. Some alcohol may be present but this would be below the legally prescribed level.

As from 1 April 2001, a new national standardised form will be introduced by the Association of Chief Police Officers aiming to assist police officers to record the results of roadside tests to see if drivers' performance is impaired by drugs. This would serve as preliminary assessment of the drivers and will be referred to as 'field impairment testing'. In these tests the police will assess the size of the drivers' pupils, comparing them to a gauge held to the side of the face. Watering of the eyes or reddening will also be recorded. Motorists will also be asked by the police to stand with feet together, tilting the head back and counting to 30 seconds. Excessive movement or sway is recorded by the officers. Other tests which will be carried out will be to have the subjects walk along a straight line and turn, stand on one leg, and touch the tip of their noses with the tip of the index finger. In due course quantified field tests may be introduced that can be carried out by the police on sweat or saliva.

MEDICAL CONFIDENTIALITY

It is important that the medical practitioner establishes his particular role in such instances with the persons to be examined. It is essential that the examinee knows and appreciates that the medical examination is carried out primarily to establish whether or not there is impairment to drive due to the taking of drugs and the results of this examination will be held in confidence but fully disclosed to the police at the time, in reports and at subsequent judicial proceedings. The rule of medical confidentiality does not hold in such specific examinations.

SCOPE OF THE MEDICAL EXAMINATION

The clinical examination that is carried out has two principal aims: to determine any physical and neurological changes consistent with producing an impairment to drive that can be due to the effects of drugs, and to differentially diagnose these from medical or other complaints. The actual examination can follow the various stages listed in form F. 97 (see Annexe 1) which acts both as an aide-memoir and as a means of recording the medical findings. This form need not be used at all but the police should always obtain a full written report from the medical practitioner which should include the results of all the tests carried out and a declaration that at the time of the examination the ability of the persons examined to drive a mechanically propelled vehicle was impaired through drink or drugs. Contemporaneous notes should always be made by the medical practitioner.

This examination should last for about twenty minutes and should be carried out in such a way that vital functions are assessed. It is not necessary to take the body temperature or to examine the ear-drums on all occasions but an examination of the eyes, of pulse and blood pressure, and tests of orientation to time, place and person, and of co-ordination of neuromuscular functions are essential in all cases.

In general the clinical investigations that should be carried out are those shown in Table 3.

TABLE 3

Function tested	Clinical Investigation
Level of consciousness	Glasgow Coma Scale (maximum 15)
Orientation	Time, place, person
Speech	Ability to participate in normal conversation, speech changes
Drowsiness	Drooping, swollen eyelids
Attention span	Backward counting
Heart rate	
Size of pupils Reaction to light and accommodation	Excessive dilation with stimulants and pin point size with opioid and opiates
Conjunctiva changes	Injection (prominent blood vessels) of the conjunctiva with cannabis smoking
Eye movements on lateral and upward gaze	Nystagmus (spontaneous pendular eye movement)
Tongue changes and smell in the mouth	Alcohol (congeners), marihuana, volatile hydrocarbons
Gait	Performance over a short distance
Balance	Ability to stand unaided on both or either foot = Romberg's test
Co-ordination tests	Finger-nose pointing, collecting an object from the floor, alternate clapping on the back of the hand, opening buttons, tying shoe laces
Mood	Elation, euphoria, depression
Psychotic symptoms	Hallucinations, delusions
Cognitive performance	Obeying simple commands, remembering an item of information eg an address given a few minutes previously.

WHICH DRUGS EFFECT DRIVING?

Different drugs are known to be associated with different clinical findings[1-3] but in the presence of several drugs in combination there may be an absence of or a change in the expected findings. The drug groups[4] which are known to cause driving impairment are:

1. benzodiazepine drugs (such as diazepam, temazepam, loreazepam, chlordiazepoxide, etc) used as tranquillisers, anxiolytics and hypnotics[5]
2. cannabis[6]
3. opioids (eg diamorphine, heroin codeine, methadone)[7]
4. amphetamines and related drugs (eg 'ecstasy')[8]
5. cocaine[9]
6. antihistaminics (used in allergy prevention and treatment)
7. antidepressants
8. other psychotropic drugs used to treat mental conditions such as schizophrenia
9. hallucinogens (eg LSD)

IMPAIRMENT

No recognised tight definition of impairment is available and thus its diagnosis is one of subjective and personal deduction by the individual doctor which depends on the results of the tests

1 Pickworth WB, Rohner MS, Fant RV: *Effects of abused drugs on psychomotor performance*. Experimental & Clinical Psychopharmacology 5: 235: 1997.
2 Seppala T, Linnoila M, Mattila MJ: *Drugs, alcohol and driving*. Drugs 17: 398; 1979.
3 Zacny JP: *A review of the effect of opioids on pschyomotor and cognitive functioning in humans*. Experimental & Clinical Psychopharmacology 3: 432; 1997.
4 *Medical Aspects of Fitness to Drive – A Guide for Medical Practitioners*, Chapters 12 and 13. Medical Commisson on Accident Prevention, London 1995.
5 O'Hanlon J F, Vermereen A et al: *Anxiolytics' effects on the actual driving performance of patients and healthy volunteers in a standarised test. An integration of three studies*. Neuropsychobiology 31; 81; 1995.
6 Moskowitz H: *Marihuana and driving*. Accid. Anal. Prev. 17: 323; 1985.
7 Zancy JP: *A review of the effects of opioids on psychomotor and cognitive functioning in humans*. Exp. Clin Psychopharmacol 3: 432; 1995.
8 Hurst PM: *Amphetamines & driving*. Alcohol, Drugs & Driving. 3: 13; 1987.
9 Siegel RK: *Cocaine use and driving behaviour*. Alcohol, Drugs & Driving 3: 1; 1989.

carried out and the level of experience in similar cases. A good rule of thumb is that if it is felt that it would be safe for the examinee to be given the keys of a car and to drive, then he would not be impaired.

Once a conclusion has been reached at the end of this clinical examination the examinee should be informed of what conclusions the doctor has reached in terms of the impairment. The two police officers involved in this arrest should be informed of the decision. A Soul and Conscience certificate is to be issued to the procurator fiscal in a sealed envelope handed to the police; a pre-prepared form is available in the police offices for this purpose. As in all medical examinations the medical practitioner has to be aware of the potential differential diagnoses. These include

1) acute anxiety state
2) withdrawal from drugs rather than their acute effects
3) sleep deprivation
4) medical conditions eg Parkinson's, Disseminated Sclerosis
5) complications of diabetes (hypoglycaemia, ketosis)
6) head injury.

SAMPLING OF BLOOD AND URINE

Although the medical opinion is sufficient on its own to indicate to the courts the presence of impairment to drive, the police would then be entitled to ask for a sample of blood or urine, the actual choice of sample being theirs. If the doctor feels that the state of the peripheral veins due to previous abuse is such that it would be well nigh impossible to obtain blood from the examinee, the doctor should express his medical opinion on this to the police. To require the arrested driver either to provide a sample while waiting for the doctor or prior to the examination is inappropriate; the sample should only be requested after the medical practitioner had diagnosed impairment.

A sealed 'drugs kit' is provided for this purpose. It has to be ensured that this is well within its expiry date. This kit contains all the requirements for venepuncture, two containers with integral anticoagulant and preservative and two sets of labels. It is important that the seal of the envelope containing this kit is broken in full sight of the detained driver. Only such kits should be used and about 20 millilitres of blood withdrawn and divided out between the two sample bottles, which are then sealed and labelled. The driver can choose his sample of the two and this is then placed in the envelope provided which is further sealed.

If a urine sample is requested by the police, the appropriate kit and the method used in procedures set out in s 5 of the Road Traffic Act 1988 should be followed in this instance. If the driver wishes to take his sample he should sign for it; if he does not want it this should preferably be retained by the police as a production to indicate that the procedure had been followed through appropriately.

In due course a copy of the toxicology report, which is both qualitative and quantitative, should be made available to the driver or his legal agents, and to the medical practitioner who carried out the medical examination. It is essential that the doctor is aware of the findings as it would be rather embarrassing if indeed it is found that he has pronounced on the presence of impairment, and in an appropriate analysis, no drugs are found in the blood-stream or urine of the driver.

THE EXPERT FOR THE DEFENCE

If an expert is instructed on behalf of the defence in such cases, it would be his role to carry out the following checks on the papers and statements provided:

1. Was the procedure undertaken by the police in accordance with the stipulations and regulations for such a procedure?
2. Was the clinical examination carried out comprehensively and appropriately?
3. Was the conclusion reached appropriate given the results of the clinical tests carried out on the driver? (Form F. 97 and the contemporaneous notes made by the doctor and his subsequent report may be necessary to give an opinion on this specific matter.)
4. Was the toxicological testing carried out appropriately?
5. Were the laboratory analytical findings in conformity with the medical opinion reached at the end of the examination?

ANNEXE 1

FORM F. 97

<u>CONFIDENTIAL</u>

REPORT ON MEDICAL EXAMINATION   F.97

Note for Examining Doctor

*The form of Report includes reference to most of the tests, etc., usually carried out by doctors. Its purpose is to inform the Procurator Fiscal of the evidence which the doctor may be expected to give at the trial. There is no compulsion, however, on doctors to carry out all of the tests and, on the other hand, they are not necessarily exhaustive of those which may be made. If the doctor carries out any other tests, particulars should be included either in the form or separately. The form, when completed, and any additional communication should be enclosed in an envelope addressed to the Procurator Fiscal marked "*Confidential*" and sealed. If, however, the doctor, obtains any information in answer to the first four questions under the heading 'Examination: History' which indicates that the person is ill, is having medical treatment or has any significant disability, he should inform the police officer in charge of the police station where the examination takes place.*

Name (in full) . . . .

Address . . . .

Occupation . . . .

Age . . . .

Place of Examination . . . .

Time of (*a*) Message Received . . . .

(*b*) Arrival at Station . . . .

(*c*) Examination . . . .

Officer(s) present at taking and Division of Urine Specimen . . . .

. . . .

EXAMINATION: History?:

Any evidence of illness or injury? . . . .

Is the person under medical treatment? . . . .

Is the person subject to fits or diabetes? ....

Are there any significant physical deformities or abnormalities? ....

....

When was food last taken? ....

GENERAL:

General Demeanour and Behaviour: ....

....

....

STATE OF CLOTHING: ....

....

SPEECH: thick, slurred, or over precise ....

CONDITION OF MOUTH, e.g. presence of dentures or any deformity ....

....

PULSE: rate and character ....

TEMPERATURE: (if thought necessary) ....

STATE OF TONGUE: ....

BREATH: odour, hiccup ....

EARS: deafness or discharge ....

HEART: ....

BLOOD PRESSURE: ....

LUNGS: ....

REFLEXES: ....

EYES: Eyelids, red or swollen? ....

      Conjunctivae ....

      Evidence of squint, etc. ....

      Any gross visual defect: are glasses used? ....

      Pupils and reaction ....

Nystagmus ....

Can he converge? ....

Manner of   (*a*) walking ....

(*b*) turning sharply ....

(*c*) sitting down and rising ....

(*d*) picking up coins from the floor ....

(*e*) standing on right leg ....

(*f*) standing on left leg ....

(*g*) standing on both feet with eyes shut ....

(*h*) touching point of nose with eyes shut ....

(1) right hand ....

(2) left hand ....

(*i*) knees bend ....

Writing: Name and address or copying from a book ....

....

Memory of incidents within the previous few hours and estimation of their time intervals: ....

....

....

....

Remarks by Examining Physician ....

....

....

....

....

I hereby certify that in my opinion at the time of my examination the ability of the above named person to drive a motor vehicle properly was not* impaired through drink or drugs.

Signed ....

Medical Qualifications ....

Date ....

*Strike out when not required

Index